Praise *for* WALKING WITH EVARISTO

"Christian Nill has written a highly engaging, disarmingly honest and evocative account of nearly three years as a Peace Corps volunteer in a Guatemalan indigenous community at a time of mounting upheaval and violence. Starting out brimming with idealistic optimism, the young Nill comes to find himself in the unwitting role of witness to terror that casts a pall over the countryside and claims the lives of those dearest to him. *An unforgettable and page-turning memoir that left me wanting more."*

—SCOTT WALLACE, AUTHOR OF THE *NYT* BESTSELLER, *THE UNCONQUERED: IN SEARCH OF THE AMAZON'S LAST UNCONTACTED TRIBES*

"This eloquent and moving account contributes in its own way to the body of *testimonio* literature from the period. ... [T]his book makes a worthwhile contribution to our understanding of this dark period in history, and we should be grateful to [author] Nill for having had the courage to write it."

—GAVIN O'TOOLE, *LATIN AMERICAN REVIEW OF BOOKS*

"Passionate and personal confessions from author Christian Nill, *Walking with Evaristo* is a captivating account of a nearly forgotten calamity."

—*SELF-PUBLISHING REVIEW*

WALKING WITH EVARISTO

WALKING WITH EVARISTO

A Memoir of Celebration and Tragedy in the Land of the Achí Maya

Christian Nill

A PEACE CORPS WRITERS BOOK

Walking with Evaristo
A Memoir of Celebration and Tragedy in the Land of the Achí Maya

A Peace Corps Writers Book — an imprint of
Peace Corps Worldwide

Printed in the United States of America
by Peace Corps Writers of Oakland, California.

For more information, contact peacecorpsworldwide@gmail.com.

Layout and Design: Robyn J. Harrison
Cover design: Damonza

In most cases I have used the actual names of people in this book. However, in a few cases I have invented names for the people I came to know, out of respect for their privacy.

ISBN-13: 978-1-950444-68-7
Library of Congress Control Number: 2024907790
First Peace Corps Writers Edition, May 2024

Dedicated to the memory of
Evaristo Cuxúm Alvarado
Guatemalan Hero

FOR MIREYA

And I come to the fields and spacious palaces of my memory, where are the treasures of innumerable images, brought into it from things of all sorts perceived by the senses. And there I come to meet myself.

—Augustine of Hippo (*The Confessions*, Book X.)

The struggle of man against power is the struggle of memory against forgetting.

—Milan Kundera (*The Book of Laughter and Forgetting*)

CONTENTS

WALKING WITH EVARISTO

Preface

My aim in this book is to provide an accurate, unflinching account of a period of roughly three and a half years that I spent in Guatemala during the late nineteen-seventies and early eighties. During most of this period I was serving as a Peace Corps volunteer in the town of Rabinal, a *municipio* of some twenty thousand inhabitants situated in the middle of the department of Baja Verapaz, which itself is situated quite nearly in the middle of the country. My account of this extraordinary time will be seen as "unflinching" in at least two distinct senses: I will try to relate the darker moments in this story without sparing the reader the fullest sense of grief and loss, and at the same time I will not spare myself any shame or discomfiture as I try to examine my own failures, foibles, pretensions, and disconnects.

When I started writing these pages a number of years ago, I conceived of the task before me as a trifold effort. I still see it that way today. Everything that I aim to record here will fall, I believe, under three broad categories: *light, enigma, confession.* First of all, I want to celebrate the life of a community that I came to love more than any other community I have ever known, and I want to try to illuminate its colors, texture, sounds and idiosyncrasies. At the same time, I also want to shed some light on the dark forces that would eventually try to suppress the spirit of Rabinal—and even murder its people.

But a full treatment of the charm and allure of this community called Rabinal must also come to terms with, or at least touch upon, the sometimes haunting, ever confounding enigmas that are also part of the fabric of life there. Enigmatic occurrences were never in short supply during my three years in Rabinal, and at the very end of my tour there would still be one last, unforgettable enigma that I ponder the meaning of even today.

Finally, I cannot fail to include here my confessions as a man, as an actor, and as a witness. It goes without saying that my failings during the time I spent in Rabinal were many, because I am an imperfect being. Yet it is not enough to say that "it goes without saying." No, I must try, for the sake of a complete record, to confess these failings to the best of my ability to my readers, to my wife and family, and to the people I knew in Rabinal who are still among the living.

Confession, to me, is not so much a religious act as it is a sort of social compact. It is a compact or promise, on the one hand, between me and the people of Rabinal and all the *rajawales* or spirits of the dead who guard her destiny. And at the same time, it is also a compact between me and you, the reader. Though I may trip and stumble at times, I will try at all events to follow in the footsteps of the classical rhetorician and Catholic saint, Augustine of Hippo:

> I wish to act in truth, making my confession both in my heart before you and in this book before the many who will read it.*

Light, enigma, confession. That is about it. You see, in many ways this is a simple story. Since it is not my intention to make it appear more obscure or challenging than necessary, I might as well set forth a few clarifications at the outset. The 'X' that appears in many proper names (Xecambá, Xococ, Raxjút, etc.) is sounded out like our 'sh' sound, as in shock or shit. Whenever I refer to "Guate," I mean Guatemala City, the capital. "Xela," on the other hand, is the popular K'iché name for Quetzaltenango, Guatemala's second largest city. (Think of "*Luna de Xelajú,*" a popular Guatemalan waltz composed by Paco Pérez in 1944, and sung so beautifully today by Gabby Moreno.)

During the timeframe of this narrative, the Guatemalan quetzal was nominally at parity with the U.S. dollar. Though towards the end of this period (around 1982) desperate Guatemalans were already paying a premium of ten percent or more on every dollar they could get their hands on.

A hectare is about two-and-a-half acres. A kilometer (which I often refer to as a "click") is six-tenths of a mile. A *quintal* is a hundred pounds; a liter is a couple gulps more than a quart.

---

*Augustine, *Confessions*, X:1

Guatemala

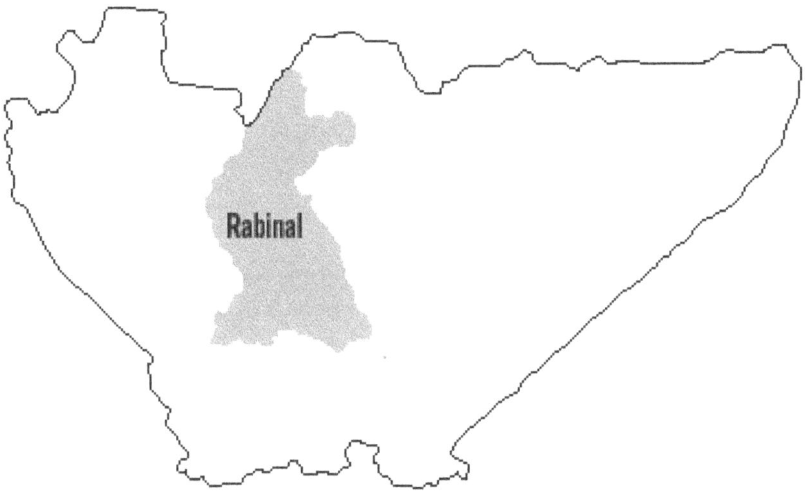

Baja Verapaz Department

Río Negro
Chitucán
Xococ
Patixlán
Vegas de
Santo Domingo
Panacál
Nimacabáj
INAFOR
Tree Nursery
To Cubulco
To San Miguel Chicáj
Pichéc
Pachalúm
Chiác
Chiticoy
Guachiplín
Xesiguán
Chirrum
Chixím
N
Concul
San Luís
Chicupác
0 1 2 3 4
Kilometers

Rabinal Municipality

CHAPTER 1

Cascading Memories, and a Meditation on Heroes

> There are times of ripening when the true element of the human spirit, held down and buried, grows ready underground with such pressure and such tension that it merely waits to be touched by one who will touch it—and then erupts.
>
> —Martin Buber, *I and Thou*

We all want to have heroes in our lives. From a tender age we are taught the importance of having heroes, and in order to nurture our incipient hero worship along healthy lines our earnest and hopeful teachers point us in the direction of exemplary heroes who are accepted by the dominant culture. The great presidents whose images are carved into the granite face of Mt. Rushmore; the renowned thinkers and agents of change like Albert Einstein or Susan B. Anthony. Sports figures. Jesus Christ. And, some years later, after he was finally accepted by the dominant culture because he was safely dead, Martin Luther King, Jr.

Like most people, I had different heroes at different stages in my life. During the 1960s, the Space Race was an exhilarating, hopeful, and widely televised national enterprise—even though that enterprise was set against the inexorable backdrop of poverty and racial injustice here at home, as well as the terrifying specter of nuclear holocaust and an escalating war halfway around the world. Still, the Space Race offered everyone—especially kids like me—something to dream about. So my first heroes were those brave, white-suited astronauts who led our country into space, and ultimately to the moon. I read colorful picture books about space travel; I patiently glued together all the plastic spacecraft model kits I could lay my hands on, and had them hanging by gossamer filaments from my bedroom ceiling. I even collected bubblegum cards with astronauts' pictures and bios instead of those other cards featuring mere baseball players. When three of my heroes were incinerated in a horrible fire before even lifting off from Cape Canaveral, I wept bitterly while lying in bed that night.

By the time the *late* sixties came around, the momentous changes in our nation's social and political climate coincided with my own awakening as a young adolescent in America. For many kids my age, and definitely for me, it was a frustrating period, for we could only watch the transformation unfold on TV without really participating in it. I kept wishing I could be ten or twelve years older, like my brother and sister.

I overcame that frustration with my own little, personal rebellion: I wouldn't be like others my age. Not necessarily smarter (for I definitely wasn't). Just different. My new heroes now were the late Mohandas Gandhi—and Pete Seeger. One rainy Sunday afternoon I found myself engrossed in a film on TV called *Nine Hours to Rama*, a gripping drama that offered a fictional account of as many hours in the life of the assassin who shot Gandhi, culminating of course in the murder itself. The main focus of the movie was on the assassin, yet because of it, I became fascinated with Gandhi himself, and fascinated with the whole idea of India. I went to the library searching for anything I could find about my hero, and I signed out a slender volume comprising a collection of his most memorable utterances and writings. The book had no dust jacket, but the faux burlap cover was embossed with an oversized reproduction of Gandhi's signature.

Gandhi introduced me to India and its struggles, its caste system, and its post-independence partition into separate Hindu and Muslim states. The whole caste system in India puzzled and saddened me, and I wondered how untouchables got by in the world, faced with so many social obstacles. To try and answer this question, one of the next books I checked out from the high school library was Mulk Raj Anand's *Untouchable*. That book opened my eyes to the experience of one untouchable by the name of Bakha who, faced with the gross injustice of prejudice and discrimination that was baked into the predominant religion, nevertheless struggled to find his way in the world. His main job for years—indeed, it was his assigned role in life—was to clean the latrines of all the other Indians in his neighborhood who possessed absolutely no inherent superiority over him other than the good luck to be born into a higher caste. I thought the ending of the book was deeply poignant, though perhaps only because at that age (fifteen, maybe) I still had very little experience with the feeling of poignancy: one day the Mahatma Gandhi comes to Bakha's town to deliver an important speech about ending the caste system. While much of the speech goes over Bakha's head, the one part that he can easily understand and grasp the significance of is when Gandhi incidentally mentions the imminent arrival of flush toilets in India.

* * *

It was around this same period, in 1968, when I heard on the nightly news a short report about nine people who broke into a draft board office located on the second floor of the Knights of Columbus building in Catonsville, Maryland. They pulled hundreds of files classified as "1-A" from the file cabinets and packed them all into a couple of wire trash burners, then hastened back downstairs with their informatic quarry and regrouped in the parking lot, where they dumped the files on the ground, doused the whole pile with homemade napalm, and then watched as one of the nine lit the pile ablaze with a single match and nimbly backed away. Each of the nine then tossed in a symbolic match. "*We are all in this together.*" They all stood around the conflagration, a couple of them gave voice to some spontaneous meditations uttered with quiet conviction, and then all joined hands and said the Our Father together. And then they calmly waited for the police to arrive.

Almost none of these details that I relate here were revealed to the American public in the national news reports. There was only one camera and sound crew present from a local TV station, because they alone had been tipped off about the event before it unfolded. Their footage never made the nightly news anywhere in the country—not even on the local station they worked for. But these days you can easily find their black and white video preserved on the Internet.[1] It's some nine minutes long, and while the soundman clearly needed either better training or better equipment, the shaky and sometimes rapidly panning video nonetheless shows exactly what happened in that parking lot in front of the Knights of Columbus on May 16, 1968.

I've watched that nine-minute video many times, and I've tried as best I can to peer deeply into the faces of each of the nine people standing around the conflagration. While I myself have never committed an indictable crime of conscience, still when I look into those faces—every one of those faces of the Catonsville Nine—I see myself.

The nine were carried off in a paddy wagon to the station house, where they were all ID'ed and fingerprinted. Then, less than an hour later, they somehow all managed to get together again in the precinct station to pose for—*a group photo*!

I now have this black and white group portrait, which I recently captured from the Internet, pinned to a bulletin board above my desk. All of the nine faces in the picture look earnest yet quite casual. The whole group pictured there might easily be mistaken for any local church committee taking an impromptu break before they return to the job of planning their next rummage sale or spaghetti and meatball fundraiser. I'm sure that the photo pinned above my desk was part of the plan. As army veteran George Mische put it, they wanted to convey through their appearance and their actions one simple message: "*Everybody* can do this!"

* * *

Heroes always begin their life's journey as ordinary people. Heroism is often something that simply happens to you, as fortuitous as breaking a leg or pulling the right lever at the right moment, almost by accident. It's ridiculous, really, but nevertheless heroism happens: most of us have a hero or two, and we rightly admire them for what we call their feats, no matter the degree of serendipity (or God's grace) that may have been involved in those feats. While I don't think I've ever done anything truly heroic in my life, when I peer into the faces of some heroes, I can't help but see a common background, a common humanity. And it is the sudden realization of that which I have in common with heroes that becomes the greatest inspiration of all.

It does seem in some sense odd that I, with my Presbyterian upbringing in a conservative upstate New York community of engineers, salesmen, factory and utility workers, and homemakers, would settle on Father Daniel Berrigan SJ as one of my heroes. Odd, too, because the one heroic act that I associate with him took only half an hour of his time and has since fallen so far below the radar of American consciousness and memory. And yet there you have it. Father Daniel couldn't *not* be a hero to me. He did what was necessary when he was called upon to do it.

Father Daniel's eight co-defendants were of course heroes, too, and not only there in Catonsville on that sunny spring morning. Thomas and Marjorie Melville were also among the nine, as I discovered only recently when I began my research to recover the past in order to supplement my poor memory. Thomas and Marjorie were both Catholics of the cloth in Guatemala until a year or so before Catonsville. Both had worked in the hinterlands of Guatemala—collectively known as the *campo*, an ecologically diverse paradise ranging from rich and verdant lowland rainforest to alpine highlands. Both Thomas and Marjorie had independently witnessed the inequality and injustice inherent in Guatemala's longstanding system of land tenure. Both had seen the disparagement, subjugation, and outright murder of poor *campesinos* who under the law had no right to anything in this world beyond a half-acre plot of land from which to eke out a living. And both of them ended up sympathizing with the workers' rebellion and the guerrillas in the mountains whose numbers were growing every day. I have no question but that they did what was necessary under the circumstances.

It was that crime, the crime of aligning their faith and their respective acts with the growing forces of social change in the country, that got them both sent back to the States. Soon after returning, the two substituted vows to each other in place of their vows to the Church.

In 1968 when I heard the Catonsville story on the news, I was a thirteen-year-old boy who knew absolutely nothing about Guatemala. Much later, as a twenty-three-year-old recently accepted for a Peace Corps posting in that country, I happened to sign out a book by the Melvilles that I hoped might help to prepare me for my imminent adventure—without having the slightest clue that the two authors of the book had also been among the nine in Catonsville holding hands around the conflagration and praying the Our Father. I was only able to put it all together—to uncover this, to me, remarkable connection—when the whole memory of Daniel Berrigan and the Catonsville Nine fell, as it were, from the sky a few days ago and took up residence in my brain and wouldn't leave. That was when I started to look stuff up on the Internet. I suppose readers who cannot possibly pay so much as a brief visit to that court of memory where I dwell all the time might think this connection an unremarkable, if not trivial coincidence. But to me it shows a pattern, a continuum, that weaves the disjointed experiences of my life into a narrative that has at least some semblance of meaning.

* * *

Daniel Berrigan, for his part, committed at least one other heroic, indictable act after Catonsville, one which invited the ridicule of many. In September 1980, he and his brother Philip, along with six other activists, spirited their way past security guards at a General Electric nuclear missile plant in King of Prussia, Pennsylvania, armed only with hammers and bottles of human blood hidden in their coats and backpacks. Once in there they set to work doing what was necessary. Daniel and others hammered away with gusto on the aluminum nosecones of the missiles, causing big dents, while their *confrères* spilled blood (mostly their own) on the papers and blueprints laying on the worktables. The King of Prussia Eight did what was necessary, even though it was all but certain that their actions would make no difference whatsoever. Pure theater, sublimely ridiculous in every respect. That made them all heroes, in my book.

By the time that event happened I was already in my second year in Guatemala. I don't even remember reading about it in the scant American press we received. I had been assigned to a town called Rabinal, located in the department (province) of Baja Verapaz—a small, unassuming grid of unpaved streets laid out in the middle of a semiarid valley surrounded by more verdant mountains. I ended up spending three years in Rabinal, and by the end of that period I felt as much a part of the community as I've ever felt in relation to any community where I have ever lived, either before or after. My assignment in Rabinal was to assist the national reforestation effort, which at the local level meant helping to develop and manage a tree nursery, teaching the *campesinos* about the importance as well as the techniques of planting trees, and handling all of the planning and logistics of local reforestation efforts. Another, but by no means secondary, part of my assignment was to teach soil conservation "best practices" on the tiny farm plots scattered through the countryside.

The work kept me busy most days, and nights I read a lot. One volume which occupied me for several weeks was a masterful biography of the German pastor and theologian Dietrich Bonhoeffer that was given to me as a gift by my hometown pastor, the Reverend Richard Manzelmann. That was the book where I found the next hero in my life's journey.

The remarkable blond-haired, blue-eyed German who arrested my attention for several weeks while I read his biography—sitting there in my hammock under a dim light in Rabinal—interested me in part because the book in my hands was a gift from a man whom I admired a great deal. Why had Rev. Manzelmann gone to the trouble of sending me this volume? After all, he had had scores of other youngsters in his annual communicants' classes. I'm sure he didn't send books to all of them. Maybe (I thought to myself much later), since he was a very worldly pastor who was well acquainted with happenings in Guatemala and elsewhere in the world, maybe he thought I showed some promise, such that with the right sources of inspiration I might become a valuable witness who could come back someday and report the truth to those in his community of faith who might not have a clue. So I guess he was sending me some of 'the right sources of inspiration.'

As a young man seeking adventure after college, I still considered myself at least nominally Christian, albeit of the questioning, non-practicing variety. So, when I first read the words of praise printed in bold letters on the back cover of the Bonhoeffer volume, calling the man a Christian "hero of our time," and calling Eberhard Bethge's account of his life "a spiritual experience," I was immediately drawn in. Bonhoeffer's Christian Lutheran theology matured rapidly while he was still a young man, and the swiftness of development in his thought was partly in response to the equally swift developments that were unfolding in German society. By the time Hitler came to power in 1933 he had already succeeded in purging the German churches of all but its most nationalistic clerics, and barely two days after his installation as Chancellor, Bonhoeffer delivered a radio address denouncing him.

As the next few years wore on and the aftereffects of the Great Depression abated, the ugly realities of the Third Reich came into sharper focus for Bonhoeffer. Jews disappeared, rumors slowly found substantiation, and the national cry of *Lebensraum!* grew louder. And so it was that only two or three years into the Second World War Bonhoeffer had become, by reason of faith and conviction, deeply involved in the July 1943 plot to assassinate the *Führer*.

Needless to say, the plot, which involved secretly placing a bomb under a conference table in Hitler's bunker, failed. The timing was off. Bonhoeffer was ultimately arrested and imprisoned, and was hanged by the Gestapo, along with several of his co-conspirators, on April 9, 1945—almost exactly one month before Germany's surrender to allied troops.

Dietrich Bonhoeffer had heard the calling and *he did what was necessary*. He has been a hero of mine ever since I first heard his name.

* * *

When I was in college, just before the Central American adventure that is chronicled here, I had several fine teachers that I remember fondly, but only one who stands out as someone I have wished to this very day I could emulate. From the very first day of his class in comparative literature, I believed that I alone—among my twenty or so classmates—was capable of a sympathetic understanding of Professor James McConkey's worldview, as well as his approach to art. Prof. McConkey taught me the value and importance of personal memory, and even though I had little personal memory to look back upon at the time, I was already (as I would say to myself later in Guatemala) *looking forward to the looking back*.

Among the several great books that Prof. McConkey guided us through that semester, always with his singular enthusiasm and quiet wit, was *Don Quixote*. I read *Don Quixote* again during those tropical evenings lying in my hammock in Rabinal, and I found I had more patience to really appreciate it this time around. Later, while visiting Guatemala City to pick up my paycheck, still pondering the nature of Don Quixote's particular heroism and his poignant demise, I stopped in an English-language bookstore where I came across Miguel de Unamuno's *The Tragic Sense of Life*.

Unamuno establishes Don Quixote as the great role model for the modern era, and he exuberantly extols the value of passion and conviction over mere rationality in the path to knowing. For me, all of this came together in one supremely enigmatic passage that nonetheless made perfect sense to me. So much sense, in fact, that I had to copy it out onto an index card which I pinned above my work table so that it could peer back at me almost every day and make me think, and think again, about heroes and about what truly matters.

> The greatest height of heroism to which an individual, like a people, can attain is to know how to face ridicule. Better still, to know how to make oneself ridiculous, and not to shrink from the ridicule.[2]

The remainder of this book is, in some sense, a meditation upon Unamuno's words. It is a story about heroes. It is also a love story.

CHAPTER 2

Training

Listen! I will be honest with you,

I do not offer the old smooth prizes, but offer rough new prizes,

These are the days that must happen to you …

—Walt Whitman, *Song of the Open Road*

When contemplating a radical move from one's own comfortable world to an unknown world, it's helpful to have a muse for some inspiration. Or an enabler.

I applied to join the Peace Corps shortly after my college graduation. I had met a few times with a Peace Corps recruiter on campus, but it still took time to find a suitable position. It took a long time. The wait was excruciating, and I began to despair of ever finding a route out of Ithaca, out of this country. In the meantime, I drifted from one menial job to another, and devoted my evenings to drawing and painting. I did send out resumes to try and get a regular professional position in the States, but I had only a shifting, inchoate notion of what my so-called profession actually was. And anyway, with unemployment at six percent and annual inflation close to nine, volunteering overseas began to look more and more like an attractive option.

Pitamber helped me get through this time. I got to know Pitamber Sharma while working in the college library shelving books. He was a grad student from Nepal working on his dissertation in regional planning, and his research brought him frequently to the library where I worked. Eight years my senior, Pitamber was himself a professor of geography at Tribhuvan University outside of Kathmandu, but he was now on sabbatical to advance his credentials by getting a doctorate at Cornell. He had a wife and kid waiting for him back in Nepal, so he clearly knew the meaning of sacrifice.

We'd meet at least a couple nights a week, Pitamber and I, for coffee and snacks in a sterile break room located in the library basement, and it was there that Pitamber began to tell me the most vivid and enchanting stories about life in Nepal. I listened with rapt attention in the neon-lit room amid the hum of half a dozen vending machines lined up against the wall behind us as he told me about the traditional gift-giving customs in Nepal's small rural villages. Or the annual festival of colors, during which people rich and poor, young and old, would fill the streets and gleefully smear each other with powdered dyes of the most boisterous, picturesque hues. I couldn't get enough of Pitamber's stories, they totally absorbed me, and he clearly enjoyed telling them. It seemed as though his own stories transported him back to the homeland he missed. They certainly transported me.

Pitamber told me about the political repression in Nepal under the absolute monarchy of King Birendra. And then he shared with me, in a spirit of openness that might only have been possible outside his own country, that he was a Marxist. For my part, I shared with him that I wanted to get into the Peace Corps; that in fact I already had an application in the hopper, and that, thanks largely to our many conversations, I had listed Nepal as my first choice among possible assignments. I suppose I must have felt a little surprised that my friend Pitamber, *qua* Marxist, should accept and even broadly approve of my intention to join the Peace Corps. But he did. Perhaps we had simply gotten to know one another well enough. We had established a basic level of trust, so that my Marxist friend could feel reasonably confident that I would never become some shallow U.S. propagandist—or worse, a CIA operative.

Pitamber loved good movies, and there was an excellent film club on campus that offered many of the recent and not-so-recent classics five or six nights a week. Fellini, Bergman, Antonioni, Buñuel, Altman, Godard, and many others besides. In the absence of Internet streaming services which would not appear for many years to come, we were truly spoiled by the surfeit of cinematic entertainment. Pitamber and I saw all kinds of films together, but most of them remain with me now as nothing more than vague but pleasant memories. There is one film, however, that I distinctly remember seeing with Pitamber, and that was Gillo Pontecorvo's *The Battle for Algiers*. I remember that one because Pitamber made a particular point of getting me to go with him to see this film, and I can only imagine that perhaps he did so because he considered the film essential preparation for anyone who was about to embark on work of any kind in the developing world.

So, we went out one night to see the film, and I must say, it certainly altered my view of things as I continued to dream of working overseas. Indeed, the scenes of torture, terrorism and conflagration in Pontecorvo's neo-realist drama set in Algeria were as revealing as they were shocking to my young, inexperienced mind. It was an awful lesson to learn, yet it was a necessary lesson, the memory of which would remain with me forever. *The Battle of Algiers* shined a bright light on the inhumanity and indifference of a European overclass drinking and partying through a torrid Saharan afternoon while their confréres the colonial administrators enforced an oppressive legal code called *Indigénat* that conferred inferior legal status upon all of the non-European Algerians. But the foreign occupiers would themselves eventually meet a terrible fate at the hands of the Algerian National Liberation Front, and thus the cycle of violence continued. For years it continued, until a newly minted Democratic Republic of Algeria finally gained its independence from France in 1962.[3]

It was hard to look at many of the scenes in *The Battle of Algiers.* Yet at the same time it was impossible to look away. After the movie Pitamber and I walked back to Collegetown together, since both of our spartan accommodations were located there. We smoked and talked about Pontecorvo's masterpiece all the way, and we stopped in at Johnny's Bar and Grill for a drink, and we talked and smoked some more. (I will not easily forget Pitamber's cigarettes: they were clove cigarettes from Nepal, and they crackled audibly, almost musically, with every drag he inhaled.) Pitamber reviewed, in a tightly organized monologue, as if he had done this before, several of the main plot elements of Pontecorvo's film, and we had a pretty lively exchange analyzing the motives of the freedom fighter Ali La Pointe, as well as the countervailing strategy of suppression orchestrated by the French Colonel Mathieu.

Pitamber earnestly wanted me to understand one basic truth, which was that, notwithstanding the particular cultural milieu of the film, *this is the way of all popular struggles everywhere.* I nodded assent to this general proposition, but I have to acknowledge now that while sitting there in a cocktail lounge close by the cloistered college community that I belonged to, there in that peaceful and prosperous corner of upstate New York, it was in truth a sort of naive assent arising from a baseline of total ignorance.

Shortly after that movie outing with Pitamber I received a letter from the Peace Corps offering me a position in Guatemala in the area of reforestation and soil conservation. But only later—nearly three years later—would I finally understand the truth of Pitamber's assertion concerning liberation struggles, from the standpoint of immediate experience of blood and terror.

Self portrait 1978

* * *

I arrived at the airport in San José, Costa Rica with all my baggage. We all arrived carrying the things we thought we'd need, with little idea of the things that would be needed of us. Stuffed in my brand new, forest green backpack, I brought with me a couple pairs of jeans (bell-bottoms, already fading from the fashion scene), several T-shirts, a couple light jackets, toiletries and underwear, sleeping bag, and a portable shortwave radio I had bought in Miami during staging. In 1978, before cell phones or personal computers or the Internet, a shortwave radio was *de rigueur* for anyone going overseas for an extended period. A shortwave would connect us with the world outside, mainly through the Voice of America. BBC, if you could pick it up.

... Oh yes, and my backpack also held three tattered paperbacks: *Don Quixote*, Saint Augustine's *Confessions*, and Walt Whitman's *Leaves of Grass*. Two of these books still sit on my bookshelf today, the pages more fragile and yellow than ever, but still readable, and still read.

There were about thirty of us in the group. all embarking on what would become one of the most memorable experiences of our lives. We had arrived in Costa Rica for three months of training to "prepare us" for our two-year stints in Guatemala, Honduras, and Nicaragua. I use the scare quotes here advisedly. Nicaragua was already stirring with the beginnings of a Sandinista uprising. And Guatemala had—well, it had its history. Before departing for this adventure, in order to get familiar with the country where I was about to spend the next two years, I had read *Guatemala: The Politics of Land Ownership* (which had been reprinted in the United Kingdom under the more ominous title, *Guatemala: Another Viet Nam*?). Thomas and Marjorie Melville wrote an unsparing account of the country's social and political landscape during the years following the 1954 *coup d'etat* that was orchestrated by the CIA—a notorious intervention that brought an end to two popularly elected terms of progressive government and introduced decades of extreme right-wing hegemony lasting through the day of my arrival—and beyond.

But books, really, were part of my baggage in more ways than one. Back in New York, I had learned to prize books above nearly everything else as a source of knowledge. I learned about conservation and ecology from books by Aldo Leopold, Barry Commoner, and a thick ecological tome I had by a brilliant young academic named Ricklefs. And a couple years before embarking on this Central American adventure, I had learned about the rewards of the examined life by reading St. Augustine.

But books, it turns out, can only whet the appetite for experience. I could scarcely have called myself "well-read" by any of the usual academic yardsticks, yet even the handful of classics that I *had* read could never have prepared me for what I—what all of us—were about to experience.

I carried with me other baggage as well. Self-doubt that was never in short supply, lost loves that would take a separate book to write about, recurring bouts of depression, religious questioning. And a sort of post-undergraduate angst exacerbated by my parents' expectation that I would get a "real job" upon graduating from college. All this, and more, I carried with me to the airport in San José, Costa Rica. Perhaps most of my new-found Peace Corps friends were carrying lighter baggage—or perhaps not.

Friends. Maybe it took a while, but that's what we indeed became. Friends joking with one another, consoling and encouraging one another, and on countless occasions helping one another. There was Tony, at 44 the eldest among us: Tony, God rest his soul, was a really easy going Californian whose experience everyone respected; who owned his own commercial tree nursery in St. Helena and had worked as a fireman in Berkeley. Tony had a great deal of trouble with Spanish (not uncommon when one reaches middle age), so he was assigned to San Juan Ixcoy high up in the mountains of Huehuetenango[1] where, he later reported to us over a beer, the deeply traditional Maya Q'anjob'al people in the *aldeas* (small villages) generally knew even less Spanish than he did. Perfect match.

There was second-eldest Ralph, a Vietnam vet who only three years earlier had seen the fall of Saigon. I've always tried to imagine what sort of personal quest had brought Rafa to Guatemala after slogging through the fog of war in Southeast Asia. Redemption? Enlightenment? Some sort of penance? I'll never know, but I do know that in Rafa I had a true friend who always listened and cared.

The rest of us in the contingent were all in our twenties, including the four of us who would be sent to Baja Verapaz department. Carlos from Texas would go to Salamá, the departmental capital of Baja Verapaz, while Bruce would be assigned to Cubulco, the end of the road. Thus, after training in Costa Rica, the two of them worked to the east and west of me, respectively, and not more than twenty kilometers away from me, who was right there in the middle, in Rabinal. A fourth young man, Mike from Minnesota, went to San Miguel Chicaj, the next town to the east of me, to work in animal husbandry with the small farmers.

* * *

I had arrived in Central America with zero *español,* so that was a challenge for me. In the beginning I wasn't exactly a quick learner; nor were my three years of high school German (expected of me by my immigrant parents) any help at all. But somehow, after maybe two months in Costa Rica, all of a sudden the logic of the language started falling into place, and eventually I found myself at least a little bit ahead of the curve.

Our training took place on a medium sized farm near the center of the village of La Guácima, a largely agricultural community not far from the capital, where all the families tended to be related to one another and where soccer matches were central to weekend entertainment. Each of us was assigned to live with a host family where we ate and slept, and it was only when we got together for training sessions each day that we learned, upon comparing notes from snatches of conversation, that most of our host families all came from the same limb if not the same branch of the tree.

The farm that was our training site raised mostly corn, but at some earlier time must have raised chickens as well, for there were chicken coops on the site that we as volunteers would become rather familiar with. *Ah, yes, those chicken coops!* We took our Spanish lessons every day in converted chicken coops that had been subdivided into tiny classrooms with dirt floors, corrugated metal roofs, and, instead of windows—what else?—chicken wire. I started smoking more during training, and I would flick my spent butts through the chicken wire, often just in time to respond to an instructor's question in Spanish.

"*¿Y tiene usted novia, Cristián? ¿Cómo va a responder usted?*"

A pretty latina asking me if I had a *fiancée*? Always ready with the smart rejoinder, I replied, "*No, señorita, no tengo…una…novia. ¿Quiere usted mi novia…ser?*" DAMN, though, still putting the friggin' verb last, like in German. Ah, but I had a long, *long* row to hoe! At least I got a laugh out of the pretty teacher.

Receiving tech training in the chicken coops. (Author on the left. Photo credit: PCV Bernie Rafalski)

Our training consisted of four hours of language immersion in the morning followed by four hours of technical and cross-cultural training in the afternoon. All of our training was conducted in the chicken coops under the corrugated metal roofs. Our three-month training period began on September 15, 1978—a Friday, and, as it happens, also a universally observed national holiday throughout Central America, for it marks the day in 1821 when the Spanish Empire finally relinquished control of all of its Central American territories. This fact was noted by our hosts and trainers during their introductions with a hint of chagrin, since but for us gringos who had descended upon them, they all might have been relaxing at home with a cold beer and a good soccer match.

We were still in the rainy season, and the showers arrived like clockwork every day around three in the afternoon, sometimes making it hard to hear our instructor Gilberto Ugalde as he patiently walked us through the process of setting up a nursery and introduced us to the varieties of tree species we'd be raising there. We listened to the lectures, but we also had a good deal of hands-on practice setting up germination boxes and seedling beds out near the corn fields, shaping a patch of sloping cropland into terraces, and learning how to make a proper compost pile. The rains continued every afternoon for at least the first four weeks or so. Around the middle of October the weather began to transition into the dry season.

Among other topics in our tech training, we learned about pest control in the tree nursery and in the field. It was here that the principles of ecology and sustainability that I had learned in school would collide head-on in Central America with the cold realities of disingenuous marketing by the multinational agrochemical companies and the sheer ubiquity of those companies' products all over this tropical paradise.[4] The pervasive use of hazardous agrochemicals in every single stage of plant husbandry in Central America, from seed germination to plantation management, was alone sufficient to make each of us acquiesce under the pressure, to forget that we had ever read Rachel Carson's *Silent Spring*, and essentially to become co-conspirators against the natural environment that we had come to defend. We had, in a sense, become hypocrites before we even began our tour of service in Guatemala.

We learned to apply Dipterex on the tree seedlings to control beetles, pill bugs and aphids. Dipterex was the Bayer Corporation's brand name for the organophosphate trichlorphon, which years later would be banned by many countries, and by the European Union. (Although notably *not* by the U.S.)

We learned to use another organophosphate, phoxim, known under the Bayer label Volaton, to combat the cotton bollworm larvae that fed on corn plants.[5] Phoxim has been banned by the E.U. for use on food crops since 2007.

Then there was the nasty stuff: Bayer's Agallol, a mercury-based fungicide that we learned to apply to our seedboxes in the nursery; and Mirex, which was to be applied on reforestation sites in the field to control the ubiquitous leafcutter ant. Mirex readily accumulates in aquatic and terrestrial food chains, often reaching harmful levels. It has been shown to cause cancer in lab animals. And it was banned in the United States the very same year we were standing there under a Costa Rican sun learning how to apply it.

* * *

We finished our training every day exhausted, yet full of new information, ideas, and inspiration. But less than six weeks into our training program in this idyllic, rural hamlet called La Guácima, all of a sudden one day I got desperately sick. Stomach cramps, fever, diarrhea—the works. I barely made it through the afternoon training session, and I walked back to my host family's house in a daze. When I refused dinner because I couldn't even look at the food, my host mother *doña* Mathilde knew something was up. I went straight to bed. I lay there decked out on a cot that was much too short for me, breathing shallow breaths and quietly telling myself, "Chris, you are not going to puke. You are *not* going to puke," while the kids and *doña* Mathilde were sitting on a couch in the next room listening to and laughing at the slapstick antics of *El Chavo del Ocho* on TV, at full volume. Thankfully, I did not puke.

After the show was over, *doña* Mathilde came into my darkened room to see me, and she carried with her a small glass bottle. By this time I felt almost delirious. Our conversation was rudimentary because I was still struggling with Spanish, but with gestures and the simplest of words she persuaded me to take off my shirt and lay on my stomach on the bed. Then without further ado came the rude surprise which any self-respecting *tico* would have welcomed as a godsent respite from suffering: *doña* Mathilde splashed my naked back with copious amounts of *aguardiente* straight from the bottle she was holding. At first I turned around and protested, "*¡No–no–NO señora! ¡Por favor que no!*" Not that it hurt, of course, or even felt the least bit uncomfortable. The cool alcohol on my skin actually felt sort of refreshing. But I was just so utterly shocked by the strangeness of this treatment which had no precedent in my whole darned background as a child of middle-class suburbia from upstate New York. In the end I had no choice but to relent—I was weak, nearly delirious, and my host mother was confident and deliberate in her ministrations.

The next morning I still could scarcely eat, but I think I ate something. And because I ate *something* at least, *doña* Mathilde was satisfied that her bedside attentions the night before had been rewarded. Rising from the breakfast table I put a jacket on because I felt chilly, which seemed odd in this tropical clime, and then I schlepped my things with unsteady gait over to the office of the training center where I would report myself as hopelessly ill and unfit for duty. The people in the office—probably recognizing the symptoms—took care of me right away, and I was driven to San José for tests. I was stricken now not only with illness but with the abject fear that this would put a perfunctory, unavoidable end to my adventure, no questions asked. Christ, a few weeks earlier they had shipped Paul Hlina back home to Maine because he had become just as sick, or sicker. Poor Paul, though, must have been much sicker, because I somehow eventually pulled out of it.

As it turned out, it was a case of giardiasis. The water, of course. Get used to the water.

* * *

Our Spanish instructors were a small group of young Costa Ricans, three or four women and one guy. One day the male trainer—let's call him Edilberto—sat down with me at the snack bar, and during this blessed little break in the middle of a four-hour stretch of Spanish immersion we talked for a few minutes about where we had come from. (Still in Spanish, of course, but we were on break, so it was more relaxed.) The snack bar looked for all the world like another chicken coop, except that it sat on a cement slab. While we talked I was distractedly casting sidelong glances at the two Shell No-Pest strips that were dangling from the low ceiling by the opposite wall, each of them covered with hundreds of fly cadavers.

We talked, and I mentioned to Edilberto I had recently come out of a place called Cornell, and I felt sort of pleased when he said he had actually heard of the place. Edilberto told me that he himself was studying economics part time at the university branch in Alajuela. And then, as if it somehow naturally followed from that piece of information, Edilberto told me he was a communist. Not just a believer in communist ideals, but an actual party member. The communists in Costa Rica had organized in the 1930s as the People's Vanguard Party (PVP), and in the early years their enthusiastic program of reforms had attracted quite a following. But later, between 1949 and 1970, they were effectively banned from the political arena. So for Edilberto and many others his age, now in the late 1970s, the resurrected PVP was, for all intents and purposes, a brand new political alternative.

My brief conversation with Edilberto highlighted one of the many disconnects between our training experience in Costa Rica and the mission that awaited us in Guatemala. For Costa Ricans have enjoyed, throughout most of that country's history, a degree of political freedom that can only be envied by their Central American neighbors. Sitting down over Cokes in a busy snack bar while Edilberto openly shared with me his leftist political affiliation was no more unusual than, say, Pitamber sharing with me his Marxist sympathies over a couple beers at a crowded eatery in upstate New York. Yet, as I was soon to find out, such unreserved sharing of one's beliefs and alliances could get you killed in Guatemala.[6]

But that wasn't the only disconnect we had to deal with. Indigenous communities in Costa Rica are non-existent, while nearly half of Guatemala's total population (about eight million around the time of this story) is indigenous Mayan. Indeed, virtually all of us in our training group would eventually be assigned to small, deeply traditional rural communities in the highlands where the indigenous percentage was actually closer to eighty percent. Given this stark contrast between the two countries, our cross-cultural training (which was a crucial third leg of the stool after language and technical

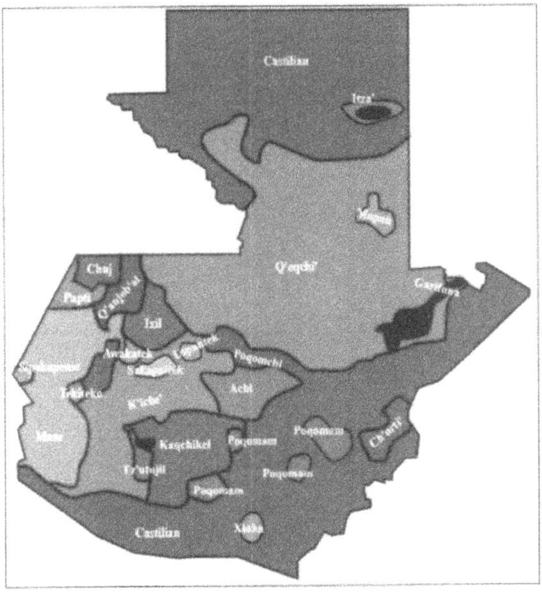

Mayan language groups in Guatemala (Source: Wikipedia)

training) became a largely theoretical exercise completely devoid of the immediacy of first-hand experience.

Language itself contributed even further to the disconnect. There are no fewer than twenty-three indigenous languages across the territory of Guatemala, in addition to Spanish. Mayan dialects with exotic and challenging names like Q'ekchi', Kaqchikel, Tz'utujil. In Costa Rica, Spanish only, unless you counted the English and German spoken by the expats who lived in the mountains or on the coast in their well-appointed retirement homes.

One final disconnect that could not be ignored: While Costa Rica abolished its military in 1949 and to this day has no standing army, Guatemala has a robust army that in the late 1970s numbered around 14,000 conscripts[7], including an elite special ops force known as the Kaibiles—a highly trained wing of the army formed in 1974 that, during our time in the country, would be assigned to undertake some of the most brutally effective counterinsurgency campaigns.[8]

The other "helping hand" extended by Americans: U.S. Marines training the Kaibiles in Guatemala. (Photo credit: U.S. Marine Corps Cpl. Brittany J. Kohler, Public Domain.)

Costa Rica was a beautiful country to visit, and I do not regret one minute of my three months there. But Costa Rica was not

Guatemala. And given the stark contrast between the two countries, for all practical purposes we might as well have been training in Pensacola or Phoenix.

* * *

An overview of Guatemala's history was most definitely *not* part of our training in La Guácima. Had it been, then it might have gone something like this:

It was the year 1896 when a seventeen-year-old by the name of Jorge Ubico pedaled his single-speed Barnes White Flyer bicycle to Guatemala's Hippodrome, and then, to everyone's surprise, raced it like a jackrabbit to become Guatemala's first national champion of the new sport known as *ciclismo*. Not only was the young Ubico a champion bicyclist, but he could also acquit himself quite admirably in a fencing match or in the boxing ring. As an adult, Ubico rose through the ranks of the military, and in 1931 he became president of the republic through an election in which his was the only name on the ballot.

President Ubico believed his most fundamental mission was to lead all of Guatemala in a "march towards civilization." Efficiency was the watchword of his administration, and in the name of efficiency Ubico promulgated a set of "Vagrancy Laws:"

> Those owning from 1 to 6.5 acres of land had to give one hundred days of work a year for wages. Those who owned

> less than an acre were obliged to give 150 days a year … If at the end of a year a man had not completed the allotted work days, he would either be imprisoned as a vagrant or else work out the incomplete time on the construction and repair of the roads. The vast majority of the peasants owned less than 6.5 acres, so that the needed labor for the plantations was easily assured.[9]

Efficiency. The Vagrancy Laws, it turned out, were only the beginning of a series of oppressive measures that aimed to harness the energy of the Guatemalan peasantry in service to the largest landowners in the country, including the notorious United Fruit Company. In the framework of later agrarian laws under Ubico, a form of debt peonage was reestablished, holding nearly the entire peasantry of Guatemala in a state of virtual slavery to the rich landowners. All of these measures aimed to please one large landowner more than anybody else: the United Fruit Company.

Jorge Ubico was a totalitarian dictator who had professed admiration for Adolf Hitler, and in fact was not unlike the German monster in many respects. Indeed, Guatemala during the thirteen-and-a-half year Ubico regime has been likened to "a modern jail."[10]

When Ubico suspended freedom of speech and the press on June 22, 1944, though, that was the last straw for most middle-class professionals, students, and his own junior officers. He was overthrown by a popular revolt the following day. Elections were called—the fairest and freest elections the people of Guatemala had seen—and a formerly exiled professor of philosophy by the name of Juan José Arévalo won the presidency in a landslide with over 80 percent of the vote.

Under Arévalo, Guatemala began to see almost immediately the democratic opening people had yearned for. The grossly unequal distribution of land in the country became a top priority for reform. In Guatemala 2.2 percent of the landowners owned 70 percent of the arable land, and the annual per capita income of agricultural workers was 87 dollars.[11] Under Arévalo, many foreign estates, especially those not under cultivation, were confiscated and redistributed to the *campesinos*. Landowners were obliged to provide adequate housing for their workers; new schools, hospitals, and houses were built; and a new minimum wage was introduced.[12]

Arévalo was succeeded by Jacobo Árbenz in a second fair and free election in 1950 and Árbenz continued the social reform policies of his predecessor. The centerpiece of his policy was an agrarian reform law under which uncultivated portions of large land-holdings were expropriated in return for compensation and then redistributed to poverty-stricken agricultural laborers. Approximately 500,000 people benefited from the decree, the majority of them indigenous people.

One entity that remained decidedly displeased by the reforms of the Árbenz administration, however, was the United Fruit Company. UFCO executives lobbied the Eisenhower administration to do something about Árbenz and the perceived attack on U.S. economic interests, and the result was the 1954 *coup d'état* sponsored, organized, and efficiently executed by the CIA, through Guatemalan operatives.

The outcome of the CIA-backed *coup d'etat* became clearly evident to every Guatemalan in very short order: the democratic

Frida Kahlo and Diego Rivera, 11 days before Kahlo's death, during a peaceful protest against U.S. intervention in Guatemala. (photographer not identified; July 2, 1954).

opening was reversed, brand new civil rights almost entirely rolled back, and the important land tenure reforms that had given so many poor Guatemalans the hope of at least a modicum of prosperity were entirely undone. The 1954 coup ushered in an era of violent suppression of the voices of justice and equality that would last another quarter century, up through the time of our arrival on the scene in late 1978.

The Guatemalan government's suppression of any and all popular movements aimed at national liberation was mainly the job of military intelligence, the feared "G-2" unit of the armed forces. The G-2 (and its rural counterpart, the S-2) had been trained, advised, and assisted by a succession of CIA operatives at least since the mid-nineteen-sixties.[13] This notorious unit—only mentioned in hushed voices, or never spoken of at all—performed its job with brutal efficiency, in the finest Ubico tradition.

None of us in the Peace Corps training program in La Guácima had more than a scant, cursory knowledge of Guatemala's troubled history. Yet, as volunteers we'd all soon be settling into rural communities all over the country's western highlands to become witnesses to the latest chapter in the whole turbulent saga.

* * *

Our most important choices in life often involve ambiguous value judgements and tradeoffs that twist some people into hopeless knots of indecision and inaction. It wasn't that way for me when I decided to join the Peace Corps to become America's representative in the developing world. I was well aware of the countervailing views at the time (and the tension between these views persists even today). But after considering them, what it came down to for me was simply my desire for adventure, my desire to *get out* and *do something in the world.* That was the urgent motivation that, for me, cast the deciding vote.

Still, there were at least three views or perspectives to think about in this matter, and I thought about them. They are: the view from altruism, the view from imperialism, and the view from self-determination. On the one hand, we like to think that an altruist would freely give of his or her knowledge and experience, without thought of recompense, in order to make some positive change happen within a community. But there's the rub, for it is distressingly common that it is only *the altruist's* knowledge and experience that the modern altruist is concerned with, simply because these are presumed (by the altruist, and by his or her teachers) to be superior to any knowledge or experience that already exists in the community. Thus, to the extent that any of the altruist's proposed solutions result in some positive change in the community, they are nonetheless solutions superimposed on the fabric of society, like a crude patch on a torn garment. And like a patch on a garment, the solution that is superimposed by the modern altruist is unlikely to be integrated and adopted by the society as a new way of life.

The imperialist, by contrast, exports knowledge and experience to an exotic land simply in order to feed the empire. To the extent that the people in a conquered territory gain new knowledge from their conquering masters, it is knowledge whose only end is to make the people more efficient cogs in the machinery of imperialism, whether that machinery takes the shape of a British East India Company—or, for that matter, a United Fruit Company.[14]

The only view that pays the respect that is due to an exotic culture is the view from the standpoint of *self-determination*. On this view we can only serve as *catalysts* for change, and in the process our own experience and knowledge must inform, and feed off of, and ultimately merge with the knowledge and experience within the community in order to create a productive synthesis.

We all came to Guatemala as modern altruists, and some, over time, grew into the role of serving as a mere catalyst in a vital process of self-determination. Over most of the past seventy-five years, America's policy towards Guatemala can be characterized as one of self-interest poisoned by a particularly virulent strain of anti-communism that clouded our vision. Clouded to the point where progressive social change with expanding justice for all could only be interpreted as another form of the Red Menace. That was America's failure. That was the cause of the CIA-sponsored *coup d'etat* in Guatemala in 1954, a *coup* that removed from office the country's last freely elected, truly progressive president of the twentieth century and installed in his place an almost uninterrupted lineage of generals and oligarchs who continued to rule the country through the day of my arrival.

Though I arrived at my posting in Guatemala as a naive, modern altruist, over the course of three years living in the community where I was assigned, I became increasingly committed to Guatemalan self-determination. And I think it was somewhere along the way that I learned to despise American imperialism.

* * *

There certainly was a prevailing mythos that undergirded the Peace Corps mission: We, the volunteers who came in peace from the United States, represented the greatest and most beneficent civilization the world had ever known; we were secular missionaries sent abroad by the dominant culture. We were highly trained technicians in forestry and agriculture, in fisheries and small business development, and politics were utterly irrelevant to the performance of our duties. We were expected to eschew politics at every turn and just focus on our mission. Our mission was to promote world peace and friendship by doing the job we were called upon to do, to help promote a better understanding of Americans on the part of Guatemalans, and to help promote a better understanding of Guatemalans on the part of Americans.

Some of the elements of the mythos that underpinned our mission were easier to digest than others. With respect to politics, as a trainee I felt confident and comfortable that I could passively observe political developments without getting directly involved in them. *Not a problem.*

What was harder to digest was the notion of American Exceptionalism which was implicit in the whole enterprise. If "exceptionalism" was intended to denote some sort of moral superiority, or worse, some kind of exempt status with respect to the rules of international law, then you could count me out. But that subtext was never explicit, except insofar as we were all clearly representatives of the very same government which had sabotaged Guatemalan democracy a couple decades earlier.

Our mission was to promote peace and friendship, but at the same time we were clearly pawns of a sort—instruments of a Cold War mentality which sought to win hearts and minds in a region of the world that might otherwise have become subject to the same "domino effect" that President Johnson and Secretary McNamara had once feared would shackle all of Southeast Asia under the yoke of Communism.

* * *

The mission, the mythos, and the man. "The man," meaning me—meaning each of us. Some kind of reconciliation was in order, but that reconciliation eluded me, at least for the duration of my training. To do the thing that was *necessary*—wasn't that at the heart of our mission? And wasn't it obvious what we needed to do? Plant trees; teach others to plant trees; save the crops growing on the mountainside from the inexorable forces of erosion. Simple plan, really, albeit complicated in the execution.

But was that the only task or service that would be needed of us?

* * *

Ah, but I was just a callow youth searching for a purpose. Ah, me—the memory of it all! And then there are the things that I have forgotten. What *was* the name of that guy who ran the *cantina* in town where we spent many an hour almost every evening? *Don* ______? And who can remember the name of that Costa Rican lager we all drank?

What the heck was the name of that lively, vivacious, and occasionally flirty gal who ran the *tienda* in the training camp? She was a real charmer, and always so solicitous whenever I stopped at the counter to buy a Coke or a chocolate bar with my miserable little training allowance. Ah me! There are just so many details I can't remember anymore, though I've often struggled to reach ever deeper into the recesses of my memory to recover them.

Hell, my story here *depends* on memory; I must work harder to plumb the depths.

> "Has it ever occurred to you that life is *all* memory? Except for each present moment that goes by so quickly you can hardly catch it?"

... Lines of Tennessee Williams (uttered by Elizabeth Taylor) in a moody, offbeat film called *Boom!* Tennessee Williams must have read Saint Augustine.

Yes, to catch each present moment, every single moment that races past us, and to feel its full intensity! And to fully grasp its *import*, its hidden meaning in the scheme of things. That is the elusive goal.

Each. Present. Moment. *Now.*

Then again (rising from my reverie), I suppose just remembering a name or two might be a win. My Internet lifeline reminds me now that the beer we drank was Imperial.

So it was that after three months of training, we stored away our memories and packed our bags and said goodbye to Costa Rica.

* * *

Left: The author during a break from training in La Guácima. (Photo taken by Raul Tuazon.) Right: The whole group on our last day in Costa Rica. (Photo by Bernie Rafalski.)

We finally arrived in Guatemala City (or just say, as we all said, "Guate") on December 18, 1978. Our plane touched down on the outskirts of the capital city after what seemed a rather harrowing descent from the blue skies above. Once on the ground, though, we breezed through customs, and then we were whisked across the city to the Peace Corps office in Zone 2, where we attended a short welcome session to meet the local staff. Country Director Mick Zenick greeted us there—the first of four CDs I would get to know during my time in Guatemala. After the dog and pony show at the office, we each picked up a check for our "settling-in allowance" from a pretty secretary named Sheny, and then we took off and walked uptown to cash our checks at the *Banco de Occidente*. Then on to 4th Avenue to catch one of the several buses to Antigua that were parked there and ready to roll.

Our very first bus trip from Guate to Antigua took well over an hour because once we left the city behind we mostly had to follow a rocky and rutted, dirt-road detour in order to reach the old colonial capital. We had to follow this more fatiguing route because the men from *Caminos* were busy carving a new four-lane, divided highway out of the hillsides and over the *arroyos*. Our detour around the highway construction was a long, bumpy ride through dust and debris. The clouds of brown dust from other passing vehicles on a particularly narrow piece made it hard to distinguish the barest outline of the huts and shanties and little brake and tire repair shops that lined either side of the road.

The bus ride got smoother towards the end, though, and at length we finally reached the picturesque cobblestone streets of Antigua. We had a rough idea when to yell, "*¡Aquí no más!*" (Stop here!), and then we pretty much followed our instincts to get to the *pensión*. We found our pre-paid *pensión* situated right under Antigua's picturesque cross-street arch, and it was appropriately named *La Pensión del Arco*—the place that would be our home for the next three weeks while we received the last of our technical and cross-cultural classes.

Christmas was right around the corner, and our three-and-a-half months of training were finally drawing to a conclusion. It had been a long, hard slog for all of us. I think it is fair to say that we were all impatient to get out to our respective postings around the country, and just get to work. The new training venue for our last three weeks made our anxious anticipation even harder to bear: We were *in Guatemala* now, surrounded by Guatemalans and Guatemalan culture, so the prospect of settling into our assigned communities was no longer just an idea or a theoretical possibility. It was now real. It was imminent.

We were chomping at the bit and feeling a little dispirited by the remainder of the training program because it seemed like overkill and redundancy at this point. The lectures were getting boring. We needed an adventure—like, *now*. Next Monday would be Christmas Day. It was Friday, and we had a weekend to kill. So, a bunch of us decided with alacrity: fuck, let's *do it*! Let's go climb Volcán de Agua, that massive conical prominence that towers above the whole town, let's do it tomorrow while we're still here and have the chance! Who knows when we'll get this chance again? We plodded impatiently through the afternoon sessions, and then those of us who were game raced back to the *pensión*, dropped our stuff there, and then rushed over to the nearest little *tienda* (store) to buy some food and drinks that looked portable enough for a long day's hike. A few guys who planned to stay overnight on top of the volcano needed more food and supplies, but I wasn't up for that.

We rose before the break of dawn on Saturday morning, got a quick breakfast for fifty *centavos* at a *comedor* in Antigua's main market, and then we hustled over to the *terminal de buses* to catch a ride to nearby Santa María de Jesús at the base of the volcano. It was a short uphill ride with many switchbacks climbing maybe five hundred meters or so in altitude. When we got to the town, we found it to be much more rustic and down-to-earth than tourist-bedeviled Antigua. Despite the signs of poverty, which were everywhere, I felt the town had a distinct charm and tranquility all its own. The streets were quiet.

Eighty-six years before our visit—almost to the day—the archeologist Alfred Percival Maudslay and his wife had walked these same streets before climbing to Volcán de Agua's summit. Maudslay's wife Anne described the town using characteristically Victorian pejoratives: she walked through the "miserably dirty village street"; entered "the huge, ugly church," and saw everywhere "the men [who]

Volcán de Agua as seen from Santa María de Jesús in 1895. (Photograph by Alfred Percival Maudslay public domain)

Halfway up *Volcán Agua*, 12/23/78 (with Volcán Fuego smoldering in the distance).

almost without exception were drunk with *chicha*."[15] The Victorians were so damned judgmental.

Our ascent to Agua's summit, some 1,500 meters above Santa María de Jesús, took nearly four hours. Halfway up the mountainside I stood at a lookout point and gazed upon the same vista that Maudslay (standing at the summit) had once found so disappointing, but which to me was utterly enchanting: as it was still morning, the entire *Valle de Panchoy* was swathed in billowy white clouds which concealed every bit of evidence of civilization down below, and only the highest peaks in the distance emerged like noble islands in a great, troubled sea. The smoldering summit of Volcán de Fuego was prominent among the islands. For Maudslay this ethereal scene frustrated his intention of getting good pictures, and it maddened him; for me it made for one of the most precious photographs of my whole time in Guatemala.

* * *

It was Christmas Eve, exactly one week after our arrival in Guatemala, and a restaurant down the street from our *pensión* was advertising a special holiday buffet featuring turkey and smoked ham with all the trimmings for the expats in town, and for anybody else who was willing to cough up some twelve quetzales or so for the *prix fixe* menu—which was a lot for a meal in those days. Dinner at the restaurant turned out to be a rather crowded affair, as the place was not huge and the advertisement in the window had definitely worked—but in the end we all left more than satisfied. There was wine to go with the dinner, but hell, we were just a bunch of slovenly Peace Corps volunteers who had come off the street, so we each had a bottle of *Gallo* lager parked by our plate.

Dinner taken care of, what to do next on a Christmas Eve far away from home? I wandered around along the cobblestone streets with a couple of my buddies as the night grew darker. We walked and talked and then I think we stopped for a minute to look at some pretty girls, all in tight jeans, who were gathered by a bench in the park laughing and talking. Too young. And anyway, it was Christmas Eve. We walked along some more, and then I guess we lost track of each other, and next thing I knew I was walking alone. Walking down the streets of Antigua all alone on Christmas Eve, I started wondering what my family was doing back home. They had surely all gathered for Christmas Eve in New Hartford, and by now they were probably finished opening presents—the German way, the night before.

But in Antigua the night was still young, as they say, and by ten or so I found myself following one of the last *posadas* before Christmas—a joyful procession of a couple hundred local citizens walking down the middle of the cobblestone street carrying bright candles on lantern poles, young and old walking together shaking their colorful, pebble-laden *chin-chines* and tortoise shells, and a few young mothers here and there carrying their infants wrapped in colorful, striped shawls. The rhythm of their hand-held percussion pieces was a mesmerizing repetition of just five beats over and over and over. *Clack-clack-CLICK-cla-lack. Clack-clack-CLICK-cla-lack. Clack-clack-CLICK-cla-lack.*

Then, over the sound of those five mesmerizing beats, a pair of autochthonous flutes called *tzijolajes* joined in unison—*twee-twee-DEEE-tweelee. Twee-twee-DEEE-tweelee. Twee-twee-DEEE-tweelee.* It wasn't a melody so much as a wordless incantation. *Our tireless progress—clack-clack-CLICK-cla-lack!*

In the middle of the procession, following the lantern-holders, six men carried on their shoulders a religious float, or *anda*, featuring life-sized figures of Mary large with child and Joseph wearing an ivory-colored straw hat on his head, a *sombrero* like the kind that any *campesino* would wear in the fields, the two of them surrounded by flowers and fruits and Christmas tree lights covering the whole ambulatory platform. The *anda* looked like it must have been a pretty hefty burden for six men to carry, but they solemnly walked along at the pace set by those in the lead. More people followed behind the *anda*—many, many people—mothers and daughters, fathers and sons, fathers carrying little ones on their shoulders, all walking along, most of them rattling their hand-painted *chin-chines*. And with the *chin-chines*, a new sound was added to the sounds in the street:

Ras-carás, ras-carás, ras-carás-carás.
Ras-carás, ras-carás, ras-carás-carás.

I walked along with them, but I kept on the narrow sidewalk. I felt like I was part of something, but at the same time I felt isolated, like a mere spectator.

At length the *posada* arrived at its destination, which was a home or business chosen for the honor that night, but the front door of the place was tightly closed. And so, in accordance with custom, a small chorus at the head of the procession began singing their hymn of supplication[16]:

En el nombre del cielo,	*In heaven's name*
yo os pido posada,	*I beg of you lodging,*
pues no puede andar,	*for my beloved wife*
mi esposa amada.	*cannot go on anymore.*

Inside the white stuccoed adobe building, behind the heavy oak door, a group of singers who were alert to the visit sang out in response:

Aquí no es mesón,	*This isn't a hotel!*
sigan en su camino,	*Keep going along your way,*
yo no puedo abrir,	*I cannot open up for you,*
no sea algún tunante.	*So don't be such a rogue!*

This exchange goes on for several stanzas, with lines like *Don't be inhuman; grant us some charity,* getting only cold responses: *leave me alone and let me sleep!* But when Joseph incidentally mentions his own name in a later stanza, and his wife's as well, then there is sudden recognition within the compound—there's a 'for heaven's sake why didn't you say so!' moment—and only then the great front door opens wide to reveal that everything inside is already prepared for the festivities of a warm welcome. There are *tamales negros* and *paches* laid out on deep, wide serving dishes, there's a giant, steaming cauldron of *ponche de frutas*, and many folding chairs are all lined up against the walls inside.

Dichosa la casa
Que abriga este dia
A la virgen pura
La hermosa Maria
Entren Santos Peregrinos
Reciban este rincón
Que aunque es pobre la morada
Os la doy de corazón.

Happy is the house
that gives shelter this day
To the pure virgin
The beautiful Maria.
Enter Holy Pilgrims,
Receive this little corner
for although my home is poor,
I give it to you from my
heart.

After seemingly endless wandering through the dark, uncaring city of Bethelehem, Mary and Joseph have finally found their *posada* for the night.

I stopped and watched as the *peregrinos* were milling about on the cobblestone and entering the compound in small groups to partake of the abundance that was laid out. Everybody who wanted to got a chance to go in and get a bite to eat—a steaming *tamal* wrapped in a dark green, wet and slimy banana leaf, a *pache* similarly wrapped, or maybe a sweet roll which was more convenient for carry-out—and of course some hot *ponche* in a disposable cup. No charge; it was an honor for the host to serve you. I watched from the other side of the street, but I could not pretend to be a part of this congregation of souls. I felt very much in the moment, I even felt a fleeting sense of joy among these people, yet as a fair-skinned, bespectacled, six-foot-three gringo on the street corner I felt also those ineluctable degrees of separation and isolation that would make me once again sad and lonely: my first Christmas alone, abroad among strangers.

It was time to move on now, so I started walking back down the street the way we had all come. Suddenly, behind me near the street corner that I had just stepped from—

CRACK-CRACK-CRACKETY-CRACK-CRACK-
CRACKETY-CRACKETY- CRACK-CRACK-
BOOM!

Somebody had lit an *ametralladora* on the street near the *posada*, a long red belt of firecrackers all strung together, fifty or sixty in all, with a cherry bomb at the end for the grand finale. *Ametralladora*: meaning, literally, machine gun. Because it almost sounded like one. Merry Christmas to all, and to all a good night.

But things would surely be going on at *La Merced* church, for I'd been told a procession of *peregrinos* with Mary and Joseph would be arriving there as well. It was now a little past eleven, but I felt energized walking through the brisk night air. I walked fast over the cobblestone streets, trying hard to leave my feelings of solitude behind. It sort of worked. I was just a few blocks from *La Merced*, and the church itself was scarcely a block from the *Pensión El Arco* where I had started out before dinner.

When I got to the church there was a huge crowd of locals surrounding the plaza in front of it, only here the crowd included a few tourists as well. The whole area in front of the church was bathed in bright, sparkling, incandescent light. Floodlights illuminated the enormous alabaster and saffron colored facade, and the tall jacarandas on either side of the plaza were brilliantly ablaze with strings of thousands of white and yellow Christmas lights wrapping round and round each majestic trunk. Most of the plaza in the middle was vacant; everybody was patiently milling around the perimeter watching, waiting, chatting with their neighbors, purchasing little bags of *golosinas* (sweets) from the street vendors.

The steps up to the church entrance were clear, because another group of *peregrinos* carrying their *anda* with Mary and Joseph would be arriving soon, and the whole procession would surely be entering through there. But why so much empty space in the plaza? I looked around and I saw the faces of *antigüeños* all around me in a celebratory mood, little children playing with sparklers while some older kids lit firecrackers here and there, couples embracing in the moist night air which was getting cooler and cooler. It was getting close to midnight.

A guy my age standing nearby looked like he might speak English, so I acknowledged him first with a friendly nod, then with a tentative "Hey, how's it going, man? Whaddaya think of all this?" He answered in vaguely accented English, "This is marvelous! It's really quite exciting. I think we're all waiting for something to happen here!" It seemed oddly comforting to find in a total stranger a face that seemed somehow familiar, but that was because I was still thinking about life back home on this night. We exchanged a tentative handshake and introduced ourselves. The guy's name was Emil, from Denmark, and he was there as a tourist to see the sights around Guatemala. He had just arrived a few days earlier, he said. I told him what I was doing in Antigua, about the job I was preparing for, and he nodded and said something above the din of a few firecrackers, but otherwise not much reaction. Still, he was a friendly sort, and we somehow forged a mutual, unspoken agreement to hang together, at least for a while.

Over on the other side of the empty plaza space we now saw a very Mayan looking fellow, short and stout and uncharacteristically hatless, who with the help of others was mounting a large lattice frame of sticks and spindles over his head in such a way that the weight of the whole elaborate arrangement rested on his shoulders. We watched as the stout figure, now partially hidden, shifted his weight from side to side to get the unwieldy frame of sticks and spindles balanced just right on his shoulders, and then he grasped a horizontal wooden bar at the level of his chin and walked with a solemn gait over to the massive stone crucifix in the middle of the plaza. There he knelt on one knee before the giant cross, and I suppose he prayed. Maybe it was a standard liturgical prayer that he prayed, something from the rosary, or maybe he was praying for his own personal safety in the act to come. Within the space of a minute he stood up, crossed himself with some difficulty while holding the grab bar with his other hand, and stood there hunched under the weight of the lattice frame.

Then a man who was well-dressed in suit and tie—the *only* man dressed so formally in this crowd of *campesinos* and simple folk who were really the salt of the earth, came up from behind and lit one tiny corner of the wood frame with a cigarette lighter. It was only then that I noticed the figure of a bull's head painted in black on a small panel affixed to the front of the frame of sticks.

And so began *la quema del torito*. The burning of the bull. It took less than three seconds for the first bombs and sparklers to ignite, and from there the spectacular fury of the blaze quickly spread to the entire elaborate armature resting on the man's back. A brass band that was waiting off to the side now struck up a happy little melody of the oom-pah, oom-pah sort. The entire lattice framework was laced with dozens of sparklers, spinners and Roman candles that erupted into flames and sparks seemingly all at once, crashing and whistling, all while the diminutive Mayan who carried these shooting and spiraling pyrotechnics on his back skipped and danced around in figure eights all over the whole plaza, forward and backward, gracefully to and fro, making several mock-threatening passes very near the people crowded around the perimeter, then skipping around in smaller circles in the middle as people in the crowd responded with oohs and ahs and small children cried out, some with delight but others out of pure fear.

The noise of the booms and cracks and hisses and whistles during this whole display of animated pyrotechnics made one worry for the sense of hearing of the intrepid performer who kept on skipping and dancing from one end of the plaza to the other. Soon we were all engulfed in a blue haze with a distinctly sulfurous odor, and then at last the frequency of the bombs and whistles began to dissipate a little. But the dancing bundle of sparks and flames kept on going for a surprisingly long time, and we both wondered out loud, the Dane and I (for we were still standing there together with our mouths agape), how anybody could carry that much pyrotechnic firepower on their back. And dancing with it besides!

The pyrotechnics in the plaza in front of a brilliantly illuminated *La Merced* church as midnight approached on Christmas Eve filled me with an ecstatic sense of wonder and amazement like nothing I had experienced before in my life. This was an experience, the first of many, that would seal my love affair with the people of Cuauhtēmallān, the place of many trees. Or, as the travel brochures call it, the land of eternal spring.[17]

CHAPTER 3

Settling Into Rabinal

With hungry hearts through the heat and cold,
We never much thought we could get very old,
We thought we could sit forever in fun,
And our chances really was a million to one.
—Bob Dylan, *Bob Dylan's Dream*

Ah, the sheer excitement of embarking on the next stage of your life! You want to immerse yourself in the all-encompassing present during every waking moment—though our history makes that impossible. Recollections of the recent or distant past always seem to impinge upon my being in the moment.

On the four-and-a-half-hour chicken bus ride from Guate to Rabinal I spent almost the whole time looking out the window. I did not want to miss a single kilometer of vistas, people, or the most incongruous or insignificant detail along the way. A few clicks outside of Guate, on the jagged rock face of a big, deep road cut, the words "TRABAJEMOS JUNTOS," urging us to all work together, were painted in five-foot, peeling white letters. A couple hours later our bus traversed the Río Motagua, and after stopping briefly in El Rancho where everybody could buy refreshments through the bus window, we began the winding ascent to Santa Elena junction where the bus would stop for another few minutes, then turn off to the left and make the equally winding descent down into the valley of Salamá. After the El Rancho stop, I lit a cigarette and watched out my window as caliche and cacti were transformed, in the space of an hour's uphill climb, into the lush greenery of a cloud forest.

At the next stop *en la cumbre de Santa Elena*, women carrying baskets and broad, wicker trays on their heads crowd onto the bus or meet our hungry faces at the passenger windows, each calling out the particular item she is selling.

"*¡Semilla de marañon a veinticinco la bolsa!*" Fresh cashews sound like a good idea.

"*¡Chocobananos a veinte len! ¡Chocobananos!*" Chocolate-covered bananas on a stick—even better.

"*¡Tayuyos! ¡Hay tayuyos! ¡Calientes y sabrosos!*"

Tayuyo. I love the playful sound of the word. *Tayuyo* is the name given to the adobe slabs which, glued together by mortar, make a home. It is also the name given to a pair of flour tortillas with a helping of mashed black beans, like mortar, in the middle.

"*¡Dos tayuyos aquí porfa!*" I call out.

"*Son cincuenta len, señor. ¿Quiere chile? Pués aquí está—¡tiene que chilearse! Gracias, señorón. ¡Que le vaya bién!*"

Two *tayuyos* with a sprinkle of chile make a good lunch. To wash it down, I bought a Coke from one of the small boys, *patojos*, who were chasing from window to window all around the chicken bus. I received the Coke in a plastic baggie with a thin, frail straw.

All of this took less than ten minutes. The bus driver blew his loud klaxon, and we began our 2,000 foot descent to the departmental capital of *Tz'alam Ha*—Salamá, where one of my fellow volunteers, Carlos, got off the bus because that was his posting. From that point on, it was another forty-five minutes through San Miguel Chicáj and over the narrow and treacherous mountain road that rose a thousand feet or so and descended once again to reach the long, semiarid valley of Urram: Rabinal, which would be my home for a while.

I got off the bus in the central plaza of Rabinal, and the *ayudante* (the driver's helper) climbed up on the roof and threw my backpack down to me. Then I stood there in the dust behind the bus, which was already headed for Cubulco, and a strange and remarkable feeling came over me. *Me*, alone at last along the way, far, far from colleagues and trainers and teachers and supervisors, here on the path I had chosen, I suddenly felt all past regrets and failures peel away from me, and I felt an invigorating freedom and hopefulness that, I swear, might have almost made me forget all physical constraints such as the fifty pounds of belongings on my back.

I looked all around to try to take in every feature of this plaza that soon would become a familiar part of my daily life. Facing the gazebo in the middle of the park, I turned around and saw the *municipalidad* behind me, a long, white façade comprising (from left to right) a tiny sub-office of the *Policia Nacional*, a post and telegraph office, a grand ballroom locked tight on this sunny afternoon, and the municipal office where I supposed the *alcalde* could be found if I ever needed him. (The 'him' turned out to be a 'her,' as I discovered a few days later. She had been appointed by acclamation some few months prior to my arrival, as the previous mayor had been run out of town for stealing from the coffers.)

There was a shoeshine boy sitting on a concrete bench nearby, so I figured I might as well take care of that before heading off for the house I was seeking, the house that my PCV predecessor was calling home.

"*¿Cuánto me cobra por un lustre, patojo?*" I inquire.

"*Un par de chocas, señor,*" was the boy's reply.

"*¿Chocas?*"

"*Cincuenta len.*"

I was still learning the local currency. Or rather, the local slang for the local currency. One *len*, one *centavo.* One *choca*, twenty-five cents. Four *chocas* to a quetzal, which at this juncture in the country's history still remained at unfaltering parity with the U.S. dollar. The boy who shined my boots—let's call him José for that might well have been his name—looked and acted like a perfect street urchin straight out of central casting, and not in the least afraid to hold a conversation with a very strange-looking stranger.

"What are you doing here," José asked, while earnestly scuffing away at my boots with his brush.

"I came here to work. Plant trees."

"And how long will you be here in Rabinal?"

"Two years—I hope."

"Yaeeeeeeeee," he whistled, looking up at me, making a dramatic gesture I would soon get accustomed to. "That's a long time!"

"For a little boy, yes," I said. Then I thought and added, "I guess for me, too." As José thought about this he put down his brush and grabbed the flat tin of shoe polish from his little bag. He daubed some polish onto a rag and went back to work on the boots.

"Where is your home, *señor*?"

"*Los Estados Unidos*," I responded. Though, truth be told, I wasn't at all sure what 'home' I might go back to in the States if I had ever to leave. I was acutely aware that my parents would not take kindly to an adult boarder if I unexpectedly showed up at their doorstep, blood or no blood.

"Yoo - NIGHT'd - Staytz," the boy parroted back to me, in his staccato version of English. Where he had picked that up is anybody's guess. This was another rhetorical flourish, though, that I would grow accustomed to in the days to come. The locals, especially in the *campo*, liked to repeat any foreign sounding term or expression they have heard, but after their own fashion, drawing out the syllables in order to savor, or ponder, the idea of it.

"*Así es*," I responded.

* * *

The itinerant carnival rides rolled into town a couple days before the week of Rabinal's *feria titular de San Pablo Apóstol* in late January. The disassembled girders, chains and machinery of the rides were towed behind aging pickups from another decade, or else loaded onto a flatbed truck with badly worn tires. Given all the tight curves and hazards of the narrow dirt road through the mountains, it was amazing that they all made it to Rabinal in one piece. But there they were—the Ferris wheel, the wave swinger, the super slide—and within a few hours all three or four of them had set up shop in a tight corner of the main plaza between the church and the *alcaldía*. I imagined that each concessionaire must have kept a pocket calendar showing the *feria* dates for all of the towns in Guatemala. That way I supposed they could just drive from one town to the next, basically all year long. San Rafael Pie de la Cuesta in October, San Andrés Xecul in November, Santa Cruz del Quiché honoring their *Santa Elena de la Cruz* in August, *la feria de Santiago* in Cubulco (the next town down the road from us) in July. And then there's the ever-changing date of that *feria* in the ancient Mayan city of Zacualpa, because that one always occurs forty days after Good Friday.

The carnival rides in that little corner of the plaza lent a familiar atmosphere reminiscent of a small-town fair anywhere in upstate New York—or for that matter, anywhere in America. But that's where the familiarity ended. For beyond that little patch of ground in the corner of the plaza one immediately became immersed in the full experience of celebration, inebriation, and mystical rites that have characterized the annual *feria* in Rabinal ever since the Spaniards laid down their swords and came to the *Valle de Urram* instead with their cross (which must have looked for all the world like another kind of weapon), to settle a land that was already well settled by native Mayans who called themselves the *Achí*. Because the Spaniards had come here to conquer the land with a cross rather than a sword, this whole region in the middle of the Guatemalan territory became known by the name of *Verapaz*—True Peace.

Vendors had come from far and wide to sell their wares during the *feria*, each one of them having set up a makeshift stall in a ragged line by the side of the park. I was shacking up with a sleeping bag on the floor in the house where Don, my PCV predecessor lived. My first or second night there, Don had a friend stay over for the night, the departing volunteer who was finishing up in Cubulco. Don's pal was pretty crazy, I thought, but we sat around and talked and drank beers through much of the night. It was getting quite late when I decided I had to get out of the house and check out the *mercado*, hopefully to find a good woolen blanket for the cold January nights in Rabinal. I'd been drinking liters of *Cabro* with the others all evening, so by now I also felt I just needed to get out of the house and work off some of that buzz with a brisk walk. Trouble was, though, once I started walking I realized it was more than a buzz and I was actually quite drunk. Nevertheless, I found my way to the *mercado*, found myself a vendor from Momostenango where they weave some of the finest wool blankets in all of Guatemala, and ended up paying the guy his initial asking price because I was too drunk to haggle. Damned good blanket, though; I still have it here and it looks like...well, almost new.

* * *

I lived in a three-room house that I shared with another volunteer by the name of Gene, who went by Eugenio in his work with the *campesinos*. Our wood frame house was a little atypical for Rabinal, but by no means ostentatious. (All of the homes in town were made either of adobe—the most prevalent material—or concrete block, or, in the poorer outskirts of town, simply bamboo-like sticks called *vara* that were lashed together with makeshift twine.) We had a nice little tiled veranda out back which doubled as an open-air kitchen, and a small yard with an achiote tree close by and, in the far corner by the adobe wall, a burn pit for trash. We were lucky enough to have hot water for showers (but for showers only), thanks to a *calentador Goliath* that was installed on the shower head. The *Goliath* was a frightening device, at least on first view, with its live wires only a couple inches above the downward water stream. Notwithstanding the sense of terror one had to suppress when standing under it, the device actually heated our water very nicely as it came out of the shower head. And mornings between December and February were indeed chilly.

A home made of *vara*: one of the humblest living arrangements. (Photo courtesy of Lewis Johnson)

There was also an accessory shed by the house which I would be using to store the two or three tons of "food for work" that I would always have on hand to help promote my soil conservation projects. Most of the food commodities that I stored in that shed came on a truck from CARE every few months, though later on there was a West German relief agency known as COGAAT (the German-Guatemalan Food for Work Cooperative) that got into the mix as well. The CARE food consisted of surplus commodities from the United States, while the COGAAT food consisted of local commodities like corn and black beans that were generally preferred by the *campesino* beneficiaries because they at least knew what to do with corn and beans. Most of the CARE food was sold for cash—especially the white enriched flour, which easily netted several quetzales per bag at the local bakery.

Our little shed by the house, stacked high with *quintal* bags of COGAAT food and scores of *medio-quintales* from CARE, turned into a real pest magnet. I had to move the food through my storeroom and out to the *campo* quickly enough to avoid an infestation of *gorgojos*, beetles, which you knew you had if you could hear the bags of bulgur softly crackling. As for the mice, it didn't matter how quickly I could keep things moving along— because they were always a menace. Every couple months or so I would enlist the help of my counterpart Juan Pablo and maybe an additional *vivero* worker, and the three of us would spend an afternoon slowly prowling around the storeroom—each of us with a machete in hand—and if we were lucky we'd decapitate maybe a couple of the buggers in an hour's time.

Eugenio didn't have to deal with these food commodity issues, but he had to put up with me dealing with them. Eugenio worked in the promotion of family fish ponds, which were intended to introduce a supplementary source of protein in the rural Guatemalan diet, as well as an opportunity for income generation. (I joked once with Eugenio that my *gorgojo*-infested flour might be a good source of protein, too.) Eugenio traveled far and wide among the *aldeas* of Rabinal and nearby Cubulco teaching *campesinos* how to build their own fish ponds, how to stock them with carp and tilapia, how to maintain them, and later how to harvest the fish for dinner or for sale.

Eugenio and I had inherited not one but two cats from my PCV predecessor, named Leo & Felix. (*Que original, ¿no?*) They were my constant company (and yes, good mousers when they felt like it) for almost all of two years. I was definitely a 'cat person'; still am to this day. I bought my cats Purina chow from a small, crowded but well-stocked supermarket near the Peace Corps office in Guate. Leo and Felix were the best fed cats in Rabinal—probably in all of Baja Verapaz—and they repaid me by helping to control the rodents that always threatened the ton or two of P.L. 480 Food for Work stored in the house.[18]

Leo and Felix became my companions every evening as I sat reading in my hammock on a poorly lit veranda. But then one day well into my second year in Rabinal, Leo didn't come back home, and I never saw him again. He just disappeared. A few months later Felix came home with his tail missing, but still alive. Obviously some kids (or possibly an adult) had messed with him. This was harder to take than the disappearance, since poor Felix was obviously terrified and hurting badly. I wanted to help him with some first aid, but I didn't know exactly how to go about it, other than to put some Neosporin on the wound. He was so terrified that he no longer even trusted me. He ate a little (only in my absence), and died a couple days later. I buried him in the backyard.

The experience with Leo and Felix seemed almost like a metaphor for the life of the *pueblo* that would reveal itself to me only much later.

* * *

Rabinal, Baja Verapaz, is a *municipio* of over three hundred square kilometers set in the heart of Guatemala. If you were to look at a map of the country and then place your finger on what appears to be more or less the dead-center middle of it, the tip of your finger would probably be resting pretty near Rabinal. And around the *municipio* you would see a departmental boundary shaped (if you use your imagination) like a fat bird spreading its wings—that is Baja Verapaz. The town lies in a long, broad valley called *Urram,* at an altitude of 970 meters, while its thirty-five hamlets or *aldeas* are scattered both within that valley as well as in the mountains, which reach an altitude of over two thousand meters. The total population of the *municipio* in 1973 was 20,393, only thirty percent of whom lived in the town center.

The indigenous people of Rabinal, like their neighbors living east, west and south of them, all speak a Mayan language known as Achí. The guttural sounds of Achí, supported by an alphabet comprising twenty-two consonants and ten vowels, are closely related to other native Mayan languages such as Kaqchikel, Tzu'utujil and K'iché. All told, Achí is spoken by over 160,000 Mayans living primarily in the Baja Verapaz department.[19]

The climate in Rabinal is tropical: records from 1978 show an average annual precipitation of about seventy centimeters. That's close to the annual precip in, say, Rochester, New York. The rainy season runs from May or June to September or October; the hottest, driest months are March and April. That's when the cicadas sing.

Besides maize and beans, peanuts and watermelon are grown in the *aldeas* that go by the names of Xococ and Patixlán, sugar cane in various *aldeas* at intermediate altitudes, and then there is the famous Rabinal orange, a delicious product of the *regadío,* the irrigated land on the edge of town. Coffee is grown everywhere.

Public water supply in the central town was available from six in the morning until two or three in the afternoon. Electricity, check. Police substation with two cops, but no patrol car. Military garrison on the edge of town, but no bank. One telephone in town, which was located in the post and telegraph office. (And I never got a chance to use it.) Personal computers not invented yet, nor cell phones nor the Internet. The daily newspaper was usually, but not always, to be found. And finally, leave your credit card at home; all transactions in Rabinal were strictly cash.

The physical presence of the Guatemalan government in Rabinal included the schools, the Ministry of Agriculture's extension service known as DIGESA, a community development agency known as *Desarrollo de la Comunidad*, our tree nursery representing the National Forestry Institute (INAFOR), a two-man post and telegraph office, the two-man detachment of the National Police that I mentioned, and the *destacamento militar* on the edge of town where thirty to forty soldiers were based.

Then there was also the humanitarian organization *Centro de Integración Familiar* (CIF, also known as the *Hogar Rural*) in Pachalúm, an *aldea* located just a kilometer outside of town on the road to San Miguel Chicaj. The *Hogar Rural*, founded by a Jesuit priest a couple years before my arrival, was devoted to a variety of community development activities in four or five target *aldeas* including Chichupac, Pichec, Nimacabaj, and Chitucán. The organization was now under the capable leadership of a Spanish priest who hailed from Madrid, *padre* Gregorio Donoso.

My predecessor Don Washco had worked with the folks at CIF, so it made sense for me to continue doing the same. And so every Saturday morning I sat down for an hour or so with four or five *promotores forestales* representing the aforementioned target *aldeas.* We sat under the shade of a big old ceiba tree near the CIF office in Pachalum and we talked about maintaining the small tree nurseries each of the *promotores* had set up under Don's guidance. They told me what tools and materials they needed to keep things going, and I dutifully took note so that I could later put together a CARE requisition for them. It would take time to get the items they needed, I told them, but I promised to make it happen. We also talked about best practices in soil conservation such as terracing the farm plots located on steep slopes, and I tried engaging the men in some casual conversation in order to learn more about the communities where they lived. I promised to go out and visit each of them very soon.

On the day of my first meeting with the *promotores forestales*, Padre Gregorio wanted to show me around before my class started. We walked around the grounds of CIF together, and he pointed out the small main office, the *cursillo* (teaching) rooms, the rabbit hutches, and the rustic kitchen area where the women from the *aldeas* received lessons in domestic hygiene. The good *padre* then insisted I walk with him the short distance from the office to a spot nearby where a steady old ox with sad eyes was harnessed to a horizontal pole and was walking in a slow, endless circle around a central cistern. Water bubbled and trickled around the lid of the cistern, and a short pipe guided a steadier flow of water down to a steel drum that was positioned off to the side. It was in fact a serviceable water well with a pump of the *padre's* own design: a *noria*, in fact, straight out of Spain's La Mancha, an ingenious device that for centuries had relied on a harnessed draught animal walking in circles to draw up water from the ground below. Padre Gregorio, lisping his c's and z's in fine Castilian, asked me if I was familiar with *Don Quixote*, and I proudly told him I was. *"Pues, yo soy Don Quixote,"* he told me with a wry smile, *"¡y esto es mi molino!"*

Besides the conservation classes every Saturday, there were also weekly planning and coordination meetings with Padre Gregorio, Güicho the CIF administrator, the itinerant doctor who came from Salamá, and Julio, the *agrónomo*. Our exchange of information during these meetings was mostly concise and confined to a small number of topics: the current state of the rabbit hutches and their recent progress in promoting them among the *aldeanos*; the doctor's progress report on vaccination efforts; my own report on the weekly class I was giving; and my visits to the *aldeas*. Padre Gregorio always listened with slightly condescending patience to my halting reports, but on the whole I think they were all supportive and even appreciative of my presence among them. A more fraternal relationship with the CIF staff—especially with Güicho—would come only much later. But it did happen.

* * *

During our Peace Corps training we all had to become thoroughly familiar with the scope of our duties. Manage a community tree nursery; grow it larger if you can. Talk to people about planting trees. Talk to anybody who would listen to you—farmers, schoolchildren, men, women, elected leaders, shop owners in town, ag extensionists from DIGESA; the small landowners, the larger landowners, and even the landless. Don, the volunteer who served before me in Rabinal, had set up a very functional, nicely terraced tree nursery north of town, close by a stream where the women from the nearby *colonia* washed their clothes and then would spread out their colorful *huipiles* and *cortes* on the rocks to dry. In the nursery we raised pine species as well as deciduous seedlings—mostly *Pinus oocarpa, P. tenuifolia, Cupressus lusitanica, Ceiba aesculifolia, Casuarina equisetifolia, Swietenia macrophylla,* and *Gravilea.* The *Gravilea* was a preferred shade species for coffee plantations. *Swietenia* is mahogany—very slow growing, but the idea of having it in my nursery simply intrigued me. Later we started raising *Leucaena* seedlings because they were being promoted by INAFOR and the Organization of American States (OAS) as a fast-growing fuelwood species that was well adapted to our ecozone.

In Guatemala, nearly eighty percent of all consumption of forest resources is for fuelwood. We're talking nearly two million families, most of them scattered throughout the Guatemalan *campo* in these tiny hamlets called *aldeas*, everyone cooking two to three meals a day, every day, on an open, three-stone fire. This is a cooking method dating from Neolithic times that wastes eighty-five to ninety percent of the heat that is generated. Not only does it deplete the forest resources faster, but it also results in very poor air quality in the home, which in turn leads to a much higher incidence of respiratory diseases, particularly among the women who do all of the cooking, and the small children under their care.

So another activity that we were all encouraged to pursue was the promotion of improved, fuel-efficient cookstoves that could be easily fabricated from local materials. With an enclosed hearth, more efficient burning; ergo, less fuelwood consumed for every meal. Manage demand through conservation, manage supply through reforestation—*problem solved*. That was the theory, anyway.

Nevertheless the triadic pattern itself is deeply rooted in ancient Mayan beliefs about the creation of the world and therefore is not easily or thoughtlessly abandoned.[20] *Oxip abaj. Siempre tienen que ser tres piedras, porque así ordena dios.* Always a three-stone fire, for it is part of God's plan. If we wanted to manage fuelwood consumption through conservation in the countryside, this is what we were up against.

Next on the agenda, talk to everybody about best practices in soil conservation: terracing, contour cropping, vegetative barriers in the gullies, composting. But soil conservation turned out to be a whole different kettle of fish. In this case we weren't giving anything away (like the free trees available in our tree nursery), so there had to be a hook to get the small farmers involved. The hook was the "food for work" from CARE, or from COGAAT. With food-for-work incentives we hoped to encourage wider community participation in soil conservation. And in fact, with the food I handed out, more people did participate in the projects. But in most cases they were doing so just to obtain the food—either for their own consumption or (much more frequently) in order to sell the commodities for desperately needed cash. When the incentive was suspended, which after a period of time was inevitable, interest in the objectives of soil conservation was lost, and in many cases the work already carried out was abandoned.[21]

Arriving in Patixlán with DIGESA extensionists to give a short course in soil conservation (the young lady pictured came along to provide instruction on preparing the CARE food commodities); local farmers receiving instruction.

Staking out contour lines on a farm plot, using a rustic A-frame level; making the terraces.

* * *

"*What?* You just got here, man, and now you say you have to leave again?" So exclaimed PCV Don Washco to me, though he quickly realized that yes, it had been about three months since he himself had attended a quarterly meeting of the whole reforestation gang in Xela. "Well I won't be here when you get back, 'cause I'm outta here!" So we said our goodbyes that evening, I got from Don a couple of last-minute pieces of advice, and the next morning at daybreak I was boarding a Salamateca bound for Guate. It was an unremarkable ride on the chicken bus, and four-and-a-half hours later I was walking down 7th Avenue to get to the *Galgos* bus station for the next leg of the trip. *Galgos* is Spanish for Greyhound, and when I got there I found on the sign above the depot entrance the same familiar logo featuring a sleek silhouette of a long-legged dog in a hurry to get somewhere. It was Q4.50 for the Salamateca to Guate, and another Q3.75 or so for the Greyhound to Xela. Halfway across the country for about the cost of half a dozen *litros* of Cabro. It was a different time.

Xela (as Quetzaltenango is known to everyone in Guatemala) was a new experience. At more than twice the altitude of Rabinal, it was pretty darn cold walking in the late afternoon from the *Parque de*

Centroamérica up a narrow sidewalk to the hotel address that I had scribbled on a piece of paper. It was February, and everybody I passed on the street was bundled up for winter. Cars, trucks and *motonetas* all jockeying for position on a narrow street which climbed steeply towards the hotel, but the traffic moved at a snail's pace for everybody except the lucky, breakaway maverick. Which, as a pedestrian, I found was reason enough to keep your wits about you at the end of each block, lest one of the mavericks should run you over.

Many of my pals were already checked in at the hotel. There was Tony from San Juan Ixcoy, and John O. from Nahualá. Raul was checking in at the desk, having just pulled in from Esquipulas Palo Gordo. And the Quiché crowd was there, too: Ken from Sacapulas, Rafa from San Andrés Sajcabajá, and Alan from Joyabaj. (Alan would not stay with us for very long after the first trimestral in Xela. His father passed away suddenly back in the States, which won him an unexpected Pan Am ticket home for the funeral. Alan never rejoined us in Guatemala. Life can be an awful bitch, and I'm sure he had his reasons for not returning, and I'm sure they were really good reasons.)

We got some dinner at a budget eatery nearby, and after that some of the guys went out for beers. I was really beat from the long trip, though, so I decided to turn in early.

The next morning after breakfast we all set out for the CARE sub-office, a good half hour's walk from our hotel. Somebody had a roughly sketched map with directions, otherwise we'd never have found the place. Our APCD Basilio Estrada was already waiting for us there, as were the expat CARE rep John Mosher and several of the subregional CARE coordinators. Rodolfo Guzmán was also there, our program coordinator representing INAFOR. The meeting started promptly at nine o'clock, and we spent the whole day learning the various routines for all our dealings with INAFOR and CARE.

By the end of the day we had all gotten our fill of tech info, requisition procedures for tools and supplies, monthly report forms, Food for Work ration proportions, and even alternative seed sources. It was time now for some serious entertainment. We all headed back to the *pensión*, took a short siesta to recharge our batteries, and then regrouped to go out for a late dinner. It was shortly after dinner when somebody in our group, I can't remember who, came up with that memorable plan for the rest of the evening:

"So whaddaya all say we check out this place called Miriam's?"

"What's this place called Miriam's?" There was a short pause, pregnant with possibilities. Was it a bar? A nightclub? A strip joint on the edge of town?

"Well, I hear it's a whorehouse—but we'd have to go check it out and see. Who's up for some action, eh? If we all go, hell, we can have our own party when we get there!" So we all went. Even the gal in our group decided to tag along, out of sheer curiosity. Very much a gal she was, but eager to show us all she could be one of the guys for an evening.

So we paid up and ambled out into the cold night air of Xela in February, with only a rough idea which way to go. Our leader (who I do remember now, but nevertheless shall remain nameless) said it was somewhere up past the ritzy *Pensión Bonifaz*, so that's where we headed. We climbed the steep and narrow cobblestone alley past the *Bonifaz*, and at the next intersection we were lucky to find an oldtimer to ask for directions.

"*Disculpe, señor*, do you know of a place called Miriam's that's around here?" He didn't seem to recognize the name, so we furnished some additional detail. "That place where the *señoritas* are. Somebody told us it was around here. Do you know the place?"He knew the place, alright. He pointed down an alleyway off to our right, kissing the cold night air with an exaggerated pucker of his lips: "Half a block down that way." Then he gave us a wan smile, turned and went on his way.

Indeed it was just a few more steps down the way, and then we were pretty sure we were in the right place. There was a big, black sheet metal door with a tiny frosted window in the middle of it, and no other doors nearby. No sign anywhere by the door; not even a clever decoy like "*Sastrería Ordoñez*" or something. There was however a dim red light shining inside, barely enough to suggest there might be somebody there to greet us. It was cold outside, in fact it was getting real cold, and it was dark, too, as the whole alleyway was completely unlit.

We knock. A short guy opens the little window, cautiously looks around at us standing outside, closes the little window, and then opens the door wide. "*¡Pasen adelante, señores!*" Seven or eight of us shuffle in through the narrow anteroom—our own gal, god bless her *por su valor*, heavily protected by our rear guard. The warmth of the place, the beat of the Latin rhythm, the smell of sweet perfume all conspire to make us feel right at home in this happy little den of iniquity where all cares are forgotten and all causes lost. Soft lights, colored lights, two girls in short, diaphanous dresses sitting there on the couch, I swear one blew me a kiss, but hell, there's the bar—"I'll buy the first round!" somebody shouts. Beers are passed around while Miguel Gallardo softly croons away a lusty little love chant with some ethereal pan flutes in the background.

Our eyes adjust, we look around, and oh my lord, there are girls everywhere. There's a girl on a barstool with her legs crossed, smoking, but not drinking. There's a girl coming out from the back room in her pink satin dress, a Latin cowboy trailing behind her. Another girl is chatting with the bouncer, and then she laughs a boisterous laugh, and what, hey, who's this over in the corner, she just got up now and she's walking towards us, *Hola nena, ¡venga para acá!* (Which sounded so ridiculous in this setting because none of us gringos had any experience with the familiar *tu* form, so instead we're all addressing these lovelies with the formal *usted* as if they were salesgirls in a department store. Crazy shit, but we made ourselves understood.) *Venga para acá mi amor y siéntese conmigo.* And she does, she comes over and she sits right down on the closest chair which is *very* close to me and she holds my hand and hangs a shapely leg right over my faded jeans. Now a new song blares, it's Donna Summer in her disco mode, what the fuck, as if somebody all of a sudden wanted to set the mood here for us gringos.

I tell the girl my name, and she tells me hers. No, I don't remember forty years later. She moves in closer, and now she's sitting on my lap. I ask her if she'd like a beer, but she insists on a glass of wine because they're all trained to say that because it brings more cash into the till. So wine it is; I've still got half my bottle of Gallo (the popular local brew). I offer her a cigarette, which she eagerly accepts, and I light hers with mine and I place it between her ruby red lips. I take out my wallet, Number One, to make sure it's still there, Number Two, to pay for her wine, and Number Three, to check and make sure I've still got that rubber from the nurse's office tucked in there behind the bills. We chit-chat for a while—stupid stuff—and then we get up to dance, and we slow-dance to—of all things—Abba singing "Chiquitita" in

Spanish. After the dance, which is hot and close and fragrant as hell, I ask her if she wants to, and she says Yes, of course, let's go.

We walk over to the bar, I slip something to the bartender for the room, and then Michael Jackson's falsetto *a todo volumen* follows us down a narrow corridor out back. *Don't stop, now ... don't stop ... don't ...*

Fade out. It was a night to remember, yes; and in the end, it was a night to forget. All these poor young women, all of them from broken families or broken *noviazgos* or broken whatever, with broken dreams, or just plain broke. Mothers with children who knew no father. (You could bet on it.) Women who could *be* something, do something, anything but this. Five quetzales a pop.

Yes, this too we did as ambassadors of the Yoo-NIGHT'd - Staytz.

I spent a while longer there after the deed, talking and joking with Raul and wondering about the strange world that awaited us outside. There was another round of beers, I had another smoke, then Raul asked me for a cig and that surprised me, but I gave him one anyway and he just tucked it behind his ear; no matter, cigs are cheap, and then we all departed in the early hours of the morning because we still had another half-day of meetings in a few hours.

* * *

The following morning was hell to get through. None of us had a hangover exactly, but most of us could hardly stay awake as the CARE rep droned on about the requisition process to get picks and shovels, Dipterex and poly bags, and of course Food for Work. When somebody raised their hand and asked a detailed question, others in the room groaned and gave him menacing looks that said, "Shit, man, don't prolong this ordeal any longer than necessary!" The guy with the question might have been me.

We adjourned before the noon hour, and as we said our goodbyes Basilio Estrada handed me a slip of paper with an address on it. *Instituto Geográfico Nacional, Avenida Las Americas 5-76, Zona 13. Bus #2 (verde) desde la Zona 1.* Perfect. I would definitely have to check this out on my way back to Rabinal. I thanked Basilio and as I headed for the door he added, "Just ask for Col. Himmelfarb.".

"*Y a propósito, Cristián,* don't forget that other address I gave you—the *tramites* for your driver's license," Basilio called to me as I pulled the door open.

"Don't worry, I won't!" And we left it at that.

That evening back in Guate I walked into the *Misión Francesa,* laid my Q1.50 on the counter, and got myself a short, narrow cot in the men's parlor where a couple other volunteers were playing cards on a mattress, another was brushing his teeth far from the sink, and yet another was already fast asleep. I was headed there myself in a heartbeat, no question. I was dog-tired from the long bus ride, the mind-numbing morning session in Xela, and of course all the lost sleep from the night before. I took care of my evening ablutions as quickly as I could, made some notes to myself for the IGN visit the next morning, and then I turned in, thank God, before anybody could start a conversation with me.

The next morning I boarded a green Number Two, dropped my *cinco centavos* in the fare box, and got myself a decent window seat so I could watch for signs. This tired, dilapidated crate of a bus whisked me all the way out to *Zona 13* with surprising efficiency, borne along by a somewhat reluctant motor that quaked and wheezed to get started after every single stop. As we rattled down the long avenues of the city I noticed that the entire side of the bus where I was sitting waved and shifted from side to side with our forward progress like a starched bedsheet hanging from a clothesline, and the couple times when the bus veered left the whole right side actually parted from the rest of the body and drifted to the right, revealing down below a generous view of the pavement we were traveling on. The green buses of the Number Two route were among the most abused and dilapidated of Guate's entire urban fleet, having weathered years of bottomless potholes, violent armed robberies and city-wide bus fare riots. But somehow, by the grace of God, they still worked.

Walking into the clean and bright IGN offices in Zone 13 felt like a visit back to the remote sensing lab I knew in college. There were several attractively framed aerial photographs and topo maps mounted on the ivory walls of the lobby, and off to the left I glimpsed a couple of technicians quietly working at drafting tables in a side room.

Somehow even the smell of the place reminded me of Fernow Hall where I had once spent hours working on my own natural resource inventory that covered a little practice slice of upstate New York.

I asked for Col. Himmelfarb at the front desk, and after a short wait he came out to greet me. Though a colonel, he was dressed in civvies. *El Coronel* seemed pleased to receive my visit, and when I introduced myself saying I had studied remote sensing with Professor Ernest Hardy, he grew warmer still. He seemed to know the name, or at least maybe had seen it in the tech literature. We started talking like professional colleagues, and he showed me around the place. While we were walking around I explained what I was doing in Rabinal, and what I wanted. I told him about my reforestation gig with INAFOR, and then went on to explain how I wanted to do this "secondary project," a comprehensive natural resource inventory of the whole *municipio*.

Col. Himmelfarb listened intently to my *spiel* as we walked down the hallway. We stopped in one room where a worker was hunched over some black and white imagery spread out like an unfurled Egyptian scroll over a long, wide table. "Are you familiar with the SLAR imagery, *señor Cristián*?" I told the colonel I had heard of it. "Side-Looking Airborne Radar," he said, in his best attempt at English. Continuing in Spanish: "This is the latest thing we are investigating, and I think we will have a great deal of use for it."

The tour was really quite interesting, but it was taking a lot of time, and I still had to get a bus back to Rabinal. I got back to the point of my visit, and told the colonel that what I really needed was a complete set of topo quads and air photos covering all of Rabinal's territory. The colonel smiled and took me to a secretary at the front desk.

"Please help this *caballero norteamericano* identify exactly which items he needs, and then help him fill out the necessary forms."

"Por supuesto, señor coronel, con mucho gusto," was the attractive young lady's succinct reply. And that, really, was it. I sat down and made out a list with the secretary, she would notify Basilio when the items were ready, and then I'd pick it all up on my next visit to Guate. I thanked the colonel for his time and his hospitality, and he thanked me for whatever it was that I was doing for Guatemala.

That last part I hoped to figure out later.

* * *

During my first few months in Rabinal I worked with *campesinos* in the communities of Xococ and Xesiguan, establishing small tree nurseries there to support local reforestation efforts. Our central tree nursery in the *pueblo* would always be the main supplier of tree seedlings for the *municipio* as a whole, but by setting up these "satellite" nurseries in the *aldeas,* the hope was to get the locals to take ownership of the reforestation campaign in their respective localities, while at the same time saving a little on the cost to truck our seedlings out to these communities. Xococ in particular was a primary target, as it was in the middle of an area that was desperately in need of reforestation, according to an O.A.S. advisor I had met with in Salamá. If the Xococ and Xesiguan nurseries got off the ground, I hoped to do the same thing in other places like Chiticoy, Pachalúm, and Guachipilín.

And so I met with Juan Cortez in Xesiguan and Mariano Alvarado in Xococ to see if I could help them get something started. They organized a group of maybe half a dozen men in each community. I got them hand tools and fertilizer from CARE and food for work from the German NGO that went by the name of COGAAT[7], and I paid them a few additional visits to see how things were going. Both men were, of course, grateful for the implements, the technical assistance, and the food commodities, and I'm quite sure they sold most of the food for cash and used the tools and fertilizer on their farm plots. Still, they managed to produce some seedlings—about a thousand in Xococ and maybe twice as many in Xesiguan. I could only hope that all of the seedlings would be outplanted somewhere in the community come the next rainy season. You can't be everywhere at once to make sure these things happen.

Little did it matter, though, because both nurseries failed after the first year. The Xococ nursery fell into disarray and was abandoned because after the maize harvest men took off for the south coast to cut sugar cane and pick cotton to supplement their meager income. (They did this every year. On the large *fincas* of the coastal plain *campesino* laborers earned about a dollar fifty a day doing this work.) In Xesiguan, the failure was largely my own fault, for the people might have actually been around but I didn't get out there often enough to follow up with *Señor* Cortez and the others in order to prepare for the next season.

Mariano Alvarado, Juan Cortéz. We shall encounter these names again later, *si dios quiere.*

Promoting small tree nurseries in the *aldeas* was not a bad idea, but in the end it required of me more than I could put into it. If nothing else than for the sake of efficiency, it seemed to make more sense to focus on developing the central nursery in the *pueblo*, where we were already putting out more than a hundred thousand seedlings a year. Our central nursery was growing quickly, albeit within a tight space on a terraced slope.

Around this time we also started a fruit tree program, planting a thousand cashew trees in the nursery for sale to the public. This was pretty successful and we made some money at it, so in the following season we expanded on the idea and planted native Rabinal orange tree seed in addition to acquiring more cashew seed. The funds raised by the fruit tree sales were used to purchase materials and to pay a modest per diem allowance for Juan Pablo, because sometimes he had to make trips to the subregional INAFOR office in San Jerónimo.

We always had four or five *peones* working in the nursery tending the germination boxes, filling the thousands of seedling bags with rich, black soil, watering everything with the garden hose, and taking care of half a dozen other odd jobs. Juan Toj Mendoza, Antonio Ramírez and Venancio, who were all close to my age. Luciano López Ortíz and Tomás Lajuj Oxlaj, two middle-aged fellows who worked tirelessly in the dirt every day. And then there was Alejandro, an ancient man whose powers were largely dissipated, who I am guessing must have had advanced prostate issues because he told us once he had trouble taking a piss, but who nevertheless had a wry sense of humor that occasionally surprised us all. We usually let Alejandro handle the soft work, like watering the seedlings.

A couple of the nursery workers were on INAFOR payroll, but the others didn't receive salaries in cash at all, but rather weekly distributions of food for work which they picked up at my house every Friday afternoon. The CARE food commodities consisted of white enriched flour, gallon tins of peanut oil (later on, soybean oil), and other agricultural surplus items from the States that varied from time to time.

Sometimes a fortified corn-soy-milk blend; or maybe bulgur, which absolutely *nobody* in the Guatemalan *campo* knew what to do with.

There was a modicum of paperwork to take care of in order to keep things moving in the program and to keep our supervisors satisfied. Monthly reports to CARE, INAFOR, and the Peace Corps. Requisitions for tools, materials, and food commodities that were sent to CARE on an as-needed basis. Occasional letters to the INAFOR subregional office in San Jerónimo to coordinate upcoming meetings, resolve issues, or request assistance. None of us had a typewriter, so everything had to be written out by hand and posted to the appropriate office. When I went home to New York for the holidays after the first year I brought back with me a lightweight Olivetti portable that was a hand-me-down from my sister.

Having a typewriter helped. At least until the ribbon ran out.

CHAPTER 4

Chitucán

Alas,
we look for good on earth and cannot recognize it
when met, since all our human heritage runs mongrel.
At times I have seen descendants of the noblest family
grow worthless though the cowards had courageous sons;
inside the souls of wealthy men bleak famine lives
while minds of stature struggle trapped in starving bodies.

—Euripides, *Electra,* 366-372

The first test of my commitment to the *aldeas* where CIF worked was Chitucán, the remotest of them all. Then a community of maybe two hundred people, Chitucán was situated more than twelve kilometers as the crow flies from the *pueblo* where I lived, but closer to eighteen clicks following the route we had to walk through the *Valle de Urram* and over the rugged mountains to the north. There was no road to Chitucán, nor would there be electricity nor running water when we got there.

At the end of our class one Saturday morning, I left the CIF compound in Pachalum with Nicolás Siano, and we started out on our trek. (Truth be told, while it was certainly a "trek" for me, it was a routine weekly trip for Nicolás.) It was easy enough to get a ride in the back of a pickup headed out to Xococ, but Xococ was not our destination. About halfway out to that village we pounded on the roof of the pickup cabin, and with an assertive shout of *¡Aquí no más!* the pickup came to an abrupt halt. From that point on we'd be making our way on foot into the mountains, a long, occasionally strenuous hike of close to three hours. Along the way I asked Nicolás once or twice how much farther it was, and he would say to me, "*Ayy, don Cristo, todavía faltan como tres leguas.*" Still some three leagues to go. I could not possibly find his response very helpful, though, as I had absolutely no idea how far a *legua* was. We kept on walking under full sun because it was the dry season, and a few times we stopped briefly so I could drink some water and take in a glimpse of the breathtaking scenery in the mountains. We'd have chatted a little more on this lengthy hike, but Nicolás exhibited a quality of quiet meekness that kept our conversations short.

A mountain vista around Chitucán.

The footpath to Chitucán was narrow and at times unforgiving, and I stumbled once or twice, but I nevertheless managed to follow Nicolás all the way out to the *aldea* without any serious mishap. Our arrival at his humble lodging high up in the mountains was memorable because of the utterly different air we now breathed. No longer the hot, dry air of the *Valle de Urram* some five hundred meters down below, but here a sweet, fresh, and slightly cool air with the fragrance of pines all around us. Nicolás motioned to his wife to come over and greet me, and she did so with a cautious smile and a small, barely audible voice. I could tell from her enunciation of *buenas tardes* that those were probably two of the very few words of Spanish that she knew.

(Nicolás himself, a little more worldly wise because as a man he got out more than his poor wife, spoke a sort of pidgin Spanish that was nonetheless effective and usually easy to follow.) Two children were standing nearby, a small boy and a girl, both of them neither playing nor working at chores but just standing there staring at me in silent amazement. I took off my canvas knapsack and set it on the ground while Nicolás dropped his *morral* on a rustic bench near the doorless entrance to their dwelling.

"Bueno, don Cristo, aquí estamos. ¿Quiere usted ver el vivero ya?" This, of course, was what I had come all this way for, to see his tree nursery, so I immediately assented. We walked a short distance from his little one-room house, and the very first sight that confronted me and indeed arrested my attention was a magnificent panorama of forested mountains stretching as far as the eye could see. Somewhere deep in the distant valleys near the horizon lay hidden the Rio Chixoy (also known as Rio Negro). This unforgettable sight was at least as stunning as any mountain vista I had seen previously on my long hikes through the Adirondacks or the Blue Ridge back in the States. For a moment I stood there transfixed, and Nicolás waited patiently for my moment of idyllic transport to pass. This was a scene, after all, that he and his wife and his children saw every single day. Could it mean the same thing to them? Did they see the mountains the same way I did? Could Nicolás, there at my side, possibly conceive of the thing in itself, this scene of rolling mountains spread out before us, as something inhabited by a God or gods, as something truly divine? He saw these things, probably, more clearly than I did.

"Aquí abajito está el vivero, don Cristo—venga." ("Right down this way is the tree nursery, sir Christ—come.")

"¡Ya voy!" ("I'm coming!") I snapped out of it and followed him downhill a short piece until we reached a tiny patch, not bigger than your typical bedroom floor plan, crudely fenced in with sticks and chicken wire. This was Nicolás' *vivero*, where he had (as my contemporaneous field notes faithfully record) exactly *"300 arbolitos de ciprés y 50 de casuarina,"* all of them neatly lined up in rows of black plastic bags.

"Ayy, que bién, que bién, Nicolás. Lo felicito mucho por lo que ha logrado aquí. Muy bién hechito." ("Ahh, how nice, how very nice, Nicolás. I congratulate you on what you've accomplished here. Very nicely done.")

Nicolás looked at his little collection of seedlings, and then looked at me. This was his chance to make his pitch. Like almost all of his fellow *promotores forestales* in the other *aldeas*, he lacked good access to water for the seedlings. Some garden hose would be a big help. (And pray tell what tap might a garden hose be hooked up to? Who knows, seeing as how there was no public water supply anywhere in sight.) Oh, and a couple *azadón* heads would be very helpful—not to worry, though, he can fashion the long wooden handles himself. And more seedling bags. He needed more seedling bags. *Y un medio-quintal de fertilizante—este, ¿como se llama?— ¡triple quince!* (And a fifty pound bag of fertilizer—that, uh, what's it called?—15-15-15!)

I told Nicolás I would see what I could do. It might take time, I said. I'd let him know at a future conservation class down in the valley, and he could then pick up the items at my house. Of course I had no idea what advantage might be gained by throwing money at this sad little tree nursery, but then Nicolás wasn't asking for much and so I figured what the hell. My cynicism was taking over even as I continued to pursue the ideal. That, I confess, happened to me often in my work with the *campesinos.*

Nicolás responded to most of my questions with a phrase that I would hear a lot during my three years in Rabinal: *Sí como no*. As in: "Do you have a water source nearby for these seedlings, Nicolás?" "*Sí como no.*" (We shall see very shortly how accessible his water source actually was.) Or again: "Do you know how to apply *triple-quince* so as not to burn the roots of your corn crop?" "*Sí como no.*" (But on further questioning I find that he really doesn't know.) *Sí como no* is actually a common expression in Spanish almost everywhere, yet the maddening frequency with which it was uttered by the Guatemalan *campesinos* always seemed to shroud under an impenetrable cloud of ambiguity much of the information I received from them. Literally: Yes, like no. Yes, but not really, not today. Yes, but I'm afraid to say, actually no.

We walked back up to the little cabin where Nicolás's wife was shaping tortillas over a hot *comal*, slapping them back and forth between two small hands until each tortilla achieved the exact, perfect thickness and diameter that her mother had taught her when she was very young, and which she herself was now teaching to her little girl who stood in a corner watching and biting her lip.

"Necesitamos jalar agua," Nicolás said to me, *"Si quiere me acompaña."* ("We need to go get water; come along with me if you like.") I assented to his proposal because I thought it would be interesting to see where he got his water from. Nicolás then pulled out two very beat up plastic jerry cans of five gallons each that were sitting on the ground inside the darkened doorway of his *casita*, and he proceeded to empty the little remaining water in one of them into a pot by the fire.

Fetching water, it turned out, was an ordeal I hadn't bargained for. It involved walking uphill a short distance, each of us with his empty jerry can, and then turning sharply downhill into a very steep-sided ravine where I had to hold onto available tree trunks, roots and limbs in order to brace myself against slipping and falling headlong towards the bottom some eight or nine meters below. Nicolás, for his part, seemed to have little need for any bracing against vegetation on the descent—partly, perhaps, because his feet were much smaller than mine and therefore easily gained purchase among the nooks and crevices—but mainly because this was a routine daily chore he had performed a thousand times before. Needless to say, it was a first for me.

We reached the bottom of the ravine, where we were greeted by the refreshing sight of a gurgling spring that seemingly emerged right out of the side of the mountain. Taking turns, we each uncapped a jerry can and positioned it in the gravel to best advantage so as to capture the flow of water. In very little time Nicolás had a full jerry can, which he capped tightly and then waited for me to fill mine. My jerry can ended up not really quite full, and I realize now that this was an involuntary (or, who knows, maybe fully conscious) act of cheating, for I knew very well what we had to do next.

"¿Listo? Vámonos entonces." And with that we began the ascent back up the steep slope of the ravine. My memory now surely exaggerates reality, but that slope seemed for all the world nearly vertical. Nicolás hauled his completely full jerry can on his back using a *mecapal*, suspending the entire heavy load from his forehead, and he did so with a nimbleness and sureness of footing that amazed me. Always at least a couple meters behind him, I myself struggled (without the benefit of a *mecapal*) to pull and heave my jerry can, which was at

best only three-quarters full, back up the slope, my sturdy Vibram-soled work boots slipping more than once on a patch of loose soil or a wet and slimy fallen leaf. We made our way back up to the edge of the ravine, and from there I carried my load on either shoulder down the gentle slope to the *casita*. This was Nicolás's chore almost every afternoon, though he admitted to me that sometimes if he was busy his wife took care of it.

I would eventually need some dinner there at his house, because after a whole afternoon with Nicolás, by now it was far too late to start walking back to town. We sat outside his *casita* and talked for a while as it began to grow dark: I asked Nicolás about the condition of his *milpa*, and he asked me about life in the United States. *"Ahí dicen que puede ganar bien uno, ¿verdad?"* To all his questions I gave him my succinct replies, because sometimes the answer was complicated. (In truth it had occurred to me that I might turn the tables on poor Nicolás and simply answer with a concise *"Si como no,"* but I thought better of the idea.) After a while the food was ready and we sat down to dinner. I say "we" meaning just Nicolás and myself. His wife and kids would eat by themselves later. Nicolás gave me the Stool of Honor at his rustic wooden table, and I squatted to sit down on it. His wife then brought me a blue and white glazed metal plate of *frijoles parados con tortilla*, along with a metal cup full of weak coffee that was strongly presweetened to suit a universal *campesino* taste. Sitting down to dinner with Nicolás while his wife silently tended the fire with the kids at her side, I experienced a sudden epiphany, a feeling of grace like I had never felt before. Here I was, sitting down to eat a meal with the poorest of Guatemala's poor—eating *their* food which they had grown, prepared, and freely given to me—and I didn't know how or if I'd ever be able to adequately thank them for this moment. *Maltiox cha'lá.*

We all retired for the night scarcely an hour after finishing dinner. For what else do you do where there is no electricity, no books, no light, no television? I unrolled my sleeping bag and laid it out in the spot that Nicolás showed me on the dirt floor of his *casita*. After I had settled in for the night, his wife lit three small candles which she placed on the ground near me. *But no, no*, this is the point where I now struggle again to remember, to recall the moment just as it occurred so that I might portray it accurately. Were they really three candles?

Or only two? Or one? It was light, and I fell asleep that night with the little light by my side. The candles, I felt absolutely convinced at the time, were a sacrament of sorts, a sacrament perhaps offering the whole family some measure of protection as they slept near me. For despite my earnest intent and my abiding aversion to violence, I was, after all, the Other, the Unknown among them.

I believe I slept very well that night.

The next morning, which was a Sunday, Nicolás's wife served me breakfast, and I recall it being very much like the dinner of the night before. After breakfast I reiterated to Nicolás my promise to get him the materials he had requested, I said my goodbyes, and I started out on the long walk back to the *pueblo*. On that walk I was all alone with my thoughts for more than three hours, and I had a lot to think about. The puny little tree nursery; fetching the water from the ravine; the CARE supplies Nicolás had asked for; dinner with the family; the little candlelight by my side as I fell asleep lying on the hard ground. Suffice to say that it was an experience I could not possibly forget, even forty years later. The walk back to the *pueblo* was mostly downhill, and I took an inadvertent detour near the end of the descent, so that I ended up not reaching the road where we had jumped off the pickup truck the day before, but instead I reached the village of Nimacabaj where there was a narrow road that eventually joined the road that I was seeking.

There was only one Rabinal *aldea* farther north than Chitucán, and that was Río Negro, five clicks in a northwesterly direction. Rio Negro was where all the trouble would soon start to brew. Those troubles would spill over into Chitucán itself, and many lives would be lost there as well. I will never know if Nicolás Siano and his family survived *la situación*, but I hope that by the grace of God they might have, and I hope Nicolás' *vivero* continued producing more seedlings with the supplies I eventually got him. If they did not survive, then it is Guatemala's tragic loss. Maybe somebody else up there can use the *azadones*, the garden hose, and whatever's left of the *triple-quince*.

* * *

My regular Saturday morning sessions with the *promotores de* CIF continued for several more months. We'd sit together on small wooden stools or sometimes on the ground under the shade of a broad, leafy ceiba tree while I talked to the group of five or six about reforesting the hillsides, terracing their steeply sloping farm plots, and getting tools from CARE to help them do this work. Then, too, explaining about their weekly Food for Work rations, which were—let's be honest—their main incentive for sitting down with me every Saturday in the first place. Spanish was a second language for all five of them, just as it was for me. Only *their* first language was Achí. All but one or two of them spoke Nicolás's halting pidgin Spanish, which consisted of a limited vocabulary punctuated at every turn with the stock filler phrases *vaya pués* and *sí como no.*

One Saturday morning I arrived punctually at the CIF administration building to start my regular weekly class with the *promotores*, only to find a bunch of people and a lot of commotion under the ceiba tree next to the building. My *promotores* were standing around with several other *campesinos* in a tight circle under the shade of the tree, Güícho and Julio were talking excitedly behind them and seemed to be directing something, and the rotund doctor who drove over from Salamá every Saturday to attend to the sick was at that moment squeezing out of his little orange Datsun. A lot of commotion going on—*so what the hell?* I walked over to the group, the circle under the ceiba opened up for the gringo, and two of my *promotores* greeted me with "*¡Hola don Cristián! ¡Mire!*"—and then I saw the object of their excited attention on the ground at our very feet: one huge snake, maybe eight feet long, lay there motionless, stretched out straight as a two-by-four, with a conspicuous bulge just past the middle of its smooth, scaly body. The thing was deader than a doornail.

Now the debate began among those assembled under the ceiba tree, and all considered opinions were heard. Translating loosely:

"What the fuck are we going to do with it now?"

"We'll *eat* the sonofabitch!"

"Have you ever eaten a serpent like this?"

"Of course I have. They're mighty tasty, in fact. Roasted on the fire and—"

"Well, we'll see about that later. First let's look into that evidence I see there in the middle of its belly." Indeed, that conspicuous bulge in the middle definitely looked like a piece of circumstantial evidence that might be pertinent to the case. At this point I came in close, kneeled on one knee, and stroked the serpent's sleek, scaly skin.

"WHOA, look out, look out!" shouted Julio rapid-fire as he nudged the head of the serpent with his foot and then raised it menacingly in the air with his hand. Always the prankster, Julio wanted to startle me into thinking there might still be some vitality left in the carcass. For a second there, the prank worked. Then everybody laughed.

"So who killed it?" I asked. "I mean, what the heck happened here?" Judging from the bulge in its belly the answer should have been obvious, but Julio condescended to explain.

"We lost a couple rabbits from the hutches over there on the other side, so we knew something was up. Güícho said we should put together a team to be on the lookout, so I gathered a few of the *muchachos* and we looked around the hutches early this morning. Armed only with machetes and *azadones*. We prowled around for an hour over there, checking all around, between the hutches and under them. One guy saw the serpent slithering and sneaking away on the ground, and so we all came running over and we nailed the bastard over the top of its head!"

As we all stared at the carcass on the ground, Julio stood there triumphant.

"Haha, I think *Cristián* ought to show us now what he can do with this malevolent serpent. *Cristián*, let's see you pick the thing up and carry it! C'mon, I dare you! C'mon and show us all what big balls the gringo has!"

So of course, being new to Rabinal and new to this whole experience, I had to show them all that *Cristián es un cabrón de véras*—shit yeah, that bastard Christian has definitely got the balls! So I bent over and picked up the serpent in the middle of its length, then stood up straight and heaved its tail end over my shoulder. It was pretty heavy, and I almost buckled under the weight. The head end still dangled, so Julio himself came to my aid (using the term advisedly); he held up the head end, some four feet in all, lifted it over my head so it rested on my other shoulder, and then held the head right in front of my face and gestured with it mock-menacingly, suggesting (as before) that the creature might still have the strength to seek vengeance. "Don't mess

with me, Julio; you're dealing with the gringo serpent-master here!" ... Thought it, but didn't say it. Truth is, I had never held a fer-de-lance[22] before, much less worn one on my shoulders.

Everybody present got a huge kick out of the gringo's wild and wacky display of *huevos* (call it guts?), and there was laughter all around. The doctor hurried back to his car and pulled out a camera, then returned to where we were all standing under the ceiba and snapped a picture.

"...Better still," said Unamuno, "to know how to *make* oneself ridiculous and not to shrink from the ridicule." But here there was no heroism; only good-natured tomfoolery. And a fervent desire on my part to be accepted in this (to me) strange, new setting.

* * *

Oh, and then there was that one nasty little existential threat to my continued existence that I suppose we need to talk about. I would be remiss if I did not address it here, and my friends would probably think of me as some kind of mendacious skunk if I were to simply gloss over it.

But let's back up. Sometime after Xela, maybe a month afterwards when I went into Guate again to collect my living allowance, I had to follow up with that *tramitador* address that Basilio Estrada had given me. Now, let me be clear that a *tramitador* in Guatemala is basically a small-time fixer. What I needed "fixing" was simply to find a way to obtain a Guatemalan driver's license without having to present an American driver's license as evidence of competence to drive. Simple matter, really, and indeed there was a simple solution. For a nominal fee I could fill out and submit some papers swearing that I did in fact have a license back in the States; I just didn't have it with me now. (The truth was that I had *never* had a driver's license back in the States, thanks to an idiotic misdiagnosis of epilepsy that had followed me around since childhood and caused my involuntary withdrawal from driver's ed in high school.)

My *tramitador*, a young, city-bred fellow about my age who was earnest and efficient in all his attentions, patiently guided me through the paperwork, and then submitted it on my behalf. (Because only he knew *how* to submit it—what kind of subtle manual flourish to use to give the bureaucrat at the National Police a sneak peek at your bills under the table. This is what you paid him for.) A few days later he delivered to the Peace Corps office a Guatemalan driver's license with my headshot on it. I picked it up on my next trip to Guate.

Fast-forward another month or so, and I'm now driving the CARE pickup truck around Baja Verapaz, with Bruce from Cubulco at my side for guidance and reassurance. On the first day out we took care of some deliveries of tools and tree seedlings and Food for Work around Cubulco, and then I dropped Bruce off at his house. I was now on my own, headed back to Rabinal behind the stiff, bucking wheel of the truck. I had maybe ten hours of driving experience, but I cruised down that road out of Cubulco, cocksure and relaxed as if I'd been driving those dirt roads for years. Headed down the straight, bumpy road before the hills ahead I lit myself a smoke and rested my arm on the doorframe, thinking about all the things that needed doing once I got to Rabinal.

But Rabinal would have to wait. For as soon as I got into the hills—I believe it may have been on the first or second curve—I was distracted by God knows what, I lost control of the wheel, and I went careening off the side of the road, bouncing down the steep hillside until further progress was arrested by a well-positioned tree. Or maybe it was a gully. I'll never know, as I was barely conscious. My kneecaps had crashed hard into the dashboard. The pickup had landed in a vertical position, with the front radiator grill firmly planted in the rocky ground, the tailgate facing skyward, and the whole body of the vehicle buttressed by that life-saving tree. Or gully. I still had enough presence of mind to notice that the smell of gasoline was beginning to grow stronger. Though my whole body was crumpled and contorted, I somehow managed to push open the side door and fall the short distance to the ground, and then crawl a few feet away from the cab.

This was my existential calamity on a lonely road between Cubulco and Rabinal. How I was found and saved I'll never know. But somehow somebody found me and went for help. Then Bruce came rushing out to the crash site on his *moto*, I was transported to the *Centro de Salud* in Cubulco, from there to the hospital in Salamá where I spent a night, and from there in an actual ambulance to the Herrera Llerandi hospital in Guate.

My very first solo trip driving the CARE pickup became my last, and I ended up with a couple broken ribs, two badly mangled kneecaps, and a visit to my hospital bed from CARE rep John Mosher who stopped by to wish me a speedy recovery and to put me on notice in no uncertain terms that I was not to drive a CARE vehicle again for the rest of my term of service in the country.

After I was released from the hospital I managed to get on a city bus and schlep my way over to the Salamateca terminal in order to find a *bus extraurbano* that would take me back to Rabinal. Me, hobbling through the city streets with my new aluminum crutches.

Once I got on the Salamateca, I paid a fare just to get to Salamá so that I could stop by the house where my Peace Corps buddy Carlos lived. I wanted to pay him a visit to let him know what had happened. After that I was out on the street again, just waiting for the next Salamateca to pass through on its way to Rabinal. That's when I had a small stroke of luck: who should pass by but Armando Garzona, driving his big red, diesel stake-bed truck. Armando lived down the street from me in Rabinal, and he owned the hardware and dry goods store where I occasionally stopped in to purchase life's necessaries. Armando pulled up beside me on the dusty avenue in Salamá and rolled down the window.

"Cristián, *mi amigo,* where are you headed?" I told him where I was headed, and then he just said to me, "Come on, get in!" So I climbed into the cabin with difficulty and sat beside him, feeling grateful for this first-class berth to finish off the remaining, bumpy, twenty-odd kilometers to Rabinal. Much more comfortable than being packed like a sardine in the back of the Salamateca bus.

The ride took less than an hour, and we talked a bit along the way. Of course, I had to begin by explaining how the hell I had ended up on crutches. But Armando was mercifully uncurious about the details. Instead, he spent much of the trek over the mountains to Rabinal telling me about the year or two he had spent driving a delivery truck in Chicago. He loved to talk about this; about the windy and stormy winter there, about the respect for traffic regulations there compared to Guatemala, about the Bears and the Cubs. All the while interspersing his monologue with phrases of broken English, seemingly to impress me. He was a tad disappointed when I told him I followed neither baseball nor American football.

At length we finally rolled through Pachalúm, and a few blocks later Armando deposited my hurting, sorry ass at my front gate. Standing there at my gate, I said *gracias,* Armando, *se lo agradezco mucho,* and then I waved goodbye to the big, red truck.

* * *

> Ah, to love and to have my love returned was my heart's desire, and it would be all the sweeter if I could also enjoy the body of the one who loved me. So I muddied the stream of friendship with the filth of lewdness and clouded its clear waters with hell's black river of lust.[23]

St. Augustine knew a thing or two about the carnal delights, but in the end he shunned them in favor of some ethereal form of divine love that's just really hard to focus on in Latin America today, thanks to halter tops, spandex, rouge, and lipstick.

Ah, but that sinuous river of lust—need it really be so black, so terribly bleak? I was still recuperating from my accident near Cubulco when Eugenio, the fisheries volunteer, and I were walking back home from dinner one evening, headed back to the house that we shared where our only companions were the cats Leo and Felix. We were talking in English along the way and we were maybe halfway back to the house when we heard a pair of young women talking and laughing a few steps behind us.

"Good-bye my love!" one of them called out, the salutation followed this time by vaguely concupiscent giggles. Eugenio and I must have heard that silly English phrase half a dozen times every day, usually coming from a gaggle of schoolchildren traipsing home from classes. But it was evening now, and when I turned to look behind me, these were no schoolgirls but two fully formed, smartly dressed young women.

"*Buenas noches, señoritas.*"

"*¡Pués muy buenas noches, señorón! Y estos caballeros, Judith, ¿qué estarán haciendo por aquí en Rabinal?*"

"*Pués no se, Sandrita. ¡Preguntémoslos!*"

What might these two gentlemen be doing here in Rabinal? I don't know, Sandrita. Let's ask them! All this, so far, with a coquettish sex appeal that definitely aroused our interest. Judith was a pretty *señorita* with wavy shoulder-length hair, while her companion Sandra sported a short, black bob not normally seen in this neck of the woods. We got to talking (by now all four of us standing around at our front door), and Eugenio and I explained to the girls what we were doing in town, how long we expected to be here, and where we were from in the States. Sandra and Judith wore identical light tan outfits with white blouses and dark pumps because, as Judith explained, they were both doing their *práctica* in home economics for a couple weeks with the *educadoras del hogar* over at DIGESA. I guessed that both of them were around nineteen, judging from the clues we got. The school they were attending was in Xela, where Sandra was actually from. Judith, for her part, was a born and bred *rabinalensa*; in fact, her father *don* Celso Sesam lived just around the corner, maybe a block away.

We invited the girls in, but Judith said they had to go home first. They promised to come back over in an hour or so—and so they did. Only now they were both dressed much more casually, Judith in a lovely floral blouse, and Sandra—slender Sandra, ever the enchantress—was now wearing slacks and a close-fitting stretchy mesh top revealing a bare midriff. We invited them inside and followed behind as we all walked out to the veranda. This was my opportunity to send a secret signal to Eugenio that, if he didn't mind (and he shouldn't), I'd take Sandra, thank you very much.

We sat around and drank beers and talked for a couple of hours. I put Fleetwood Mac on our dinky little *radiograbadora*, but the band was unfamiliar to them. Then Sandra reached for her purse and pulled out her own cassette to help set the mood, and the cassette happened to be the Bee Gees. No less Anglo than my selection, but in the wake of *Saturday Night Fever* the Bee Gees were really big all over

Latin America, and no self-respecting *chica* would call their music unappealing. Sandra and I got up and slow-danced beneath the dim light of the veranda to "Massachusetts" and "How Do You Mend a Broken Heart," my arm wrapped around her waist and an oversized hand resting on her small shoulder. Oh my.

In the end, of course, neither Eugenio nor I saw any action, and it's probably just as well, for there surely would have been hell to pay afterwards. Never do it in the town where you are living unless you plan to get serious very quickly.

We all said our goodnights and promised to get together again someday soon. Alas, that day never came. Yet for me the evening with Sandra and Judith was revelatory. I started thinking I actually might have a chance with some other eligible Latin American woman someday. Maybe, someday, somewhere.

Out of town.

* * *

I resolved early on to try and make the rounds to visit each of the four *aldeas* where my *promotores* lived. Though I was now able to check off the most inaccessible one on my list, Chitucán, I still had to pay a visit to Chichupac, Nimacabaj, and Sacachó. All four were tiny hamlets of less than five hundred inhabitants each. Like Chitucán, Chichupac was also situated high up in the mountains, but way up in the southern Chuacús range, far from Chitucán. At least there was a road there. Nimacabaj and Sacachó both lay in the broad *Valle de Urram*, essentially at the same elevation as the house where I lived, and not far from it.

In order to get out to Chichupac I'd need to find a ride first, so at our next Saturday meeting it seemed easier to ask Cristóbal Pérez, the youngest of the *promotores*, if I might join him on his return to Sacachó after we adjourned. Cristóbal couldn't easily say no, so after talking for an hour about trees and pests and soil quality and general nursery upkeep under the shade of the ceiba tree in Pachalúm, we walked back to Rabinal's central plaza together and without much trouble found a pickup for the ride out to Sacachó. While we sat in the cargo bed of a beat-up Datsun riding out of town, I asked Cristóbal the most burning question I had so far: if this *aldea* we were going to was called Pichéc on my maps, why was he calling it Sacachó? Where were we going, anyway? "Pichéc-Sacachó," Cristóbal replied, as if the answer was self-evident. Well, *of course*. Sacachó, it turned out, was a particular sector of the *aldea* of Pichéc. And what are the names of the other sectors? Silence.

We bounced along in the back of the pickup for another couple clicks.

My visit to Sacachó with Cristóbal turned out to be a stark contrast compared to my earlier visit to Chitucán. No lengthy hike high up into the mountains, and hence no need for an overnight stay. After our short ride in the back of the pickup, we only had to walk a kilometer or so along a single sundrenched, rocky hillside of unchallenging slope before we reached the one-room adobe structure that Cristóbal called home. Part of the space by the door was devoted to a humble little *tienda* sparsely stocked with hard candies, exactly one brand of cigarettes, a row of *octavos* (hip flasks) of that powerful *aguardiente* known as Quetzalteca Especial, a basket of unwrapped caramel popcorn balls called *alborotos*, and some stale-looking sweet rolls that sold for five *centavos* each. Oh yes, and a plastic crate half filled with Gallo beer, along with a choice of Coke or Orange Crush. All of the glass bottles unrefrigerated, since there was no electricity. The sun's heat was oppressive in Sacachó, and it seemed the only thing this place had in common with Chitucán was the lack of electricity. Yet on the other hand you could say that here in Cristóbal's domain we were still closely connected to all the modern trappings of civilization: there was a radio broadcast of *norteñas* coming from somewhere in the dark end of the room, and the inside of the door to Cristóbal's abode was incongruously adorned with a full-length poster of Michael Jackson standing poised in his tuxedo and ready to rock.

I put down fifteen centavos for a warm bottle of Coke, and I sat on a ledge while Cristóbal talked to me about his tree nursery which we were about to see. He told me he had fifteen thousand seedlings ready for outplanting, and he had several men helping with the daily upkeep. He wasted little time getting to the same point that Nicolás Siano had brought up in Chitucán, namely that he needed tools and garden hose, fungicide and fertilizer, and of course Food for Work for himself and the guys who were helping him. But Cristóbal's approach to this appeal was utterly different from the halting but earnest humility of our man

Nicolás. I couldn't help but get this feeling that Cristóbal was really on the take, and that this whole charade of a diligently maintained satellite tree nursery contributing to the national reforestation campaign was just a ruse to get as much merchandise as he could get his hands on, which he would then hand out to his relatives or resell to his neighbors. Inwardly I congratulated myself for using good gringo judgment in my estimation of Cristóbal as a person, and I wasn't about to be hoodwinked into giving him more than he really needed. After all, there were needs everywhere, and supplies were not limitless.

As it turned out, reality was more ambiguous than my supposedly razor-sharp perceptions might allow. I finished my Coke, and we walked down the hill to the tree nursery. To start with, there were nowhere near fifteen thousand seedlings there. Probably fewer than five thousand, though raising that many was still an accomplishment. I didn't see any men there helping out, but then it was a Saturday. Okay. The main problem, though, was that nearly all of Cristóbal's seedlings were a meter tall and hopelessly rootbound in their little black poly bags. Hauling them out to a prospective reforestation site and transplanting them there would be exceedingly difficult, if not impossible. And there were still weeks to go before planting season.

I advised Cristóbal to try and get his five thousand seedlings outplanted as quickly as possible after the first good rains. Give them out to friends and neighbors. Plant a bunch on that hillside over there, and you might have a nice little woodlot close to home in a few years. But you have to get them all planted, like *real soon*, before they all take root right here in the ground underneath your *vivero*.

"*Sí como no. Gracias, don Cristo.*" Sir Christ, again. I thought I saw Cristóbal smirk right after that reply—but maybe it was just his nature. Or maybe I had just read his face wrong.

After our meeting in Sacachó I walked all the way back home. Clouds were gathering on the horizon as I got closer to the *pueblo*, and a few minutes after I walked through the door of the house it started pouring cats and dogs.

* * *

"Shit, so you mean, then, we've got the truck for the weekend?"

"Sure looks like it," said Bruce to the two of us. "I mean what the hell, it's been a full week, and we got a shitload done today, didn't we? Got you your *tierra negra* out of the road cut up there by Chichupac; got you almost a ton of it. And now your *campesinos* out in Xococ should be happy too, because we hauled all those bags of food for work right to their doorstep. So now maybe we oughtta do something for ourselves, whaddaya say? I can't drive the truck back to Chimaltenango until Monday, anyway, because there's nobody there to receive it."

"Of course, I suppose you could just drop the keys in the box there," I volunteered, stupidly undermining the whole direction of the conversation.

"Forget it. I'll tell them on Monday I didn't feel comfortable doing that. C'mon, Chris, get with the program!"

Bruce's logic was impeccable. All that remained was to make a good plan for tomorrow, Saturday. Something new; something interesting. Each of us, Bruce, Eugenio and myself, reached almost simultaneously for our respective beers and we each took a long, thoughtful swig. Bruce and I were drinking from *litros* of Cabro; Eugenio, from a regular, 12-ounce Gallo. It didn't take long to come up with a plan.

"Chuitinamít!" I exclaimed. "Let's all go out and explore the ruins of Chuitinamít! Look, I can show it to you on my topo quad—even got it on my air photos here." I think Bruce was impressed that I even had these resources. We were sitting together on the veranda, Bruce reclining in the hammock with his Cabro on the floor beside him. Of course we *had* to check this out, so we all got up and marched into my bedroom, where I happened to have the maps all laid out on my rough-hewn, pine work table.

"Look, we just drive out towards Xococ like we did this morning, stop and park right after Las Vegas de Santo Domingo, and look, there's the trail right there. Whaddaya think, maybe an hour's hike, tops?"

"Gentlemen," said Bruce, "I think we have a plan." And indeed we had an excellent plan. Leave early in the morning, park off the dirt road right where the trail intersects it, hike a few clicks up to the ruins; hell, we could spend an hour or more at the site of this Mayan fortress and still be back by mid-afternoon.

We left the house with a good buzz and walked over to *doña* Anita's *comedor* for dinner, and then after we ate we stopped at the *tienda* nearby to get some victuals for our adventure the next day. I bought a couple cans of Ducal refried beans and half a dozen *panes franceses* (which were not in the least French, but rather had a texture and consistency vaguely resembling Italian ciabatta). Also an extra pack of cigs.

Next morning we started out around 7:30. Rumbling past the *destacamento militar* on the edge of town, we caught a look from the soldier manning the sentry post there, but it was nothing more than an idle look. His hands remained clasped, as if in prayer, over the top of his mounted 50-calibre.

It was less than half an hour out to the point where we'd have to park the pickup and start walking. After we passed the schoolhouse in Vegas de Santo Domingo, however, we had to go real slow so as not to miss the foot trail. (Trails crisscross the Guatemalan countryside everywhere, but the *campesinos* don't need signs or markers because, unlike us, they know where the hell they are going.) Peering over the *caliche* and cornfields off to the north, I spotted what looked like a plausible path, so I gave Bruce the signal, "*¡Aquí no más!*"

We got out and grabbed our lightly packed *mochilas* from the back of the truck, and we set off on our little walk. We started out at a leisurely pace, passing within shouting distance of a few humble *casitas* with tile roofs and thin walls of *vara*, making sure at all costs that we wouldn't traipse right through their fields of maize, squash and beans.

When we reached the top of a hill, we heard somebody calling out to us from way back, far behind us on the path. We turned around, and there in the distance we saw a local farmer gesturing excitedly at us. The gestures seemed to say "Keep Out", and I think the words he shouted were a warning to the same effect, though we couldn't really hear him very clearly. We shouted back to him and said in as few words as possible that we were simply on a hike out to Chuitinamít. But that couldn't have sounded very reassuring to our interlocutor. After all, we were strangers in this territory, humanoid creatures who looked utterly unlike anybody who lived around here, possibly unlike anybody the old man had ever seen before. We sounded different with our gringo accents, and those bags slung over our shoulders might not be carrying victuals but deadly weapons. The old man's consternation was understandable.

Still and all, having offered our explanation we were satisfied to just turn around and keep walking, leaving the old man standing there frustrated, and perhaps angry. Was his warning an omen of some sort? We just kept walking.

After an hour's climb we finally reached the site of the ancient fortress, some three hundred meters above the floor of the valley, and we were not disappointed. Though heavily overgrown with weeds and small, scraggly trees, one could clearly make out not only the general layout of the first plaza we saw, but even the details of the stonework in the walls of each building. We found a couple low-profile Mayan temple pyramids; we saw an ancient ball court. The place seemed enormous: nearly four dozen separate buildings (this the archeologists tell us, for we didn't actually count them) spread out over a high ridge overlooking the *Valle de Urram*. This was the very heart of the Rabinaleb domain during the late postclassic period, more than a century before Columbus's fateful arrival in Hispaniola.

Left: Peace Corps volunteers Bruce and Eugenio walking past one of the 44 ancient structures that comprise Chuitinamít. Right: Detail showing one of the heavily overgrown walls.

We sat down on a gentle slope right below one of the temples, and there we ate our spartan lunch of day-old *pan francés* and cold refried beans right out of the can. A modest picnic, to be sure, but then we weren't there for a banquet. Afterwards we got up and looked around some more. At one point we stood on the edge of a precipice overlooking the wide valley below, and in that moment the three of us were struck almost with a sense of religious awe. For a while we stood there taking in the breathtaking sight of the green and azure vista that was spread out before us. Behind us, around the perimeter of an empty, gray plaza, the long, low council house and two imposing temple mounds stood erect, the massive structures garlanded for all the ages under twisted vines and desiccated weeds. Still, they seemed to preserve a quiet sense of dignity, even nobility.

The three of us felt like pioneering explorers in the silent realm of an ancient, dead city. But of course, we were not the first non-Mayans to discover the ineffable mystery of Chuitinamít. Over the course of a century the archeologists Alfred P. Maudslay, Ledyard Smith, and John Fox had all left their footprints here.[24] The Frenchman Alain Ichon would make the same climb up the slope of *Cerro Chuitinamít* a few years after our visit, and Marie-Charlotte Arnauld did so even later, near the close of the twentieth century.

Not one of us on this trip had the least training in matters archeological, so all we could do was to stare dumbly at the twin temple pyramids, the sunken ball court and the altars, and idly speculate about the way people might have lived there seven hundred years ago. We spent quite a while walking around, dreaming and speculating about that fabulous, ancient world.

There was some renewed interest in this whole region during the 1980s and '90s. Recent field work has thus shown that Chuitinamít and other nearby sites, like Kaj'yúp near Rabinal, show marked characteristics which are not to be found in El Quiché to the west of us: central pyramid-temples rather than lateral ones in the main square, "council houses" with stairs on the four facades of the platform, and "long houses" with monumental stairs on a single façade. These traits define a layout that has come to be called "Plaza Verapaz", because it is well distributed between the late sites of Baja Verapaz and Alta Verapaz, as well as in the Chixoy river valley.[25]But what really mattered, according to the French archeologist Marie-Charlotte Arnauld, "was the alliance of the Rabinaleb of Kajyub [sic] with the people of Kawinal (some ten kilometers northwest of Chuitinamít)—an alliance that made it possible to actually form a *single political territory* that we can evaluate to almost 2,000 km^2, that is to say the current department of Baja Verapaz from the summits of the Sierra de Chuacús to the north."[26]

Quite a kingdom. A past grandeur sealed forever inside of mute stones. The three of us wandered around the quiet desolation of

Chuitinamít for almost an hour. I touched the stony temple facades and the dried-out weeds that grew out of them and over them, and I struggled hard to imagine the pride and glory of an age long past. These ancient builders, these priests and warriors and watchers of the sky at night were all ancestors of the men and women we saw every day on the street, the people we worked with, the ones who would take the tools we brought and follow our instructions because we brought knowledge they supposedly did not possess. We brought methods and means, to be sure, but knowledge?

They possessed so much knowledge that we knew nothing about.

Cumulus clouds began to gather on the horizon to the south, and by that sign we knew it was time to go. It had been a good visit; an enlightening visit. In the end the old man's warning had come to nothing, thank goodness, for we never encountered any trouble to be reckoned with amidst the ruins of Chuitinamít. Only silent stones, empty plazas, weeds and vines, and a rumor of secrets that might be revealed someday.

* * *

I wish I had a picture.

In 1979 one of the many *aldea* visits that I made was out to Xococ, some ten clicks west of Rabinal. There was a dirt road out there, fairly straight and level, except for a couple twists around Patixlán, and early in the morning I hitched a ride on the back of a pickup to get out there. Santos was one of the very few drivers going out there just about every morning. I can't forget that name, because the letters were hastily painted in all-caps on both doors of his yellow and heavily dented Datsun *pickupito*. My purpose in going out to Xococ on this occasion was to do some farm plot consultations with the local farmers whom I had met a few days earlier during a short course I had given back in town.

During this period very early in my service things were still pretty calm in Rabinal. The civil war might have been well underway in other parts of the country, but in Rabinal in early 1979 there was little evidence of this. Or perhaps I was still just too naive or uninformed to perceive what was really going on.

I met with a few farmers that day in Xococ. We talked about laying out contours on their farm plots and making terraces, we talked about planting trees, and I promised to get a truck soon to bring a couple hundred seedlings out there for them to plant. By late afternoon, though, I gradually realized there might not be another ride back to the *pueblo*, and certainly no time to walk ten kilometers before nightfall. Hoping against hope, I headed down to the schoolhouse facing the river where a pickup would likely stop, I was told—if one ever showed up. Not one showed up.

So I walked back up the hill and I humbly asked one of the local leaders, *don* Mariano López Alvarado, if he could put me up for the night at his house. Maybe he felt 'honored' or maybe he felt a trifle put out, but he gladly offered me a dinner of beans and tortillas and a hammock that hung beneath the posts supporting an overhang of the corrugated metal roof. *Don* Mariano was what we volunteers called a 'community sparkplug,' but his home was as simple and unassuming as anybody else's in Xococ. Wife prattling over the fire with her daughter; other kids gawking from afar at the unearthly sight of this six-foot-three gringo in their midst. After dinner *don* Mariano and I talked for a while in the black of the night—a night rendered so black for lack of electricity in the town. We retired by nine o'clock, and silence reigned throughout the whole town.

I slept quite well that night in the hammock. Next morning, I offered my thanks and said my goodbyes, and headed back to the *pueblo*. It soon became apparent this would be a long walk, though, since this early in the morning no one would be driving *out* of Xococ.

A mile or so into the hike I was coming over a gentle hillside passing through *aldea* Patixlán when I saw it—I saw the image that is indelibly painted (not so much 'imprinted,' but *painted*, I say) in my memory. Spread out before me I saw the most peaceful, idyllic panorama of dense morning mist in the valleys, with hills and mountains emerging like islands in a vast, calm sea. Chuitinamít Hill itself was one of those lonely islands emerging prominently out of the dense blue haze. It was very still all around me, as there were few houses nearby. It was a quiet serenity that suddenly filled me with an ineffable sense of optimism and confidence. The self-doubt that had plagued me so often in the past simply washed away, and it seemed as if the very spirit of this land that I beheld before my eyes might somehow see me through the next two years.

Standing there in the road on the hillside I might well have recalled Augustine's own meditations on religious ecstasy,

> If the tumult of the flesh fell silent for someone,
> and silent too were the phantasms of earth, sea and air,
> silent the heavens,
> and the very soul silent to itself,
> that it might pass beyond itself by not thinking of its own being,
> would not *Enter into the joy of your Lord*
> be this, and this alone? [27]

And I knew in that moment there on the hillside that I had glimpsed the same spirit of Creation that is known by many names—Lord God ... Holy Spirit ... Vishnu ... Itzamná ... Kinich Ahau. *Shāntih, shāntih.*

Breathe, now. Breathe in and keep walking, I said to myself. I continued my hike for quite some distance as the blue haze slowly dissipated under a bright morning sun. I eventually made it back to my house in Rabinal, and the seasonal rain arrived around two in the afternoon, like clockwork.

I will never forget that remarkable scene I beheld from a Patixlán hillside in early 1979. That scene has come back to me in occasional daydreams over the last forty years. I never felt a greater sense of peace than I did in that moment. We were young then, and everything mattered.

These days I wish I had a picture of it all. But then again, I do—it is a priceless picture ensconced in a silent court of memory in the deepest recesses of my mind.

CHAPTER 5

Xecambá

"Only connect!...Live in fragments no longer."

—E.M. Forster, *Howard's End*

Memory doesn't actually play tricks on us. Damn, but it just falls apart and deteriorates! The distant memory of one episode in life's journey is like a precious, hand-painted piece of crockery sitting high up on the shelf. Some crockery is quite durable and wears well over time. Who knows why. Maybe the porcelain is more substantial, or maybe it spent longer in the kiln after it was shaped. Or maybe it was just made from better mud. But most crockery is fragile, and the briefest handling—just to turn the piece over and read its provenance stamped on the bottom—may lead to a careless slip and then a mess of jagged shards scattered across the floor.

But the individual shards on the floor are themselves interesting, and some might yet possess an intrinsic beauty all their own, inasmuch as they capture and preserve at least one corner of the lovely pastoral scene that was painted on the china plate or soup tureen when it was whole.

In the rooms of that mansion which is my memory, there are episodic events from whole cloth that are preserved in all their rich detail—coherent and often compelling stories with a beginning, a middle, and an end. I remember the people involved, their faces, their names, their attitudes, the time of year, the time of day, even the weather. I can remember all the specific circumstances of these stories, and I usually can even remember *why* I remember each one so well. I can recall these stories that are all of a piece and set them down on paper without too much struggle—indeed, I have done so here—and then the rest depends only on my language mastery, my ability to construct a narrative, and luck.

Then there are the fragments. Pieces of visions and experiences, moments of insight totally disconnected from their broader context, abstract portraits where the mouth is blurry or missing, the liquid eyes deceptively authentic yet missing something unnamable. Nevertheless these fragments are as real as the stories from the past that play out in my mind in all their fullness. All that is needed is the thread of imagination to stitch them together to create a coherent account worth sharing.

I have a box full of these broken shards stored away in a corner of my mind. Here is one such attempt where I've mended them back together, recollecting a number of vividly recalled memory fragments and bonding them each to each with the sparest use of imaginative invention, in order to arrive at some kind of meaning.

* * *

It is late morning in the bone-dry Mesoamerican valley. The *feria titular* which welcomed me to Rabinal is long past, but I am still in the first few months of my stay. In the plaza, bright shimmering patches of blue and white and gray move in tightly spaced rows under palm trees. Little arms and legs swing like sticks in unison. Heat rises from the white earth like a clear fluid curtain obscuring the details. The shimmering forms seem to float above the ground as they rhythmically advance, marching to a cadence set by the music of squawking brass and a static-ridden chorus of disembodied voices. Two figures stand taller than the rest, they stand at ease, and their featureless faces shimmer. The fluid shapes produce the effect of an impressionist painting set to motion. The shimmering forms of marching schoolchildren move as a single unit across the plaza past palm trees with white painted stems. Behind them, even the chalk-white face of the church appears as a liquid edifice diffracted by the calm but incessant heat. Great timber buttresses angle up against the sides of the chalk-faced church, as if the whole massive façade were really nothing but a plywood studio prop in a Hollywood movie. The broad steps of the church are crumbling, and in places the rises and runs have resolved into something resembling the slope of a hill. Gleaming white saints peer out from a dozen niches in the white façade; a pair of them gaze heavenward with beatific longing, though the twin belfries above their heads are empty.

Four soldiers in boonie hats clank past the broad church steps, their Galils slung low, the stocks folded. They too are shrouded by the fluid curtain as they slouch indifferently past the marching schoolchildren. One soldier sips through a straw from a clear plastic bag filled with orange soda.

Pharmakos. This is the life of the plaza at the end of the old polluted year. I nudge my glasses up with a smooth, pallid finger and try to walk at least a bus length behind the soldiers.

In front of the church the stall belonging to *don* Juan Lux is open. It faces the church, the first in a long row of merchants' stalls stretching to the opposite end of the park. The rest of the stalls are shuttered with gray sheets of corrugated metal, for it is Monday and there is no market. Besides *don* Juan, only la Mari is always open—the *comedor* where you can get a modest breakfast of eggs and black beans for fifty *centavos*, a small slab of shoeleather "biftec" or a greasy *recado* of tripe with amoebic horchata or sweet dishwater coffee for dinner. The tripe is to be avoided. You eat on a bench by the fire, smoke watering your eyes, and there's a truck driver and a police officer on either side of you, or a traveling salesman or a *campesino*.

Muchas gracias, señora, buen provecho. Maltiox cha'lá.

Don Juan's stall is open for business even when it's not market day because he sells plastic goods. Shiny red and blue baskets, assorted combs and cooking utensils, plastic sandals, pails and *palanganas*, and the colorfully striped pinch-necked *tinajas* that the women carry on their heads with such grace and skill. The big plastic *tinajas* hang from his stall in rows. *Don* Juan gets a new shipment of plastic goods every week from the capital, and his sales are brisk. He is the only merchant in the plaza with wheels. His dirty yellow VW bus is parked by the stall; the chrome VW that used to adorn the front end is long gone, and the rear bumper's gone, too. One whole side of the bus looks like a mottled, mustard-colored relief map of the surrounding countryside. A bumper sticker in the rear window says "*YO AMO GUATEMALA*," only there's a big red Valentine heart in place of the word *AMO*.

An old Mayan woman stoops in front of *don* Juan's stall in the shade of the corrugated *lamina*, pouring slowly from one plastic *tinaja* into another on the ground. A thin trail of steam rises from the creamy chocolate-colored gruel as she pours. *Don* Juan is sitting in his stall watching with a mournful look.

The old woman will carry the sacred libation to the men of the *cofradía* in a darkened room off the park. She will arrive at their doorstep—*buenas ta-a-a-rdes*—and then she will lower the *tinaja* off the top of her head in one deft move and set it on the ground, placing the cloth *yagual* in her lap as she crouches at the door. She will froth the chocolate once more before she ladles it into brightly painted calabash gourds. In low voices the men will thank her, *maltiox cha'lá*, and then they will drink from the calabash gourds while passing around a bad cigar. They drink the sacred libation, they drink from the skull of One Hunahpu, they drink and pray and talk among themselves in low voices, dreaming of deliverance.

Beyond the church in the park a naked, dun-colored hill stands alone, impassive except for the shimmering shoulders near its base. The hill known as Xecambá stands out singly and prominently among the many that form a ragged horizon surrounding the plaza. Thorny Place, Meawan. Hills of ancient legend. To the west, Plaster House, along the Black Road leading to the bloody conquests of the Quiché lords. Chuitinamít, the easternmost sentinel of Utatlán, where kinship and ballcourts are inextricably linked.[28] The wavy distortions of heat rising from the sunny plaza and from the hood of a pickup parked nearby set the whole scene to liquid motion, while the dun-colored face of Xecambá rises above it all, solid and bare.

Xecambá, place of blood sacrifice and fount of legends involving gods and men, remains indifferent to the lives that animate the plaza—the children marching, the old women prattling in the marketplace, the straw hatted men all crowded standing up in the back of a battered pickup, the priest in his darkened door, the soldiers, the merchants—even as it guards their destiny.

Now the clear fluid curtain of tropical heat begins to evaporate, and the fluttering illusion congeals into a starker reality.

As I draw near, things come into focus. The air is motionless, but the martial music now is blaring. As I nudge my glasses up again to the notch on the bridge of my sweaty nose, a shadow falls across my left shoulder and the staccato syllables of a native dialect surprise. An indigenous woman passes me quickly and crosses the dusty street to the other side, her three small children in tow, one of them a baby wrapped in a brightly colored *sarape* on the back of his sister. The wide stripes of purple and green and yellow strain tightly across the young girl's chest, and she leans forward under the weight of her infant brother. The woman looks old enough to be their grandmother. She adjusts the enormous bundle on her head as she utters an urgent phrase in a secretive voice that is barely audible. The younger child looks up at the woman, and *mamita* repeats the guttural sounds with yet more urgency. The boy skips along and then trips and scurries behind his older sister and covers the face of the sleeping infant with a loose flap of the striped serape. They hurry on until they turn the corner and pass out of sight behind a brown mud cake wall.

Mal de ojo. I silently form the words with my mouth. *Mal de ojo*. I hope I will never be on the receiving end of the evil eye.

I walk across the plaza past the marching children, all of them identically dressed in pale blue shirts and blouses, gray trousers and pleated skirts. Some of them are wearing their Sunday shoes, others wear simple homemade sandals cut from old tires; none are shoeless. They march in five parallel files sloping from the tallest up front to the shortest in back. Now I can make out that the two taller figures off to one side are a man and a woman, and the woman holds a megaphone. The man is bobbing at the knees, clapping his hands to the beat of the anthem. He's really getting into it. Beads of sweat glisten on his forehead. Ahead of the marching files of children two girls carry opposite ends of a long banner with bright red letters. *Escuela Normal Rabinalense*. At the very head of the parade one tallish boy lifts high a pale blue and white flag. The flag is actually made of cloth, what a surprise, and it is attached to an aluminum staff. Bird of paradise, the iridescent splendor of a lonely quetzal perched above crossed flintlocks. Freedom and order. This same national heraldry is plastered all over the place in drugstores, *tiendas*, schools, on utility poles, and at nearly every civic meeting place, but only on cheap plastic, often in long banners of repeat patterns. It is rare to see a single real cloth flag. Much less a staff. The ubiquitous plastic flags are found even in the remotest *aldeas* up in the mountains, where they adorn soot-covered walls next to Jesus Christ, the Virgen de Guadalupe, and the occasional Michael Jackson poster. Every last citizen, no matter how poor or isolated, shall know his country's patriotic colors. Flags for all. Plastic patriotism of the masses. Bearers of life-giving libation, pray for deliverance.

And today, plastics make it all possible.

I stop again on the other side of the plaza by the church and turn around. Across the way, beneath the painted palms, the teacher who was clapping a beat sees me approaching, and he waves to me with a hand raised high in the air.

"*El nuevo gringo!*" he cries.

Now, gringo can be a really ambiguous term in Spanish. It's a word that is not at all like those more execrable epithets denoting origins or race that we all know as English speakers. "Gringo" actually can mean many things, depending on the circumstances. It can be said with something like affection—or with baiting hostility. Beneath the mask of small-town civility, the sentiment of the speaker is often inscrutable. That's how it was today. A place like this where you're the only gringo around, usually they simply mean, "He who stands alone and apart from us."

I wave back. The fetid odor of rotting mangos makes the air feel heavy. The children are now marching in an amorphous circuit near the round gazebo in the middle of the park. They look hot and tired yet stoic as they march in full sun.

"Square the corners! Remember to square the corners!" shouts the woman with the megaphone. She lowers it to below her chin and smiles in my direction. As I approach, the man says, "*Que calor, no?*"

"*Sí hombre*, there is much heat."

"Two more weeks and the rains will come. One can feel it."

"Yes, I suppose one can."

"Do you know how one feels it?"

"No, I do not," I admit.

"The cicadas. Did you hear the cicadas this morning, *señor*? They drone on late in the dry season, and their singing gets louder and louder as the first rains draw near. The cicadas are calling for rain, and the sky will soon answer them."

"I didn't know that."

"Well now you do. Two more weeks."

It is hard to talk above the blaring anthem coming from the boom box that sits squat on a cement bench. The children keep marching, and with alternating glances in either direction the teacher with the megaphone tries to divide her attention between her uniformed brood and this halting conversation in the sparse shade of a palm tree. She has the most beautiful indigenous face, and her black hair is curled and coiled rather than straight like the women in the marketplace. She is conservatively dressed with a white blouse and a plain gray skirt of undaring length.

Guatemala feliz! que tus aras
no profane jamás el verdugo;
ni haya esclavos que laman el yugo
ni tiranos que escupan tu faz.

The anthem's lyrics speak of slaves and tyrants. Standing near the high curb of the park I contemplate the irony in those verses.

"How do you like our town so far?" The woman smiled and glanced again at the children. The anthem blared.

"Rabinal is a wonderful little town. I am enjoying myself here very much." Always quick with the winning smile and the judicious compliment. Because I know that this approach will go a long way towards breaking down barriers and easing my way into the culture. My compliment, though, obscures the fact that when I first received the posting half a year earlier, my initial reaction had been that Guatemala was not "exotic" enough. Too Catholic, I thought, and much too close to America. There didn't seem to be any other opportunities, however, given the qualifications I had alleged on my application, so I had come to Guatemala after all, though it wasn't exotic enough. Hopefully I could accomplish something useful here.

"I call myself Cristián," I say, thrusting out a hand as I approach.

"I am Luz de Carmen Mendoza, *a sus ordenes*. And this is HeIio—"

"Alvarado Coloch." He shakes my hand firmly. "*A sus ordenes.*" He actually clicks his heels, though his glazed eyes betray a hangover. Helio's hirsute arms and face make him look quite the animal beside

Luz de Carmen's radiant beauty. He utters Spanish with a lazy drawl, while the woman's speech is precise, almost staccato.

The woman lowers her megaphone, holds it at her side with her finger on the trigger mechanism, and turns to face me.

"Have you been up Cerro Kaj'yup yet, *señor*? Have you not seen the ruins?"

Xecambá is to the east of the *pueblo*; Kaj'yup to the north. I had heard something once about a legendary connection between the two hills, something involving the traditions of the ancient Mayans—but I lacked many details.

"No, not yet. But I intend to go up there soon."

"I have been there many times. Last year I took the children to see the ruins." This seems a matter of great pride to Luz de Carmen.

"Perhaps then you could be my guide to the ruins." I proffer another winning smile. But the girl—for Luz de Carmen, I can now see, is but a girl, barely twenty—demure, giggling and glancing back towards the schoolchildren.

"You would have to meet my father first," she says. She laughs, and Helio laughs, too.

"She is quite a catch, *señor*. In this you must not vacillate."

He says this in the sportive, fraternal manner that is customary between two men with common interests.

"But I—I only meant to see the ruins. Really."

Despite the awkwardness, through all of this exchange the girl has not once blushed, but now it is I who feels my face redden.

"The ruins up there are really quite interesting," Luz de Carmen says, and it is evident now she has not for one moment lost her composure.

"Like our princess, here, a real treasure" adds Helio.

"Forget Helio," says Luz de Carmen. "I am no princess. And I cannot accompany you to visit Cerro Kaj'yup, for we have just met—and anyway I have a *novio*. But *you* must go see the ruins, *de veras*. They will reveal to you much about the history of our little town."

"I will certainly go see them. Though 1 am not sure when."

"A ver que dice dios."

"Si, a ver que dice." I have heard this expression several times during my short tenure in the country, and I am getting used to simply

agreeing and responding in kind. But the phrase strikes me as odd. "To see what God shall say." It seems it is always said with a voice of wistful resignation, as one might refer to something that is completely out of one's hands. Yet it comes up in conversation even when talking about mundane eventualities that one could unquestionably plan for and execute. Cerro Kaj'yup is not yet in my planner, but it will be as soon as I return to the house.

I lifted my chin and kiss the air with an exaggerated pucker in the direction of the gazebo. "And the children over there—?" I'd grown accustomed to using this very Latin gesture, and had learned to deploy it casually once in a while in conversations. Luz de Carmen is walking back towards the children now, and she raises the megaphone to her mouth.

"*Desfilando,*" she says, turning back to me from several yards away and speaking through the megaphone. She has the sweetest voice, but the trigger-activated device turns it into something inertly rasping, like a voice coming from a cheap transistor radio. She lowers it again and over the cacophony of the recorded anthem says in her own voice, "It has been a pleasure, *señor* Cristián. Then she turns and rejoins her brood.

"But what are they marching for?"

"For the Fifteenth, our Independence Day," Helio replies.

"But that is in September." I already knew about the Fifteenth. "That is months away."

"Our children must practice a great deal for the Fifteenth. It is a very important celebration for us. Lucita and I will take the children out of class every Monday, Wednesday, and Friday for an hour. When the great day is very close, we will do this every day. There is much preparation. As you can see, our littlest ones—especially those *chiquilincitos*—well, they are not the best of soldiers. *Hay que darle, darle...* You have got to give it, give it, give it to them so they will march well on the Fifteenth."

"But that means you lose a lot of classroom time, no?"

"Ah, *señor*, but there is time for everything. Everything has its priority, you see. Besides, here they get exercise, they learn discipline, they learn to be proud of their appearance and their country. These things are important, are they not?"

"*Pues, sí. Es muy cierto.*" Yes indeed; so very true.

"Very well then. Look, it is already the hour for lunch." Helio turns towards Luz de Carmen, who is calling out marching orders to the schoolchildren surrounding the gazebo, and he raises his arms high in the air, one hand fingering the wrist of the other. She simply nods. "Let's go see what la Mari has for us today. You will join me, no?"

"Yes, I have much hunger," I reply. "But what about Luz de Carmen, can she not join us?"

"Lucita will finish up with the children and march them back to school. She always eats at the school. Somebody has to watch the children during recess."

I thought this arrangement a little unfair, but I had resolved to be open and accepting of the new climate of morals and manners I found myself in. Sometimes, as now, this required a conscious effort. This was just one of many things I would say 'yes' to and condone, not because I thought that all values were relative, but rather because I simply wanted to adapt and try to fit in as best I could.

We walk across the park to the *comedor*. The oak smell of the cooking fire mixed with that of over-grilled beef hurries us on to Mari's open door. I have to duck to get inside.

"*Hola* Mari! What do we have today?" Helio rubs his two hands vigorously and bares his teeth in a grin. On a wooden shelf by the fire there is a radio, and it plays the fadeout melody of the daily *radionovela*. Over the staticky sound of melodramatic strings and horns, a narrator sums up the action of today's episode, and poses questions to entice people to tune in tomorrow. The voice speaks in the sonorous tones of high Spanish. Mari stands over the fire clapping corn flour tortillas between the wetted palms of her hands and lays them on the hot *comal*.

"*Hay biftec*," replies Mari. La Mari always seems so cheerful. Never a frown, never a sign of indifference. Yet today—there is a certain hesitation in her voice. I had eaten at Mari's several times already, as it was a convenient stop on the way to the *vivero*. Helio and I sit down on the long wooden bench, and in one deft move Mari sets the plates before us. A dog pokes its head in the doorway, a pariah dog straight out of Malcolm Lowry's Cuernavaca, and it raises its mangy snout in the air as if to sniff some meager nourishment out of the cooking smells in the *comedor*.

"*Chucho, fuera!*" Mari turns and hisses at the mutt, then reaches for the plastic bowl she has used to wet her palms and splashes out just enough water to anoint the ground before her. The pariah dog dodges the water and hurries off, nose to the ground and tail between its legs.

"*Házme la campaña, Mari—un remedio, porfa.*" Without comment or complaint, Mari prepares the *remedio* in a small glass adorned with Flintstone cartoon characters. She cracks a raw egg into the concoction, and tops it off with a spritz of *aguardiente* from the flask on her shelf. I watch wide-eyed as Helio empties the glass without once removing it from his lips.

"*Un remedio para picar la piedra en su cabeza,*" Mari says, and we all laugh. *Pica-piedra* was the Spanish name for the Flintstones.

"So, you have been here a month so far," says Helio, restraining a belch. "Will you be with us long, *señor* Cristián?"

"I suppose I may be here for a couple years. Maybe more." I stick a piece of beef carcass in my mouth and set to work chewing on it. "I see you have a very accurate account of my stay so far."

"Ha ha! When you are the only gringo in town, people notice." Helio laughs volubly and looks over at Mari, who turns and smiles back while stoking the fire with another log. As we talk, the radio on the shelf emits a constant white noise of midday news and football scores laced with raucous advertisements for batteries and stomach remedies; pickup trucks and aspirin.

"La Mari here, she tells me she has been admiring you. I think she likes you."

"*¡Usted se calle!*" is Mari's rebuke, but the shape of her mouth suggests mock anger mixed with—and this surprises me—something like pleasure at the insinuation. "*Don* Helio, you are worse than the dog!"

"She is a spirited woman, as you can see. And she cooks."

"I will be sure to make a note of this in my journal," I reply, trying my best to keep up with the banter. "Spirited woman. Good cook."

The radio broadcast punctuates our conversation with advertising jingles alternating with telegraphic news headlines that sound off like machine gun bursts.

...Ultima hora! Ultima hora!

"*Señor,* you are still an unknown here in Rabinal—a cipher only, whose value we do not yet perceive."

I make no reply to this, but instead work on my shoeleather *biftec.*" I still had many questions about Rabinal, but I wasn't sure this was the time or place to try to fill in the gaps.

"What, then, is your title, *señor* Cristián? You are an *ingeniero*, no?"

"Yes, I suppose you could call me that."

"But what kind of engineering? What is your branch?"

"That is a little hard to say. Call it natural resources."

"Natural resources? Then you are an *ingeniero forestal*?"

"Close enough. Actually, that's a pretty big part of what I do, yes."

"Everybody who comes to help us has a title. Some are *médicos*, some are *licenciados*. But most of them are *ingenieros*. Is that because engineers are what we mostly need here, or is it simply because that is what mostly comes out of your great universities?"

"I think it is a little of both."

"Me, I was to become a priest, but I became a teacher instead."

"You were to be a priest?"

"*Así es.* I was raised in a very Catholic family. *Mi mamá*, she was *católica rematada*. She very much wanted her eldest son to take the vows. But Felipe, he was killed many years ago, so the burden of fulfilling my mother's dream fell to me instead. But forget about me, you see what I do here now. I teach. What about your work here?"

I am cautious in my reply only because I want to forestall any misunderstanding. "I work in natural resources, and I will be managing the tree nursery down by the river, across from the *colonia*."

I take a long draught of the *horchata* that Mari has poured, and I start cutting away vigorously at the carcass on my plate. "I hope I can help people and maybe get them to plant some trees around here." I chomp on a piece of meat. The radio blares out a lively jingle –

...¡Soy el rey del camino cuando en mi Hino voy!

I wish the volume could be turned down. Helio listens attentively, considers this information on the new stranger in town, and then says, "I see. You will get the *campesinos* to plant these trees, and then in ten years you will be back to harvest them."

"No, no," I was quick to respond. "I can absolutely assure you—"

"They say the gringo comes and teaches us many new things, but the *campesino* knows that the tools and ideas that the gringo hands out so freely come with a price. He has no doubt that you will come back later to take his trees, take his land away. It has been that way before, and it will happen again."

...Señora, ¿cómo blanquear su ropa a modo de que... ?

"But surely they understand that things can be different. This gringo..." I struggle for the right words in Spanish.

"What our *campesino* understands, *señor*, is one vast circle. History is a circle, and there is nothing new under the sun. That is why it is so hard to make progress here. We are all trapped in this great circle."

... ¡Ultima hora! En la capital, mueren dos agentes de seguridad cuando...

"But this idea of endless exploitation. Maybe they bring it on themselves. This circle, I think maybe it is a trap of their own making."

"Ah, but there you are wrong, my friend. *Los maya*, they did not invent time. God gave these people the calendar round, they just keep the days and watch the cycles pass. If torment there be in the world, then torment will return again and again."

"But they must have goals in life. I don't know, but I'm a pretty goal-oriented *muchacho*. I have certain goals here and—"

Alivio rápido y seguro. ¡De la marca que usted confia... !

"That is precisely what worries our *campesino*. Your certain goals here."

"*Mire*—I can assure you that my goals here are completely honorable!" I protest. If it were not for Helio's garrulous tone, I would be offended by the insinuation. Here is a man who could hold forth on any subject, it seems. An intelligent native, educated beyond the borders of this dusty town. Only now he chooses to hold forth on the question of my intentions.

"*Cálmese, señor*. I do not accuse you. I am sure you are an honorable man. But in accordance with the gringo's sense of honor. For the gringo, is there not honor in dominion?"

"Now you are trying to trap me with words. Well, I will answer you. No, I do not think there is any particular honor in dominion. Anyway, I have not come here to dominate anybody, but to learn. To learn, and to try to help." I mean this sincerely, and try to sound sincere. "Maybe I am different from other gringos. Maybe that is why I came here in the first place."

"We shall see. *En su debido tiempo verémos.*"

For all his challenges to my integrity, Helio seems a likable fellow. He knows how to argue, and I respect him for that. Helio talks of Mayan concepts of time, and my intentions here in town. Suddenly everything about Rabinal seems far less transparent and prosaic than I am accustomed to dealing with in my maps.

... los desconocidos se huyeron, habiendo dejado un saldo de siete muertos,
entre ellos dos niños de escasamente cinco años, y una mujer en pleno embarazo ...

We eat in silence while Mari rinses dishes in a plastic bucket. When Helio speaks again, he adopts a more conciliatory tone. "You have come here to plant trees, then—that is good, that is very good. The deforestation of this land, it is a very great problem. Look at the hills around us. My grandfather remembers when trees grew everywhere, and the water flowed clear. That was not such a long time ago. We have always been poor, *señor* Cristián, but by the grace of God, our poverty was bearable. Now it is a day's journey just to gather enough firewood for a few days of beans and tortillas. The plagues on this land are many. Our water makes us ill, and our children die from curable diseases before they are old enough to go to school. During the dry season whole families travel to the coast in crowded buses, they go to harvest cotton on the great farms near Mazate, and at the end of the season they bring back a few *centavos* in their pockets and all the rich farmers' chemicals on their hands, in their blood. Here in Rabinal, only death grows rich."

"I read much about these plagues while preparing to come here," I say. "You may be surprised to learn that many of these problems have been quite well documented by scientists and other experts from all over."

"I am not surprised. But you are the expert we look to now, there is no other. Do you know of another gringo who lives here? You are the only one, and we will be grateful for your guidance."

> *... Recuérdese, para insecticidas, BAYER es el nombre más respetado en el mundo ...*

I see this as an auspicious turn. Helio's change of tone from raw challenge to earnest solicitude surprises me, but I decide to accept it at face value. I will accept the garland of recognition as Resident Expert, and in the days to come will take concrete steps to earn the respect already bestowed on me. In the background, the radio program shifts back from news to sports again.

> *En fútbol anoche, el equipo capitalino DEMOLlO al de Quezaltenango, cinco dos ...*

Mari places more tortillas in the basket on the table. She looks at Helio and says, "We haven't seen Dionisio since Thursday. Have you not seen him, *don* Helio?"

"Dionisio ... Dionisio. Which Dionisio?" Then, "Ah! The one from the pharmacy, no?"

"Right by the pharmacy. He lives with his mother there. He is cousin to my brother's wife. Nobody has seen him since Thursday, and his mother is very worried. He works as a *peón* at the construction site that belongs to *don* Maco. The others there have not seen him, either."

"I know who you mean. I for my part have not seen him, but—Thursday, you say? Wait. Thursday in the market there was an army truck, I mean a truck commissioned by the army. It was a red truck, like the one that comes through every summer to haul away the poor bastards who go to work on the coast. I believe they were rounding up *reclutos*, at least that is what *don* Chente said. It looks like they have taken your Dionisio and made him into a *tamalito de chipilín*. Not likely you'll see him again for a couple years." Mari's face stiffens. She looks at the *comal* on the fire, and then back at the table where we sit. She dries her hands on her apron. Her dumb stare falls on the ground before her, then shoots across towards the fire. Does this news merely confirm her worst fears? Dionisio has been snatched off the street and drafted.

"*Más tortillas, Mari, porfa!*"

I look up as Mari sets more tortillas on the table. Our glances meet only for a second. Her face looks different. This is one of those moments. I will encounter many more like it in the days to come. The desire to offer comfort to another soul; the barriers that make it impossible.

Later it is *muchas gracias* and *buén provecho*. We both get up and each give two quarters to Mari. "Seventy-five *centavos* for you, *don* Helio. *El remedio*." Helio gives her the extra change in his pocket and says, "*Porque eres un amorcito, linda Mari*." He kisses the palm of his hand exuberantly as Mari drops the money in her smokey and grimy apron.

As we are about to head off our separate ways, Helio says to me, "Many people will be counting on you, *señor* Cristián, for they are sorely afflicted. Only remember, for their sake and for your own, you can perhaps end the plague and heal the affliction that you see before you, but the plague that you cannot see—that is another matter."

The radio blares.

...GOOOOOOOOOOOOOOOOOL!

The plaza is quiet now, so quiet that the syncopated shuffle of my boots over the hard white dirt seems to draw all eyes upon me. Only gringo, all alone—the afflicted one. Well, everybody has some kind of affliction, some in their minds. Is ignorance an affliction? I continue walking as I think about this. Wisdom of the jaguar. To see the patterns of chaos, to move without fear in the darkness. *Revoltijo*, he said. "In this you must not vacillate, *señor*." I need to get home, I need to get back to my maps. Juan Pablo must be waiting. But if time is a circle, then he'll be back anyway. We will all be back here, back to the beginning of time.

Behind the dun-colored face of Xecambá, a procession of tall white clouds hugs the distant horizon, advancing northward ever so slowly. *Hoy no*. The cicadas will sing louder before the sky opens up. Two more weeks.

As I walk by the church steps the fetid smell of rotting mangos grows stronger. Another little microclimate of local putrefaction. I try to draw shallow breaths, but that doesn't help. The source of the odor is not far off—a flattened, fly-covered mango pit is laying on the ground not five yards away, baking in the afternoon sun. The overpowering fetidness hangs in the air like the sweet smell of death.

Walking briskly past the foul odor, I saw walking towards me along the ragged barbed wire fence a stout young girl with hair disheveled and a hobbled gait. Her clothes were very dirty, her forehead appeared bruised, and her puffy face had no chin to speak of. She looked maybe twelve. As she hobbled along the fence she ran her fingers along the middle run of barbed wire, scarcely avoiding the menacing barbs every few inches.

"*Ten cuidado, niña!* You will easily cut yourself there." The girl stood still and gaped at me, now holding the run of barbed wire in a tight fist. She opened her mouth, but no words came forth.

"*No seas tontita!*" Don't be stupid. No sooner had I made this exclamation than I regretted my choice of words. The girl held fast to the barbed wire and stared at me. I approached her and placed one hand lightly on her clenched fist. I shook my head 'no', but the girl still held on tight. She seemed frozen in amazement at my tall figure.

"*No hay que—*" But I did not finish the sentence, for I saw that it was no use. With both hands I tried to gently uncurl the fingers of the girl's fist, one by one. When I finally succeeded in releasing her grip, I noticed she had already acquired a small cut. I looked into her squinting black eyes and held up one index finger and mouthed "*Espérese,*" wait a minute, without saying it. I swung my backpack off my shoulder and fumbled among the things inside. At last I grabbed a dirty white plastic box with a red cross on it.

The girl looked at me and stretched out her uninjured hand and grunted—or moaned. She curled the fingers of her outstretched hand as if to clutch an imaginary coin. She did this several times. I reached in my pocket and pulled out a tattered bill, which I put carefully in her hand. Her eyes grew large at the sight of the bill—was it surprise or indignation in her expression? She was probably used to getting only *centavo* coins; would she even know what to do with this miserable looking piece of wrinkled paper? She clutched the bill and quickly stuffed it in a pocket of her faded dress. Our eyes met for what seemed an eternity, but the poor girl just blankly stared. Her inscrutable expression confounded me even more when she dropped her jaw as if to begin a long, wailing howl. Then she pursed her lips as if to make the sound of 'M'. She said nothing, but only moved her lips. I wished I could pull the words from her mouth.

As I kneeled down to examine her hand, the girl took a step backward. When I looked up at her I saw that her face had contorted into a grimace of horror. Yet she said nothing, she just stood there. What wisdom lay behind those black, squinting eyes? What secret knowledge lay dormant in a deep recess of her afflicted brain? I could only imagine the torment and hardship she must have suffered in her short life, yet I felt a connection, almost electric, or deeply organic like symbiosis, between myself and the poor bedraggled girl with wild black hair. We stared at one another for a long minute, as if we could communicate without words or gestures. When I regained the analytic presence of mind to reach down and open the first aid kit, the girl stepped back again—then turned and ran. "*Ven acá*," I called out, though I knew it was pointless if she wasn't even looking at me. The girl ran down the street behind the church as I squatted on the ground by my kit holding a fresh packet of gauze.

Pharmakos. The old polluted year. Only gringo, the afflicted one. But no, the afflictions here are legion. Look around you. No sense—some people just ain't got no sense. Can't see the danger. Forest for the trees. Danger all around—I guess they're inured to it. Time is a circle. Ambiguities, eternal ambiguities. Medicine is for healing; can medicine be the poison? Same old story, only with a new twist. Progress is necessary—but time is a circle, and life here is cheap.

I gather my things off the ground and start walking again. I walk past the *cantinas*, the cemetery, the *destacamento militar*. The streets are quiet now except for the music of a wailing Mexican ranchera that spills into the street from a *cantina* called, appropriately enough, "*El Refugio*."

I walk past the *destacamento militar*. In front of it a lone soldier stands in a makeshift sentry post covered with a ragged roof of thatched palm branches, his mounted machine gun at the ready, the bipod resting on the rough-hewn edge of his rustic cubicle. I make a conscious effort to pass at a normal pace, being careful not to trip on the speed bumps.

They call these speed bumps "sleeping patrolmen." Crude security measures, but effective. Parked by the army barracks I notice two canvas topped jeeps where I was used to seeing only one, and beside the jeeps there is a civilian pickup. *What's that pickup doing there?*

Well before the cemetery on the outskirts of town I turn back onto the right road heading home, and as I continue on I begin to make mental notes concerning the lay of the land, *el plan del pueblo.*

* * *

Tuesday, Apr. 10, 1979

Made some progress today. Got most of the maps that will be needed for a full survey, though San Cristóbal quad turned out unavailable. (Checked this on my second visit to IGN in Guat City; the *Coronel* there politely refused my request, made a vague ref. to disputed land claims in that area.) Enough work here to keep me occupied for months. Finished first overlay today of at least 75% of the central quad (Rabinal, *pueblo*); need more mylar to continue. They say the rains will come in two weeks or so. Native wisdom. Need to get out and recon the whole area—or as much as I can—before the serious wet season begins. Get Vol. II of dendrology guide ASAP.

I lit a cigarette. That colonel with the German name at the IGN—the place where I got the maps—his name almost sounded like some parody of the old Teutonic order. Himmelfarb. The color of heaven. Who knows, maybe he's actually the son of an old Nazi war criminal. Hmm ... *could happen*, I suppose. Field Marshall Adolf Himmelfarb, seeing at last the likely outcome of the war and the certainty of his own fate, deserts his battalion of jackbooted comrades fighting on the sands of Egypt and finds his way to the New World, where he settles down and takes a Central American wife. Goes into coffee, raises a son, later a daughter, becomes a citizen, erases the past. But the past lives on in his son, who graduates with honors from the *Politécnica*, spends three quarters of his career in uniform, and now heads up the *Instituto Geográfico Nacional.*

"Shit, Chris, cut the BS and get back to work." I reopened my notebook.

> **Wednesday TO-DO:** Go to *vivero* – Do seedling inventory and monthly reports – Check out that reforestation site on Kaj'yúp *ladera* – Afternoon back home, count how many FFW bags left in bodega – Do CARE requisition and post it – Work on altitude zone map based on topos – Make posters for presentation.

Okay, ready at least for tomorrow. I figured I better get going if I was to get through the tree nursery tasks *and* get out to the reforestation site all before lunch. I stubbed out my cigarette in the moist ground just off the veranda and threw the remaining coffee in my cup out into the bushes. I grabbed my *morral*, slipped my notebook into it, and headed out the door, striding quickly past the CUC graffito on the wall, scarcely thinking about it.

Some kind of sacrifice will be needed to ward off evil from this place. Perhaps many sacrifices.

Pharmakos.[29]

The Baja Verapaz forestry crew, (L-R): Carl Schattenberg, the author, and Bruce Jeffrey.

CHAPTER 6

Kaj'yup

> We must feel the reality and presence of God through all external things, without exception, as clearly as our hand feels the substance of paper through the penholder and the nib.
>
> —Simone Weil (*Waiting for God*, p. 44)

Rabinal. How can I even begin to know you? How might I finally glimpse your soul? For once, just for once dammit, don't be so coy and mysterious with me. Speak to me. What hidden meaning can you reveal to me? Place of the Daughter of the Lord, a place that is watched over by the spirits of Xecambá and Kaj'yúp,

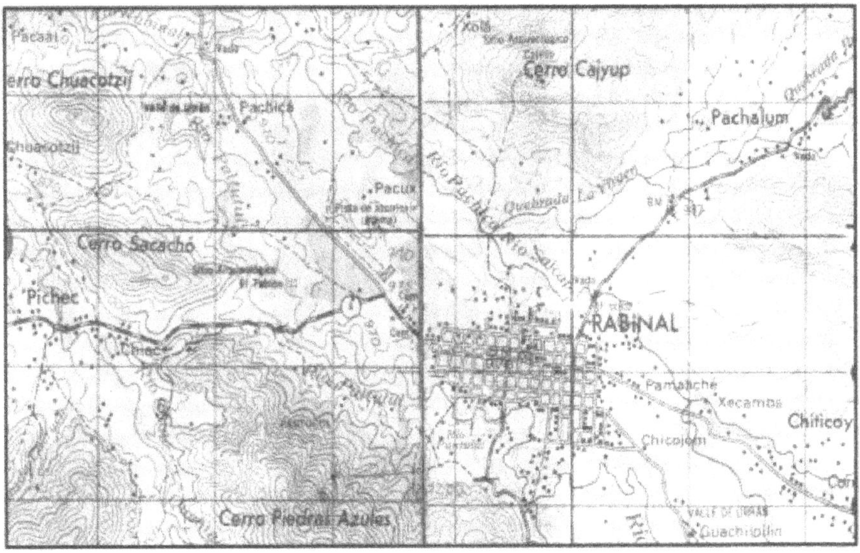

Rabinal is one of the oldest communities in Guatemala. Founded in 1537, they say, under the name of San Pablo. But the souls of the Achí dwelled in this valley for many, many years, long before the Spaniards coming from Mexico ever laid claim to it.

Rabinal. Her beauty astonishes me every single day, yet her secrets always lay just beyond my reach. Still and all, the best way to get a feel for this town, without question, is to simply take a walk along its streets and pathways. *Just take a walk.* Take a long walk from one end of the town to the other. Be sure to greet the people you pass on the street, buy something in the *mercado*, stop to admire the church façade. And be sure to leave your camera behind, because it might only separate you from the lived experience. Pay attention to the details.

So let's take a walk. C'mon, let's do it—I mean right now, just you and me, my friend. Look, I just finished my spartan breakfast of *pan de a cinco* and strong coffee, I've taken my meds, and I've already tossed the dish and mug into the *pila* out back. I'll put out my morning cigarette in a minute and we can take off. It's 7:15; if we leave now we should be in the *vivero* by eight. Yeah, forty-five minutes more or less; only because of the stops we'll be making. Wait for me out front; I'll be there in a minute and we'll walk down there together. And hey, don't freak out when you see that CUC graffito painted on the wall facing us over there. Rest assured this is not CUC headquarters. I guess I figured that painting it over when I moved in here would have made a statement to my neighbors, and I didn't want to make any kind of statement. Though leaving it there on my wall for all to see I suppose makes a statement, too. Don't ask me how it got there; it simply came with this place I rented. I mean fuck it, it's just CUC, *el Comité de Unidad Campesina*. Don't worry, ain't nobody here's gonna think *I'm* CUC; everyone here knows who I am and what I do. Let's go now, jes' lemme lock the gate here.

My street is like all the streets in Rabinal: unpaved everywhere and uneven in spots, but relatively tidy in spite of the dust and the ruts. Oh look, there's Augustito across the street; he's always climbing way up on the *malla* fence around their veranda. *Hola Augustito—¡yo te veo, muchachito travieso!* I see you, you naughty little boy! His parents call him *el mono* because he just climbs and climbs everywhere all the time, like a little monkey. Nice kid; rambunctious. Immersed in the joys of childhood—a world that we no longer know, you and me. This is the *familia Jerónimo*; the boy's dad is Augusto, and he's, like, the town photographer. A previous gringo volunteer years ago got him into that trade, and now it's his main source of income. He takes everybody's headshot for their *cedulas*. Wedding photography, too. I swear Augusto must've photographed every head in town here over the age of eighteen—even from the *aldeas*. He's a terrific guy, Augusto, you'll definitely have to meet him. His wife Carmen is so sweet—and very well educated. *Tiene su maestría en educación.* Okay, hold on a sec, let's walk quickly here; the fetid odor of that discarded mango pit covered with flies and rotting in the sun over there is a sensory experience you'll not easily forget. Briskly now, until we've passed it.

Oh, hey, look who's approaching on his black bicycle—

"Buenos días don Cipriano, ¿como le va?"

"Bien, señor Cristián, ¿y usted qué tal?"

"Pues, ahorita vamos para el vivero—¿pero venía usted para traerme algo? ¿Un telegrama?"

"No-o-o, señor, todavía es muy temprano. Más tarde tal vez sí."

Cipriano is the mailman here in town. The *only* mailman. He generally comes by in the afternoon with a letter or two for me. Telegrams, though, might come almost any time of day, each one neatly folded and taped into a tiny packet that would fit in the palm of the smallest hand. I get telegrams every once in a while—one, two, maybe three a week. Get'em from the Peace Corps; from the CARE rep; from INAFOR; once in a while from a volunteer in another town. Since you are visiting from another land, another time, you should understand that telegrams are our text messages here, and Cipriano delivers every single one of them, and all the mail, on his old, dusty black bicycle.

Across the street and just a couple doors down from the three-room house I'm renting now is the wood-frame house I once occupied, which I shared with Eugenio who worked in fishpond culture. Eugenio got sick of my sloppy housekeeping (among other things) and moved to Cubulco, saying he had more work there. Later a couple groovy chicks moved into the house— sisters, I think—and I thought about them many a night as I sat on my bed smoking and listening to VOA on the shortwave. No fun and games with the locals, though. That was my rule.

Those girls played "Funkytown," I swear, over and over *and over again* on their Victrola, like it was the only record they had. Disco funk was never my cup of tea, though, so in order to show them what real pop music was I played everything I had from The Boss just as loud as I could crank up my pathetic little *radiograbadora*. "Born to Run;" "Rosalita;" "Thunder Road." I threw at them everything I had, but they probably never even heard it. After a few months the Guatemalan chicks left, and then lovely red-haired Susanna moved into my old wood-frame house—a Peace Corps nurse who would later share with me the most disturbing stories about *campesinos* who came into the *Centro de Salud* with grave machete wounds which she and the local nurses there had to patch up as best they could. *Who was doing these terrible things?*

On the corner of my block we pass by the wretched little *tienda* that Chente's wife is still trying to keep running, even though she hasn't received new deliveries in weeks or possibly months. She threw alcoholic Chente out of the house last year, and now she sits on a low stool in the tienda surrounded by packs of cigarettes and chewing gum and big glass jars full of bonbons and *galletas* gone stale, *sentada ahí dándole de mamar a su chirís*, just sitting there giving breast to her baby, and hoping that somebody will come in and buy something. Chente just sort of wanders around town, usually drunk; I ran into him the other day and he asked me for money.

Let's keep moving, for we still have a ways to go. By the way, right now we're walking down *Segunda Calle*, headed for the central plaza which is just a few blocks to the west. Behind us, that big barren hill is Xecambá, *el Cerro de Tinajas*. Straight in front of us, way over the hazy hills over there in the distance, lies Cubulco, the end of the line. No more road after that, though I suppose you could hike over the mountains and eventually reach Joyabaj in the Quiché department. Rabinal itself is divided into four zones, and right now we're in *la Zona Cuatro, San Sebastián*. Zone One is *El Apóstol,* Zone Two is *El Mártir*, and Zone Three is *Santo Domingo*. I live in a particular *barrio* of Zone Four known as *El Tamarindo,* so named for a tamarind tree that grows somewhere along my street. Don't know if I've ever seen it.

"Buenos días hermanas, ¡que Dios les bendiga a ustedes!" Good morning sisters, may God bless you!

"Que le bendiga mejor a usted, señor" said one of the two in a small but cheerful voice. Better that He should bless you, sir. They're nuns from the *parroquia*, whom I actually don't see too often out on the street. Their tan habits almost match the color of the dust in the street.

How much farther, you ask? Well, it's about two clicks from my house down to the nursery, and I'd say we've scarcely walked more than three hundred meters so far. It is pretty warm this morning, under this hazy, blue sky. I hope you're not getting tired already. It's just that I like to stop every so often to say hi or sometimes just to look at something. *Wait, listen—do you hear that?* You can hear the cicadas singing every year around this time, all day long. *Cicada pennata*□thousands of them out there in the trees. Though the climate right now is still bone dry, the cicadas announce the beginning of the rainy season, which should be upon us in a couple weeks or so, around mid-May. Pretty darn loud, no? And yet they're far away from us, sittin' in the trees way over on the edge of town. Friggin' obnoxious, they are□their so-called song is this deafening, high pitched monotone. But they're part of the rhythm of life here.

Over here on the right is *el Almacén de la Familia Garzona. Electrodomésticos*, mainly—small appliances, some hardware. And a little furniture. I bought my tape player there, *a plazos*. Armando Garzona owns this store, and his brother Roberto runs the only gas station in town, which is on the road headed south out of town towards Xesiguan and the capital. What? Xesiguan? It's an *aldea*. Pretty small, maybe four hundred people live there. Not too far, maybe seven or eight kilometers. I helped them set up a small tree nursery last year, but it failed after the first year due to lack of interest and my own inattention to follow-up. Not a shining success for me. But anyway, this Armando here, he's a *ladino* through and through. He always likes to get chummy with me in his broken English, and he tells me about how he spent a year in the States driving a truck around the Chicago area. Lately he's telling me big stories about the resort he's going to build someday on the edge of town to attract tourists; I guess I'll believe it when I see it.

What's a *ladino*? Well, mostly they are the Guatemalans who can claim Spanish heritage. But an indigenous Mayan, it turns out, can become "ladinoized" if he or she abandons the language, the customs, and the traditional attire of the indigenous culture. There are definitely some ladinoized Mayans here in Rabinal. You'll see.

But listen, this Armando Garzona, you need to know something about him. This thing will happen more than a year from now. It will happen on September 15, 1981. I can only tell you this now because we're time-traveling at the whim of our narrator (my older self) who wants to foreshadow something important. What I'm about to tell you will certainly happen. Right now we're just taking a brisk walk down to the tree nursery, but dark times lie ahead. I will run into Armando again; I will see him on Independence Day in the year 1981. I'll be walking towards the main plaza on this very street—in fact almost right here where we stand. I'll be walking along, and I'll greet him as I always do. But something is about to happen in the plaza two blocks away, something terrible is about to happen. And Armando knows something. He doesn't look like his usual jocular self; he looks really upset and worried. He stands in front of me, blocking my way.

"Mire, no hay que pasar a la plaza ahorita. Está muy malo ahí. Mejor véte a casa, Cristián. Váyase a su casa. Por favor."

"¿Qué pasa, Armando? Qué es lo que pasó ahí en la plaza?"

"Mejor solo váyase a su casa. Creeme, ahí no hay seguridad ahorita."

Another moment, and then he says to me the words which I shall never forget for as long as I live:

"¿Sabe que? Estos indios, ¡hay que matarlos todos!"[30]

2a Calle at 5a Avenida, looking west. (Photo credit: Lewis Johnson, ca. 1967) There's now a cell tower on the NE corner, and the street is paved.

So what's he saying, you ask? He's saying to me look, you can't go into the plaza right now, it's very bad there. Best you go home, Christian. Go home. So, like, I say to Armando, what's going on? What's happened in the plaza? And he just says, go on home. It's not safe here now. And then *that's* when he says to me: You know what? *These Indians, we've got to kill them all!*

We'll get to that day. Just wait. But for now, just fuck it. Let's stop in this *tienda* for a second, I need a pack of cigarettes. Careful of the wet soil there; *la mamá de Letty* is hosing down the street before the heavy trucks come through later today. Ha—what trucks, you ask?—never mind, you'll see.

"*Buenos días, seño.*"

"*Buenos di-i-i-as, don Cristián. ¿Como eśtá uśted? Pase adelante.*"

"*¿Está Letty adentro?*"

"*Si-i-i, ahí está. Ahí le va a atender ella.*"

"*Muchas gracias.*"

We enter a smallish *tienda* that is much better stocked than the first one we passed a while ago. Not only cold beer and *octavos de aguardiente*, but also chocolate bars, *chocobananos*, bubble gum, *champurradas, pan de a cinco, pan francés,* soda, assorted confections, *pepitoria*, pens, school notebooks, batteries, devotional candles—and, of course, cigarettes. All of it neatly displayed under a glass countertop the length of a small car, or in baskets sitting atop said countertop, or on the two or three shelves on the wall behind our pretty Letty still in her schoolgirl uniform. I've spent all this time in Rabinal reminding myself that Letty is just a little too young for me. Though I've had this vague and perhaps not unfounded feeling that Letty's parents might be happy to see me take an interest in her.

I buy a pack of Rubios, and I open it walking out the door, as I need another smoke. Leaving the *tienda*, a light tan, skeletal pariah dog trots behind us, anxious for a scrap of anything as we continue towards the central plaza. The long lateral wall of the *catedral de San Pablo Apóstol*, over here on our right, is these days reinforced against potential collapse by three dark ochre buttresses fashioned from rough wooden beams some seven or eight meters in length. The church was heavily damaged by the 1976 earthquake which left much of the country in

Another favorite tienda, this one just a few meters NW of the central plaza.

ruins, and now three years later is judged unstable and therefore closed to the public. On the other side of this massive structure there's a squat, unassuming, provisional *capilla* that was built by the townspeople out of adobe and timber sidings after the earthquake, and this is where *padre* Melchor now gives mass.

Well, my friend, here we are in the central plaza of Rabinal. I love this place. Behind that long colonnade on the north side you'll find the *alcaldía* and the *salón municipal*. There, too, is the tiny office of *correos y telegrafía*, where Cipriano and his boss the *telegrafista* work, as well as the equally cramped police substation where *don* Felipe and his *subteniente* will often be seen standing outside surveying the whole plaza. Over here on the left is the south side of the plaza: a row of adobe buildings featuring Osorio's *tienda agropecuaria* where I've brought in soil samples for testing a couple of times, *el Taller Hernandez, la farmacia*—and the *Cine Popular Rabinalense*, where tonight they're showing—well imagine that!—*"Fuerza 10 de Navarone"* starring Harrison Ford. On the west side, there's the *Restaurante Las Diamelas*, my favorite place for *frijoles volteados*. A very nice dinner there, including a tough strip of beef, boiled *güicoyitos*, and of course that perfect *maleta* of refried beans will cost you Q.2.50. We'll pass right by there in a minute, once we get through the plaza.

But hey, turn around now for a second and look up: isn't the facade of this church absolutely magnificent in its brilliance? And at this hour the sun is not yet even shining on it. Just wait till this afternoon. Those saints in their niches—each one has a name, each has a blessing to offer.[31] So they say. I pass by here almost every day, and I often wonder if those alabaster saints standing in their niches for all these hundreds of years still have any blessings left to bestow on us. Or were all of their blessings exhausted long ago? And without a blessing, then, who will deliver us from evil?

(Here is revealed the soul—my own soul—between doubt and faith. The beautiful life of this town and the things that I eventually shall witness here will only make my struggle harder. My theological bearings were all confused in those years, and I guess you could say they remain so today.)

Catedral de San Pablo Apóstol, right after 1976 quake. (Credit: Augusto Jerónimo)

The provisional chapel constructed after the earthquake. (Credit: Augusto Jerónimo)

As you can see, roughly one-half of the wide expanse of this plaza is our municipal park with its gazebo for public functions, its geometric pattern of well swept sidewalks, and its tall palms, the stems of which you'll notice are whitewashed up to a height of at least a meter. (That's the custom in public spaces everywhere here in Guatemala.) Wait, I think I see José sitting on a park bench over there; maybe we can pick up a copy of today's *La Nación* before we head down to the tree nursery. Chepito, as we all call him, he's a regular fixture here around the park, and he's the same little urchin who will shine your shoes for a couple *chocas*.

"Tienes La Nación, patojo?"

"Sí señor, aquí está. Viente y cinco len, porfa."

"Gracias, Chepito."

"Gracias a usted, señor. Que le vaya bien."

Patojos. Kids. They call'em *chamacos* in Mexico, but here they're *patojos.* Stuffing the newspaper in my *morral,* I turn around, and there across the plaza in the middle of the row of *comedores* and *tiendas* I spy our sweet, lovely Mari, the Achí girl who serves us fifty-*centavo* breakfasts and lunches. I often eat there to save a little money—unless she's serving *tripa.*

"*¡Hola Mari!*" I call out to her across the way as she stands in the doorway of her tiny *comedor* throwing out a bucket of dishwater.

¡Buenos días don Cristián!"

"Voy para el vivero ahorita, pero tal vez regreso para almuerzo ahí contigo."

"*¡Vaya, está bien don Cristián, aquí lo esperamos!*"

We shout our brief exchange across the plaza for all to hear, and now once again, like many days previously, I wonder what it would be like to be close to Mari. Lovely Mari, dressed every day in her colorful *huipil y corte* saturated with the smell of woodsmoke and charred tortillas. I've watched her often prattling over the fire with her mother, pouring a glass of *horchata,* or drying her hands on her apron before fixing me a plate of *biftek y frijoles parados*, serving the plate to me while flashing a coquettish smile and later dismissing an uninvited pariah dog with her *¡Fuera, chucho!* Get out of here, mutt!

On the west side of the park near the restaurant, there sits Santos in his dented, dirty yellow Datsun pickup, while a couple more *campesinos* climb into the *palangana* where seven or eight are already crowded in the back standing together. Santos makes the trip out to Xococ (about fifteen clicks west of here) generally twice a day—but not every day. He covers the gas and makes a small profit hauling *campesinos*, sometimes twelve at a time, in his *palangana*. They come into town for the market, or to run an errand or catch a bus. I've taken the ride to Xococ with Santos several times, and each time he insists I ride up front with him in the cabin. I did so once or twice, but I usually prefer to ride with the *campesinos* standing in the back. I was never great at spontaneous chit-chat, so I feel awkward riding up front in the seat beside him. It doesn't seem fair, either. It's much more fun to hold on tight to the rails in back with the *campesinos*. It must be quite a sight, though, me at almost two meters towering over them as we bounce along the road out to Xococ.

Neither yellow nor a Datsun, but this could be the very same Santos in his pickup in later years. (Rabinal plaza, 1998)

Every town everywhere has its secrets. Rabinal holds secrets and enigmas in abundance—but Rabinal has also its afflictions. Pestilence, hunger, poverty, illiteracy, to name but a few. And the general strife that is imminent. There are many afflictions here. And there are remedies, too.[3] *Pharmakon*: the medicine, the drug, the poison, both sickness and cure, which may cause healing or bitter destruction, including self-destruction. The ancient Greeks remind us that the medicine may also be the poison.[32] The old men of the *cofradia* pass the flask of *aguardiente* around the darkened room and each man consumes his copious portion, each seeking with his brethren some measure of protection from evil through a solemn invocation of the *rajawales*, the spirits of the dead.

Then there is the *pharmakos*: the unloved, the scapegoat, the community's sacrifice of its own in order to deliver us all from evil. Ultimately the *pharmakos* dies (or is grievously maimed like Oedipus), so that we might live. Here in Rabinal, a human sacrifice not unlike another Oedipus will be needed in order to lift the plague of violence that will come. Perhaps many such sacrifices will be needed.[33]

But the mortal threat of imminent plague, the strife that looms, is not yet even fully visible to us here in this town, so the sacrifices that are made are small and seemingly insignificant. Even when they are significant – involving, say, the death of a neighbor— the connection with the broader plague of violence is lost on us. And if the ritual connection is lost, then the plague is never lifted, it only grows worse. A broken ritual will doom Rabinal.

As we approach the western edge of the plaza, behold: here we find a perfect example of futile self-sacrifice lying on the sidewalk in front of Las Diamelas, stone drunk. His legs splayed, he wears a white shirt unbuttoned at the top and he leans his back against the white plastered adobe wall of the restaurant, right beside the entrance. It is Joaquin, younger brother of the woman who serves me dinner in the restaurant. Standing over Joaquin, I can see this is not a case of "Deliver us from evil," but rather, "Deliver me from this world." It's almost eight in the morning, but Joaquín slurs a slow but unexpectedly loud greeting as if it's still midnight in the *cantina* he went to the night before.

"Go-o-od MORNING, my friend!" I must credit Joaquín with the fact that his English today sounds almost unaccented in spite of his present sad state. It's one of the few English phrases he knows. I squat down and sit on my haunches to talk with him.

"*Hola*, Joaquín. *¿Qué le pasa, hombre? Es muy temprano para estar así, ¿no crees?*" What's the matter, man? It's much too early to be like this, don't you think?

"Pues no sabes, Cristián, tu no sabes. No te puedes imaginar. Estoy perdido. De veras que estoy perdido, hombre, estoy bien jodido." You have no idea, he says, you just don't know. You cannot imagine. I am lost. I am truly lost, man, and I'm fucked.

"¿Qué pasó, Joaquin? - ¿cuál es el problema? Cuénteme." But my expression of concern goes unanswered.

"Ay, Cristián, no sabes, no sabes que pena. Estoy jodido, pero bien jodido. Y estos tiempos que estamos viviendo. Yo digo, pues, que estamos bien jodidos todos. Mira, Cristián, tú eres un buen hombre, tu eres muy noble. Tu vienes aquí para enseñar a la gente. ¿Y yo? Pues, yo enseñaba, yo también enseñaba. A los niños en la escuela les enseñaba. Mirá—¿somos cuates, no? Tu y yo, pués, SOMOS CUATES, Cristián."

He says to me: Ay, Cristián, you do not know, you've no idea what sorrow. I'm fucked, really fucked. And these times in which we are living. I tell you, we're all fucked. Look, Cristián, you are a good man. You are noble. You come here to teach people. And me? Ah, I once taught; I, too, was a teacher once. I taught the children in the school. But look, we're buddies, aren't we? You and I, *we're buddies*, Cristián.

"Pues si, Joaquin, claro que somos cuates, y le quiero ayudar si puedo, se lo juro, pero cuénteme, ¿qué es lo que realmente pasó?" Yes, *Joaquin,* we're buddies, and I want to help you if I can, I swear, but just tell me, what really has happened?

Unfortunately our conversation does not progress, but rather devolves further into futile repetitions of lamentation and self-abuse from Joaquin followed by my own anodyne, insipid replies. I've spoken with Joaquin only a couple of times before, when he was sober, or nearly so, so it's a bit of a stretch to acknowledge that we're *cuates,* meaning best of friends. Still, I've always wished him well and I've always hoped he might someday go clear. But in the end he never went clear.

As for that *"tu eres muy noble"* bit, this actually isn't the first time that I've heard this kind of embarrassing, over-the-top and sadly misinformed appraisal of my person. Thing is, though, I've always only heard it coming from a drunk. So, looking at it that way, from a drunk's perspective, I've more or less accepted their inflated estimation of me.

After a few minutes I straighten up and say goodbye to Joaquin, for we must be on our way. No one else comes near Joaquin, for he is a polluted entity in the community. *Pharmakos*. This, too, is the life of the plaza.

A month after our encounter on the street corner, I will hear that Joaquin has died. Dead from incurable cirrhosis of the liver.

> *Padre santo, Dios eterno y Todopoderoso, te pedimos por Joaquín, que llamaste de este mundo. Dale la felicidad, la luz y la paz. Que él, habiendo pasado por la muerte, participe con los santos de la luz eterna, como le prometiste a Abraham y a su descendencia. Amén.*

As we move along down the main street headed towards *el Calvario*, we pass two soldiers from the *destacamento militar* on the edge of town. Two young Mayans, barely eighteen, maybe not even, who look like any of the other Mayans I live among here in Rabinal, only we know without asking that they actually hail from Huehue or Mazate or Xela, or maybe even Olopa—anywhere but Rabinal, because that's the way of the army. The two slouch by in their slightly faded camouflage khakis and soft-sided boonie hats with the brim folded up on the right, each with his Galil slung over a shoulder and pointed down low. One of the soldiers is sipping orange soda through a straw stuck in a clear plastic bag as he walks by. No words. I never speak to the soldiers I pass on the street, and I see two, four, maybe six of them almost every day. They always patrol in pairs, never more than a pair.

Hate the killing, never the killers. Well, maybe their commanding officers—I mean I think I could hate those guys. But it hasn't yet happened here in Rabinal. I know it's happened elsewhere, but not here. Not yet. At least not so far as I know.

Let's keep walking. Ahh, now take a deep breath and just smell the fresh bread coming out of that *panaderia* across the street. I always get my *pirujos* there, and I know exactly when to come by to find them fresh out of the oven. All of our nursery workers who receive food for work come by here too once a week to unload their *medio-quintales* of white enriched Alliance for Progress flour in exchange for cash. They need cash to live on, not flour. And the baker, the *panadero,* he knows when he's got a good thing going so he keeps it all low profile and then just pulls out of his oven the best tasting bread in town.

The son of the *panadero*, the bearded fellow over there climbing into his pickup, that's Julio Vásquez. He's a *perito agrónomo* who works with CIF over in Pachalum—that's the *aldea* you passed by just before your bus arrived here in town—and working with CIF he handles all of the agricultural extension, including animal husbandry. Okay, I see the quizzical look so I'll explain: CIF is the *Centro de Integración Familiar*, also known as the *Hogar Rural*. They work in several target *aldeas* in the areas of education, health, agriculture, and home economics. They do literacy and Spanish language training; vaccination campaigns; latrine building; demonstration plots, crop diversification, rabbit hutches, fishponds, potable water systems, and more besides; and the Spanish *padre* who runs the operation ties it all together in his homilies under the theme of social advancement through Christian worship. Base communities in the best sense. Only they don't dare call it that, because words like that can get them all killed. I do hope you'll have a chance to meet *Padre* Gregorio later on.

WHOA! - look sharp there, my friend! Better hop up here onto the sidewalk. Here, lemme give you a hand. Take a look down the street, that's the Salamateca coming in from Cubulco, and judging from his speed that must be Carlos at the wheel. He's haulin' ass, and he ain't stoppin' for nobody unless they make a sign that they want to get on, so watch out! *Bueno pués*, coast is clear. Wait a sec for the dust to settle, and then let's get a move on, as we're not quite halfway there.

Down the street there on the other side, those two businesses belong to the Garcia family. *Doña* Candelaria is usually running the *tienda agropecuaria*, and I've bought a few small things from her, like a funnel, a hammer, or a bag of nails. But most of our tools and supplies come from CARE, so I don't get in to see her too much. Then there's the *pensión* business, if you can call it that, right next door. They've got, I dunno, ten maybe twelve rooms, and they might have a handful of guests at any given time. Traveling merchants, mostly, or the occasional bureaucrat or *ingeniero* from Guate. More business, of course, during the *feria titular*. When's that? Oh, that's in late January. The 25th is the *dia de San Pablo Apostol*. That's actually the day commemorating his conversion, they say, when he quit persecuting the early Christians and decided to follow Jesus instead. Honestly, you'll have to be here for the *feria*. It's not to be missed.

Doña Candi's son Güícho is the admin guy over at CIF in Pachalum. Funny piece of trivia: when I first started working with Padre Gregorio, Güícho, and Julio Vásquez over there in Pachalum, I saw that all three had full beards, that's when I said what the hell and started letting mine grow out, too. All three, at least in the beginning, were rightly skeptical of my potential contribution. I think they tolerated my presence and just tried to extract what benefit they could out of me. Like more tree seedlings for their target *aldeas*. I owe a lot to Güícho, though, for it was with him that my political awakening here began. More about that, later.

Just up ahead by that rough adobe wall—the one lacking plaster—right there we'll be leaving *Primera Calle* and heading off to the right, down to the tree nursery. But let's hustle now and make the turn before that overloaded flatbed that's approaching covers us completely in dust. He's hauling out *barita* from the open pit mine that's located over the hills past Xococ. The mine is actually over the border in Cubulco. We've seen a lot more truckloads like this lately, maybe four or five a day. Every one of them is dangerously overloaded for the terrain, and they all trail a suffocating cloud of dust behind them, which is why so many store owners along this main drag try to find the right time every day to hose down the street before they come by. I mean, every store owner around here leaves the front door open for his customers, so all his merch that's laid out would end up covered in a thick layer of dust if he didn't take precautions. Out in the countryside towards Xococ these overloaded trucks are wreaking havoc with the access road that was cleared years ago by the poor farmers of the area with no help at all from *Caminos* or anybody else from the government. They made that road all by themselves, and now the trucks from the *mina* are trashing it.

Okay, good, we've made the turn and we'll miss the truck by a few seconds. Look behind you now—the diesel exhaust and that big white cloud of dust are what we narrowly missed!

What's barite good for, you ask? Hell, it's just a rock. Okay, but seriously, there's a story here. What's happening is the country's pouring millions right now into oil exploration in the Petén. They've sold exploration concessions to Texaco, Getty, Elf-Acquitaine and others both in the Petén and in Alta Verapaz. (And guess who owns a ton of the land up there where the oil fields are. The generals, of course, including Lucas García, our current president.) So how does barite come into the picture? Well, the drillers combine ground barite with bentonite, water, and other stuff to make a mud at the drill sites, and then they pump the mud down the drill hole to control high formation pressures and to prevent explosive releases of oil and gas from the well. Barite has a high specific gravity, which makes it the best rock to increase the density of drilling muds.[34]

Halliburton scoped out this area for the barite mine. My older self knows this only because of a remarkable coincidence that will happen years later back in the States, around 1994. I will be working in upstate New York at that point, and my new boss there, Bill Webb, will be a geologist twenty years my senior who, back in the day—*this* day, as we're walking down to the tree nursery—worked for Halliburton and was flying over Rabinal and Cubulco with his geology buddies to get an overview of the whole area where they expected to extract the barite. We didn't know each other yet, but Bill was up in the sky appraising the barite operation while I was on the ground planting trees and watching the overloaded flatbeds tear up the road every day—five, six trucks a day—upwards of twenty thousand tons a year. (Trust me, I did the math.) Most of the barite rumbling through Rabinal goes to the oil fields north of here, like the Chapayal and North Petén basins where the generals have their ranches. The escalation of violence that is yet to come will arise from a ruthless imperative to establish a secure investment climate for the Guatemalan state and all the *ladino* investors.[35] The nickel in Izabal, the oil in the Petén, and the barite in Baja Verapaz that makes the oil drilling possible. Always the poor pay the price.

Okay, up ahead it's mostly downhill to the nursery. But look, over there on the right you can see the casuarina treetops over the roofs—a really nice, mature planting swaying in the breeze right there in the *patio* of our Centro de Salud. They did a great job with that planting; very pretty trees that have been there for maybe fifteen years or more.

At this point we leave behind the dense settlement of the town proper. On this gentle slope down to the tree nursery you'll see small parcels with new *milpa* on either side of the road, and the road itself will narrow. We're approaching the *colonia La Ladrillera*, and our nursery is set up right across from it. *La Ladrillera,* so named because there are clay deposits all around here, and they do in fact fabricate a lot of adobe bricks. The local artisans come here also for the clay they need for their distinctive Rabinal pottery. More than fifty families live tightly packed together in shanty housing in the *colonia*; running water comes from two or three communal standpipes.

Half a click to the west is another settlement, *Colonia* Pacúx, which is just being built. The National Electrification Institute INDE is building it to house the *aldeanos* from Rio Negro who are all going to be dispossessed of their homes because they will be flooded out by the rising waters of the river once the hydroelectric dam is finished. They call it *el Proyecto Chixoy*, and they say it'll have a capacity of about three hundred megawatts of power.[36] There's also a significant reforestation goal associated with the hydro project. I met with some O.A.S. reps a couple months ago in Salamá, and they said the target is to plant two million seedlings in the Chixoy watershed, at a cost of about 15,000 person-days of labor. Huge effort by any measure, but we'll first have to win the confidence of the people in and around Rio Negro in order to enlist their help with the planting. Right now trust and confidence are in short supply among the people of the Chixoy region□especially in Rio Negro□as their land and their livelihoods are soon to be submerged under the bright and peaceful waters of an engorged river made so by the dam that is to be built. If anything comes of the reforestation plan, the seedlings would come from here, and from whatever satellite nurseries we can set up.

Look to the north, my friend. From here you can appreciate the round prominence that they call *Cerro Kaj'yup*. There's a Mayan ruin

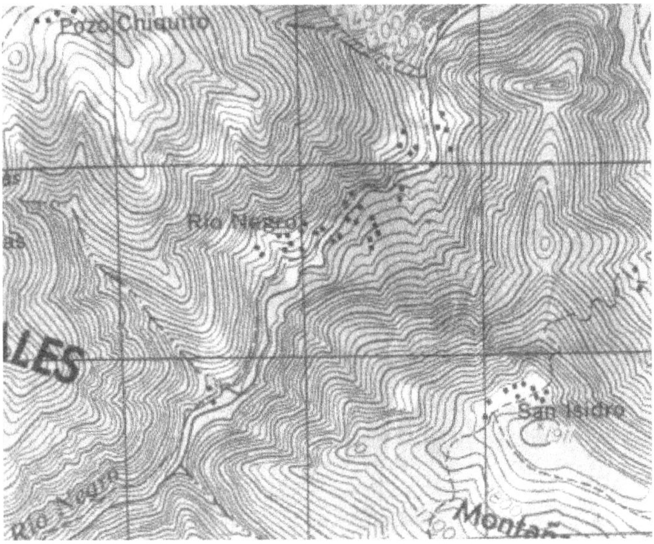

1964 topographic image of Chixoy region (above), and 2021 Google Earth satellite image of the same area (below), showing clearly the extent of the new reservoir that was created upon completion of the hydroelectric dam in 1983.

up on top, like a lookout, with dry, twisted trees growing out of its sides. The name is a concatenation of two words: "Kaj," for sky, and "u'yub" which means hill or mountain, so the meaning is "mountain that touches the sky." It's only about three hundred meters higher than the spot where we're standing, but up there you'll get a spectacular view of the whole Valle de Urram. You can see quite far, especially towards the west where the Ki'che' enemy would have advanced from. We'll have to go up there someday and take a look around. The place was originally a Poqomchí settlement and was invaded by the Rabinaleb' who made it their capital during the Late Post-Classic Period. The strategic location of the citadel on top of this hill had defensive purposes and you can still see evidence there of defensive arrangements formed by high terrace walls and lookouts that served to spot the incursions of enemy tribes. The place is mentioned in the famous Rabinal Achí dance-drama, which narrates the conflicts between the K'iche' and Rabinaleb' princes.

But with the Spanish conquest, the internal armed conflict, the passage of time, and the carelessness and disinterest of the authorities, there is not much of the original site that is left to see—mainly just a couple of walls and a building—which, according to the ancestral Achí tradition, is home to the *rajawales* or *nahuales*, protectors of the Rabinal community and the region, and that is why the people here still revere it. Let me repeat that: the *protectors* of the Rabinal community. The *cofrades y brujos* around here go up there now and then to pray and sacrifice a chicken over the altar that is inside a little hut. It is said that the roots of the trees up there reach the heart of the Earth and Xibalbá.

Xibalbá: think *Hades.*

The post-classic remnants of Kaj'yup. (Photo credit: Daniel Arturo Chen Siana)

And the *vivero*? Ah yes, the tree nursery. Well, my friend, *here it is*, right across the road from the *colonia*. We're finally here. Let me introduce you to everybody. First, there's Juanito here, Juan Pablo Osorio, my Guatemalan counterpart and right-hand man. Juanito handles the day-to-day management of the tree nursery, and occasionally he goes out with me to the *aldeas*. He draws an INAFOR salary that's smaller than my own living allowance, which barely exceeds two hundred quetzales a month. His wife Rosalía does my laundry every week□at home, by hand, scouring each item of my clothing on the rough, concrete *pila*. I pay her a couple quetzales. Juan Pablo has completed *tercero básico* in the schools here, roughly equivalent to our ninth grade in the U.S. He's really *listo*; he's on the ball, believe me, and he's not bad with figures, either. One of the accomplishments I take great pride in here is that I got him to read *Don Quixote*. I should put that on my resume.

There are two others here who receive a small salary from INAFOR: Juan Pablo's brother Miguel, and Venancio Mendoza down there by the seedbeds. The other fellows in the nursery all receive food for work, and you see them here working at their various tasks: some filling more seedling bags with *tierra negra*, another one weeding the *tablones*, watering all the seedlings, or spraying *abono foliar* all over the *tablones* to help the seedlings grow faster. Here's Chano, Luciano López Ortíz—he's one strong, humble *mensch*. Then there's Antonio Ramírez, who like Juan Pablo is close to my age. Antonio likes to go on a binge every once in a while, but he's an okay guy; hard worker.

Over there is Tomás Lajuj Oxlaj. Tomás walks into town every day from his home in Nimacabaj, an *aldea* some four, maybe four and a half clicks from here, out on the road to Xococ. Now look down a couple terraces below, and there's *el anciano*, *don* Antonio, watering the *tablónes* like he always does. He must be in his seventies, this guy, and his age is catching up with him, so we have him do the watering most of the day and leave it at that. As I said, most of these guys collect wages in the form of weekly distributions of food for work. Unfortunately that's all we can do for them, since INAFOR doesn't have a budget for more salaries. The guys stop by my house every Saturday morning because I always have literally a ton or two of CARE food for work stored in the back room, and each worker earns a fifty-pound bag of white enriched flour every week. They also receive a measure of some other commodities like bulgur or corn-soy-milk blend, plus a gallon of peanut oil. The bags of flour they take to the *panadería*, the bakery, to exchange for cash, because cash is what they need. They might consume some of the CSM, because it's a little bit similar to Incaparina, a locally processed cereal which they know, and the cooking oil they'll either sell or use. The bulgur they don't know *what* the hell to do with, and they can't even sell it, because bulgur simply isn't known here. Who knows where the bulgur ends up.

USAID (P.L. 480) food commodities provided by CARE: cooking oil and bags of Corn-Soy-Milk blend. (Source: *The Guardian*)

We're lucky to have a municipal water line that runs to the nursery, and we're about fifteen meters below the *pueblo* so the pressure is pretty decent. When there's water. That's usually a little more than half the day. We need another water source for all these seedlings, and we're working on that. As you can see, this nursery sits on five levels of terracing, and beyond the fence down there is a small creek where all the women from the *colonia* wash their clothes. The women wash by turns all morning long squatting on the creek bank or wading into the slow, shallow current, their Ambar soap suds mixing with the fresh, clear water, Maybe you'll see one of them slapping her water-drenched *corte* on a big rock, and the *huipíles* and the other articles of clothing are all laid out on the stream bank to dry.

The *alcalde* has been nagging us lately that we use too much water here and they don't have enough pressure in the *colonia*. To be honest, all the municipal water we use here is actually scarcely enough. Our idea is to get a gasoline pump and some water supply ducting, and we'll pump that creek water right up to the *vivero* where it should fill a couple of 55-gallon drums in, I'd say, less than five minutes. I'm working on getting the materials from CARE, and hopefully in a couple months we can set it all up. This morning, though, we're going to use a sight level to figure out first what the slope is and the vertical distance down to the creek. With that data in hand, we'll be able to estimate how much horsepower we'll need to bring the water up here to, hmm, let's say the third terrace level where we can place a couple steel drums. I think it's nearly a twelve meter drop to the creek, so a five or six horsepower pump will probably do the trick.

Before we tackle that job, however, we need to take inventory of all the seedlings we have here, as the rainy season is fast approaching. We'll simply count the length and width of each *tablón* of seedling bags, and then add it all up. That'll take us an hour or so, and then I want to make sure we apply some fungicide on the seedbeds down there now that the casuarina has germinated. We'll mix up some Cupravit or Agallol for that.[37] After that we'll discuss our plans for the new tool shed with office space that we want to build right up here close to the road. The plan is to get some lumber and log sidings from INAFOR for that project, and the corrugated metal roofing we'll get from CARE. (I pull out another cigarette and light it, cupping my hands against a light breeze.) What I have in mind will be a nice upgrade from the dinky toolshed you're looking at right now. It'll be cool—we'll even have a desk in there for Juan Pablo to do his monthly reports and seedling inventories. I really can't wait to get started on it.

Bueno, I think it's probably time we head back now. My plan for this afternoon is to do some cartography work back at the house, using the topo quads I got from the Instituto Geográfico Nacional in Guate. I can also show you the air photos I have there, too; I've got a stereo viewer, so you can check out all the territory here in three dimensions. But first—*wait*—here's an experience that every Rabinal visitor must have …

"Bueno, muchás, ahí viene la señora. ¡Ya es hora de chilate!"

Doña Mencha arrives at the *vivero* gate carrying an enormous earthen kettle on top of her head. Now, without any help from anyone, she reaches up with both arms and deftly lifts the heavy kettle off of her head and places it on the ground. All of the men from the *vivero*

A typical community tree nursery not unlike the one we had in Rabinal, but imagine it on a terraced slope.

Table 1. Inventory of the Rabinal Tree Nursery, INAFOR/CARE/Peace Corps (from field notes dated April 23, 1979)

Species	Common Name	Total
Cupressus lusitanica	Mexican Cypress	25,101
Cedrela odorata	Cedar	11,975
Casuarina equisetifolia	Casuarina	17,825
Salix spp.	Willow	450
Enterolobium spp.	Conocaste	7,100
Eucalyptus spp.	Eucalyptus	3,462
Swietenia macrophylla	Mahogany	84
Pinus oocarpa	Ocote	2,581
Pinus michoacana	White Pine	3,654
Tabebuia spp.	Matilisguate	8,880
Enterolobium spp.	Guanacaste	5,600
TOTAL		**86,712**

gather around and greet her in Achí as she settles herself on the ground and uses a small hemispherical *guacal* (that's half of a hollowed-out calabash gourd) to ladle out the creamy, off-white *atól* made from corn, carefully pouring it into additional *guacales* which she has brought with her□one for each of us who wants to partake of this steaming, late morning beverage. *Cada porción, diez len.* To each *guacal* that she serves she adds a pinch of salt and optional chile to add some heat to the experience, if you like. I always ask for extra chile. Nearby a young girl who can't be more than seven sits on the ground, dressed just like her mother in her *huipíl* and *corte* and cute as a button, and she has brought an old galvanized pail full of water to rinse the used *guacales* after we finish.

Though it's only late morning, the heat of the day is already upon us, the cicadas are singing their long monotone hymn in the trees, and I suppose the folks living in some different latitude might not necessarily enjoy a thick, hot beverage on a day like this, but Juan Pablo insists (and has in fact repeated to me many times), that a *guacal* of steaming hot *atól* on a hot morning actually cools you down. As any good skeptic might say—*a saber.* Who knows? Anyway, the *atól* is good, and the heat of the chile definitely makes the whole experience more interesting. I throw my head back to drink up the last of it, and I return my used *guacal* to *Doña* Mencha. *Maltiox cha'lá.*

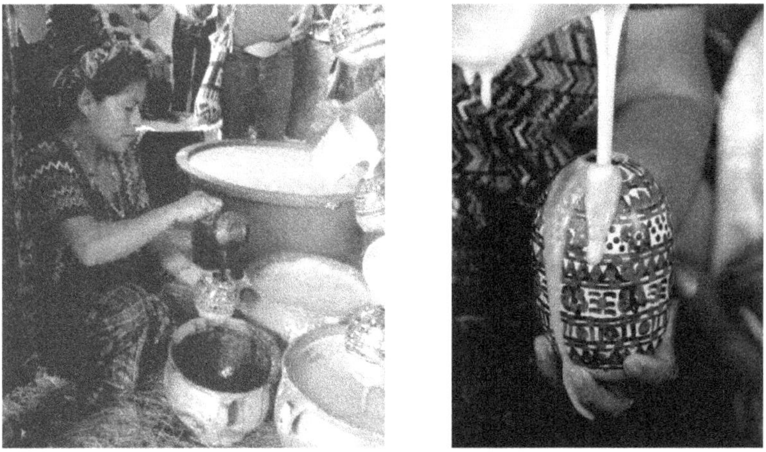

Steaming *chilate* in the background, and chocolate (*atól negro*) being served in *jicaros* in the foreground. (Photo credit: Helios Villatoro)

Let's get going now, we have to head back to the house because I've got stuff to do. We say our goodbyes to the men, and Juan Pablo asks me if I'll be back tomorrow. Probably not, I tell him, as I plan to work on the natural resource inventory in the morning, and in the afternoon I'll be taking off with Güicho from CIF to talk to some *aldeanos* in Nimacabaj. As we leave the *vivero* and walk back up the road towards the *pueblo*, billowing tufts of cumulus slowly drift over the Chuacús range to the south. It won't rain for another couple of weeks, but the fair weather clouds gradually build up this time of year, like a silent prologue to the rains that are imminent. Above us the sky is a hazy azure, and the monotonous song of the cicadas accompanies us all the way back up the hill.

We're back to the main drag in town which is *Primera Calle*: from here we have to head east to the plaza—but wait a sec and look now to the west. Five blocks down the street, there stands the brilliant white edifice of the *Calvario* chapel, which serves as the entrance to one of two cemeteries here in town. And right across the street from the *Calvario*, there's the *destacamento militar* which houses some thirty soldiers, give or take. The *destacamento* is partly shaded by an enormous ceiba tree, and a soldier wearing a camouflage boonie hat is the lone soul manning the small, sandbagged and thatch-roofed sentry post, his hands resting on the stock of a Belgian MAG 7.62 mounted on a bipod. The machine gun is pointed at anybody and everybody who might walk past.

Beyond the *destacamento* on that same side of the main drag there's another cemetery—the one for the poor. The cemetery behind the *Calvario* is a miniature city of multicolored mausoleums, but every single burial in the other cemetery on the opposite side of the road is marked only by a small, rough-hewn, wooden cross over a mound of earth. When I first came here I thought the distinction between the two was *ladino-indígena*, but that is not strictly the case. Rather, it is simply a distinction between those who have some means, and those who have none. But rest assured, there are no *ladinos* buried in the cemetery of the poor.

As we turn around and face the plaza, two more soldiers are strolling just ahead of us with their Galils slung low. Always two by two. They're going our way, so it looks like we'll have to pass them.

Not to worry, they really don't give a shit about us. The *comandante*, he may give a shit about my presence in town, but I don't think he issues any special orders to his grunts in regards to me. Benign neglect. Or so I choose to believe. Actually, the army here puzzles me. I don't like them, but I also don't know what to think about them. I don't know what the hell they do all day long except patrol around town, always two by two. I am so ignorant, really. What goes on here that I cannot see? But I've never dared to ask a question. Not about the *ejército*.

We pass the two soldiers without acknowledging them (nor do they look towards us), and we pick up the pace a little so as to leave them well behind us. Another couple blocks down the street I am surprised to see *padre* Gregorio, a Spaniard from Madrid, walking towards us with his striding gait almost as long as my own; surprised because he's usually driving a pickup from the Hogar Rural whenever I see him around here. Dressed in crisp blue jeans, clerical collar and a wide-brimmed hat, *padre* Gregorio, tall and slender, an unmistakable figure even at a distance with his full black beard and the thick black frames of his glasses, greets me with his customary geniality:

"Hola Cristián, ¿cómo estás? Mira que cosa, me parece que ya tienes unos meses de vivir aquí con nosotros. ¿Y te está gustando nuestro Rabinal?

"Pués sí, me gusta mucho aquí."

I really admire *padre* Gregorio a great deal, and I admire what he has done with CIF in Pachalum. I want him to know that I am not just some curious interloper here in Rabinal, and I do not necessarily represent everything that America stands for. I question a lot of things. I am not my predecessor (though my predecessor did very well here), and I am not CIA. I seem to find tacit acceptance by the *padre*, but in the final analysis he has a mission here, and I am either part of his mission in Rabinal, or I am of little consequence.

Near the plaza I spot one of the *aldeanos* I visited a few weeks ago in Xesiguan, a tireless worker who on this day in town is dressed in a gray, worn-out New York Yankees T-shirt and light colored pants thoroughly soiled from hours tending his *milpa* back in the mountains.

"¡Buenos días don Cristo!"

"Bue-e-enos días don Vinicio, ¿cómo está usted?"

Don Cristo. During my time in Rabinal I've found that many of the local Mayans—especially those from the more remote *aldeas*—either cannot grasp or simply cannot remember that my name is Christian—Cristián. It's not a common name in their social universe. So "Cristo" seems to them an acceptable substitute, and the questionable piety of referring to this *gringo* who swears, drinks and smokes as our Lord and Savior is entirely lost on them. As with so many things here in Rabinal, I just go with the flow and savor the irony of the moment in the back of my mind. I answer to "*Don Cristo*" always bemused, but never for a moment hesitating to reply.

Well, we're back in the central plaza, and will you look at that church now! The sun is almost at its apogee, and the brilliance of the facade at noontime almost seems to make the saints come alive. There's *San Pablo Apóstol* robed and seated in his premier niche at the very top beneath the highest belfries, holding his staff, with *San Pedro Apóstol* to his right and *San Pedro Martir* on his left. A martyr for Rabinal; but with the things that are going down, I fear in the days to come there will be more. Did you know that the CUC was formed around here only a couple years ago?

We'll come back to the plaza later to eat, but I think it's best we head home first to shower and take a break. Oh, look over there—the kids have gotten out and they're all headed home from school. Watch out, because here they come.

"Goodbye my luff!"

"GOODBYE my LUFF!"

Who knows where they all picked up that phrase; it's truly one of the most inscrutable things about living here. Sometimes I respond in kind, "*¡Adios mi amor!*" and they run along giggling, or sometimes I just wave and smile. Only the ones who are a little older really know what the heck they are saying; the younger ones are just parroting meaningless syllables. This too is life in Rabinal.

Well hey, let's stop here in the *tienda* again and get some beer for tonight. If we store it in the water in the *pila* out back it should still be kinda cool by the time we want it. I've got some Jack Daniels in the house too, so we'll be all set for tonight.

We step into the same *tienda* where I bought cigarettes this morning, but pretty Letty is not there now to help us because her classes at the *colegio* don't get out till much later. Her mother *doña* Matilde helps us out instead.

"Buenas tardes, seño. Como está usted?"

"Pués no tan bién como usted, Señor Cristián. En qué le puedo servir?"

"Pués sólo queremos dos litros de Cabro, si fuera tan amable."

"Dos Cabros, si señor. (Goes to the fridge.) *Aquí tiene sus dos litros, señor. Son cuatro quetzales con cincuenta centavos, porfa."*

I pull out my wallet and pass the money to her. *"Y la Letty todavía está en el colegio, ¿verdad?"*

"Pues si-i-i, Señor Cristián. Pero ya no tarda en venir."

"Ayy, pues cómo me gusta verla siempre. ¡Tan bella la sonrisa de su hija!"

"¡No se preocupe, Señor Cristián, que la Letty va a estar aquí para servirle cuando usted quiera! Don't you worry, Mister Christian; our Letty will be here to attend to all your needs!

At this point you and I exchange glances, and I have to suppress a smile. Yes, it's been a long time all alone here in Rabinal, but let's not read into *doña* Matilde's reply more than she actually intended.

The *litros* are a little too heavy to stuff in a *morral*, so we carry them off grabbing each bottle by its neck. Five short blocks and we're back where we started this morning. I'm ready for a little break, aren't you? We'll clean up at my house and then go back out and find some lunch. Cigarette? No, I didn't think so. Sorry.

Around the next corner we pass another pair of soldiers, but this time they're carrying their Galils in a sort of low "ready" position. Third pair on patrol that we've seen today. That's a little strange; usually I see only one or at most two on this trip to the *vivero*. But not to worry; they pretty much ignore me, and they behave themselves. No story here, trust me. Nothing much has changed in the five months that I've been here. Everything's cool, and life is good. For the *gringo*, at least. Jeez, I can't wait to get washed up; I feel so sweaty.

As we come down my street approaching the house I rent, something looks different. What do I see there all around Augusto's place across the street? Black drapes? What's going on? A wide swath of pleated black fabric now crowns the entrance to Augusto's home, and as I peer inside towards their concrete patio slab I can see that there are a few people sitting in plastic chairs who I haven't seen before, and there too are Augusto's brothers Baudilio and Paulino and Gilberto. Augusto never has this many visitors at one time, so I ask his wife

Carmen, who happens to pass near the gate, what's going on. Carmen tells me in a soft but deliberate voice that there has been a death in the family, and they have all gathered to grieve as they all learned this news only a couple of hours ago when Gilberto came back into town from Salamá. Gilberto was in Salamá because he was seeing his wife Hermelinda who lay there in the hospital. He had been there for several days with her and was staying by her side almost all day long every single day, because Hermelinda, I am told, had somehow contracted tetanus and Hermelinda was not vaccinated against tetanus, and her case was terminal, and there was nothing to do but stay with her and hold her hand as her illness got worse and worse and worse, until one morning, this morning in fact, during the first hours of the new day, Hermelinda died and left her husband and her children all alone to cope with life and loss in a sad, gray block house down the street.

Dios te salve, María, llena de gracia,
el Señor está contigo.
Bendita Tú eres entre todas las
mujeres y bendito es
el fruto de tu vientre, Jesús.
Santa María, Madre de Dios,
ruega por nosotros los pecadores ahora
y en la hora de nuestra muerte. Amén.

You and I will now walk the few steps back to my side of the street, and I will unlock my gate and we will both go in, we'll walk past the CUC graffito on my wall and inside I'll offer you a towel so you can go out back and take a cool, bracing midday shower before the water runs out which it will in a couple of hours. Meanwhile I'll just sit down here and wait my turn. And so, to kill some time, I pull out of my *morral* the newspaper I had picked up in the plaza, and I glance at the main headline splashed across the front page in big blue letters.

"***Repudio generalizado por el asesinato de Colom Argueta***"

The progressive new mayor of Guatemala City has just been assassinated; he probably died just a few hours before Hermelinda.

CHAPTER 7

Palimoníx

Pueblo rabinalense! Your attention, please! The Ministry of Public Health has determined that we must adopt extraordinary measures to protect our community from the deadly threat of rabies. In accordance with this directive, be advised that tomorrow, Wednesday, your Centro de Salud will undertake a sanitary campaign throughout Rabinal to rid us of those vectors which transmit the deadly virus. KEEP YOUR SMALL CHILDREN INDOORS, as well as those domestic animals that belong to your household and are under your care. The placement of strychnine baits will be supervised by our technicians during the pre-dawn hours, and said baits will remain in place until the end of the day. STRYCHNINE IS POISON! Do not touch these poison baits, on risk of death. Also, do not approach any animal you may see on the street, as it may be contaminated with rabies or poison, or both. This is a message from your local *Centro de Salud. ¡Adelante Guatemala! ¡Adelante pueblo de Rabinal!*"

The red pickup jerked its way around the corner by the fertilizer dispensary, leaning heavily into each rut and bouncing back with rocking spasms. A chipped and battered megaphone was mounted on top of the cab with duct tape, and the insignia on the door said "*SALUD PUBLICA*" in stenciled letters, with "*Gobierno de Guatemala*" arching over it.

I stopped as the pickup turned onto the street where I was walking—I had to, for the street was narrow, and the pickup had veered wide. I waved a salutation, and the Mayan *técnico* who was driving waved back. Dr. Martínez—a balding, middle-aged *ladino* with wire-rimmed glasses and a thick brush mustache—was beside him, the voice behind the mic. He said "those vectors," as if the whole plan were a neat diagram with lines and circles and a perfectly clear legend. As if *doña* Matilde or the kids on the street corner across from the dispensary knew what a vector was. The good doctor's frail, white-shirted torso jounced about in the cab; he held onto the grab bar above his door, and with his other hand clutched the mic close to his mouth. Dr. Martínez was one of the few people in town with an advanced professional degree. The *técnico* who drove the pickup was almost always at the good doctor's side, like a faithful sidekick.

The rest of the way home, I thought about medicine—Tropical Medicine, and my own case of the trots. My bowel was loosening, I had to go bad. The Flagyl was on the shelf in my bedroom, crammed between books, but I kept putting off starting the two-week regimen because a) I wanted to force my body to adapt, and b) you couldn't drink alcohol during the regimen. And c) the amoebas would come back anyway, because there was no way to avoid them. Sort of like the clap, I thought: you keep screwing around, you eventually pay the price.

"Good-bye-my-LUF!" A small group of schoolchildren on the next corner shouted out to me between titters and giggles as I passed by. I smiled and waved and shouted back at them, "Good-BYE, my love! *Adiós, pués.*"

That was on Tuesday. Early Wednesday morning I walked the very same route from my house down to the *vivero*, only this time when I got close to the plaza, there on the street corner I noticed a group of kids having a time of it laughing and joking while they surrounded something that was in the road. As I got closer I saw what it was: a lean, brown pariah dog that I had frequently seen sauntering around the marketplace begging for scraps, now laying on its side in the dusty street gasping and foaming at the mouth in its convulsive final death throes, a hapless victim of the strychnine purge announced by the good doctor just the day before. The children were almost savagely indifferent to the poor dog's agony as they dared one another to touch or kick the near-carcass. One boy pulled a blue straw from the plastic baggie of NeHi Orange he had been drinking and bent over the dog to place the straw in its gasping mouth. All the other kids got a really big kick out of this and laughed and shouted with even greater glee at the dying dog with a thin, blue straw in its mouth. The whole macabre sight and the cruelty of the children were too much to take in, so I walked along quickly, wishing to God I could forget what I had just seen. But I still can't forget.

I spent most of the rest of that morning in the *vivero* working with Juan Pablo on monthly reports and supply requisitions. We looked carefully at our germination beds, ordered some of the sprouts to be transplanted to dirt-filled poly bags, and then we walked over and checked the status of the cashew seedlings in our fruit tree corner. Coming up nicely. I had one of the men mix up some Dipterex to spray on the eucalyptus seedlings. As a rule I would tell somebody else to mix and apply the pesticides whenever it seemed warranted, but I almost never did the job myself. Over the long term this might have been a dangerous job with clear health impacts, a fact which I never adequately shared with my workers, rationalizing instead that they would never have paid any attention to my warnings anyway. Somebody had to do the job—but (I confess now) it wouldn't be the tall, white gringo who only stopped by to visit a few hours every week.

On my way back home after the *vivero* visit I passed through the *plaza* again. The brown dog was still there, now an inert, short-haired mass of flesh lying on its side by a yellow adobe wall, with a thin, blue plastic straw still hanging from the black lips of its mouth.

* * *

I've always loved my maps. Maps, I think, are the crowning achievement of our Western Enlightenment. People today take maps for granted, I thought to myself as I fished out my keychain and opened a Coke. The fact that they do is testimony to maps' conquest of our imagination. Take measure, make symbol. Take measure, make symbol. The symbols laid out on a broad sheet of paper help us focus on what's important by omitting extraneous details. If the details are anything more important than the ripples on the surface of the pond or the color of a cornfield, they'll be the subject of another map. Someone else's map.

One map, an early map, depicted a flat world on ancient vellum, with spectacular maritime monsters prowling near its edge. Now the monsters are gone from our maps, and we know the flatness is illusory. There's no longer anything to fall off the edge of. In that way, maps conquered our imagination; they have tamed our religious excesses, which we now recognize as old superstitions. We so honored maps that we named an entire new world for an Italian mapmaker. Maps are the graphic distillation of human reason on a messy, chaotic world that otherwise seems to defy reason. Nature, red in tooth and claw, gets mapped into submission.

This was my ritual during many an afternoon, and often into the night. Hunched over a rustic plank table, straining to focus, I would follow a sinuous brown line with the tip of my drafting pen on a sheet of mylar. With calm diligence I applied stroke after stroke, and the black ink made a rivulet on the mylar like the path of a drunken soldier. On the map underneath the mylar the line wanders through a soft green haze over a flat plain, now bisecting a tight cluster of tiny black squares, now winding past short rows of letters that form names like Patixlán, Chixím, Pachalum. Most of the clusters are quite small, except for the one labeled Xococ. There the black squares, all the squalid little houses of the *aldea*, form a dense nucleus surrounded by more sparsely scattered squares that resemble the toss of a hundred tiny dice.

The thin brown line I traced made a pronounced, angular V as it crossed another line that was blue. There are brown V's above it and more below it, V's hooded over V's, and the pattern reminded me of how *don* Juan Lux stacked a dozen straw-colored *sombreros* in his plaza stall on Wednesdays and Saturdays.

"Where the contours cross a stream, they are shaped like arrowheads pointing to the source," I said to Juan Pablo in a whisper. I followed the course of the thin, blue stream over to the edge as far as I could go; there it was summarily curtailed by the broad, white margin with tick marks for latitude. "It continues on the next quad."

"And where is that?" Juan Pablo asked.

"We don't have it."

"What about the brown lines?"

"Each one winds around until it comes back to where it began. Every point on a single brown line is at the same altitude. Think, like terraces on a hillside."

"Is the whole *municipio* on this map?"

"No, it takes several quads to cover the whole area. Rabinal is pretty big, once you get outside the *pueblo*!"

"And the stream?" Juan Pablo placed a finger on the blue line where it met the white margin. "The source would be—?"

"On the next quad. The one we need to get," I answered. "San Cristóbal Verapaz," I added, reading the name off of the margin.

"You will not obtain San Cristóbal."

"Why not?"

"*La situación*. Believe me, you will not obtain San Cristóbal."

"Then we'll have to work with what we have," I said.

"The next quad over is an important one. Over here to the west. That is where the barite mines are located."

"*La barita?*"

"*Sí, hombre. La mina* and their *malditos camiones. Chingados.* I wonder how much precious landscape and forest they have stripped for that operation." I pondered. "Look, Juan Pablo. Work with me on this. I need someone like you to escort me through these *aldeas*—you know, to introduce me to each one of those little clusters of squares on the map. These maps are my bible, but I need someone like you to show me around. Will you do this for me?"

* * *

During the rainy season from May through September the storm clouds appeared like clockwork every day over the high peaks of the *Sierra Chuacús* looking south. I would try to plan most of my outdoor activities for the morning, because by two in the afternoon there would be a downpour you could almost set your watch by. The rains were pretty much unfailing in their arrival every day, except during the *canícula*—a short dry spell of roughly two weeks that fell right in the middle of the rainy season. The *canícula* punctuated the *invierno* every year like an em dash in the middle of a sentence, and later when the daily downpours resumed they were generally more severe than they were in the earlier half of the season.

The order of the day in late July of 1979 was for some important government officials to visit our tree nursery by the *colonia* in the morning, and get out of there by noon. The year 1979 had been designated by federal decree as *El Año Nacional de la Reforestación*, and the officials who were coming included Gen. Leonel Vassaux Martínez, who was charged with overseeing this national effort, as well as the governor of Baja Verapaz department, Sr. Hugo Conde Prera. I had received an official telegram about the planned visit, which gave me enough lead time so that I could prepare some crude visual aids on cardstock before their arrival.

Recalling the meeting I had attended in Salamá some three months earlier, during which OAS planners wanted to get me and my fellow volunteers on board with their ambitious plan to outplant two million seedlings over the next twelve months, I thought it might be appropriate to give the officials who were coming to the nursery a reality check concerning reforestation outcomes. I'm all for the plan, I thought, but let's go into this with open eyes. The inevitable dry season mortality, the leafcutter ants, and a short list of additional factors which I wrote down in neat, four-inch letters on the sheets of cardstock I had bought would certainly reduce those two million seedlings (*if* we ever found the many hands needed to plant those seedlings in the first place) to a few hundred thousand at best.

Half an hour before the officials arrived at the nursery on the appointed day, an army jeep from Rabinal's *destacamento militar* came bouncing down the road and stopped at our gate, and a *ladino* lieutenant with a neatly trimmed mustache jumped out, along with three or four Mayan grunts carrying their Israeli Galils slung over their shoulders. The soldiers all wore soft sided, camouflage boonie hats—decent protection against the sun, but certainly not against any potential enemy—while the lieutenant himself was bareheaded and carried a holstered nine millimeter Beretta on his belt. The soldiers quickly dispersed to nearby positions and peered around in every direction while the lieutenant casually walked up to me and Juan Pablo and told us that they were there to provide security for the imminent arrival of the officials.

The lieutenant looked over our nursery, asked us a couple questions about it, and then said he wanted to get some people together soon to plant some trees. We politely assured him that yes, we can certainly coordinate that anytime you want. But I felt distracted from the conversation. In my mind I was just trying to focus on the presentation I was about to give, how to best deliver it in Spanish, and how to calibrate my message so as not to alienate the government officials. I started to wonder if maybe I should change my tack with them and just keep it all rosy and upbeat. But no, let's be honest and real about this. I wanted to tell them when they came, Hell yeah, let's get out there and plant those two million seedlings, but let's not kid ourselves about the anticipated results. Let's—

Never mind, because next thing we saw was a black Jeep Cherokee with tinted windows barreling down the dirt road even faster than the army jeep before it, and it trailed behind a cloud of dust that made passing *campesinos* cover their faces and look away from the road. The Cherokee came to a halt on the opposite side of the road from our nursery, and the general and the governor emerged, both of them wearing crisp guayaberas and office slacks. Two portly men, fifty-ish, accompanied by two plainclothes bodyguards toting Uzis. It definitely seemed we had enough protective firepower on hand for the visit. Greetings and handshakes, and then Juan Pablo gave them a short tour of the nursery. So far, so good. The general reiterated the reforestation goals for Baja Verapaz, emphasizing that the government hoped to see a substantial amount of the outplanting of seedlings occur around Xococ and over in the Chixoy region, the latter being a remote part of Rabinal *municipio* around the Río Negro, also known as the Río Chixoy. (How could we possibly know at the time what fate would soon befall the people of Río Negro, at the hands of the people of Xococ? A fate that would perhaps even be sealed under the tactical guidance of the very same army officer who was now watching us right outside the gate.)

After the general finished speaking it was my turn to deliver the presentation I had prepared. With a couple hand-lettered poster boards hanging from the barbed wire fencing around the nursery to illustrate my points, I took a deep breath and began my *spiel*, which to my own dismay, as I spoke, was already sounding a little too much like a lecture. Yet I pushed on, systematically describing all the environmental and cultural factors militating against the survival of tree seedlings. I explained how the goal of planting some two million seedlings in the Chixoy watershed, even if we had the level of nursery production needed to support such an ambitious goal, would likely result in the survival of only a few hundred thousand mature trees. Now that's not bad, really, but I wanted everybody to be realistic about anticipated outcomes. *Debemos de emprender esta tarea con los ojos abiertos.* Let's make sure we approach this task with open eyes.

The general and the governor patiently listened to my presentation and then thanked me for my candid appraisal of the prospects for success. They were clearly not happy with my message, and the remainder of their visit did not take too long. Juan Pablo cast me a sidelong glance from across the *vivero*, and I could see he was really pissed. It was only afterwards I realized that while I may have convinced myself of the inescapable logic of the reforestation challenge, my approach to political engagement on a human level was utterly inept.

* * *

A couple more weeks passed, and the tree nursery was emptying out very nicely. *Campesino* farmers arrived at the gate every day to get their free seedlings, sometimes a dozen or more of them in a day. When we had access to a truck from CARE, we used it to haul hundreds of seedlings at a time out to the barren slopes and byways all over the countryside. Meanwhile, Juan Pablo and his men were already planting seeds for the next year. Business (if you can call it that) was brisk, and we were happy to report to INAFOR several thousand outplantings every month of the rainy season.

Then, one day, the young lieutenant from the *destacamento* paid us another visit at the *vivero*. He arrived in his jeep, accompanied as always by two soldiers with their Galils, and he called out to us at the gate, "*Buenos días señores, ¿cómo les va?*" In these circumstances it is of course always best to accept the army on its own terms, for there are no other terms. The lieutenant probably wanted something. Let's see what he wants.

As it turned out, the lieutenant wanted to make us an offer that we couldn't possibly refuse. If you want to get some trees planted—a lot of trees—then I'm the man you need to help you do it, he told us. He would assemble a group of *campesinos*—no problem with that, he assured us, no problem at all with the help of the *comisionados militares*—and he would bring them all here to the *vivero*, and each man would carry away ten, no, fifteen seedlings, and the lieutenant would then "escort" them all out to the village of Palimoníx on the road going south towards El Chol, past the Esso station. He proposed to do this next Sunday because it would be market day and that's when everybody typically comes into town. The plan was to plant all the seedlings along the road for several hundred meters, if possible, to create a nice, attractive *alameda* in years to come. Do you have any casuarinas? *Me gustan los casuarinas. Son más bonitos.* They're prettier, the lieutenant said. He said it like a little boy who was admiring the beauty of trees for the first time.

Hey, this is the National Reforestation Year, and every agency has to do its part to help out, including the army. And by the way, the lieutenant added, the mayor really wants to see this happen, too.

Listening to the lieutenant's plan, and realizing finally that he sort of needed us, I found my *huevos* (that is to say, my balls) and set my conditions. Sure, we can help you do this, I said, and yes, we definitely still have plenty of casuarinas over there in the *tablones*. But we have to do this in an orderly fashion, and I want to talk to all the people you bring here before they start taking the seedlings out. I also want to go with them to the outplanting site and supervise their efforts to make sure they do it right. Two meters apart; eight-inch holes; no J-rooting. Can we agree on these things? (Of course I would have liked to add a final condition: "And I want only volunteers, no forcible recruits!" But I knew that would be a non-starter with the lieutenant. Or else he would have simply said, "*¡Sí como no, señor!*")

Sunday morning arrived, and so I walked down to the nursery to see if we had a reforestation project or not. By the time I got there, there were already close to forty *campesinos* milling about near the gate, and the lieutenant was standing by his jeep waiting for me. I greeted everyone present with my best show of earnest enthusiasm, though I already started to have a little bit of doubt as to whether we'd be able to pull this thing off. The lieutenant addressed the assembly of men first, just to remind everybody what they were expected to do, and to be sure to do a good job of it. Then it was my turn, and I spoke to everybody while standing on one of the lower terraces where the casuarinas were all neatly lined up in rows.

"*¡Buenos días, señores! ¿Listos para sembrar árboles?*" My query was immediately answered with a couple enthusiastic rejoinders of "*Aqui estamos*—¡listos!" along with several slower affirmatives mumbled by the others, who sounded less than enthusiastic— all of the responses in any event belying the fact that everybody was there with me under duress. Indeed, they lacked only the chains around their ankles. What if you were to say that you simply had things to do and you didn't have time for this little project today? Who knows what would've happened—but the lieutenant had your name.

So, standing by the casuarinas, I went on to explain once again what we were about to do, and how we were going to do it. Spacing, depth, no J-rooting, *señores*—but the men were already lifting their seedlings from the *tablón* and walking off with them, and any pretense of organization that had prevailed was already beginning to fall apart. Before I could finish talking, most of the *campesinos* were standing on the road outside the *vivero*, each man carrying at least fifteen seedlings on his back with a *mecapal* wrapped across his forehead. I rushed out of the *vivero* to join them and start the walk back up the hill when the lieutenant crawled by in his jeep and offered me a ride. This was a delicate moment for me, because I wanted at all events to avoid *any* appearance of alliance or common interest with the military in Rabinal. I was already beginning to perceive forebodings of troubles ahead in town, and the image of the gringo riding alongside the army lieutenant in his jeep would remain an indelible one for many. Anyway, the outplanting site was just two clicks away on the other side of town, so it made a lot more sense to show solidarity with the forty or so *campesinos* and walk alongside them instead. As politely as I could, I declined the lieutenant's invitation. "Thanks, sir; I'll walk."

At length we all made it to the outplanting site along the road out to El Chol, and there the men stopped one by one along either side of the road, each man setting down his load of seedlings on the ground, and then with hands or sticks they all began to dig their little holes. There was little respect for the planting distance I had recommended, and some seedlings ended up much too close to the road. Everybody seemed eager to finish quickly, which I perceived as an alacrity born of mixed intentions. Perhaps they all wanted to demonstrate to the lieutenant who watched from his jeep their energy and enthusiasm, but they certainly all had other things to do as well. And on top of that, their brisk pace probably evinced an element of fear.

The work was finished in half an hour and everybody quickly dispersed and the lieutenant drove back to his *destacamento* on the edge of town out by the two cemeteries. I am guessing the *campesinos* planted maybe six hundred trees along the road to El Chol that day, which actually in a few years might have become a nice alameda to welcome visitors on the back road from the capital as they came into Rabinal. But today, forty years later, there is not a shred of evidence that such a project was ever undertaken. Nor should there be, I suppose. Maybe the trees were harvested for fuelwood long ago. Or maybe the little casuarina seedlings fell victim to poor transplanting technique, to neglect, to inexorable development along the roadside due to population pressures, or to *zompopos* (those nasty leafcutter ants with their ravenous appetites) —in short, to all the cultural and environmental factors that so often militate against a successful reforestation effort.

On the road to El Chol through Palimoníx *aldea*. (Source: Google Earth.)

* * *

I spent all of three years in Rabinal striving almost every day to live fully and vividly in the present. So great was my obsession with *the present moment* that on most days I quite consciously forswore those habits and behaviors that I thought might separate me from the mystery, the frequent beauty and even sometimes the helpless terror of the present. For the most part I stopped taking photographs during those years, as I believed that the camera lens would inevitably prevent my total immersion in the present moment. This "immersion in the present" seemed to me all the more important during those particular moments, and quite a few of them there were, that I suppose most people would regard as uniquely "photogenic." The men of the *cofradía* passing by on the street with their autochthonous flute and drum from which emanated a solemn and mysterious strain. Or the panoramic vista of the whole *Valle de Urram* as I stood near the ancient ceremonial altar atop *Cerro Kaj'yúp*.

I reminded myself of this resolve almost every day, but because I did not actually stick to it every single day I am lucky that I possess today at least a small collection of a couple dozen photographs documenting the life of the town that I came to love. I've kept these pictures through many moves over the years, and for me every single one of them has almost talismanic properties revealing the entire, vivid gestalt that surrounded the moment in which each picture was taken. Looking at one of these photographs today, I can see—or rather *feel*—not only the image that is before me, but also many of the details that remained outside the camera's view, and even the sounds and the smells that accompanied the scene.

There were many scenes, of course, of a less picturesque quality—a *campesino* hurriedly planting one of his fifteen casuarina seedlings by the roadside, for instance, or the army lieutenant sitting in his jeep by the tree nursery—that I sometimes wish I had a picture of now. But perhaps it is because I *don't* have these pictures that my memory of each of these scenes is not only more vivid and detailed, but almost incandescent. I sometimes regret that I have so little photographic documentation of my experience in Rabinal, yet my resolute desire back then to eschew picture-taking and live instead in the present to the fullest extent possible helped, in the end, to preserve the memory of those moments.

CHAPTER 8

Chichupac

To have his path made clear for him is the aspiration of every human being in our beclouded and tempestuous existence.

—Joseph Conrad, *The Mirror of the Sea*

It was late into my first rainy season in Rabinal when I had to make a trip out to the *aldea* of Chichupac, high up in the Chuacús mountain range. My job there was to look at a couple small satellite tree nurseries that were being managed by the CIF *promotores* there—two Mayan farmers named Romulo Chajaj and Dionisio Sic Osorio. I was also going to give them some instruction on soil conservation techniques. Chichupac was only ten kilometers south of the *pueblo*, yet during the rainy season the journey could take a while, as the daily rainstorms that time of the year always made a sloppy mess of the narrow dirt road which was the only way to get there.

Having no vehicle at my disposal, I hopped onto the *Cobanerita* early in the morning. The *Cobanerita* was a *bus extraurbano* that, like almost all the other buses that crisscrossed Guatemala, was made by the Bluebird Company out of Georgia. And except for the variegated color scheme of these buses, and of course the long roof rack on top, each one looked for all the world like an American school bus. We volunteers called them "chicken buses," because on any given trip out of town you might be riding beside a *campesino* carrying a basket with a live chicken inside softly clucking away under a brightly colored cloth.

I got on the bus in the main plaza, and I was lucky to find a spot right up front for the jostling ride that went by twists and turns high up into the mountains. For those who had the patience and the intestinal fortitude, one could stay on the *Cobanerita*, if they wished, as it bounced along through the mud for another seventy kilometers on its way to Guate.

"*¡Aquí no más!*" I called out as we approached a muddy side path on the left side of the road that would take me into Chichupac. I got off the bus and started down the path towards the *aldea*. At nearly 1,600 meters above sea level, the clean, cool damp air here was a bracing contrast to the atmosphere back in town. I was actually walking through the soft, misty underbelly of a dense cloud cover that shrouded the entire mountaintop and which was unlikely to lift for several hours. There was only the damp mist, and there was silence. I hadn't gone far, though, when I passed two Mayan women who came walking uphill in small, quick steps towards the road behind me, each one balancing on her head an enormous bundle wrapped in a traditional *peraje* with brilliantly multicolored zig-zag striping. "*Buenos dias,*" I said to the women as they passed me, because that's what you do, I thought. You say hello. But the two women scurried right past me in silence. Back in town I could always greet the Mayan women on the street or in the plaza, and they would usually respond in kind, however tentatively. But up here in the lonely spaces of the mountains I think I had terrified the poor women, so they had hurried on past me, and I suddenly felt ashamed of my uncouth forwardness.

During our class at CIF in Pachalum the previous Saturday I had set it up with Romulo and Dionisio that I would meet them at the schoolhouse in the center of their village. The schoolhouse was not hard to find. It was the drab, cinder block building with the corrugated metal roof standing right there at the end of the path—no bigger than a trailer home, yet bigger than any other structure in the whole village. And there was Romulo—*and there, too*, was the CIF pickup parked on a patch of grass! The driver was nowhere to be seen, but either Güicho or Julio had to be around somewhere. *Púchica*, so I could have gotten a ride here this morning with CIF if I'd been paying attention during the weekly planning meeting a couple days before!

"Romulo, did you see who came here in the vehicle?"

"*Si, don Cristo,*" he answered, "It was the *Señor Administrador* del CIF." That would be Güicho. And as if on cue, Güicho suddenly emerged from one of the nearby huts beside a patch of tall cornstalks.

"Gracias, entonces, cuídense, nos vemos," he spoke towards the darkened door of the dwelling, and I heard some unintelligible response from inside.

"I didn't realize you were going to be up here today," I said.

"Si, pués fue una diligencia," answered Güicho. He had to take care of an unspecified "diligence." Okay, none of my business, I guess. I asked Güicho how much longer he'd be around, and he told me, and anyway he'd wait for me, he said. I told him I had to talk with Romulo and Dionisio about their tree nurseries, and maybe talk a little about making some terraces or contour ditches on their croplands, and then I'd be done. "That is good; I'll wait for you here," Güicho replied.

So I went with Romulo to go see his *vivero*. Dionisio never showed up. The two of us walked down a hill through wet grass and past fragrant pine trees, and I couldn't help it but my senses took me back all at once, back to the Adirondacks. Not just the Adirondacks, but one specific place in the Adirondacks: Tirrell Pond, off the Northville-Lake Placid Trail, where I had camped a few years ago and had heard the laughing loon through the dense morning mist on the water. The sense of smell is without question the most powerful sense we have to elicit nostalgic recollections of the past. It transports me every now and then, and I have to brace myself to remember where the hell I am.

"¡Pués aquí está en su casa, don Cristián, y esto es mi vivero!" ("Make yourself at home, *don* Christian, and here is my tree nursery!") Romulo's voice woke me from my reverie; we had arrived at his humble home. And he actually called me by my real name this time, most likely because he had heard Güícho greet me. The tree nursery was right beside his house, and his corn crop on a small plot of *milpa* measuring less than an acre covered the steep slope down below. Romulo's little hut was made of four waist-high walls of adobe topped with many tightly lashed bamboo-like sticks called *vara*, all standing vertically and somehow fastened or "planted" in the adobe.

The *vivero* that Romulo showed me boasted a grand total of maybe two hundred seedlings, all lined up in their little black poly bags. A fragrant mixture of pines and Mexican cypress, most of them ready for outplanting.

"When will you be planting these, Romulo? They look about ready, and the rainy season won't last a lot longer. *"Pues vamos a ver qué hacemos, don Cristián—primero dios que ya mero.*" Basically, in plain English: "Who knows? I haven't made any plans." I came to realize he might plant them somewhere, or he might not. He might give them away to a neighbor, and who knows if the receiver would ever plant them.

Such were the prospects for reforestation in the remote *aldeas* of Rabinal—of the whole country, for that matter. In my dealings with the *campesinos* in the *aldeas*, I always felt I had to try to divine their true intentions, their actual priorities. As well as their reservations, their fears. There was the well known fear I had heard about, the fear among many out in the *campo* that the strange-looking gringo who came to help you would later come back again to take your land. Or at least take your trees when full grown. Heck, here I was coming all the out to Chichupac to monitor, to *supervise* Romulo's little tree nursery, a sure sign that I must have some interest at stake. Why else would this gringo go to the trouble?

In the end, of course, I had to give Romulo the benefit of the doubt. Hopefully the trees in his *vivero* would all get outplanted soon.

While we looked at this little *vivero* that was no bigger than a child's hopscotch pattern laid out on the ground, Romulo made the now familiar pitch that I had heard before in each of the other satellite nurseries I had visited. "Here it's very difficult to get water to water the trees. But if I had some hose, not too much, maybe twenty meters, I could connect it to the faucet on the community *pila* up the hill and water these seedlings every day." I responded by noting that the spigot on the *pila* up the hill had no threads with which to connect anything. "I'll find a way!" was Romulo's ready reply. "We'll see" was mine.

I finished up with Romulo, and as we said our goodbyes I saw his wife who was standing by the doorway in her traditional *huipíl* and *corte*. No words, this time, just a furtive look as she turned her head away—and then I headed back up the hill alone. I found Güicho talking with some *campesinos* by the schoolhouse, so I joined him and hung out there, waiting for him to finish up whatever *diligencias* he had on his agenda. By the time we got into the pickup for the drive back downhill to the *pueblo*, it had started to drizzle, and the sky looked very dark even over the valley far below. We didn't get wet, though, we got into the pickup just in time, and the truth is that after walking around in Chichupac all morning, the cozy, dry cabin of the pickup truck felt so comfortable that it had an almost soporific effect on me.

"*Bueno Cristián,* how did your meeting with Romulo and Dionisio go?" It wasn't much of a meeting, of course; the little tree nursery Romulo managed was a pretty sad affair, and then Dionisio never showed up, so I didn't even bother to talk much about soil conservation topics. I put on a face and told Güicho it went pretty well, and I had a list now of things to follow up with.

"*Bueno—qué bien.*" And at that point Güicho switched on the radio. Just in time for the news bulletins[38] at the top of the hour.

> ¡Ultima hora! ANOTHER TEACHER KIDNAPPED! An elementary school teacher who also teaches at various high school locations in Mazatenango was kidnapped yesterday while he was on his way to teach at a rural school in San Francisco Zapotitlán, Suchitepéquez. The teacher, 25-year-old Jose Chavez de Leon, was walking to the rural school to teach his class when several armed men intercepted him on his route and took him away to parts unknown.
>
> ¡Ultima hora! In other news, four soldiers were killed and another nine seriously injured between Zacualpa and Santa Cruz del Quiche when the military truck they were riding in was attacked by guerrillas who detonated a Claymore mine in the road.
>
> ¡Ultima hora! ANOTHER SHOOTING AT A GUERRILLA HIDEOUT! Two guerrillas died when…

Güicho turned the volume down and gave a long sigh. "*Ayy, Cristián,* what shall we do, for the love of God? *What shall we do?*"

"I guess it's a difficult time all over the place, the way it sounds," I meekly replied. Wanting to express greater empathy, but my words sounded wooden and I was unsure where we were headed. But Güicho was just warming up.

"*Este gobierno—*This government of murderous generals and the bloodsucking, filthy rich families that support them have to come to an end someday. We can't go on like this! Look what's happening all over the countryside—they're kidnapping our school teachers now, and the community leaders."

It hit me, suddenly, that the voice on the news had said the kidnapped teacher from Mazatenango was twenty-five years old, which was exactly my age. I leaned forward and listened more intently to Güicho.

"And right here in our own Baja Verapaz the same shit is happening—or worse. They're killing all the leaders that we need the most in order to progress as a country! I'm telling you, *Cristián*, those rebel forces in the mountains, those rebels who are struggling every day with scarcely enough food to eat, they, *they* are the ones who will triumph someday—and only then will we see some changes around here. But meanwhile we continue struggling every day—you and me both, we'll continue to struggle to contribute our *granito de arena*—our little grain of sand—around here in all these blessed *aldeas*—in Chichupac, in Nimacabaj, and Pichec and Chitucán. We have so much work to do here to help the *aldeanos*.

"Listen, I am happy, *Cristián*, that you are here with us. *To be a witness*. Trust me, I'm in no way opposed to what you do here; we *need* to preserve nature and save our forest resources, for our own good, and for our children. But nevertheless you shall see, *Cristián*, you shall see that at the end of the day there is an even greater mission that awaits us—and each of us will have to decide if he will contribute his *granito de arena* to that mission as well."[39]

This moment—the telegraphic news bulletins followed by Güicho's courageously frank commentary—lasted only a few short minutes as we bounced along through the rain with the windshield wipers going *swoosh-clack, swoosh-clack*. We could talk freely there, ensconced in the privacy of a pickup truck cabin where nobody else could hear us. Still, I ask myself, how is it that I can remember this moment so vividly more than forty years later? Güicho's words (or words to that effect) made my somnolent conscience stand at attention. Not that I didn't already possess some sense of compassion and fellow-feeling for the *campesinos* who I visited in their little villages spread out over the whole *municipio*. That feeling became especially palpable whenever I encountered the poorest of the poor in their miserable hovels with virtually no land to farm. Still, it had been an almost "academic" sense of fellow-feeling, and "at the end of the day," as Güicho put it, I always had felt that I needed to just concentrate on my mission—the *professional* mission, not the moral one—and just plant those trees and make those terraces and hope that the human tragedy would somehow work itself out in the long run.

This was the day—this was the moment—when I realized that that was a fool's mission.

* * *

Nineteen seventy-nine was the year I saw my first Guatemalan Independence Day. The date, September fifteenth, fell just a few weeks after my ride down the mountainside coming back from Chichupac that rainy morning with Güicho. And it marked exactly one year since my arrival in Costa Rica for the beginning of training. Leading up to the official celebration, I'd seen the marching schoolchildren almost every day in the central plaza practicing, practicing over and over for hours on end in preparation for the big day. When the holiday arrived there were sporadic *bombas* all day long, and kids would light their long, red *ametralladoras* in the middle of the street. The *bombas* were not actual bombs, but rather inexpensive fireworks not unlike our Roman candles or M-80s. The *ametralladoras*—literally, "machine guns"—actually sounded a lot like their lethal namesake. (And in the days yet to come, would sometimes be confused with them.)

Anyone who worked for a salary had the day off *para el Quince*, and men congregated in the cantinas, some of them for the better part of the day. In the plaza near the church, a schoolteacher who I knew because we had given him loads of trees for his elementary students to plant accosted me with drunken salutations and wildly exaggerated gestures. *"Cristián, my friend, how are YOU? Let me tell you something, my friend…."* And, switching to Spanish because that was all he knew of English, he prattled on in his drunken palaver.

In the plaza there were bands, parades, *actos juveniles*, marimbas, sacerdotal blessings and mayoral proclamations amplified over a poorly wired P.A. system—and countless little plastic flags strung up like handkerchiefs hanging from a clothesline, or simply pasted to every available wall. On the school, on the pharmacy, on all the other little *tiendas*, on the wall of my favorite restaurant where I went for *frijoles volteados* over on the corner of the park, and of course plastered all over the gazebo in the middle of the plaza. Blue and white plastic flags everywhere, each with a coat of arms in the middle comprised of an emerald green quetzal perched over two crossed swords, two flintlocks, and an open scroll bearing the words: "LIBERTAD, 15 DE SEPTIEMBRE DE 1821."

It was on this day, my first Independence Day in Rabinal, that I received my first revolutionary flier—a mimeographed screed that someone overnight had slipped under the front door of the place I was calling home.

> TO ALL WORKERS IN THE COUNTRYSIDE OF THE VERAPACES:
>
> THE COMMITTEE FOR PEASANT UNITY - CUC - greets you on this fifteenth of September, a day on which once again, with parades and grand propaganda, the filthy rich and your government celebrate their independence from the murderous Spanish conquistadors because they now have become the owners of the best land and the fruits of the toil of our ancestors.

Reading through the rambling, full-page bulletin that was printed on legal size paper so that it would all fit, there was one particular passage that gave me pause:

> WE SHALL NOT WIN OUR LIBERTY until we fight the abusive authorities, the homeland guard, the forest guard and others who have forced all the *campesinos* to plant trees even while they themselves do business with the large timber concerns; who have taken away our machetes when we're in town only to sell them afterwards at five quetzales a piece.

And if that was not cause enough for some consternation, the very next sentence could not fail to alert me to some troubling intimations that the Guatemalan government, which I for all practical purposes represented locally, might be running roughshod over indigenous rights in a distant aldea:

[We'll] fight until the rights of our campesino brothers and sisters in the Chixoy region are respected by the government.

I shall have occasion to return to the whole Rio Chixoy debacle later. But at this point, barely eight months into my posting in Rabinal and lacking any source of local news other than word of mouth, I was left with little more than a vague suspicion that something very wrong might be happening in the Chixoy region, and in particular affecting the people of the *aldea* of Rio Negro, which was almost a full day's hike from the *pueblo* where I lived.

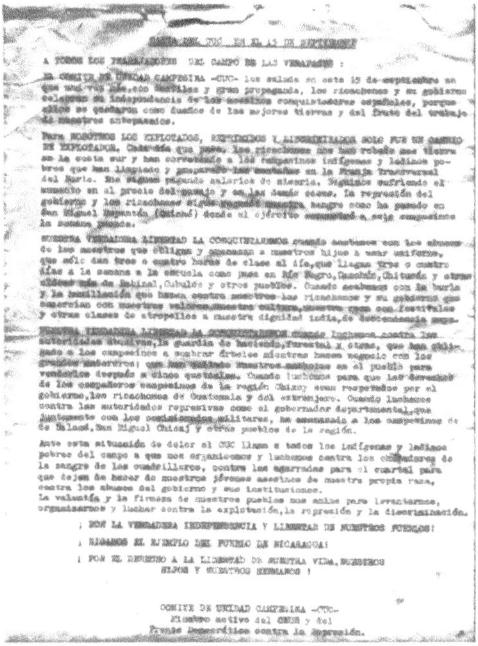

[illegible] DEL CUC EN EL 15 DE SEPTIEMBRE

A TODOS LOS TRABAJADORES DEL CAMPO DE LAS VERAPACES:

EL COMITE DE UNIDAD CAMPESINA -CUC- los saluda en este 15 de septiembre en que una vez más, con desfiles y gran propaganda, los ricachones y su gobierno celebran su independencia de los asesinos conquistadores españoles, porque ellos se quedaron como dueños de las mejores tierras y del fruto del trabajo de nuestros antepasados.

Para NOSOTROS LOS EXPLOTADOS, REPRIMIDOS Y DISCRIMINADOS SOLO FUE UN CAMBIO DE EXPLOTADOR. Cada día que pasa, los ricachones que han robado sus tierras en la costa sur y han convertido a los campesinos indígenas y ladinos pobres que han limpiado y preparado las montañas en la Franja Transversal del Norte. Nos siguen pagando salarios de miseria. Seguimos sufriendo el aumento en el precio del pasaje y en las demás cosas. La represión del gobierno y los ricachones sigue regando nuestra sangre como ha pasado en San Miguel Uspantán (Quiché) donde el ejército [illegible] a seis campesinos la semana pasada.

NUESTRA VERDADERA LIBERTAD LA CONQUISTAREMOS cuando acabemos con los abusos de los maestros que obligan y amenazan a nuestros hijos a usar uniforme, que sólo dan tres o cuatro horas de clase al día, que llegan tres o cuatro días a la semana a la escuela como pasa en Río Negro, Canchún, Chituxán y otras aldeas más de Rabinal, Cubulco y otros pueblos. Cuando acabemos con la burla y la humillación que hacen contra nosotros los ricachones y su gobierno que comercian con nuestros valores, nuestra cultura, nuestra ropa con festivales y otras clases de atropellos a nuestra dignidad india, de descendencia maya.

NUESTRA VERDADERA LIBERTAD LA CONQUISTAREMOS cuando luchemos contra las autoridades abusivas, la guardia de hacienda, forestal y otras, que han obligado a los campesinos a sembrar árboles mientras hacen negocio con los grandes madereros; que han quitado nuestros [illegible] en el pueblo para venderlos después a cinco quetzales. Cuando luchemos para que los derechos de los compañeros campesinos de la región Chixoy sean respetados por el gobierno, los ricachones de Guatemala y del extranjero. Cuando luchemos contra las autoridades represivas como el gobernador departamental, que juntamente con los comisionados militares, ha amenazado a los campesinos de de Salamá, San Miguel Chicaj y otros pueblos de la región.

Ante esta situación de dolor el CUC llama a todos los indígenas y ladinos pobres del campo a que nos organicemos y luchemos contra los chupadores de la sangre de los cuadrilleros, contra las agarradas para el cuartel para que dejen de hacer de nuestros jóvenes asesinos de nuestra propia raza, contra los abusos del gobierno y sus instituciones.
La valentía y la firmeza de nuestros pueblos nos anima para levantarnos, organizarnos y luchar contra la explotación, la represión y la discriminación.

¡POR LA VERDADERA INDEPENDENCIA Y LIBERTAD DE NUESTROS PUEBLOS!

¡SIGAMOS EL EJEMPLO DEL PUEBLO DE NICARAGUA!

¡POR EL DERECHO A LA LIBERTAD DE NUESTRA VIDA, NUESTROS HIJOS Y NUESTROS HERMANOS!

COMITE DE UNIDAD CAMPESINA -CUC-
Miembro activo del CNUS y del
Frente Democrático contra la Represión.

Up till now I felt safe and secure in Rabinal—indeed, I felt quite happy, notwithstanding occasional bouts of self-loathing and depression that were simply part of my nature to endure. But now the CUC bulletin on my doorstep introduced a whole new element of underlying tension that I wasn't entirely prepared for. What's going on up in the Chixoy region? I knew about the government's nascent hydroelectric project up there, but this early in my tour I still knew nothing about the impact that project might have on the people who lived there.

And who's the *Comité de Unidad Campesina*? Are any of my neighbors CUC? My acquaintances? The workers in my tree nursery, or the *campesinos* I meet with every week in the surrounding villages? And what opinion should I have regarding the CUC? They may have taken issue with some of the government's reforestation tactics, okay, but their rambling indictment nevertheless had the ring of truth. The National Reforestation Campaign was by no means an undertaking carried out with unassailable good will or the finest collectivist spirit—a point that had been driven home to me a few weeks earlier by the army-led outplanting fiasco. In the final analysis, I concluded that I had to try and find new ways to keep myself informed about what was going on in Rabinal, and especially up in the mountains. Seek out friends, acquaintances, *La Nación*. Hell, even *el teléfono de bejuco* (that is to say, word-of-mouth; the proverbial grapevine). Reliable information was lacking, but I hoped that by triangulating the situation from a variety of news sources—or at least the few sources I could get my hands on—I might get at something approaching the truth.

Things were brewing all across Central America. I recalled how when I was starting my training in Costa Rica exactly one year earlier, the Nicaraguan contingent that overlapped with our own group was just finishing up. I drank with them one night as they celebrated their completion of training, and the next morning they were all so excited to be shipping out to the Land of Lakes and Volcanoes. But within three months of their arrival Peace Corps/Nicaragua closed up shop due to the volatile political unrest, and everybody had to go home. The *Frente Sandinista de Liberación Nacional* achieved rapid gains during the ensuing months, and then in July, only a couple months prior to this Independence Day, Eugenio and I were sitting on the veranda listening to a shortwave broadcast when we heard the Voice of America announce that the FSLN army had triumphantly entered the capital Managua. I sat there cheering the news, because everyone knew what a bastard that Anastasio Somoza was.[40] Eugenio, though, seemed a tad more circumspect. The war in Nicaragua had left over thirty thousand dead, and over a hundred thousand Nicaraguans had fled into exile. A five-member junta entered Managua the very next day and assumed power, pledging to work for "political pluralism, a mixed economic system, and a foreign policy embracing non-alignment."[41] Now, of course, with the benefit of hindsight, we are in a better position to appreciate Eugenio's circumspection concerning the Sandinistas' proposals for change.

But it was still 1979, and we couldn't have imagined what kinds of transformations the revolutionary fervor might undergo. And meanwhile the tide continued to swell even further across the isthmus during the months following this Independence Day. In December 1979, the Cuban government brought together the leaders of five Salvadoran revolutionary groups to form the Farabundo Martí National Liberation Front (FMLN). The FMLN aimed to overturn an oligarchic repressive regime that had ruled El Salvador for decades.

Meanwhile in Guatemala the *Ejército Guerrillero de los Pobres* expanded its influence quite dramatically during the latter part of that year, controlling a large amount of territory in the so-called "Ixil Triangle" in El Quiché department, and holding numerous demonstrations in the remote towns of Nebaj, Chajul, and Cotzal. At the same time that the EGP was expanding its presence in the *Altiplano*, the insurgent movement known as ORPA, the Revolutionary Organization of the People in Arms, began to show renewed strength and activity.[42] The founding member of ORPA was one Rodrigo Asturias, son of Guatemala's Nobel laureate Miguel Angel Asturias.

What none of us could perceive at the time (certainly none of us in our Peace Corps contingent, and probably no one in Rabinal) was that we were on the cusp of civil war—or, to be more precise, we were on the cusp of the darkest chapter of a civil war that had been dragging on for the last twenty years. There had been unrest in Guatemala ever since the CIA-sponsored coup in 1954. That event ushered in a succession of right-leaning presidents who invariably enabled, if not orchestrated, the exploitation of the poor while protecting the interests of the landed oligarchy and the multinational corporations such as the United Fruit Company. The unrest had erupted in sporadic acts of rebellion since 1960. But a whole different character of unrest and bloody suppression was about to begin in the wake of the events of July 1979, when the Sandinista freedom fighters marched into Managua.

Time ... and change. By now I had been living in Rabinal for less than one of the one thousand years or more in the life of the community. When you are on the cusp of change during that tiny "snapshot in time," you have absolutely no idea how long the process of change might take. What direction will it take? In what will the change culminate? Indeed, given the fluidity of countless events large and small, day after day, how can the idea of "culmination," signaling an endpoint, have any meaning? When the apocalypse begins to unfold, who really knows how long it will last? And how bad will it be? When you see the first troubling evidence that something horrible is going down somewhere near you—but not necessarily in front of your very eyes—how do you begin to divine where it is all headed? Is there a condition that is even more horrible than horrible?

"You cannot step twice into the same river, for other waters are continually flowing on."[43] So said Heraclitus the Obscure some twenty-five centuries ago in one of his less obscure ruminations. I have always seen Heraclitus as a fundamentally tragic philosopher—enlightening and disturbing in equal measures. He speaks to us about time and strife and destiny in koan-like philosophical fragments, and even his most obscure fragments will often just seize you and make you think.

Rabinal often seemed to me like a timeless community that probably hadn't changed much in decades, but the truth was that every single morning when I stepped outside my door I was faced with a new, or at least different, Rabinal. Every day stepping into a new river. The new reality came into focus only very gradually at first, and the general trend that was the product of a concatenation of many small changes was, at least in the beginning, only dimly perceived. But the pace of change would pick up in the months to come. And things would soon become clearer.

The really puzzling and disconcerting fragment from Heraclitus comes a little later:

> Time is a child moving counters in a game; the royal power is the child's.

The idea that as we all move about in this world we are merely counters in some child's invisible game is of course deeply unsettling. But more unsettling still is Heraclitus's ominous warning to his fellow Ephesians, and to us:

> It should be understood that war is the common condition, that strife is justice, and that all things come to pass through the compulsion of strife.

Sitting in our comfortable homes and our cloistered retreats we might pray that the melancholy misanthrope Heraclitus was just hopelessly misguided and wrong in his assessment of the human condition. Yet the more we wander about in this world of tears and travail, the more evidence we find that he may have been tragically correct.

* * *

That night of the fifteenth there was a dance in the *salón municipal*, and of course I had to go and check it out. It was there that I met Carlos Enrique "Quique" Izaguirre Pérez, who invited me to dance with his pretty daughter. I happily obliged, we danced to a *son* or two played by a *marimba orquesta*, and afterwards Quique and I sat at a table talking over bottles of Gallo. I told Quique that I had come out of a university back in *Nueva York*. I told him about the job I was doing in Rabinal; I told him about my aspirations. I didn't realize it in the moment, but through our conversation in that *salón municipal* Quique was discreetly assessing where my sympathies might lie. We talked for a long while as the marimba played on, and a while later we left the *salón* and walked back to my house a few blocks off the main plaza; Quique's daughter departed separately with her mother.

Quique worked with the copper mine on Lake Izabal. Separated from his wife, he told me, so I supposed he must have returned to Rabinal mainly to see his cherished daughter. We were walking alone, well past midnight, just the two of us on an empty street, when Quique got to the point.

"The day will come. *Cristián*, when you will have to state with conviction that you never knew me. *Are you afraid?* Well, perhaps not, but when the day comes that you feel it is necessary to leave the country because you knew me, then please, go, GO."[44]

It all sounded a bit melodramatic, but Quique looked at me earnestly with a face that I swear was a face of the people. Quique belonged to the *guerrilla*, that much was clear, and by now I was not sure if I could believe his story that he worked at the copper mines. Maybe he did, or maybe he was out there organizing the workers. He showed me a rock that he carried with him. He gave this rock to me. It fit in the palm of my hand, and hundreds of tiny crystals that were embedded in the surface glittered in the moonlight. Quique wanted me to have this rock. I don't know why. I kept that rock for nearly twenty years, until I lost it somewhere in upstate New York.

That night Quique said to me:

"...*Y la gente está llorando...*"

"...*No podremos tolerar traidores...*"

"...*¿Piensas que hay libertad de prensa en este país? No creés—pues no existe tal libertad.*"

I am grateful to my younger self that I still possess a contemporaneous record of these snatches of conversation, albeit scribbled on a single three-by-five card like a telegram from the distant past. Quique was CUC, no doubt, or maybe EGP. And I was ... a listener.

* * *

One might say the trouble all began sometime before I arrived in Rabinal. How long before is a matter of historical interpretation and perspective. Shall we say nine months before, in Panzós? Let's start there.

> In the central plaza of Panzós, Alta Verapaz [10km NE of Rabinal], members of the Zacapa Military Zone attacked a peaceful peasant demonstration, killing many people. The deceased peasants, indigenous people who had been summoned to the place, were fighting for the legalization of the public lands they had occupied for years. Their fight directly confronted them with investors who wanted to exploit the mineral wealth of the area, particularly the oil reserves (under contracts with Basic Resources International and Shenandoah Oil), and nickel.[45]

But wait, no, that doesn't seem quite right. The Panzós massacre was a consequential event, but the trouble started *much* earlier than that. Maybe it actually started some twelve years earlier:

> [In March of 1966] the G-2 and the Judicial Police raided three houses in Guatemala City, capturing twenty-eight trade unionists and members of the PGT. Those captured included most of the PGT's central committee and peasant federation leader Leonardo Castillo Flores. All subsequently "disappeared" while in the custody of the security force and

> became known in subsequent months by the Guatemalan press as "the 28". This incident was followed by a wave of unexplained "disappearances" and killings in Guatemala City and in the countryside which were reported by the Guatemala City press.[46]

Or maybe we really need to go back another thirty years earlier. Yes, back to the nineteen thirties, back to the totalitarian regime of Jorge Ubico, when words like "trade union," "strike," and "petition" were literally banned from public discourse, and hundreds of thousands of poor Guatemalans found themselves working under conditions of virtual slavery.

Then again, no; actually, we need to go back another sixty years *even before* Ubico, when an earlier president, Justo Rufino Barrios, known as "The Reformer," transferred Guatemala's publicly owned wealth to the rich and influential private coffee growers. Under Barrios, peasants using village land were given six months to pay for their plot or forfeit it. Tens of thousands lost their land through this government scheme, and a majority soon found themselves ensnared in debt bondage.[47]

Was *that* the point when the intolerable oppression of the Mayan majority in Guatemala began?

Realistically, in our search for the roots of revolution, we might as well go all the way back to the beginning of Spanish occupation of the ancestral lands of the Mayan people in the sixteenth century, when the invading *conquistadores* made slaves of the Mayans in their own homeland. *Don* Pedro de Alvarado, that faithful lieutenant of Hernan Cortes and the first Spanish governor of Guatemala, was absolutely ruthless in his dealings with the indigenous peoples that he set out to conquer. Historians judge that his greed drove him to excessive cruelty, and his Spanish contemporaries denounced his extreme brutality during his lifetime.[48]

Thus, facing the historical reality of more than four centuries of violent oppression of Mayans in their own land, the leaders of Guatemala's Committee for Peasant Unity, founded in 1978, certainly had their work cut out for them. The CUC was described by its founder Pablo Ceto as a convergence of the leftist insurgency and the indigenous peoples' movements. Though it was a distinct organization, it had close ties to the Guerrilla Army of the Poor (EGP). It has been described as Guatemala's first national labor organization that was led by indigenous people.[49]

Around this time in late 1979 I was only just beginning to appreciate the complexities of the political landscape in Guatemala, and despite the flier on my doorstep and the presence of an army garrison on the edge of town, the rumor of civil war still seemed a distant concern that scarcely affected my day-to-day activities.

But the pace of change would quicken in the days to come.

* * *

Sharing a house with Eugenio had been an arrangement of convenience that was destined to be short-lived. The differences between us were too great. Though we both had been brought up in conservative households back in the States, Eugenio still carried his conservatism in his very soul, while I had abandoned mine years before even reaching college. Eugenio was a neat and resourceful housekeeper, while I was a slob. There were so many other contrasts that I could relate, but further comparison does not necessarily bode well for the reader's estimation of my personal qualities, so I will dispense with it.

So, it shouldn't have come as a surprise when Eugenio told me one August evening that he had decided to move down the road to Cubulco for the rest of his term of service. "I just have more work in the Cubulco area than I do here in Rabinal," he told me. And that very well may have been true. But in the final analysis, Eugenio was really just fed up with me, especially my failure to share in most of the housekeeping tasks. So he picked up and left Rabinal, and I now had the whole house to myself.

After Eugenio moved to Cubulco I thought I was getting along fine all alone in that little wood-frame house next door to Cipriano the mailman—until I wasn't. No surprise, though, for I really saw the problem coming as soon as he moved out. It came down to simple economics: I now had to cover the entire monthly rent of fifty quetzales all by myself, on a monthly living allowance of around 180 quetzales. I tried to economize, and that worked for a little while—taking more of my meals *en el comedor de la Mari* who charged me only fifty centavos; refraining, when I could, from buying little things to support the *vivero*, like nails or notebooks or chicken wire; drinking less beer, for sure, and not replenishing my supply of Jack Daniels. But in the end I had to look around town for a cheaper place to live.

I found a new place without too much trouble, and at first it seemed perfect. Actually, Juan Pablo found the place for me. A stout, gray, concrete block structure way over on the other side of town, my new home was now much closer to our INAFOR *vivero*, which was convenient, though I was also now just three short blocks from the *destacamento militar*. That humble house, with a brand new roof made of overlapping *duralita* panels that rattled in the rain, comprised one, single U-shaped room wrapping around a small, weedy spot outdoors where the concrete *pila* was located for washing dishes and clothes, and where there was also a rather exposed little cubicle for taking a surreptitious shower. *Sin calentador Goliath*, however, so going forward I'd have to resolve to shower in the afternoon in order to avoid freezing my nuts off. Several steps away, at a tactful distance from the house itself, there was a very crude, malodorous latrine that would be my only facility henceforth, in lieu of the perfectly good flush toilet I had left behind. But that was okay, I could live with all of these small inconveniences just to be able to enjoy the utterly decadent privilege of that one asset that was unquestionably the main "selling point" of the house—*a refrigerator*. Yes, a small refrigerator for my soft drinks, for my beer, for my occasional leftovers which were very scarce indeed because I mostly ate in the *comedores*—and really, it turned out after living there a while, for little else besides that. But at least I had a refrigerator if I needed it, and I never wanted to admit to myself that I didn't really need it.

A new home, a new beginning. In my humble little block house I threw myself into my work with newfound enthusiasm. I was happy to find that the high window facing the street offered a generous amount of natural light that was nicely diffused by the textured privacy glass; this was the perfect spot to put my desk of rough hewn timber and spend Saturday and Sunday mornings tracing lines on mylar with my Rapidograph pen to make new thematic maps based on the topo quads I had obtained in Guat City. My thematic maps, covering features like water resources, altitude zones, and forest stands, would eventually all form part of my ambitious natural resource inventory of the whole three hundred square-kilometer *municipio*. That, at least, was the plan.

Finding enough space in my new house to store all the Food for Work commodities would soon become a bit of a problem, though. When the next CARE truck arrived with a new *remesa*, we had to pile all the bags high—nearly to the roof beams, in fact—all in one leg of my U-shaped room. I had to sleep in a corner of the room facing the street, and I was bothered only occasionally by a busy little mouse scurrying across the cement floor or (this happened only twice that I recall) across my naked torso while lying in bed. Leo and Felix continued to accompany me in the new place, and for the most part they continued to do their job. But mice always showed up for the feast.

Over the ensuing weeks I persuaded myself that I could certainly live with it all—the tight quarters with the food commodities close by, the weedy, treeless yard out back, the malodorous latrine, the partially exposed shower stall that compelled me to time my showers wisely. I could certainly deal with it. After all, I had a *refrigerator*, thank you very much! So life was good.

But then the rains ended in October, and a completely unforeseen problem emerged with the advent of the dry season. I no longer had running water in the tap—or at least I had very, very little of it. The shower head became utterly useless, as the paltry trickle of water coming out of it was impossible to utilize. I now had to get used to bathing myself with *guacales*—hemispherical calabash gourds—that I filled with water scooped right out of the *pila* tank. And in order to keep the *pila* tank more or less full I had to leave the spigot open twenty-four hours a day. For a few hours every morning a thin stream of water would slowly fill the *pila*, and then for the entire rest of the day there was not another drop to be added.

A few times when the water trickling from the spigot was not enough to adequately fill the *pila*, I had to resort to extreme measures: after a day's work down in the *vivero*, where water was plentiful if not exactly constant, I would fill a plastic, five-gallon jerry can with the hose, seal it tightly, and then carry the damned thing on foot back to my house a kilometer up the hill, shifting the weight from one shoulder to the other every few minutes. The slope of the hill heading homewards was fortunately quite shallow. Still, I could not help but recall the daily ordeal of Nicolás Siano hauling water from a spring at the bottom of a deep ravine in Chitucán, and I lightened my load somewhat with an ironic chuckle.

As it turned out, I would not remain in my "perfect" little gray block house for very long. In November I took a Salamateca back to the capital for Thanksgiving; I went to the loud, drunken holiday party at the Peace Corps office where a female volunteer was selling kisses to raise money for something and I there received a most memorable and passionate kiss; I enjoyed a sumptuous Thanksgiving dinner with all the trimmings and fine California Chardonnay at the home of a commercial attaché from the Embassy where another volunteer and I were both randomly assigned to eat; I returned to Rabinal after the holiday and got busy looking for a new place to live, which endeavor once again did not take too long; and then, finally, with a date-certain to move into my new abode come January I got my plane tickets and packed my knapsack and flew home to upstate New York to celebrate Christmas with my family.

I remember only two things from my holiday visit to the States. I remember walking down a concourse in Miami to reach my connecting flight home when I passed by a Hudson's variety store where I saw several sweatshirts and tees prominently displayed out in front, each one bearing a silkscreened portrait of the Ayatollah Khomeini positioned between the crosshairs and concentric circles of a rifle scope. *Take aim at evil.* And I thought to myself, yes, there were surely other things going on in the world in 1979 besides the daily tribulations in a little town called Rabinal. Big, important things, profoundly worrisome things, and yes, some triumphs, too. But nothing seemed as real to me anymore as my daily walks down to the tree nursery, or across town to the main plaza on market day, or over to Pachalum for conservation classes with my *promotores.*

The only other thing I remember from that visit home is my awkward reticence whenever I was asked about life in Guatemala. I should have shared more. After all, that too was part of my mission as a volunteer. I had been called upon to be a witness. And indeed, there were so many things to tell. But where to begin? I couldn't think where to begin. So I said nothing, or very little, about life in Guatemala during my visit home.

I am ashamed to confess that this was one of my great failings. And coming around now, more than forty years later, to tell a story about days long past can hardly make up for it.

CHAPTER 9

A Turning Point

But if any far-off state there be
Dearer than life to immortality,
The hand of the Dark hath hold thereof,
And mist is under the mist above;
So we are sick for life, and cling
On earth to this nameless and shining thing,
For other life is a fountain sealed,
And the deeps below are unrevealed
—And we drift on legends forever.
—Euripides, *Hippolytus*, 191ff

Oxlajuj Q'anil.[50]

"Lord Tecum Uman, I come to you on this day to commemorate your spirit, and to tell you that today my heart is filled with gladness. *Mundo santo*, Lord Tecum Uman, I bring with me wonderful news—but then, you already know it. Eusebia is with child, dear Lord of the Earth, and my good son Evaristo is beside himself with happiness and gratitude for your holy providence. Remember my son always, and help keep him on the right path, for he loves and respects you, and someday, when the time is right and the calling is unmistakable, he too will become an *aj'q'ij*, a good and faithful keeper of the days. Now we are all in a great state of preparation, dear Lord, and I am here today to humbly ask for your blessings, and your guidance."

On a stone altar speckled with many layers of wax drippings, the flames of six small candles danced wildly with every slight movement of the air. The old man knelt on the ground and waited in silence. Several minutes passed as he waited for the lightning in his blood to gather strength. Soft intermittent clucks came from the plastic woven grain sack he had placed on the ground behind him. There on the hilltop, crouched before the altar, he waited. When he felt a gust of wind at his back, he knew it was time. He opened a flask and proceeded to wipe his hands with *aguardiente*. He splashed the alcohol on his face and neck and rubbed it into his skin. After doing this he stored the flask back in his *morral*. He sighed once, hands on his knees, and let his face relax. Then, lifting his chin slightly while casting his eyes down on the charred space between the candles, he spoke more words of prayer.

"*Santa tierra, santo cielo, santa palabra del Popol Vuh*. Sovereign Plumed Serpent, gods of the sea and sky: Your creation was accomplished through sacrifice; may this offering be acceptable in your eyes."

A small eddy of a light, cool breeze swirled around the sacred space where the old man knelt at the altar atop *Cerro Kaj'yup*, and one of the candles was extinguished. He relit the candle and in silence continued the prayer, moving his lips as if to form the words. The life in the grain sack stirred for a moment and calmed down again.

Next he made a small pile of the twigs he had brought with him to the hilltop altar. With a match he lit the end of a stick of resinous *ocote*, and with that stick he carefully lit the pile on four sides. The air was now calm again, and the smoke rose straight up into the pre-dawn sky. The old man stood up and looked to the east. The horizon had brightened, and now he could see the first sliver of sun shrouded in haze. It was time. He turned and reached in the sack, felt his way to the neck, and grasped it firmly. The squawking began. As he pulled it out, the chicken beat its wings frantically, and tiny black and brown feathers flew everywhere. The old man held the bird high above the fire and prayed, then crouched and pressed its head down firmly on the stone slab.

"Commander of the Quiché kingdom, Tecum Uman." The chicken flapped and squawked. "Oh, God of the World … Lady María Tecum ... City of the holy ruins of the Quiché realm … Oh God of the World, Mayor of World, President of World, Judge of World[51]: Hear our prayer, and accept this offering."

Flash of steel. The blade came down swift and hard, and the squawking stopped. The old man placed the machete by his side and held the headless body by its legs so it wouldn't move. Then he pulled a small packet of seeds from his woolen *morral.* Dawn of the new day, *Oxlajuj Q'anil.* The fullness of sun now bathed the altar in a warm yellow glow, though the *pueblo* down below in the valley was still dark.

* * *

As it turned out, two weeks back in upstate New York was more than enough for me. Upon returning to Rabinal I rang in the New Year with another new place to call home—my third dwelling in less than a year. But now at last I felt I had finally arrived. This was the house for me. No fridge, but the three rooms were definitely more spacious than what I had been calling home for the past three months. I regained a patio, too, which I had sorely missed in the previous place. No *calentador* on the shower head, so I'd still have to deal with cold showers in the cool winter months. But, BUT at last I finally had a flush toilet again, which more than made up for it. And the water flowed nicely out of the *pila* spigot the whole morning long, and didn't stop flowing until two or three in the afternoon. Good, reliable indoor plumbing is a blessing that cannot be fully appreciated until you've survived a few months without it. (Never mind that the water coming out of the faucet was still carrying the same lovely protozoans that had been making my life so—well, *interesting* ever since I first arrived in Central America.)

The yard that came with the house was a pretty decent size. There were two lemon trees right by the *pila,* with lemons always ripe for the picking, and a tall chicozapote tree offering not only some pleasant shade, but also an eternal abundance of chicozapotes that I often gave away to neighbors by the bucketload, since I did not care much for the fruit. There was a deep burn pit way out in the corner of the lot, which I'd find useful to get rid of my scarce trash once every couple months. And finally, though I hadn't a vehicle to my name, I actually had a *carport.* A carport with a most interesting graffito emblazoned on its wall (which happened also to be the wall of the adjoining house belonging to my neighbor). It said, simply: CUC.

January was the month of the *feria titular de San Pablo,* and also the first anniversary of my time in Rabinal. Preparations began all around town well before the middle of the month, as they had the year before. The out-of-town vendors all arrived in their battered trucks and pickups, and the carnival rides were set up in the very same corner of the plaza. The men of the *cofradias* (the religious brotherhoods mixing Catholic ritual with ancient Mayan traditions) sat in their darkened, windowless rooms to celebrate their mysterious ceremonies with incense, *aguardiente*, and enigmatic chants in Achí, and then they walked together in solemn processions through the streets of the town.

A Rabinal *cofradía* in solemn procession.

This time around I believe I managed to stay relatively sober throughout the week of festivities. Maybe a buzz now and then, but most of the time I just chilled and delighted in my surroundings. Several friends were coming over from neighboring Peace Corps sites to stay for a night or two: Marcos from San Cristóbal, Carlos from Salamá, and Miguel *de vacas* from San Miguel Chicaj, accompanied by his pretty girlfriend, Silvia, *la cobanera*. I had to try and make sure each of them would have a reasonably comfortable sleeping spot in the house, and in the end that simply meant having them spread their blankets and sleeping bags across *medio-quintal* bags of bulgur and flour from CARE. We worked it out.

The market in the plaza was busy every single day leading up to the big social event that was scheduled to take place in the grand ballroom of the *municipalidad* on the 25th. Vendors came rolling into town from far and wide, just as they had done the year before, and they all set up their sheets and tarpaulins around the perimeter of the plaza to sell their blankets and hats and fabrics and assorted wares from other parts of the country. The locals set up shop there, too, selling their traditional products like the brightly colored calabash gourds called *jícaras,* other gourds called *guacales* that were hemispherical with primitive, homespun patterns and pictures etched into a matte black surface. There were also plenty of examples of the traditional Rabinal pottery sitting on makeshift shelves or laid out on tarps on the ground, each piece with its contemporary rendering of ancient Mayan warrior heroes depicted in primary colors against an ochre background. I bought some of this pottery on several occasions, even though these otherwise attractive pieces were invariably inscribed with homely mottos such as *DIOS BENDIGA ESTE HOGAR,* or simply *RECUERDO DE RABINAL.*

The Rabinal market, ca. 1973. (Photos courtesy of Lewis Johnson.)

The official program of the *feria* began on Thursday morning with a solemn procession carrying the image of San Sebastián—a youthful, half naked figure seemingly reaching for the stars above—from the church on the plaza to the lodging of the *cofradia* a few blocks away. That evening a group of performers wearing traditional costumes and masks for the occasion arrived at the doorstep of the *Ishoc Ajau*, the young woman upon whom was bestowed the title of Queen of the Mayas for that year. They would then escort her over to the *salon municipal* for her coronation.

In the days that followed there were more religious processions, a crowning of the Queen of the *Feria,* then army parachutists falling from the sky over the soccer field, some spirited soccer matches, a noisy motocross rally, and speeches by the mayor and the governor; cattle shows and equestrian parades, bicycle races for the children, a crowning of the Queen of Sports, a marathon, a concert in the kiosk at the park performed by the army band from the Cobán military base, and of course the big social dance on Friday the 25th.

Nowadays every twenty-fifth of January in Rabinal there is also a performance of the Mayan drama known as the *Rabinal Achí*, a story of war and sacrifice that was originally performed by the Rabinaleb' people during the pre-Columbian decades of the fifteenth century. The *Rabinal Achí* is the earliest example of dramatic performance among the indigenous peoples of the Americas. In 2005 it was declared one of the Masterpieces of the Oral and Intangible Heritage of Humanity by UNESCO.

With slow, heavily symbolic choreography that has been likened to Japanese Noh theater, the *Rabinal Achí* is presented by a group of characters who appear within a sacred space in the plaza representing the Maya villages, including Kaj'yup, which was the regional capital of the Rabinaleb' in the fourteenth century. The narrative of the play centers on a conflict between two political powers in the region: the two princes, Rabinal Achí and K'iche Achí. The prince K'iche' Achí is captured and put on trial for attempting to steal Rabinaleb' children, a grave violation of Maya law.[52] (And, as far as that goes, anybody else's law, I suppose.) Other characters include the king of the Rabinaleb' Job'Toj, and his servant, Achij Mun; also Ixoq Mun (who has both male and female traits), the Green-Feathered Mother, Uchuch Q'uq' and Uchuch Raxon, and thirteen eagles and thirteen jaguars who represent the warriors of the fortress of Kaj'yup.

As it happened, I never got to see the *Rabinal Achí*, because the Mayan drama was quite arbitrarily suppressed during the years when I lived in the very town of its birth. At this distant remove it is hard for me to fathom how or why this ancient play with its highly ritualized storyline might have been suppressed, nor can I even imagine who might have been the enforcer of the suppression. Did the government (or, more preposterous yet, maybe the local *destacamento militar* all on its own) simply prohibit the performance, thinking perhaps that the performers might transmit, *sub rosa*, some revolutionary marching orders in the Mayan dialect that only the locals would understand?

How do you say *¡Viva la revolución!* in Achí?

The reason behind the absence of the *Rabinal Achí* during my time in Rabinal was impenetrably obscure. All I know is it was never performed, not even once, during my three years there, nor would it be performed again for several years afterwards.

* * *

But the Friday night dance was definitely *not* suppressed, and in fact it was not to be missed, as it was the biggest social event of the year. I got there early that evening and I bought myself a Gallo beer at the cash bar in the *salón municipal*. It was the end of the month and cash was tight, so I tried to sip my beer slowly as I wandered around the perimeter of the *salón* from one group of friends and acquaintances to another. Most people of course were out on the floor dancing to the vibrant tones of the *marimba orquesta*, a group that was hired from out of town and was really quite good.

I sat and talked for a while with our town photographer Augusto Jerónimo and his wife Carmen. Then at one point Augusto put his hand on my shoulder and, with enthusiasm that belied a vaguely ulterior sense of purpose, pointed out *Don* Beto Mendoza and his family who were sitting at another table nearby. "*Don* Beto has a very pretty daughter," he said to me. "You should go over and meet her!" Maybe it wasn't an ulterior purpose after all, but rather a quite clear one. At any rate, not being one to dismiss the advice of a friend and neighbor, I picked up my beer and walked over to the Mendoza table to check out what I'd been missing.

I was greeted by *don* Beto himself, the guy who drove the *camioneta* named *Dulcinea* between Rabinal and Salamá every day. I'd been on his bus several times, though he always competed with the *Salamatecas*. *Don* Beto didn't waste any time introducing me to his daughter Elizabeth, a pretty *señorita* with long brown hair who sat at the table in her crisp, white dress.

"Mucho gusto!"

"El gusto es mío."

And with those succinct greetings began my first dalliance with *la guatemalidad femenina*. I asked her to dance. Every *señorita* can dance, of course, and me, I followed along and faked it as best I could. (I'm sure this was the first defect she found in me.) We weren't on the dance floor for three minutes when "la Lisa" spoke to me in passable English. She was studying, she told me, at the Guatemalan-American Institute in Guate, where everyone learned English as a required part of the curriculum. I was impressed. By her English, by her slender figure, by her angelic aura in that dress as white as virgin snow.

We danced a couple more turns, and when we got back to the Mendoza table I found I had lost track of my beer, so I went to get another. I offered to get her one, too, but she politely declined. Lisa was in Rabinal only for the weekend, as she had to be back for classes on Monday. She lived with her mother in Guate, while her *papito* held down the fort in Rabinal driving the bus every day. I didn't have access to a telephone in Rabinal, and in retrospect that was probably a good thing. Nevertheless, we promised to keep in touch. And thus began an epistolary relationship that lasted for several months. Lisa was only seventeen.

Next day the girl in the dress as white as virgin snow got on the bus and returned to Guate, and we exchanged letters over the next several months.

* * *

During the entire week of the *feria*, I only had to pass by the *destacamento militar* once. That was when I was on my way, along with my gringo guests, to go watch the motocross race out in the *campo*. The *destacamento* itself never changed: a triangular parcel of half an hectare, with a featureless barracks building in the middle that housed maybe thirty to forty soldiers, along with an adjacent *comandancia*. Out on one corner of the triangle by the main road there was a sentry post piled high with sandbags, with a makeshift sunshade above it made of leaves and palm blades. There was always a soldier there, always alone on his watch, huddled behind a mounted machine gun. Passing by the *destacamento* made you forget there was a buoyant, magical *feria* going on elsewhere in town. *This* was reality, it said, so screw the magic, sober up, and get used to it.

But with so much going on in town it was easy to ignore reality at least for this one week. The *destacamento*, after all, was just one little spot on the edge of town, and the pairs of soldiers that continued to patrol the streets every day with their Galils slung low couldn't disturb our beautiful illusion. The *feria* events were all and everything, at least for this week, and they were perfectly timed out hour by hour in the official program of the *Feria Titular de San Pablo*. I still have the tattered, fading sheets of the program sitting here on my desk. In its concluding pages the pamphlet extends special recognition and grateful appreciation to a number of dignitaries, all of whom did little or nothing for Rabinal. Ever. Among the names recognized there is the country's Government Minister, one *Licenciado* Donaldo Alvarez Ruíz, who only a few days after Rabinal's *feria* would be responsible for murder and crimes against humanity in connection with the government's siege of the Spanish Embassy. (This, in addition to the dozens of other assassinations and disappearances he had authorized during his time in office.) Alvarez Ruíz was sacked a year later in the wake of the 1982 *coup d'etat*, and for years he was pursued earnestly by Guatemalan and international authorities. It is said that for a while he lived in Miami where he sold used cars. He later moved to Mexico and was nationalized there. When Guatemalan activists finally tracked him down, the Mexican government let him slip away.[53] He was never to be found again. If he's still alive, he would be more than ninety years old now.

> *Pues si, GRACIAS, licenciado, por sus buenos oficios—¡y ahora coma mierda y vete a la chingada, vos hijo de la gran puta! ¡Cerote matón—chinga tu madre!*[54]

The *feria* program also thoughtfully extends appreciation to one *Coronel* Guillermo Arturo de la Cruz Gelpke, the commander of the *Zona Militar 21* in Cobán, who a few years later would become a vice-minister of defense, and after that a *diputado* representing the very same department of Cobán (just north of Rabinal), and who years later would be questioned by an intrepid reporter about the mass grave that had been found on the army base under his command.

> [Carolina Gamazo]: I wanted to ask you about the bones found in the Cobán military base.
> [Col. de la Cruz]: They are from the cemetery of a village that is there within the area.
> [Gamazo]: And how is it possible that they had their hands tied, tourniquets, ropes around their necks?
> [de la Cruz]: Ahhh. I wasn't on top of that really because I got pretty far away from it. No, I didn't know.
> [Gamazo]: They found a grave with the remains of women and children from Rabinal.

[de la Cruz]: I didn't know. No...no. [55]

Pués sí, entonces, MUCHAS GRACIAS, coronel, por sus buenos oficios en pro de nuestra feria (al fin no hiciste ni cacho por nosotros)—¡y ahora coma mierda vos también, y véte a la chingada, vos hijo de la gran puta! ¡Cerote MATÓN—chinga tu madre!

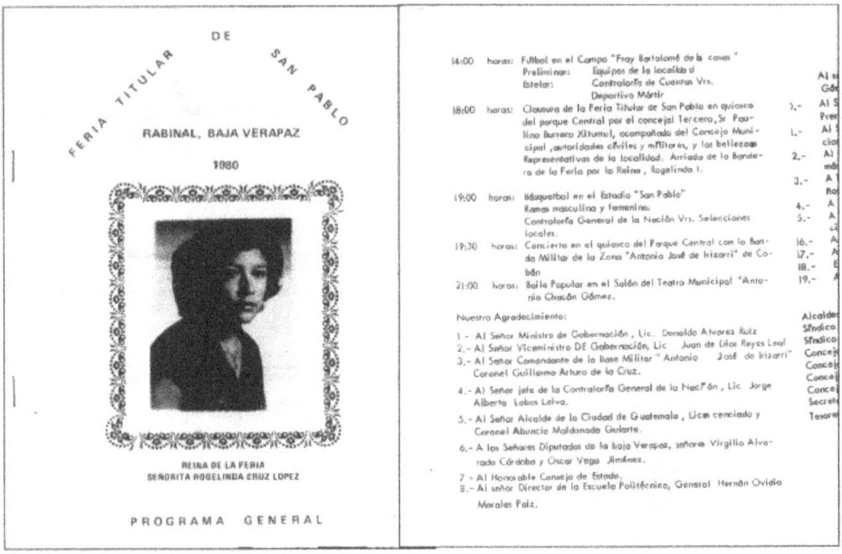
FERIA TITULAR DE SAN PABLO
RABINAL, BAJA VERAPAZ
1980
REINA DE LA FERIA
SEÑORITA ROGELINDA CRUZ LOPEZ
PROGRAMA GENERAL

14:00 horas: Fútbol en el Campo "Fray Bartolomé de las casas"
Preliminar: Equipos de la localidad
Estelar: Contraloría de Cuentas Vrs. Deportivo Mártir

18:00 horas: Clausura de la Feria Titular de San Pablo en quiosco del parque Central por el concejal Tercero, Sr. Paulino Barrera Xitumul, acompañado del Concejo Municipal, autoridades civiles y militares, y las bellezas Representativas de la localidad. Arriada de la Bandera de la Feria por la Reina, Rogelinda I.

19:00 horas: Básquetbol en el Estadio "San Pablo" Ramas masculina y femenina: Contraloría General de la Nación Vrs. Selecciones locales.

19:30 horas: Concierto en el quiosco del Parque Central con la Banda Militar de la Zona "Antonio José de Irisarri" de Cobán

21:00 horas: Baile Popular en el Salón del Teatro Municipal "Antonio Chacón Gómez.

Nuestro Agradecimiento:

1.- Al Señor Ministro de Gobernación, Lic. Donaldo Alvarez Ruiz
2.- Al Señor Viceministro DE Gobernación, Lic Juan de Dios Reyes Leal
3.- Al Señor Comandante de la Base Militar "Antonio José de Irisarri" Coronel Guillermo Arturo de la Cruz.
4.- Al Señor jefe de la Contraloría General de la Nación, Lic. Jorge Alberto Lobos Leiva.
5.- Al Señor Alcalde de la Ciudad de Guatemala, Licenciado y Coronel Abuncio Maldonado Gularte.
6.- A los Señores Diputados de la baja Verapaz, señores Virgilio Alvarado Córdoba y Oscar Vega Jiménez.
7.- Al Honorable Consejo de Estado.
8.- Al señor Director de la Escuela Politécnica, General Hernán Ovidio Morales Paiz.

Festival program, Feria Titular de San Pablo Rabinal, 1980: Cover and acknowledgement pages.

But of course the truth is I knew none of these things while I sat in my hammock in Rabinal in 1980 holding that *programa de la feria* in my hands. Alvarez Ruíz was to me just another government minister; the colonel, just another army officer. In fact, nobody in Rabinal could have known at the time the full scope and scale of the horror that these men had already perpetrated, or were about to perpetrate. People maybe had heard things here and there, but nobody knew much.

And, anyway, it was always the better part of prudence to pay fawning obeisance to those who had the guns. It was a simple matter of survival.

* * *

It was the first of February. By now all the dances, the drinking, the pageantry and the alcohol-fortified frivolity that had distracted us for days had faded into the past like a small child's balloon that slips away and drifts on the wind to distant realms. Life was back to normal.

So, early in the morning on the first day of February 1980 I was on my usual twenty-minute walk down to our tree nursery when, passing through the central plaza, I thought I'd pick up a newspaper from the same urchin we met earlier, who squatted by the same concrete bench in the park now, just waiting for customers. To be honest, I wasn't in the habit of buying the paper every single day that it could be had (and it couldn't be had every day in Rabinal), so the news I was accustomed to receiving was sparse at best. My usual habit was to glance at the headline on page one and then stuff the paper in my *morral*, hoping to read the stories in greater detail later. But occasionally I may have actually folded and stuffed the paper in my *morral* without scarcely looking at it. I don't know whether I actually saw the headline that morning, or whether perhaps I saw it later in the evening.

For now, let's call those Alternative Takes One and Two. But then there's Alternative Take Number Three: Maybe I walked through Rabinal's plaza that Friday morning, February 1, on my way to the tree nursery, but I didn't stop to buy any newspaper at all. Either the *patojo* José was not there in the park when I passed through, or maybe he was but I was perhaps too preoccupied with other things on my mind to bother with the day's news. In either case, though I had no newspaper I may have heard the news that night listening to VOA on my shortwave. Unless, that is, I never even turned my radio on that night, in which case I would have finished the day and gone to sleep that night entirely oblivious to what had happened. Technically, now we're talking two additional Alternative Takes here, Numbers Three-A and Three-B, with additional sub-permutations.

The truth is that when it comes to how I learned about the horror of January 31, I don't know what the truth is. I just don't remember. But the event itself, apart from my learning about it, is an objective fact that cannot be denied. Though the powerful and the blameworthy will always put their own spin on it.

Government ministers and president Lucas himself called the peaceful protesters terrorists, they called them psychopaths. The press, while neither confirming nor explicating these epithets, nevertheless gave them prominent play on page one.

Here, then, is a latter-day account[56] that is a good deal more fine-grained, now with the benefit of hindsight and subsequent investigation:

> A group of K'iche' and Ixil peasant farmers marched to Guatemala City to protest the kidnapping and murder of peasants in Uspantán, in Quiché department, by elements of the Guatemalan army. The peasants were organized, guided and joined by members of the *Comité de Unidad Campesina (CUC)*, a group loosely associated with the *Ejército Guerrillero de los Pobres* (EGP). The protesters were denied a hearing in Congress and their legal adviser had been assassinated. On January 28, they briefly took over two radio stations.
>
> Late in the morning on January 31, 1980, the peasants, joined by workers and students, entered the Spanish Embassy in Guatemala City. According to police reports, some of the demonstrators were armed with machetes, pistols and Molotov cocktails.
>
> Spain was considered sympathetic to the indigenous cause, especially after the Guatemalan army came to be suspected of the murder of Spanish priests in the indigenous regions. Arriving at the embassy, the protesters announced that they had come to peacefully occupy the building and that they would hold a press conference at noon. They presented the ambassador with a letter that read in part, "We ... direct ourselves to you because we know you are honorable people who will tell the truth about the criminal repression suffered by the peasants of Guatemala."

President Fernando Romeo Lucas García, police chief Germán Chupina Barahona, and Minister of the Interior Donaldo Álvarez Ruiz (... ah yes, *I remember,* the man to whom we all said thank you so much for your help with our *feria titular*) met in the National Palace to determine a course of action. Despite pleas by the Spanish ambassador to negotiate, the decision was taken to forcibly expel the group occupying the embassy. Shortly before noon, before the protesters could air their grievances, some 300 armed agents of the government surrounded the building and cut the electricity, water and telephone lines. SWAT police proceeded to occupy the first and third floors of the building over the shouts of the ambassador that they were violating international law in doing so. The peasants barricaded themselves, along with the captive embassy staff and the visiting Guatemalan officials, in the ambassador's office on the second floor.

An order was given to charge the ambassador's office. Police breached the office door and introduced a substance, most likely white phosphorus, which together with the Molotov cocktails ignited a fire. (Some academics and critics, including David Stoll and Jorge Palmieri, contend that it was the Molotov cocktails alone that started the blaze.) Exactly how the fire started and who is responsible for it has been the subject of considerable controversy. As fire consumed the second floor and the demonstrators and captive staff of the embassy were *burned alive*, police refused pleas from bystanders to allow firefighters to combat the blaze. Though firefighters were there at the ready. A total of 37 people died in the fire, including former vice president Eduardo Cáceres, former Minister of Foreign Affairs Adolfo Molina Orantes and activist Vicente Menchú, father of Rigoberta Menchú, a future politician and Nobel Peace Prize winner. Spanish Consul Jaime Ruiz del Árbol also died in the fire, along with other Spanish citizens employed by the embassy. And more than thirty poor *campesinos* who had walked all the way from El Quiché department.

Spain's Ambassador Cajal y López survived by escaping through a window. The only other survivor, demonstrator Gregorio Yujá Xona, suffered third-degree burns. Both were sent to Herrera Llerandi Hospital for treatment.

On February 1, at 7:30 a.m., the police guard at Herrera Llerandi Hospital was withdrawn. Shortly thereafter a band of twenty armed men masked with bandanas, widely believed to be plainclothes members of the Judicial Police, entered the hospital and kidnapped Gregorio Yuja Xona. He was taken to an unknown location, tortured, and shot dead. His body was dumped on the campus of the University of San Carlos. Around his neck was a placard with a note that read "Brought to Justice for Being a Terrorist" and "The Ambassador will be next." Ambassador Cajal y López escaped the hospital with the assistance of other members of the diplomatic corps and eventually fled the country.

A commemorative plaque located near the site where one of the last Mayan peasants who escaped the Spanish Embassy occupation was brutally murdered. (Source: *Prensa Comunitaria*, on their Facebook page.)

The burning of the Spanish Embassy in Guatemala City became the signal event that changed the course of the popular struggle for liberation. The government certainly could have *negotiated* a solution—not only a solution to the Spanish Embassy occupation but to the whole, painful civil war that had already left thousands dead or disappeared. But instead the government had charged inside with guns blazing and white phosphorus burning through the hallways of the embassy, and in the end thirty-seven were dead, including poor *campesinos* as well as embassy officials.

And after this, nothing would ever be the same again.

* * *

It was now February 1980, just a couple weeks past the *feria de San Pablo*, when I received another CUC flier at my house. One morning it was just laying there on the concrete inside the carport, ironically (or should I say fittingly?) right below the CUC graffito on my wall.

> *THE MURDEROUS LUCAS REGIME HAS BURNED OUR COMRADES ALIVE!*

OUR HEROES WHO HAVE BEEN MASSACRED SHALL LIVE ON IN OUR COMBATIVE STRUGGLES!

The densely formatted, two-page flier recounts in detail the whole Spanish Embassy siege as well as other atrocities in the Quiché department that had led up to it. There was another dig at the National Forestry Institute, but this time it was just a brief, glancing blow. The main demand expressed in the flier was to secure fair compensation for the agricultural workers who picked cotton and cut sugar cane on the expansive farms that belonged to the rich on the south coast. Most of those workers came from small towns all over the Western Highlands, including Rabinal. All they were demanding was five miserable quetzales for every *ton* of sugarcane and for every hundred-pound bale of cotton.

I suppose in order to get a good sense of the humility behind that earnest demand, I would have had to try and do the job myself once.

CHAPTER 10

Río Negro

After the Spanish Embassy siege, it became harder and harder to look at the newspaper. My Spanish was getting better, but with every passing day the news was getting worse. The press in Guatemala had a penchant for gore and needlessly grizzly details which, I believe, may have had the perverse effect of anaesthetizing the public from the political import of what they were seeing. Most of the newspapers would display quite prominently their most recent scenes of explicit brutality that were discovered in the countryside, or on the streets of the capital. A human skull embedded in a random pile of rubbish was an older murder only lately discovered; a severed arm or leg still wearing a scrap of dirty clothing was a fresh one. The photographs in the newspaper every day were ghastly and grisly to look at, yet hard to look away from.

It was bad enough having to flip through pages of gore in order to get to the news. But then there was this to contend with as well: the enigmatic newspaper copy that showed no blood, no protruding bones, no graphics of any kind. It was the text itself that was so haunting, and it haunted me because of what it left to the imagination. And our imagination is often far more unsettling than what we see before our eyes.

I've kept one such clipping, a tiny scrap of newsprint that I suppose most people would have lost by now, but somehow I've hung on to it for all these years. It roughly translates as:

PURE BLOOD

Owner has received confusing communications about the situation of this copy [or issue].

They ask people who know their whereabouts to communicate to clarify the negotiation in the interest

of a quick and substantial favorable resolution.
We guarantee complete seriousness.
Go directly to Club Hipico Tamaulipas, Postal Box. 00017, Guatemala City.

PURA SANGRE

Propietario ha recibido comunicaciones confusas sobre la situación de este ejemplar.
Solicitan a personas que conozcan su paradero, que se comuniquen para clarificar la negociación en el interés de una rápida y sustancial resolución favorable.
Garantizamos completa seriedad.
Dirigirse directamente a **Club Hípico Tamaulipas**, Apto. Postal **00017**, Ciudad Guatemala.

Is this about a horse that has disappeared? Or a person? Did the "owner" place this classified? Or was it actually a dear relative? Perhaps an anguished father, or mother. Who are "they"? And why were the last communications "about the situation of this copy" so confusing? Were the captors maybe a little incompetent? Or were they merely being fickle in their demands?

The "negotiation of a quick and substantial favorable solution" certainly seems clear enough: the "owner" is definitely ready and willing to pay up. *Seriously*, he says.

But then the enigma is compounded further by the final instruction, which on the face of it appears consistent with the equestrian theme. The post office box looks legit, but to the extent that I could investigate this matter it appears there never was any equestrian club in Tamaulipas, nor is there any Tamaulipas in Guatemala. It's in northern Mexico.

I've only looked at this clipping a handful of times over the past forty years, but every time I have, I've found myself on the verge of madness trying to imagine the details of the reality behind the cryptic message. Parents ready to pay a handsome sum for the freedom of their beloved son. A son, I imagined, because in the captors' calculus he would be worth more. And *los tatas* apparently have the money. And now their anguish is only made worse by the "confusing communications" they have received. And the captors? Well, if it was military intelligence or the White Hand, then hell, they didn't need the money. They would have simply killed the poor bastard, end of negotiation. Only the insurgency would have demanded a ransom, because they always needed the cash to finance their cause.[57]

There were acts of terror on both sides, but even the worst that was perpetrated by the insurgency paled in comparison to the genocide perpetrated by the state and its private actors like the White Hand.[58]

* * *

I was once told the story that in Rio Negro, an *aldea* located at the northernmost extreme of Rabinal *municipio*, the people lived off the abundance of the namesake river (also known as Rio Chixoy), *and the men there fished with bombs.* Either from a boat or from the banks of the river, they would launch crude explosive devices into the water to stun the fish. Then they simply gathered them up from the water's surface. That's what I was once told. The people of Rio Negro lived in a fertile river valley, and by all accounts life there was—well, for many years, at least bearable.

I was invited once or twice by Rabinal's agricultural extensionists from DIGESA to make a trip out to Rio Negro. It would have been a hike of several hours over the mountains north of the *pueblo*, though I was told there was an easier route by first driving to *aldea* Xococ, and then hiking to Rio Negro from there, thus avoiding most of the steep mountain climbs. (There were, actually, some even more accessible routes to get there, but not from my starting point in Rabinal *pueblo*.) At any rate, I declined the invitation because I had decided I simply had other plans or obligations at the moment. I truly regret missing the opportunity to go there. It is one of my biggest regrets from my whole time in Rabinal. I wish I could have gotten to know the people who lived on their own and fished with bombs.

My knowledge of what happened in Rio Negro months later came only from the stories I heard in town, from a few, sketchy articles in the *Prensa Libre*, and from the telling evidence I saw in Rabinal itself. Many years later, in the age of the Internet, I learned quite a bit more.

INDE, the National Electrification Institute, had been planning for several years to build a hydroelectric dam on the Rio Chixoy. By the time I came to Rabinal this project was well underway, and the inhabitants of Rio Negro were advised they would be relocated, since their *aldea* would soon be flooded. Some will recognize this as a story we've heard before—the Three Gorges dam displacing millions along the Yangtze in China; the Kinzua Dam between Pennsylvania and New York that displaced several hundred Iroquois of the Seneca Nation in the 1950s. Facing the power of capital and the illusion of a 'manifest destiny,' indigenous communities that stand in the way simply because they *exist* never seem to survive. Add guns and tyrants to the mix, and the possibility of a just outcome is even more remote.

The people of Rio Negro naturally resisted the relocation imperative. I watched as a new *colonia* was being erected not far from our *vivero forestal*, but it filled only very slowly with a few displaced families from Rio Negro. Most of the units remained empty. The government named the new settlement *aldea* Pacúx, a brand new place to live just outside town, easy walking distance to the central market. But still they did not come. After all, the people of Rio Negro were accustomed to living in a fertile river valley, living off the abundance of the river, and the government was now proposing to relocate them to an arid settlement of little boxes with no river and no land to farm.

The first evidence of trouble in Rio Negro that I saw was in 1980 or early '81. I saw at least a couple army helicopters flying up north in that direction, and an army ambulance truck—something never seen before in Rabinal—was parked in front of the *municipalidad*. I heard later that they were trying to persuade the *aldeanos* to move out, but violence had inevitably ensued. Who knows how it really played out. My only news source was the "*teléfono de bejuco*"—rumors.

I suppose that was "Phase 1" of the Rio Negro massacre. Some *aldeanos* were killed—I never knew how many—and there may have been some army fatalities as well. There wasn't much more news about Rio Negro through the rest of my stay in Rabinal, and God knows there was enough trouble going on elsewhere in the *municipio* to divert our attention. "Phase 2" of the Rio Negro massacre actually happened almost a year later. Though I was no longer there when it happened, I have a sort of indirect yet unforgettable connection to it. But this requires a digression.

You see, over the course of two years or so I had worked a lot with the farmers of Xococ, doing soil conservation courses there, planting trees, even starting a small "satellite" tree nursery near the school in the village. Among the many people I got to know in that aldea was one Fermin Lajuj Xitumul, a *listo* (meaning capable) fellow who had a farm plot near the Xococ schoolhouse. He was also, at times, unbearably obsequious. He attended my short courses, did some contour ditches on his plot, planted some trees, and received more than a couple *quintales* of Food for Work for his effort. He'd come to my house for his FFW rations, and we'd talk for a while, his voice ever solicitous and fawning. Humility is one thing, but this habit of his really stuck in my craw. Still, he seemed to be accomplishing good things on his farm plot, he appeared to be receptive to new ideas, and he was helping me accomplish *my* objectives.

Now, during my third year in Rabinal the *Patrullas de Autodefensa Civil* became quite well organized and active under the direction of the regular army. Fermin Lajuj and others from Xococ formed one of the biggest PACs in the countryside. In March, 1982 members of the Xococ PAC under army guidance hiked over to Rio Negro and slaughtered 177 of the *aldeanos* who still remained there. A few escaped the slaughter, including one very young girl by the name of Dominga, who I later learned was spirited out of the country by Catholic nuns and, last I heard maybe 20 years ago, was all grown up and married to an American guy in Iowa.[59]

I also learned much later that, following the 1996 Peace Accords, one Fermin Lajuj Xitumul, along with two other farmers from Xococ, were tried and convicted and sentenced to death for their leadership roles in the Rio Negro massacre. I do not know whether the sentence was actually carried out or later commuted. Or whether Fermin perhaps died in custody while waiting for it.

While my connection to the incident in Rio Negro is tenuous at best, just the thought that I had conversed with, worked with, and *helped* someone who later became a mass murderer still haunts me.

On a visit to Rabinal in 1998 I photographed the monument pictured below, which names the 177 victims of the Rio Negro massacre.

* * *

The exotic charm, the ineffable magic, and certainly the pathos of a town like Rabinal should have touched the sensibilities of anyone endowed with a modicum of empathy and curiosity, and a healthy sense of wonder. I've always believed I possessed those qualities, and it is true that in the end Rabinal affected me more deeply than any place I have ever been. Still, there were times during my first two years in Rabinal when I found myself wallowing in the doldrums of self-absorption and lethargy. I cannot adequately explain the causes of these occasional crises, but crises indeed they were. Each episode just seemed to paralyze my will and deepen my ambient level of melancholy.

The name for it is *acedia*—Dante's sin. Helplessness in the face of necessity. Mental torpor replacing positive action. The soul between doubt and faith. This is one of the hardest confessions to make, for all those wasted hours dwelling on my own inadequacy only served to expose my weakness for a species of laziness that justifies itself by masquerading as thoughtful introspection. Ah yes, *introspection*—an admirable quality, no? But at times I was just introspecting myself to the point of downright sloth. And sometimes the downward spiral reached a pathetic nadir that lasted for days on end.

It was hard to climb out of that deep hole of hopelessness and self-hate. It could take days. Days that were simply wasted time. Days that I could have spent doing, and learning, and loving.

The seasonal changes in the weather had a lot to do with it. Those days in April and early May were hot as hell in Rabinal, and for someone like me from the northern latitudes, the heat could become immobilizing. The thousands of cicadas droning on all day in the trees in the distance only made the heat feel hotter.

Still, there was no denying it: the acedia was really deep inside me, quite apart from any environmental factors. It was a product of my reading. (So, stop reading?) It was a product of my life experience. (Though it wasn't, I think, a product of my upbringing.) Letters between me and my friend Ed back in Ithaca had a lot to do with it, too. My letters to Ed just exuded acedia and aimless introspection on every page, and the few drafts that I've kept I now find all but unreadable.

Hell, my very *name* had something to do with it. I began reflecting on this a lot. *Christian Nill*. Christian, the impossible ideal. *¡Don Cristo!* A flawed Christian, at best, fished out of a black well of nothingness. Nill. *Señor Nada*. I am nothing.

I can do. Nothing.

I know. Nothing.

Yes, I was quite capable of wallowing for a long time in this kind of self-loathing. But my damnable spells of acedia had their objective sources as well. In moments of sober reflection on outcomes I was often led to a sense of despair. Face the facts: an inexorably growing population struggling to survive with a finite resource base in this country. Under these circumstances, could we ever recover the forest in a million years? Can't grow more land. And people can't eat trees.

As volunteers we were all doing our level best to meet the demands of our job description, and yet at times there seemed to be an undercurrent of growing futility in all our efforts. Try as I might to put on the face of the determined professional, this conclusion seemed all but inescapable. As a student of natural resources I had learned about the pioneering work of Raphael Zon, a Russian émigré who, as a researcher with the U.S. Forest Service, came to be known as "the dean of all foresters of America." Zon had spent years documenting macro trends of forest growth and forest depletion not only in the United States but across the entire world. He believed, and his meticulously collected data showed, that the reduction in forest area would simply continue as world population increased (particularly in the tropics) and required more land for agriculture.[60]

As the tropical areas of Latin America developed economically (as they surely would), their forests would be exploited 'just as wastefully as have forests in all other regions under similar circumstances.' And the consumption of wood clearly would rise commensurately with a rise in standards of living. Half a century before my own foray into tropical reforestation efforts, Zon and his fellow researchers at the Forest Service already knew that forest destruction would reach catastrophic proportions in Central America and Brazil, and it was mainly due to fuelwood harvesting, as well as the pervasive patterns and practices of shifting agriculture.[61] In the face of these macro trends, everything we were doing to try and reforest Guatemala seemed like a drop in the bucket. Possibly even misguided.

And some of our soil conservation efforts would be called into question as well (though this came later). Contour cropping to control soil erosion was all fine and dandy, but when it came to terracing one had to ask oneself: *conservation at what cost?* Terraces require a huge amount of effort to construct, and they invariably result in a reduction of tillable land. They are unlikely in almost all cases to be a profitable investment for the small farmer, unless he can be persuaded to switch from his traditional maize and beans to a more lucrative cash crop.[62] But the farmers of Baja Verapaz would rarely if ever be persuaded to abandon their traditional crops of maize and black beans. And our bribes of "food for work" to incentivize the construction of terraces would never change that. Not over the long term, which is the only term that matters.

These thoughts roiled in my brain and became all but completely paralyzing in their effect. My acedia always released me in the end, but it could sometimes take days for me to snap out of it. These interludes of mental torpor and anguish over outcomes were mostly confined to my second year in Rabinal, and by the third year I had a different outlook, thanks to new experiences both celebratory and amorous. And the darker times that awaited me just around the bend would also serve to shake me out of my navel-gazing idleness.

I regret that it took some tragedy to finally wake me up.

CHAPTER 11

A Man Called Evaristo

Personal battles aside, things started looking up during the first part of 1980. Back at the tree nursery, I was finding that my faith in Juan Pablo's carpentry skills had not been misplaced. In the beginning of the year we had decided we needed a bigger bodega, and before the rains arrived in June we had one. In the end, all I had to do was supply him with the tools and the materials, along with a few suggestions as to the dimensions we should aim for. I told him, among other things, to make sure and give the building enough height so a six-foot-three gringo wouldn't have to crouch inside. Juan Pablo replied with a wry smile that he hoped he had enough materials to comply with my request; if not, then the lone six-foot-three gringo in town would have to buy the extra lumber himself somewhere.

I suggested floor dimensions of roughly eight by twelve feet, and Juan Pablo delivered on that as well. Besides needing enough room to store all our tools and supplies in there, I wanted to make sure we'd have some space for a decent-sized work table. My aim was to get Juan Pablo more involved later on with the reporting and paperwork tasks involved with the tree nursery. Soon that would include, as well, keeping a rudimentary accounting system so we could track the use of income from our fruit tree sales. I'm no accountant, never was, but I figured hell, it can't be rocket science. And I learned a thing or two along the way.

While Juan Pablo and his men were banging away with their hammers nailing up the timber sidings that would form the walls of the new bodega, I was standing in the middle of the *vivero* with clinometer in hand, and the redoubtable Luciano who could do almost anything I asked of him was down below holding a bar so I could measure the slope we were on. The whole *vivero* was on a steep slope, which is why my predecessor Don had built these beautiful terraces for all the nursery seedlings. Now we were planning a new irrigation system that would pull water from the stream down below. We simply had to do this, we really had no choice, because the people from the municipal water network *and* the mayor's people as well had told us we were using far too much water, and they would cut us off if we didn't find another source of supply. We had already received from CARE a small, three-horse gasoline pump for the job, and all we needed now was a good, accurate estimate of the vertical distance down to the stream so that I could order the right diameter and length of PVC pipe. We had three big steel drums all ready for storage of the *vital líquido*, the "vital liquid," as they called it.

It took Juan Pablo a month or so to finish the bodega. He could have done it more quickly, but we always seemed to be needing more of something—more nails, more timber sidings, a pair of hinges for the door—and sometimes it took time to replenish our materials. But when it was finally finished we had a beautiful new bodega—as beautiful as a rectangular shed made of rustic timber sidings with tree bark still hanging off the sides could be. We moved in all the stuff that we had up until now stored in our tiny closet of a shed: the scads of black poly bags for our seedlings, the shovels, the picks, the hoes, the garden hose, the brand new pump we got, and of course all the chemicals, too. The plastic bags of Mirex and Agallol and Cupravit; the steel canisters of Dipterex and Volaton, and the bags of fertilizer. Juan Pablo and I were pleased with the progress we had achieved in the first few months of the year, and now we were just hoping for some good rains so we could start outplanting all those seedlings.

Meanwhile there was much work to do in the field as well. My efforts to promote soil conservation projects out towards Xococ and Patixlán accelerated in the wake of a couple short courses I had given earlier in the year. This campaign was being planned out by the agricultural extension agents over at DIGESA, Juán Abelino Mendoza and Abel García, though most of my visits out to those *aldeas* I did on my own. The idea was to persuade as many of the small farmers as possible to construct terraces or contour ditches on their sloping, postage stamp parcels that were planted with maize and beans. Some of the farmers were beginning to adopt these conservation techniques, it seemed, and the tons of Food for Work I had in my back room at the house were depleting quickly, as the farmers from Xococ and Patixlán and elsewhere came into town regularly to claim their rations in return for their conservation efforts.

I said I made all my trips out to these places alone, but the fact is I could never have succeeded in persuading the local farmers to invest their time and energy in these soil conservation measures were it not for one man who provided invaluable assistance every step of the way. In order to reach out to these farmers who all lived some seven or eight clicks from the *pueblo* and who had never even met this strange-looking gringo before, clearly I would need to work with a trusted liaison, a local community sparkplug whose own work for the betterment of the community already commanded the respect of his neighbors.

With the help of the DIGESA extensionists I found such a man, and now it is time for you to get to know him as well. For he will play an important role in the rest of this story.

* * *

There are some people you meet in life who will make a singular impression on you. In Rabinal that man was Evaristo. Evaristo Cuxúm Alvarado. I'll have to try to tell the story of Evaristo with as much patience and perseverance as possible, for it is not an easy story to tell. There are three parts to this story, which really are three emblematic vignettes from our relationship that lasted a little more than two years. Besides the vignette which I am about to relate, you will see him again later on, when we took a long walk together. And then we will see him once again, triumphant, standing in Rabinal's plaza.

Evaristo in Patixlán

I first met Evaristo Cuxúm through the DIGESA staff in Rabinal. Evaristo hailed from *aldea* Patixlán, some ten clicks west of the town center. He was introduced to me as this real *listo* guy who might be helpful in promoting reforestation and soil conservation among the farmers in his neck of the woods. As it turned out during the months that followed, this estimation of Evaristo's value to his community was an understatement.

Evaristo was a young man, scarcely two or three years older than me. More often than not when I saw Evaristo, he'd be clutching a notebook or *cartapacio*, because he was always either learning new things or taking notes on his work as a *promotor,* or preparing lessons for the people of his village. Besides being a *promotor agrícola* for DIGESA, I also called him my *promotor forestal* for Patixlán and nearby Xococ. He made terraces, he planted trees, and later he was even holding classes to teach the women of Patixlán how to read and write. From a photo I have I am reminded that he was the father of at least a couple small children. Evaristo had boundless energy and enthusiasm, and he always applied these to every task at hand.

So far I am writing about Evaristo from memory, but I have a journal entry here that will take us through the remainder of my first story about him. The words that follow may therefore be considered a "real-time" account, from Wednesday, Jan. 16, 1980:

> I saw Evaristo today, behind bars in the Salamá jail. I saw him shortly after returning from San Jerónimo, where I had spoken with Santizo of INAFOR about our tree nursery needs. I got a ride into Salamá and, as I was walking down the street past Carlitos's house, Juan Avelino passed by in his green Toyota pickup. He rolled down the window and called out to me. I stopped and we spoke, and at length I came to understand that Evaristo, who's one of the most *listo* guys from Patixlán, where together we gave a short course on conservation only two months earlier—this Evaristo, an eager and wryly jocular fellow my age, who is nearing completion on his new house, who wants to make *terrazas* on his land next—this Evaristo is in jail. Juan Avelino offered me a ride to the departmental penitentiary to visit him; it was only five blocks away. On the way, I recalled the sketchy and very partial details I had heard about recent events in Xococ and Patixlán.
>
> Years ago, the people of Xococ and neighboring *aldeas* had built a road from Rabinal out to their neck of the woods—about fourteen kilometers in length. It must have been quite an undertaking, as it appears they did it without any help at all from *Caminos* or any other agency. It is only a dirt road, of course, but it has served

well to provide Xococ, Patixlán, and other *aldeas* out that way with access to goods and services, contributing a lot to the development of those areas. They made the road with their own hands, with shovels and *azadones,* and I imagine they are proud of that.

I don't know when the barite (*barita*) mine was established just beyond Xococ, across the municipal border in Cubulco. It couldn't have been too long ago, because the mine's existence is part and parcel of the recent oil exploration initiative in Guatemala, and the barite is used as a drilling lubricant. Over the past months, though, the mine has been particularly active, hauling out four to six heavy truckloads of rock every day. This has contributed to the degradation of the dirt road from Xococ to Rabinal, and has contributed also to the consternation of the people of the *aldeas* who see it being used and abused every day by a private enterprise that had no hand in building or maintaining the road.

The mine employs a number of people who are residents of Xococ. Talking with a friend some months back, I learned that the pay for the workers (including this man himself) was four to six weeks behind. There was no telling when they would get paid for the work they had already performed.

In recent weeks the situation has become grave. The people are really up in arms about the daily degradation of their road. And this is where my information grows sketchy. I don't know who started it. There were some exchanges between the *aldeanos* and the *mineros,* the details of which sound pretty ugly. A van belonging to the *mina* ran over a group of people in Xococ, and it was apparently no accident. One of them lies in the Salamá hospital with a crushed chest. Another *aldeano* was shot in cold blood with a pistol. After that a group of *aldeanos* caused a mine vehicle to crash as it passed by. It was then that Evaristo was somehow arrested and charged with inciting an insurrection. It's hard to piece together how, exactly,

> the arrest might have been effected, since Rabinal had only two policemen and not a single police vehicle. The two officers in town had always managed simply by commandeering private vehicles whenever they needed one. Presumably that's what they would have had to do in order to arrest our man Evaristo out in Patixlán, some twelve clicks away from their post on the main plaza.
>
> So here we are in Salamá, the departmental capital, standing at the gate of the penitentiary. I talked with Evaristo through the gate. He wasn't in a cell at the time. Several of the prisoners milled around in a large open yard with a surface of white caliche, and Evaristo was standing there among them. The word up was that he was going to appear before a Salamá magistrate the next day. I tried to encourage and console Evaristo as best I could, but I had never visited a friend in jail before, so it was hard to find the words. Through the bars I handed him what was left of my pack of cigarettes. I offered him matches, too, but he politely refused, since after all this was a jail. He said don't worry, he'd find a light somewhere.

Things looked pretty bleak for poor Evaristo. But, remarkably, a later journal entry from the very next day simply says: "Evaristo was freed today from jail, his cousin ran up to tell me on the street today."

Unfortunately that's all I have about Evaristo in my skimpy journal. I was never much of a journal writer. I have no idea how Evaristo got released from jail. At any rate, it seems like this first story had a salutary outcome, and after the incident Evaristo returned to Patixlán and I continued to work with him on various projects. I suppose you could call it a salutary outcome; except that the overloaded trucks hauling *barita* continued to rumble through Patixlán, and through Rabinal, every day.

The first evidence you see of a hero in the making is when the authorities take notice. There are two more very distinct memories I have of Evaristo. But these must come later, at the proper time.

* * *

In 1980, guerrilla operations on the urban front as well as in the countryside intensified considerably. The insurgents executed a series of propaganda acts as well as assassinations of prominent landowners and leaders of Guatemala's extreme Right. Meanwhile, the daily average number of assassinations perpetrated by the official as well as the unofficial security forces increased from twenty to thirty in 1979, to a conservative estimate of thirty to forty in 1980.

In the early months of 1980 a farmworkers strike led by the CUC forced the Guatemalan government to raise minimum wages by 200 percent, from an equivalent of U.S. $1.12 to $3.20. *Per day.* This was considered a major victory. The strike involved 70,000 workers from sugarcane plantations, as well as 40,000 cotton pickers.[63]

In March of that year new sources of strife erupted in the farthest reaches of Rabinal *municipio*. Two residents of Río Negro *aldea* who were passing through a nearby village known as Pueblo Viejo were accused of stealing beans from the dining rooms of the workers who were constructing the enormous hydroelectric dam on the Rio Chixoy. The men were pursued by two soldiers and an officer of the *Policia Militar Ambulante* (PMA). Upon arrival at Río Negro, the two residents began shouting that they were being pursued by the military. The soldiers were somehow "rounded up and taken to the church." A community member, who was drunk, struck the officer of the PMA, who, in his eagerness to defend himself, shot and killed seven people. Immediately, the farmers reacted with stones and machetes and killed the agent. One of the soldiers, seeing the reaction of the crowd and his companion dying, left his gun and fled. The other soldier was withheld for a while, and was later freed.[64]

One day later the army commented on the incident, saying that the community had influence from the guerrillas and that was the factor that explained their refusal to leave their lands. The military claimed in their press bulletin:

> For some time the people of the Río Negro village have become troubled by the influence of subversive elements, which have benefited from the problems of land, raised on the grounds that their land will be affected by the flooding of the Chixoy dam. This, unlike other villages which have voluntarily accepted

> the transfer to safer places and where they have better life expectancies.[65]

Barely four months later two more Rio Negro inhabitants, who were going to claim titles to their land at the INDE offices, were murdered in cold blood.

On the first of September of that year, Vice President Francisco Villagrán Kramer resigned from his position. In his letter of resignation, Kramer cited his disapproval of the government's human rights record as one of the main reasons for his action.

On September 5, 1980, a terrorist attack by the EGP (Guerrilla Army of the Poor) took place in front of the National Palace of Guatemala, then the seat of the Guatemalan government. The objective was to discourage the populace from supporting a massive demonstration that the government of General Lucas García had prepared for Sunday, September 7, 1980. Six adults and a child died in the attack when two bombs exploded inside a vehicle.[66]

Later that month, in Rabinal's Pichec *aldea*, the place where I had met with Cristóbal to look at his tree nursery, soldiers dressed in civilian clothes with red handkerchiefs, accompanied by members of the Civil Defense Patrol, massacred some sixteen people including newborn children, men and women. Some of the people were buried alive, while others were executed with bullets. A civil patrolman from the very same community was guiding the soldiers.[67]

Finally, in October of 1980, a tripartite alliance was formalized between the EGP, FAR, and ORPA, as a necessary condition in order to receive Cuban support for the revolution. Thus was born the Guatemalan National Revolutionary Unity—URNG. In that same month I visited my program manager Basilio Estrada in his office and informed him of my desire to extend my Peace Corps service for another year. Basilio shook my hand and broadly approved, despite the fact that I couldn't drive anymore because only a year and a half earlier I had crashed a CARE pickup in the hills outside Cubulco. I guess my capacity in Spanish must have been the charm.

And then, in the middle of that same month, there was yet another watershed event that would worry anybody who read the newspapers—and it galvanized many into action. Irma Flaquer, a psychologist and a respected journalist with *La Nación* newspaper, was attending her grandson's fourth birthday party. It is said this was her last farewell to her son Fernando, his wife, Mayra Rosales, and her grandson, Fernando, before she was to leave for Nicaragua the next day. While she and Fernando drove back to her apartment, they were stopped a block away from her apartment by two vehicles surrounding their car. Fernando was shot in the head and Irma cried out for a doctor for her son. She herself was then grabbed and taken away. Her body was never recovered, and it is believed she was executed. She had been the first white, middle-class, professional woman to have been abducted and presumably murdered in Guatemala during that time.[68]

* * *

But it was really a lovely October in Rabinal, with a nice cool breeze almost every morning. By now the seasonal rains were much less frequent. Just back from my monthly bus trip to Guate, I was back on the job again, having been granted the one-year extension I had requested. I was beginning to get to know my new Baja Verapaz colleagues, Jeff Hudson in Salamá and John Schelhas in Cubulco. Adding to my positive outlook, we now had a greatly expanded tree nursery that boasted a brand new *bodega*. We were all pretty proud of it (as rustic as it was), but I think Juan Pablo was the proudest. Sometimes, living out in the country, you take great pride in small things.

Guatemala's *Día de la Revolución* was celebrated on October 20 every year, a national holiday for everybody in the country. This holiday commemorated, without a hint of irony, the inauguration of Juan José Arévalo's democratically elected government back in 1944—Guatemala's first truly progressive president of the modern era. The Arevalo administration had brought momentous changes to Guatemala's social and political landscape—hopeful changes which promised to usher in a new era of freedom and prosperity for millions of Guatemalans. Changes which every successive administration after the CIA-sponsored *coup d'etat* in 1954 worked their asses off to either reverse or fossilize. Hence the irony that would never be acknowledged in official proclamations commemorating this day.

It was about 6:30 in the morning a couple days before the holiday, and I was just climbing out of bed when I heard someone rattling at my gate and calling out to me. It was Juan Pablo, and he was in quite a state. With great agitation he told me to put my clothes on quickly and run down to the tree nursery with him. Then he told me that our *bodega* had been firebombed in the dark hours of the morning. I got my ass in gear as quickly as I could, put some clothes on, and I ran almost all the way to the *vivero,* some two clicks from my house.

Once I got there I simply stood in the middle of the road dumbfounded by the whole scene before my eyes. In the early morning the ruins were still smoldering, but I could see the remaining traces of smoke only when I got very close to the nursery. The structure of the *bodega* had essentially disappeared and was now just a level mass of cinders. The fire was out by the time I arrived, and all that was left was that mass of ashes and a few charred timber sidings. Shovel blades missing their wooden handles, blackened nails that were no longer fastened to anything. Curiously, amidst the ashes and the rubble we found a small mass of molten glass that had cooled and congealed into a sort of abstract sculpture, like something the sculptor Jean Arp might have dreamed up and then discarded. I think it was Juan Pablo who then recalled that one of us had left an empty Coke bottle on the desk the day before. So, then (my research now tells me), the blaze that had taken our *bodega* must have reached a temperature of at least fourteen hundred degrees. Fahrenheit.

There were leaflets everywhere on the ground outside the nursery, all on yellow slips of paper. Hundreds of them scattered across the road, fluttering in the cool morning breeze. I wish I had saved one—but you can't save everything. And anyway, I was hesitant to even pick one up and place it in my pocket, since I didn't want to arouse any suspicion as to where my sympathies might lie. The leaflets on the ground clearly declared the authors of the sabotage: it was the *Comité de Unidad Campesina.*

Juanito and I ran back to the main plaza and reported the event to the police captain who was in his office. The police in Rabinal never had any form of motorized transport, so the captain asked *don* Juan Lux, who had an old, beat-up VW bus parked in the plaza, to drive him down to the nursery so he and his sidekick corporal could assess the scene. (Yes, it would be fair to say that the police captain *don* Felipe was "commandeering" the VW, but he did so in his customary soft-spoken manner, so I am not far off the mark if I characterize it here as a firmly stated plea rather than an imperative.)

Thus Juanito and I arrived at the nursery for our second visit around eight in the morning, now accompanied by the two men in blue. There was not a great deal of conversation this time; mostly the two officers just looked around and quietly took stock of the situation. They did ask us what had been stored in the *bodega*, and we roughly itemized the lost contents as best we could from memory. In doing so, I quickly realized that these were not just the harmless remains of a bonfire smoldering on the ground; this was a fucking *toxic waste site*. All that Dipterex, mercury-based Agallol and all the other shit we sprayed on the seedlings to fend off the pestilence of Mother Nature. And a good deal of polyethylene plastic, too.

Later I had to go to the *alcaldia* to make some sort of declaration, which they carefully wrote down in a large, heavy folio book inside the mayor's office. I stuck to the facts that I knew, which were sparse. I had to sign my name below the transcription of what I told the officials, and then they made me sign another document that I was not allowed to read. "What's this?" I asked. "The confidential report," I was told. Under normal circumstances I am not accustomed to signing something I have not had the opportunity to read first. But these were not normal circumstances. I wonder sometimes what would have happened if I'd had the balls to tell them that I refused to sign their "confidential" document.

My account here is based on what I recall of the firebombing of our tree nursery in Rabinal. But I uncovered a scribbled journal entry dated 19 Oct., 1980—a contemporaneous account of the event, offering a few additional details, and a bit of reflection. Here is what I wrote at the time:

> Sun., 19 Oct., 1980 (Rabinal)
>
> Last Friday I was beginning to say something about Grace when the sensory overload of the city [Guatemala City] overcame me. Today, within the last hour, I feel I got a momentary glimpse of that condition of Grace. It was nothing more than a fleeting experience, but I felt it intensely, and it meant something to me. The feeling was triggered by sounds and images: a skyward view at dusk, patterns of far yellow clouds drifting behind the nearer purple ones, the dalliance of a couple

distant birds in the air—and a recording of Bach's Ave María off of my tape deck in the background.

I felt something, inspired by these images and sounds, that has been hard to feel during the past day and a half: a reflective calm, a momentary spiritual communion.

Could I have felt this at all, had I not experienced a bit of hell just before? Could the depth of that feeling of peace have hardly impressed me, had I not previously experienced loss; had I not previously caught a glimpse of the Abyss?

Yesterday the CUC burned down our nursery building [or so it appeared at the time], which is tantamount to saying they burned down our nursery. Between 12 and 2 a.m. Saturday morning, they descended Cerro Kaj'yup, the prominent hill north of town, cut their way into the vivero from below near the river, climbed up the broad, empty terraces where until a few weeks ago we had some thousands of tree seedlings, and they set off Molotov cocktails in the bodega/oficina we'd built only half a year ago.

The blaze must have been quite intense. Juan Pablo told me that the fire was seen from quite a distance. Antonio Ramirez told me how the women from neighboring houses tried in vain to extinguish the blaze with buckets of water, and how he ran the 2 kilometers or so to Juan Pablo's house, half naked in the middle of the night, and woke him to let him know what had happened.

As for Juanito and me, we arrived at the scene, or rather the aftermath of the scene, around 6:30 the following morning. Squinting into the sunrise, I leaned forward against two fenceposts, and gazed into the smoldering, charred remains of the building—all that was left of nearly a year's work invested by me and half a dozen others. A solemn crowd of men, women and children from the neighboring colonia gathered behind me on the dirt road. Nobody said a word.

** END OF CONTEMPORANEOUS ACCOUNT **

... I wrote that a long time ago, and by now of course I am way past the sting of the moment. At the time I thought I could understand why the CUC might firebomb our tree nursery. It represented the Government, after all, and in particular it represented INAFOR, which was hated by many for a number of reasons, not least of which was the bribes they took every day to look the other way while the rich landowners continued their forest clearcutting.

What I wasn't prepared for was the stunning revelation, more than forty years later, that the CUC had not in fact firebombed our tree nursery. It was actually the work of the army. And those hundreds of yellow leaflets strewn all over the ground? Just a clever ploy by the army to shift blame for the incident to the guerrillas. This I learned from a reliable source during a recent return visit to Rabinal.

For more than forty years I had been seduced by a devious lie. Everything, it seemed, was shrouded in darkness back then, and nothing was as it seemed. But light eventually emerges.

And our guys in the *vivero* built a new bodega within a couple months after the fire. This time they built it of adobe.

There is nothing pretty or polite in a civil war, and sometimes 'good actors' get caught in the middle. I still remain convinced that we were good actors who wanted to accomplish something positive and lasting in the community. But back there in Rabinal, in the moment, the whole experience would serve to wake me up to who I was, where I was, and what I might have represented to others.

* * *

On my next monthly trip to Guate to pick up my paycheck I stopped by the English language bookshop in Zone 1 to try and find some reading material to take back with me. I came across Dante's *Divine Comedy* on a shelf there, right at eye level, and I thought to myself, *hell*, maybe it's time I tackled that old story again. Dante had been assigned as required reading in my high school English class, but, truth be told, back then I had only skimmed through it, and still somehow I managed to fake my way through the quizzes. Maybe now, sitting in my hammock in Rabinal in the very midst of a battle between good and evil, maybe now was the time to take a more serious look at it. And so I left the bookshop called Arnell's with a copy of *The Divine Comedy* in hand, and Dante's verses carried me through a couple months of late evenings in the latter part of 1980.

Nothing seizes one's attention like a vivid picture of hell, and so I was captivated and totally absorbed by Dante's colorful imagery in *The Inferno*. It was there that I learned about the consequences of neutrality in times of moral crisis:

> ... the sad souls of those who lived
> Without occasion for infamy or praise.
>
> They are mixed with that abject squadron of angels
> Who did not think it worth their while to rebel
> Or to be faithful to God, but were for themselves.
>
> ... The world does not remember them at all.[69]

When you think about it, there could scarcely be a worse punishment after death: 'The world does not remember them at all.' Six hundred years later President Theodore Roosevelt got it right when he succinctly reprised those verses thus: "Dante reserved a special place of infamy in the inferno for those base angels who dared side neither with evil nor with good." And another half-century later these verses were somewhat inaccurately yet trenchantly quoted by John F. Kennedy when he said,

> I do not think, in trying to remain aloof from the Algerian and similar controversies ... that we have remembered the words of the poet Dante: 'The hottest places in Hell are reserved for those who, in a time of great moral crisis, maintain their neutrality.[70]

Though our Peace Corps mission strictly precluded any direct involvement in the political affairs of the country where we served, nevertheless sooner or later in Guatemala we would all have to answer—at the very least somewhere deep within our heart of hearts—that same urgent question that my adolescent hero, the folk singer Pete Seeger had once put to the coal miners in Harlan County, Kentucky:

> *Which side are you on, boys, which side are you on?*

CHAPTER 12

What Do the Birds Tell Us?

Rosendo Xolop was a respected citizen of Rabinal. Among other things, he was the president of the local ceramics cooperative, and by all accounts he performed the duties of his office with dedication and zeal. Rosendo was also a *comisionado militar*, a civilian who was responsible for coordinating with the local military officials to round up young, new recruits every once in a while. This state of affairs was customary in every community all across Guatemala, and, to be fair, it was not unlike other countries where the finest upstanding pillars of the community are chosen to form a committee to send their young men off to fight in some remote swamp, desert, or jungle. The only differences being that in Guatemala there was no committee as such, and the war was not abroad, but at home. In fact, the war was being waged in the very community where one lived. Hence, the army always made sure that the raw recruits (in essence, draftees) would unfailingly be posted to other communities far from their home of record. It's always easier to perform your assigned duty as a soldier so long as you're not looking into the face of your brother or sister, your father or your mother.

But it was in his capacity as a *cooperativista*, not as a *comisionado*, that I got to know Rosendo over the course of the year. One day, early in the year, Rosendo stopped by my house with a special request: he wanted some guidance on how to develop some good marketing tools, like pamphlets and catalogs and such, to showcase the whole wide variety of ceramic pieces that were being produced every day by his fellow *cooperativistas*. We spent some time together that evening, and we met again at least one more time later on, and in these meetings we discussed at some length how to put together some marketing paraphernalia that might be useful. Though I had no experience in marketing per se, I liked the idea of helping out with this project, and I had a veritable flood of seat-of-the-pants ideas that I hoped might at least set him off in the right direction. Among other things, I told him he'd need to get either a good camera or a good photographer in order to assemble a nice collection of high-quality pictures of all their colorful jars and urns and vases that the *cooperativistas* had fashioned from the earth beneath their very feet. "And make sure you have a simple, clean background in all the pictures," I told him.

I suggested he might take up a collection among his fellow *cooperativistas* to defray the cost of the effort, and then I recommended he might even work with our own Augusto Jerónimo who lived right across the street from me. He was our unofficial "town photographer," and he had all the tools of the trade. Rosendo walked away with a head full of ideas that night, and I was sure he would follow up with at least a couple of them.

I saw Rosendo again on the Day of the Dead—a day of solemn remembrance and alcohol-fortified celebration in local cemeteries across the country. Everyone in town congregates in and around the cemetery on the Day of the Dead. There's marimba music and *copal* incense (...oh, how I remember the sweet fragrance of *copal*!), and the people all bring gifts of flowers and *atól de plátano*, cigars and *aguardiente*, photographs and knick-knacks, transistor radios broadcasting *norteñas* at full volume, and any other favorite item that was loved or simply enjoyed by their loved ones while they were among the living. All these things are carefully arranged on the graves of the *antepasados* who exist now in another world.

At this point in time, I was nearing the end of my second year in Rabinal. My Spanish was pretty good, though I still knew only a smattering of words in the local language, Achí. I bought myself an *octavo* bottle of *Venado Especial* (the portable version of a very cheap, powerful rum) and slipped it into my back pocket. I walked down the road from my house, past the church and the central plaza, passing by the *Restaurante Las Diamelas* where I often ate dinner, and down past the military *destacamento* to the *Calvario* chapel and the cemetery to be with my friends and neighbors for this mystical celebration amidst the colorful tombs and the sad, earthen mounds. Viewing the cemetery festivities from afar (for I was still an outsider to this deeply personal mystery), I happened to run into Rosendo Xolop, and I sat down on a rustic wooden bench with him.

We sat and talked for a while. Rosendo was pretty drunk, and I was already well past a good buzz myself. We talked, very guardedly, about the difficult times the town was going through. The army was everywhere, and people were disappearing. Rosendo wept, as drunken men sometimes do, and then, to my surprise, he became all of a sudden more lucid and he begged me—*begged me*—to help him get to the United States. Rosendo was the *comisionado militar* in town, the draft commissioner who singled out young men to go into the army. And yet now he was afraid of what the army might do with *him*. The army lieutenant had recently ordered that young men be rounded up in the nearby *aldea* of Pachalum. But this was a hamlet where Rosendo had friends and family. Therefore he had resisted or simply slow-walked the order, questioning why. Rosendo begged me over and over again to try and help him get to the United States, so he could be far from the danger that haunted him.

Awkwardly, and rather stupidly, I tried to allay Rosendo's mortal fears. Half drunk myself, I naively insisted that it can't be all that bad, and surely he'd find a way out of this. Of course I knew that none of this was true, or even the least bit helpful. But I was half drunk and too inept, too much of a *coward*, really, to do what I should have done—or at least tried to do. The moment passed, and I remember little else from this Day of the Dead in the year 1980. But I do remember this much which I've told you. For this, at least, is the part I can never forget.

The longer I was in Guatemala, the more my daily experiences tended to whipsaw chaotically between celebration and pathos, between comedy and tragedy; indeed, I might say, even between love and death. I suspect that my exposure to such violent and unpredictable changes in fortune (not so much my own fortune, but the lot that was dealt every day to those around me) left its mark on me, possibly forever. How that mark shows up in my personality is, I suppose, for others to judge, but the memory of those times in Rabinal makes me wonder sometimes how I made it from day to day without the benefit of psychological counseling. Putting in a request to the Peace Corps for some sort of counseling might have been an option, I suppose. But like the soldier in the field who simply passes on reporting his frayed or jangled nerves for fear of being cut from the platoon or maybe even sent home, I tried, and often managed pretty well, to power through the events happening all around me.

Exactly one week after my unsettling encounter with Rosendo Xolop sitting there on a bench by the Calvario chapel, *hell, it was time to party!*

* * *

Did somebody say 'party'? Indeed, there was to be a party, and even *I* was invited! Right after the Day of the Dead I had gone into Guate on my usual, monthly blitz through the city to pick up my paycheck and run sundry errands. One of my reforestation buddies told me about the event, and I later confirmed the information when I passed through the office of our program manager, Basilio Estrada. Our host agency, INAFOR, was hosting the fête for all of the departing volunteers in my group who had worked in the reforestation program. A few of my compatriots had already returned home, but whoever was left was certainly invited—including myself, even though I wasn't going anywhere for another year or so. All I had to do was stick around for a couple extra days instead of heading straight back to Rabinal.

Which I was planning to do anyway. For, you see, on this particular trip to Guate it looked as if I might finally get to see Lisa again, after so many months during which we had only written each other. Why exactly I had never gone to see Lisa on previous trips to Guate is an omission I will never fully understand. For I certainly had the opportunity to do so. In retrospect, I believe that fate, or destiny, or perhaps some inscrutable astral influence may have been at work—and it worked on me.

At any rate, this was the visit to Guate, *this was the visit* when I thought I might see her again. In our last exchange of letters we had agreed on a rendezvous at her mom's place in *Zona 7*, so all I needed to do, really, was to give her a call and let her know I was in Guate and that I was on my way. Lisa was young and pretty. Yet whenever I had a moment to reflect on the matter (and I had many such moments back in Rabinal), I had started to feel some creeping reservations about our prospects as a couple. She was, after all, only seventeen when I had first met her a few months earlier during the *feria*. Maybe eighteen by now.

Hmm.

The INAFOR party was to take place the next day, a Friday, and it was going to be at the *Parque de las Naciones Unidas*, a government recreational facility outside the town of Amatitlán. I figured I'd better pick up my paycheck and go to the bank now to cash it, while I was still sober. That done, I think I pretty much goofed off for the rest of the afternoon, and I bunked at the *Misión Francesa*.

The next day several of us got a ride out to the party venue in Amatitlán with Basilio in his Ford Bronco. It wasn't yet noon, and the INAFOR people hadn't yet arrived, so mostly we sat around and talked about stuff each of us had seen over the past two years. We focused on the interesting and the amusing, and mostly steered clear of the tragic. Soon the INAFOR crew showed up, including the agency's general manager Jorge Spiegler, along with a number of his functionaries representing different departments, and a group of young women who were all INAFOR secretaries, mostly from the same departments as the functionaries. Caterers showed up from one of the best steak restaurants in Guate, and they briskly set to work in the kitchen area. And, finally, the Minister of Agriculture also showed up, his bodyguards fanning out immediately around the perimeter of the courtyard, their Uzis barely concealed under their dark sport jackets.

A couple more carloads of volunteers arrived, and it started to feel like a real party. A few of the INAFOR guys sat down with us, while others gathered in their own little groups. The enticing fragrance of steak on the grill now wafted through the air. A couple waiters went from table to table offering us all beers. Nobody declined.

During the whole fête in Amatitlán I felt the strangest mixture of emotions: laughter and sadness as I spent those last couple hours with my colleagues; energy and optimism looking forward to one more year in Rabinal; yet also some growing concern over the situation there, especially since our tree nursery had just been firebombed.

The main theme, though, was celebration, so we talked and laughed and slapped each other on the back, and pretty soon everybody was on their second or third beer. At length the secretaries finally came out, two by two, with generously mounded plates of food, which they helped distribute to each of the tables where we sat. I can smell the food even as I write this; it was quite the feast.

Midway through the whole affair bottles of Johnny Walker Red suddenly appeared, one at each table, and somebody handed out plastic cups. Then *don* Jorge Spiegler stood up and addressed the whole group, scotch in hand. He expressed profound appreciation for everything we volunteers had done over the previous two years. (Though of course he had only partial knowledge of what we had actually done!) Nice speech, though. Next on the agenda was for a volunteer to speak on behalf of the whole group, and the group put me up to the task. I got up and gave a short *spiel* basically thanking everybody, and especially INAFOR, for their guidance and their assistance over the past couple years, and for the food we were eating. My Spanish was good, and I wasn't drunk yet, so everybody seemed to like what I had to say. Basilio told me it was moving.

After the speeches the liquor flowed freely, and the empty plates were taken from our tables. Then suddenly *a miracle happened*, though I did not instantly recognize it as such: *don* Jorge Spiegler, the general manager of INAFOR, brought one of the secretaries over to the table where I was sitting, and he said to her, "Mireyita, do me a favor now—sit down here, please [he brought over a chair] and entertain these gentlemen!" So Mireya, perhaps a little embarrassed and maybe even somewhat put out by this order from the boss, sat down beside me at the table, and I introduced myself and offered her a drink. Still standing by our table, *don* Jorge incidentally asked me how things were going in Rabinal in the wake of the recent firebombing. (So, then, he already knew about it!) I told him we were all doing about as well as could be expected, and I promised him we would recover from this. We would certainly recover. He nodded approval and moved on to the next table.

Amatitlán, 1980: INAFOR's fête for departing Peace Corps volunteers. The author makes a connection that lasts forever.

Mireya and I exchanged only tentative pleasantries at first, but within a few minutes we were both drinking Johnny Walker from the same plastic cup and we were getting to know one another, at least in a desultory sort of way. We talked and talked, and though another volunteer at one point tried to horn in on the conversation, we had by now grown inseparable, just the two of us surrounded by all my pals at the wide, circular table. Somehow, even though we had known each other for scarcely half an hour, we both felt comfortable enough to set a date to get together the very next day: Nine o'clock, we agreed, under the statue of Tecun Uman, out by the zoo. When we finally parted late that afternoon, the women all lined up so we could say our goodbyes, and I tried to steal a kiss with Mireya, but she would have nothing of it. Her friends were right there with her, and after all we had only just met.

Returning from the fête in Amatitlán, I sat back in the car and relaxed, and considered my good fortune. An actual date. With an actual woman. I was thrilled. I slept well that night, even though I knew that the next morning I would have to make a dreadfully hard decision.

* * *

On Saturday morning I woke early, showered and got dressed and made myself as ready as I possibly could be, and then I walked from the *Misión Francesa* up to the *Hotel Panamericano* on Ninth Street for breakfast. The *Panamericano* had these absolutely delicious cinnamon Danishes that were simply to die for, and their coffee was good, too. I found a couple volunteers already seated there in the great, echoing hall where breakfast was served, so I joined them at their table and placed my order. The cinnamon roll was great, but it was a little hard to focus on the conversation at the table because I had so much on my mind. I didn't linger very long over my coffee; I paid up and said *adios* to the other gringos, and then I walked over to the *Parque Centenario* to get myself a shoeshine.

It wasn't hard to find a boy there to shine my heavy *campo* boots, as there were several hanging around in the park waiting for customers. Saturday mornings are slow everywhere in Guate, so the one I sat down with seemed glad to get the work. The boy pulled out a worn rag redolent of old shoe polish and started scuffing away at the toes of my boots. I sat back with one arm over the side of the park bench and watched the light Saturday traffic passing by. And I started thinking seriously for the first time about my dilemma.

Let's see, I had just made a date the day before with this girl named Mireya. Tecun Uman, nine o'clock. What time is it now? Heck, you've still got an hour. So, what are you going to do? Remember Lisa? You basically promised her you would stop by and visit on this trip to the capital. Was it a promise? Well, anyway, she was expecting you to call, because you pretty much made it out that way. "I'll give you a call once I'm in Guate, and I'll go over and see you." Didn't you write something like that in the last letter?

The boy meanwhile is scuffing away at my boots. He must have asked me a question along the way, like at least maybe he asked what tone of polish I wanted, but I scarcely had the presence of mind to reply. "Umm, *no se,* that one," I said, pointing randomly to one of the flat Kiwi canisters he held up for me.

What *am* I to do now? Well, I can get up from this bench, pay the boy, and walk down to the Guatel building where all the pay phones are lined up in a long row. I can dial Lisa's number which I have scribbled on a scrap of paper in my billfold because she gave it to me in her last letter. I can ask for Lisa (because her mom would probably answer the phone), and then I can tell Lisa I'll be over there to *Zona 7* in about an hour.

Or…*or* I can get up from this bench, pay the boy, and walk to the nearest bus stop on 4th Ave. and take a green Number Five to the Tecun Uman statue, out by the zoo. With any luck, I might find Mireya sitting there under the statue.

Hmm, Mireya. I love that name, it's just a little unusual, I thought. I'd never heard of a Mireya before. I wonder if she'd—oh heck, what time is it? *Shit*, I've got to make some kind of decision here. What shall I do? Well, yesterday with Mireya—I mean, that was a real promise. You can't let her sit out there under Tecun Uman waiting for you and then you never show up! As for Lisa, well, Number One, she's probably just lounging around at home right now, maybe not even thinking about me, and, Number Two, well, I mean that wasn't really a promise in the same sense, now, was it? I mean, you had to come to the capital anyway on other business that had nothing to do with her, you said you'd give her a call if you could, so isn't it plausible that that other business ran into a snag or a delay or something? But it's a Saturday. Well, you know, shit happens. Even on a Saturday.

The boy had by now finished the shoeshine job and was looking up at me. I paid him, including a nice little tip, and I got up from the bench and started walking. I do believe that up to the very last minute walking towards the street corner I was still deciding what to do. There were other permutations to consider. Like for instance riding out to Tecun Uman only to tell this girl Mireya I was so, so sorry, but I simply couldn't spend the day with her because something had come up, then riding back to find a pay phone and tell Lisa I'd be right over.

—Nah, too much hauling ass from one end of the city to the other. Waste of precious time.

On the street corner I waited for the light, and then I crossed over, and headed down the street towards the payphones in front of the Guatel building. Once I got there, I picked a phone from the several that were available (even this seemed like an important decision, for it had to be an auspicious telephone!), and I dialed Lisa's number and executed—well, my *modified* plan. Lisa's mom answered the phone. She greeted me ever so cordially, and then she called for Lisa to come quick. Before I knew it I was talking with the girl I'd danced with back in Rabinal—God, it seemed like eons ago.

"*Hola*, Lisa! ... Yes, this is Cristián … Yes, I know, it's been a long time since we've seen each other—so how are you? … Why thank you, I am doing well … Yes, I've enjoyed reading all your letters, too. It's been great to keep in touch like this every so often … Well, right now I'm calling from a payphone in Zone 1 … Yes, of course I still have the address you gave me; I've got it right here in my wallet. But listen, Lisa, I have to tell you something. Something's come up, and I have to go back to Rabinal this morning … Yes, really, no kidding—honest. We have a situation right now in Rabinal. [Quick, Cristián, *think*: something she can corroborate with her father *don* Beto in Rabinal!] It's, well, you see, our tree nursery got firebombed a couple weeks ago [The truth always helps!], and—well, yes, thank you Lisa, I know, it was dreadful, we're all dealing with it as best we can—anyway, so I have to get back there now because there are some things—um—I really have to take care of right away. [Lame excuse, this, especially seeing as how it was a Saturday, for Chrissake. But at least there was a foundation in fact.] So, anyway, listen, we'll have to do this another time. Yeah, I'm really sorry. I'll write you when I get back to Rabinal. Yes, thank you; okay, we'll talk later. *Adios, pués.*"

In the end, I suppose it was just that I couldn't wrap my head around the age difference. At least that's what I told myself. It's never easy, and in the end, for someone, it will never seem kind. Lisa, it's far too late to say I'm sorry, and it would be depraved of me to say, 'I had hoped you might understand.' In the end, Lisa, I'm glad I got to know you, for you taught me something about myself.

After the telephone call I looked at my watch, and I totally freaked out. I sprinted all the way up to 4th Ave to catch a green Number Five, hoping to God the sweat might dry off during the ride out there. It seemed I had to wait forever before a Five showed up, and then the ride out to *Zona 13* felt interminable. By the time I got out to the zoo, Mireya was still sitting there waiting beneath the gigantic statue of the Mayan hero Tecun Uman. I was more than half an hour late. We shared a warm-ish embrace under Tecun Uman, and I explained to her that after breakfast I had gone for a shoeshine and just lost all track of time. Instead of waiting for me for what must have seemed to her an eternity, by rights Mireya could have simply gotten up and caught a bus back home. But she didn't, instead she waited for me, for more than half an hour she waited, and now here we were alone together in the busy city, conversing under the shade of Tecun Uman.

We walked hand in hand over to the *Trebol* where all the city and inter-city buses customarily stopped, and we flagged down a bus to Antigua—Mireya's hometown. Inside the bus, a Mexican *norteña* with a bouncy accordion rhythm was blaring at full volume. We found ourselves a couple seats, and when I looked up I couldn't help but notice the stickers that were displayed up front, right above the windshield, with their messages that sounded rather less than auspicious for this date:

Eat More Beans—Our Country Needs Gas!

Jesus is My Copilot

¡De tu Educación Dependen los Machetazos!

As it turned out, though, this Saturday would become a day to mark on the calendar, a day to remember forever. Only we couldn't possibly have known that as we started off on our little trip. Once we got to Antigua we walked around the cobblestone streets and peeked into the shops full of traditional crafts and trendy clothing without buying anything, because neither of us had any money to spend. We ate a simple but satisfying lunch in a restaurant not far from *El Arco*, and then later we sat on a bench together in a forested park, away from the crowds, just the two of us, all alone, and in my heart of hearts as I write this I know that Mireya was softly singing to herself in her own heart that afternoon, and the song her heart sang, the song she didn't even know she knew, went something like this …

> *Come now, luxuriant Graces, and beautiful-haired Muses.*[71]
> *Give me Love, give me Longing now, the powers*
> *you use to overwhelm all gods and mortal men!*[72]

And then like magic she was granted the gifts that she had asked for, and she used those powers to cast her spell on me. We sat and talked on that bench beneath the pines and the pretty casuarinas, but soon words were followed by a silence, and then the silence was followed by a kiss. Mireya stood in front of me while I sat on the wooden bench, and we tightly embraced and simply lost ourselves in long, passionate kisses.

And it was a delicate, mystic raiment she wore,

> *… with every kind of enchantment*
> *woven through it … There is the heat of Love,*
> *the pulsing rush of Longing, the lover's whisper,*
> *irresistible—magic to make the sanest man go mad,*

... and mad indeed she drove me. We spent an hour in each other's embrace under the pines and casuarinas, and suddenly we both realized a page had been turned. Something new and exciting had begun. How long it might last was anyone's guess, yet deep inside I was earnestly hoping that someday, *someday* I might be able to say, with Sappho,

> *I tell you*
> *someone will remember us*
> *in the future.*[73]

Paul Gauguin, “Nostalgic Promenade” (1889). Private collection.

* * *

A few days after the fête in Amatitlán where I had met Mireya, I was back at work in the *vivero* in Rabinal when I had occasion to confront the conundrum of duty. Juan Pablo brought our laborer *don* Tomás over to see me with a request that they both believed I needed to attend to with some urgency. *Don* Tomás's INAFOR ID card had recently expired, and needed to be renewed.

Now, one of my duties was indeed to make sure that each of my workers was issued an agency-endorsed identification card. And under normal circumstances this would have been considered more like a mundane routine than a duty. There was, however, one relevant circumstance which made all the difference: by now Rabinal was becoming engulfed in the same civil strife that had already become “the new normal” in the country's *Altiplano* to the west and north. If an army *kaibil* should happen upon one of my workers and demand his

ID, it seemed quite plausible (and indeed, had been confirmed by our experience!) that some demonstration of government affiliation might advance one's interest in self-preservation. It was just as possible, however, that an armed guerrilla might stop our worker on the road, and if *he* should find evidence of the poor fellow's INAFOR affiliation (especially in light of the recent CUC fire-bombing of our tree nursery), then the outcome might be more likely to be sanguinary rather than sanguine. The INAFOR ID could, in short, become either a license to live or possibly a death certificate, depending on one's fortunes.

So, should I perform my duty, I asked myself, by writing the necessary letter of request and posting it to the INAFOR subregional office to obtain a validated ID for Tomás? Or should I simply let the ID lapse?

I could go on and on with all the philosophical equivocating (as in fact I actually did a few years later when I looked back on this whole experience while struggling with Kant and Sidgwick in a grad school ethics seminar), but let the matter rest here: I simply got *don* Tomás his new ID a few days later, and he tucked it away in his worn out wallet.

Scarcely two months later, government soldiers from our local *destacamento* entered the *aldea* known as Nimacabaj, where Tomás lived. According to the account he gave me, the soldiers interrogated the family that lived on one side of his house, and then summarily executed them all. They did the same to the family that lived on the other side. When they visited don Tomás, he managed to produce his newly validated INAFOR ID card and show it to them. As *don* Tomás himself related to me the next day in the *vivero*, the soldiers asked for some water to drink and then went on their way.

* * *

Tomás Lajuj's alarming report of the army *rastreo* in Nimacabaj provided yet more evidence that things were no longer the same in Rabinal, that our freedom of movement (among other things) might now be qualified and contingent rather than truly free.

Can I go out now to the *aldea* called Rio Negro? Because I've always wanted to go there and get to know the people who live by the great river. The place sounded fascinating.

Short answer: no. You can't.

How about down south of town? Maybe Plan de Sanchez? Can

I go out there? I've seen a few people from there on market days here in town, and I know they want to plant trees. I could teach some soil conservation techniques out there, too. Heck, it's only a few kilometers to the *aldea*, heading over Piedras Azules.

Don't even try it.

Nimacabaj, on the other hand, was down in the valley not far from town, and that little community always seemed safe to visit. I had visited Nimacabaj on several occasions in the past, I had done so both alone and with others, including once at twilight with Luís (Güicho) García when we set up a Super 8 projector in front of the little one-room school there and hooked it up to a gasoline generator and proceeded to show the assembled *campesinos* a short didactic movie on household sanitation and latrines.

I remember: while Güicho ran the movie I smoked a cigarette and looked out over the darkening fields of *milpa* to the west, as the sun sank below the horizon, and the sky was brightened intermittently by silent, random discharges of heat lightning which lasted throughout most of the presentation. It was a strangely idyllic moment, this silent electrostatic display, yet at the same time troubling, for one could easily imagine that one was witnessing the flashes of mighty guns in a war that was still far, far away.

Listening now to the testimony coming from *don* Tomás about the evening of terror he had endured I thought to myself: I might not ever again be able to make such a visit to Nimacabaj. And I wondered what precautions might be in order when next I had to visit some of the other *aldeas* in the valley like Xococ or Patixlán, Chiac or Chiticoy.

* * *

One afternoon a few weeks after *don* Tomás's unsettling account I witnessed a strange phenomenon up in the sky that haunted me and made me wonder whether it was possible that spirits of some kind might actually be governing the course of events in Rabinal as they unfolded. I was standing outside my front gate looking up at the clouds to try and see what kind of weather might be developing, when I spied a flock of maybe two dozen dark colored birds that were not traveling anywhere at all, but rather were circling, circling in a tight, vertical spiral slowly rising in the air above me. They continued to circle above me in this tight spiral for longer than a minute, and the sight of them made me think about the events of recent days and the connection or portent that might be augured.

What do the birds tell us? What omen or harbinger does their strange behavior represent? Is the birds' spiraling flight meant to punctuate the final end of strife and terror? Or is it a warning to be heeded concerning even worse things yet to come? Some say spiraling birds in flight signify imminent death, others that they are escorting the recently deceased to the afterlife.

Calchas, the ancient Greek seer, might have helped me here. Or maybe one of his professional peers from among the ancient Hittites, the Romans, or even the Mayans themselves.

> Calchas,
> the clearest by far of all the seers
> who scan the flight of birds. He knew all things that are,
> all things that are past and all that are to come,
> the seer who had led the Argive ships to Troy
> with the second sight that god Apollo gave him.[74]

Calchas himself watched the birds and uttered his prophecies, and in many other cultures individuals endowed with this same gift have always watched the birds closely, finding in their dalliances, their soaring flight and their occasional aerial combat prophecies for human conduct and a community's destiny. *Ornithomancy.* I do not doubt that there could be something to it. Yet on the other hand the spiraling flock that I saw above me that afternoon might have had a much more straightforward explanation from the perspective of natural history: the birds I saw winding upward in their tight spiral could have simply been taking advantage of a buoyant thermal in the air, as birds sometimes do, or they might have all been engaged in a coordinated effort to confuse a nearby predator.

Second sight, or sober science? In that moment standing outside my gate, I felt not at all sure that one path of knowing was more certain than the other. Are birds really messengers from the gods, or are they just reptiles with feathers?

A couple weeks later I witnessed another uncommon sight in the sky, only this time it was in the morning and the phenomenon I saw was of a decidedly more prosaic nature. I was walking down the street where I lived, headed towards the *vivero,* when I heard the distant buzz of an airplane engine. A small, white, single-engine plane—a Cessna, perhaps, or some such craft—came flying over the mountains north of town and flew right over *Cerro Kaj'yúp*, that crumbling citadel of ancient warriors and spirits eternal. And then, as it flew directly over the *pueblo,* all of a sudden I saw falling from the plane thousands of tiny pieces of paper, first one cloud of them and then another. The plane flew off to the south and disappeared over the *Sierra Chuacús* as the two clouds of leaflets fluttered in the breeze and came slowly drifting to the ground and scattering everywhere. Many of the yellow leaflets, none bigger than a standard index card, landed almost at my feet, and I stooped to pick one up. I regret that I never saved one of these yellow slips of paper that fell from the sky. I do wish I had done so, but my best recollection is that each one conveyed a message of reassurance mixed with admonition. "Reassuring" everybody that the army was there to protect us all from the evil of armed rebellion, the curse of communism, while at the same time warning us all regarding the consequences of "unpatriotic" thought or action.[75]

It's been a very long time since I held that leaflet in my hand, but I nevertheless recall that there was also a crude and unflattering little caricature of the rebel forces next to the words of admonition. The plane that had flown overhead looked for all the world like a private plane, but of course it might just as well have belonged to Guatemala's armed forces. I'll never really know. What was salient and certain about this occurrence, however, was what it signified. Rabinal was now most definitely "on the radar" as a new flashpoint in the war for Guatemala's soul, and in all likelihood *la situación* would only grow worse for us all in the coming months. Today it was a battle for hearts and minds waged with leaflets; soon it would be a different kind of battle waged with weapons of a graver caliber.

There was reason to believe, in fact, that the real battle had already begun.

CHAPTER 13

The Voyage of Life

As a young boy growing up in central New York, I became an early devotee of Romanticism. Not so much literary Romanticism, mind you. But I was definitely a sucker for every uplifting story of a passionate quest for truth and oneness with nature, and as a pre-teenager I was already beginning to grasp, however dimly, the idea of mortality. I also loved art and all types of pictorial representation, from the cheery, polychrome visions of Peter Max to the staid yet often stunning Hudson River School.

It was December 21st, 1967, a wet, gray afternoon totally devoid of snow, when my brother Butch, who was home for the holidays, invited me to go with him to visit the museum. I was twelve at the time; my brother was ten years my senior, and not yet a year out of college. We got into his orange VW beetle and made the short trip downtown to Utica's Munson Williams Proctor Art Institute. I know the exact date of this little excursion because I still vividly recall hearing the news on that scratchy AM radio in his car, and I remember the announcer delivering the headline that in Cape Town, South Africa, a man named Louis Washkansky had just died, having survived for a couple weeks with the world's very first transplanted heart. I listened to this news bulletin as Butch drove down Genesee Street—precisely at the point, I remember, where we puttered past Proctor Boulevard.

Just a random, forgettable moment that lasted less than thirty seconds, the merest ripple in the river of time that flowed by, hour by hour, day by day, over half a century ago. Why do I still remember it now as an old man, remember it as if it happened literally yesterday? The brain works in funny ways.

A few minutes after the news broadcast we pulled into the museum parking lot and walked briskly across the street to get out of the rain. Once inside, we must have spent a couple hours strolling through the galleries, admiring (and yes, in a few cases ignoring) all kinds of art. Still lifes and eighteenth-century portraiture filled much of the lower level where we had entered. Upstairs, some lovely pastoral landscapes that transported my nascent romantic spirit to a secret space where I was all alone and free. Then, later on, a haunting, eerily lit landscape by Edward Hopper; and for extra measure a sensuous canvas by O'Keefe, along with an exuberant black-and-white dripping by Pollack. Utica was fortunate to have some damned good art in town—not a lot, but enough to nourish the soul. Yet the utter silence on every floor and in every gallery attested to an all but indifferent public.

Many of the pieces were really worth spending some time with. But for me the greatest reward of all was literally at the top of the museum, on the third floor: Thomas Cole's "The Voyage of Life," a series of four enormous canvases depicting through allegorical imagery a man's passage from childhood to youth to manhood, and finally to old age. This was the first time I had ever seen Cole's paintings, and I was transfixed by the symbolism in nearly every detail. Each of the four scenes was replete with Christian symbols and iconography, but I mostly stood in awe of the purely human allegory that was portrayed, not so much the religious one. The bright-eyed youth casting off on a voyage to a palace in the sky; later, in another canvas, the seasoned mariner praying for his life on a rudderless vessel careening towards a violent maelstrom. Cole's depiction of the soul's progress from birth to mortality made a deep impression on my twelve-year-old brain, and the images stuck with me for many years to come.

Two of the four "Voyage of Life" canvases by Thomas Cole: 'Youth' and 'Manhood.' (Munson Art Institute, Utica, NY.)

I would remember Thomas Cole's paintings once again in early 1981 as I sat in a hammock late at night in Rabinal, ashtray nearly full and a liter of Cabro at my side. I raised my eyes from the book I was reading, and I peered into the darkness beyond the chicozapote tree in my small yard.

Where the hell was I, really, in the scheme of things? What was my mission here?

On one level, at least, my marching orders seemed clear enough: promote reforestation in the *aldeas* and all over the hillsides, and teach the small farmers some elementary best practices in soil conservation. That was the great goal, the dream: to foster throughout this community—throughout every community in Guatemala—the practices and habits that would eventually lead to an *equilibrium* between the growth of forest resources and their consumption by humans. We were also to promote the construction of lorena stoves[76], if we had the time, in order to conserve fuelwood in the *campesinos*' households. All part of seeking that equilibrium. And then there was the secondary project I had elected to undertake: using the topo maps and air photos I had acquired to undertake a comprehensive inventory of the forest resources covering the whole *municipio*.

But it seemed I should be doing something more. Or maybe something else entirely. This thought was nagging me of late, and in the quiet stillness of the night I had time to dwell on the matter at some length. What should I be doing here, really? I recalled my meeting many months earlier with the OAS planners, and I recalled my own presentation on our local reforestation effort that I had delivered in front of the tree nursery that day when we were visited by the governor and the general in charge of the national reforestation campaign. I'm sure they didn't like my presentation one bit—but I knew I was right. Simply put, the numbers were against us. We, all of us, all of my Peace Corps colleagues in reforestation, were waging a nearly hopeless war against the millions of three-stone cooking fires and the billions of leafcutter ants all across the country. It seemed as though all the Mirex in the world would not protect our seedling plantations from being devoured by the ants, and even if it did, at what cost? Probably at the cost of rising cancer rates in every *aldea*, and dead birds everywhere.

To compound the frustration, I had recently heard that the army had torched an entire forest along a key road connecting Quetzaltenango with Retalhuleu on the south coast. They had done this in order to eliminate all possible hiding places where guerrillas might wait in ambush for a passing military convoy. I had occasion to see that very same forest once from a bus that I took departing from Xela. (We had taken the coastal route to Guate that time, because the Pan American Highway was too risky.) Before the army torched it, all along that winding road there had stood a gorgeously lush, shady, verdant canopy that went from tall pines and oaks up near Cantel down to palm trees and sweetgum as one descended to the coast. Now the forest was all gone. The army had reduced it to blackened stumps and ashes.

Was I really doing what was necessary in Rabinal?

At the same time, I was starting to sense an undercurrent growing in Rabinal as well as in neighboring towns. First there was that *boletín de las fuerzas rebeldes* that I had discovered on my doorstep on my first Independence Day in the country. Then there was that strange, midnight walk back home on that very same date: the man named Quique whom I had befriended at the dance had walked with me, he talked with me, and he intimated to me that things were about to change soon, they were about to change in a big way, and he promised me there would even come a time when I would have to swear I had never heard his name.

At the very beginning of 1979, over in the Quiché department, less than eighty kilometers from where I was, the Guerrilla Army of the Poor (EGP) had occupied the town of Nebaj for a day, calling on the people there to join the revolution against their nonindigenous landlords and the army of the rich.[77] In Guatemala City there had been a number of disappearances and assassinations throughout the year, including the murder of the capital's progressive young mayor, Manuel Colom Argueta. And on a regional scale, by mid-July of 1979, close to the time of my talk with those hotshot officials in our tree nursery, the Sandinista liberation forces were marching triumphantly into Managua and seizing the reins of power there. That signal event would become a major catalyst for the changes that were about to unfold in Rabinal and surrounding territories, though I could hardly yet discern the scope of the changes that were just around the corner.

In light of all this, was I really doing what was necessary in Rabinal?

But in the end, I did not rebel. After all, I had a job to do, however Sisyphean it might appear—and I had a future to think about. I could sympathize with the rebels' cause, to be sure, but all of my background growing up in New Hartford and later in college had inclined me towards pacifism, and I knew in my heart of hearts that I could never carry a gun. Could I somehow perform some act that would not require me to resort to violence? But it would have to be something I could do without calling any attention to myself. And under the circumstances I had no idea anyway with whom I might share in confidence my willingness to assist in furthering the cause of revolution.

Revolution. Did I really want to be part of a revolution? *Should* I be part of the revolution? The whole idea seemed far-fetched, even absurd, yet it intrigued me. After all, there must be a hundred things I could do to help out without necessarily holding a gun. Carry messages; translate dispatches for the foreign press; provide shelter to a confrere or two for a few nights in the back of the house where I lived. But how could I possibly find out who had the to-do list? And even if I found that person, how could I start the conversation? It just seemed so utterly implausible. At twenty-five I was still so very young, yet I was already starting to feel morally whiplashed and rudderless at sea. And the turbulent waters that were roiling just around the bend would soon test my convictions like nothing else in my life ever had before.

And every step of the way I would continue to look forward to the looking back. And here I am now, looking back.

* * *

These aimless ruminations all but consumed me many evenings in the early part of 1981. But, to be honest, I couldn't really dwell on these things for too long, since there was also the rest of my life to contend with: I was falling in love. Mireya had already been over to see me once in Rabinal for a weekend visit, enduring nine hours on the Salamateca bus out of and then back to Guate, just so we could be together for our weekend tryst lasting barely a day and a half. We had by now exchanged several long letters—letters filled with romance, dreams, and confessions. Now Mireya was to come over again to spend a couple days with me during the *feria titular* at the end of January. I was overjoyed, ecstatic, and I'm sure it showed every time I walked down to the *vivero* now to talk with the men and make plans with Juan Pablo. Yes, the year 1981 was shaping up to be a very good year indeed—even as I began to ponder what the hell this romantic dalliance might come to at the conclusion of this, my third year of service in the country.

Mireya and I were definitely hitting it off, and our love for each other seemed to grow day by day despite the odds, despite the distance. At the same time I realized, however, that I would very soon have to perform some delicate emotional repair work in letting down the other girl, Lisa, as gently as possible. I imagined I might see her soon at the big dance for the *feria titular*, and I knew I'd be dancing with Mireya that night, so it seemed prudent to start the awkward separation process right now with a short, preemptive letter stressing the bonds of friendship rather than love. I can't remember what I wrote, but if I was smart, I think I must have played the age card first, seeing as how Lisa was several years my junior and barely out of high school. I mailed this letter well before the week of the *feria*, and I think it might have been my last letter to the girl.

With the *feria titular* right around the corner, I learned that fellow volunteers Tex from Salamá and Juanito from Cubulco were both coming over to spend the night; maybe David French from San Miguel Chicaj as well. Everybody always loved to see the traditions and festivities in Rabinal. Of course my door was always open to PCV guests; it was fun to have a few gringos around for a change. The guests could sleep in a hammock on the patio, or on top of *medio-quintal* bags of P.L. 480 white, enriched flour in the back room. Mireya and I would have my bedroom (which was also my office) all to ourselves.

Mireya and I went to the big dance in the *salón municipal* on the last official night of the *feria*, and we danced to several numbers, probably more than I had ever danced to before anywhere, and it was mainly because Mireya simply loved to dance and could not get enough of it.

I followed along as best I could. Lisa was nowhere to be seen anywhere on the dance floor.

* * *

The *feria titular* had been a blast, but it was over now, and there were many tasks to keep me occupied in and around town. The DIGESA extensionists were keeping me busy with new requests to go out and visit and help the small farmers with soil conservation consultations in Xococ, Patixlán, and other *aldeas* a little closer to home. I was also making some progress with the mapping and air photo interpretation for my forest resource inventory, and I wanted to keep up the pace with

Two different processions of the *cofradia* during the *feria titular* in Rabinal, exemplifying a syncretic faith mixing Catholic rites and Mayan traditions. (Photos taken by the author, 1980).

that work so that I might have something to show for myself before the end of my service extension.

In the tree nursery there was a lot of work to do, too, because at the same time that the men there were laying adobe and raising rough wooden siding for the new *bodega*, I was busy sighting and measuring the steep slope down to the creek below with a handy little Abney level, and I was drawing up plans for the pump and piping system that would bring us a badly needed supplementary water supply for all the tree seedlings, which now numbered well over a hundred thousand. Our fruit tree sales were starting to take off, and the small income from that venture would be used to acquire some small supplies and establish a modest per diem allowance for Juan Pablo's occasional errands to the subregional INAFOR office.

And finally, after the end of the official workday, I often continued working late into the night, typing away on my now rather hefty-looking "Guide to Reforestation and Soil Conservation," which upon completion I aimed to share with my Guatemalan colleagues and their successors. I figured if I could do all my research, perfect my written Spanish, and then try to make that little tome as authoritative as possible, I might be able to get it duplicated ("published" was still a stretch, I thought) for other communities around Baja Verapaz, and maybe beyond.

The first of February rolled around, and it was time once again to make that four-and-a half hour bus trip into Guate to collect my salary. Only this time the trip to the city also meant I'd get to see my love, *¡Mi Mireyita!* Of course we had just seen each other during the *feria*, but what the heck, we'd do it again! Besides, St. Valentine's Day was coming up soon, and I wanted to get her something special with my meager "living allowance."

So I boarded the Salamateca in Rabinal's central plaza with a sense of enthusiasm bordering on euphoria. Climbing onto the bus behind several others, I saw that it was already nearly half full with *campesinos* who had started their trip as far back as Cubulco, which was the beginning of the route some fifteen clicks to the west. I took a seat towards the back of the bus, across the aisle from a *campesino* couple who had a basket on the floor with a chicken in it that was partially covered with a blue and green, hand-loomed *sirvieta*—the chicken peeping out as it twitched its head and softly clucked. The wife, like all the other *campesino* women on board, wore her traditional, elaborately embroidered *huipil*, and a brightly multicolored *corte* that was hemmed well below her knees. Husband and wife both wore rubber *kaites* on their feet: old vulcanized tire retreads cut down to roughly the shape of a human foot, and fashioned into a sandal with additional cords of the same rubber. The husband had on a dark blue long-sleeved shirt, nondescript work pants, and of course the customary white *sombrero*. A knitted woolen *morral* that hung from his shoulder would have carried his tattered little wallet with his government-issued *cedula de vecindad* carefully folded up inside, plus whatever other small items he carried with him, like maybe a few stiff tortillas, a loose cigarette or two, and maybe even a tiny cellophane bag full of *pepitoria* which would be their shared snack later on the trip. And of course, his machete in its leather scabbard, which for practical reasons he had to lay down beside him on the bus seat.

Across from me, one row forward, a pretty little Mayan girl, maybe seven or eight years old, was standing in the aisle by the bench where her mother was seated. She was looking back towards me and smiling while she held her mother's hand. The mother, facing forward, did not notice me, but the little girl did, and so I started making silly faces at her. That made her giggle, and then her mother looked and made her turn around and sit down, but every so often she continued to cast furtive glances back towards me, and each time I acknowledged her glances with a smile.

Sitting there in the back of the bus, cramped tightly in my seat with my kneecaps pressing hard into the metal back of the seat in front of me, all of a sudden I felt sublimely at peace with my surroundings. As the *camioneta* turned left onto the road out of town and started gathering speed through the *aldea* of Pachalúm, I felt a moistness in my eyes—a skipped breath, yes, and then I just sat in my seat absolutely transfixed, and I was overcome by a mystical sense of oneness with all the other passengers seated around me. For a minute there, barely a minute, I felt inseparable from everything around me—the Mayan couple sitting across from me, the beautiful little girl who kept stealing glances at me, and *everyone else on the bus*—and in that minute a small tear slowly fell from the corner of my eye.

> And then my mind attained to *That Which Is*, in the flash of one tremulous glance. Then indeed did I perceive your invisible reality through created things....[78]

I was at peace in that moment. I was headed to Guate to see my love Mireya, but I already couldn't wait to get back to Rabinal.

I've held the loving memory of that moment in my brain for more than forty years, and for more than forty years I've wanted to record it on paper. Today I finally recorded it. On paper.

* * *

But in late February 1981, with a little over two years of service under my belt in Rabinal, it finally all came down to a Punctuation Mark that would change absolutely everything.

> (March, 1981, n.d.)
>
> I almost didn't recognize them when they arrived in what appeared to be Basilio's Ford Bronco. There were two of them: Carlos and ______. Displaced from their familiar environment in the Peace Corps

> office in the capital, it was somehow extraordinary watching them approach me, smiling a greeting, there on the dusty streets of Rabinal. Yet the thought registered even before they said a word: It had to be about Dad.
>
> Indeed, it was about my father. "¡Hola Cristián, we're lucky to find you so quickly! I'm so sorry to bring you some bad news, but it looks like your dad back in the States is *algo malito*."

The drivers from the Peace Corps office simply appeared one day on the street, picked me up, and drove me to the capital. They had come to fetch me because my father back home was "not too well." Within less than 48 hours I was on a plane to Miami, and from there it was an unexpectedly circuitous route to upstate New York. Hoping—God, just hoping—to get a last chance to see my dying father. It was the nineteenth of February.

When I got to Miami I had a coffee in the airport cafeteria, and walking down the concourse I passed a departure board where I found that my flight to New York was delayed for another hour. Sitting down, then, at my gate I somehow fell into conversation with (or rather, listened to the monologue of) one Tony ________, a Puerto Rican from Philadelphia who was returning to the States after being jailed for a week in El Salvador because he had snapped pictures where a mass killing had taken place and soldiers were still about.[79] Though part of my mind was obviously elsewhere, Tony's story was gripping, and I felt glad for him that he had made it out of there alive.

It seemed that for all the sleek monorails and people movers and brightly lit concourses lined with upscale shops and bars and restaurants in the Miami terminal, even here I could not escape the gritty Central American reality.

My delayed flight to Syracuse finally took off, and I was mainly just hoping I could get back in time to see my father alive once more before his time was up. Because I somehow knew his time was up. My plane arrived in Syracuse at 12:15 Friday morning. My brother Butch and his wife Lin were waiting in the terminal to meet me and drive me home to New Hartford. They must have waited hours in the airport for my delayed arrival. On the drive home Butch warned me not to be shocked when I saw Dad.

On Saturday, the last day of February (according to the contemporaneous notes I still have, scribbled on a fading scrap of paper), "I saw Dad alone, because Mom was down with a bad cold. Conversation by now was difficult, at best. First thing on arriving, Dad asked me to help sit him on the edge of the bed. There he sat, hands folded on the faux wood-grain table top, just staring out the window at the bleak, snowless February landscape outside. Very quiet. Just staring. He wouldn't eat anything, and he became aggravated at my anxious pleadings."

This was my father's third heart attack, and, as it would turn out, his last. I was able to visit him in the hospital for a couple weeks before he passed. During that period I got telephone calls from the Peace Corps, and a Guatemala desk officer asked me impatiently whether I planned to return to my assignment—or if I intended to quit. I was absolutely resolved not to quit, so I begged the guy on the phone to please be patient a little longer. He then gave me a final date to "make up my mind." How do you tell the guy your mind's already made up, you're just waiting for your father to die?

Meanwhile my mom and I went every day to see my father in the ICU. During one late morning visit I showed him a picture I had in my wallet of my new girlfriend, Mireya. Dad's response to the photograph was minimal, or maybe it was just difficult to register. He was uncomfortable in bed, and he had trouble breathing. Outside the hospital window there was a steady drizzle. I visited my father day after day: we didn't talk much; I mostly just sat there and watched over his gaunt shape lying very still in the bed, and I stared out the window at the gray clouds and the rain. Then one day I stayed home while my mom paid him a visit all by herself. The following day, around five in the morning, our phone rang at home and I jumped out of bed to pick it up. It took the nurse on the other end less than a minute to give me the news.

We buried my father on a cold, snowless afternoon in early March. After the ceremony at the gravesite, we walked through wet, matted grass back to the car that was parked on the cemetery path. My eyes to the ground, I noticed when we reached the automobile path how the old, cracked asphalt still held water, and there was a long puddle there. Standing at the puddle's edge I looked down and saw my reflection in sepia tones, a silhouette of my figure rippled by the breeze,

My father building the back room addition to our house in 1964.

and the reflection of the overcast sky above me. It was at that moment, as near as I recall, when I made a commitment to commemorate the occasion: I promised myself that I would dedicate the remainder of my service in Guatemala to the memory of my father.

* * *

Many other details that I still remember are left out of this upstate interlude that lasted three weeks. But never mind, because the purpose of this story is not so much to tell you about my father's last days and his passing. Rather, I want to tell you about the before and after. Before I got that unexpected visit on the streets of Rabinal, before I sat alone in the sterility of an American hospital watching my father die, things had been going pretty well. I would even say *quite* well. Yes, there was violence in the countryside, but I seldom heard anything but the most fragmentary accounts uttered in hushed voices. I could still travel around, at least to the closer *aldeas* in the valley, and life in the *pueblo* where I lived seemed quite normal. I drank with friends and went to wedding parties; I joined my Guatemalan neighbors almost every time I could in the cycle of local pageantry and festivals that punctuated the year. Times were getting tough all around me, all around the country in fact, but the magic of Rabinal—and now the elixir of love—held me in a narcotizing trance.

That was all before the upstate New York interlude. When I got back to Rabinal three weeks later, many things—no, *everything*—had changed. It was like a change of scenery between the acts in a play. There was a totally different mood that now prevailed in town; a completely different feeling just walking down the street to the *tienda* to buy a pack of cigarettes. "Difference between day and night" is such a cliché, but that's what it amounted to. All of a sudden, people weren't on the street at night. The soldiers from the *destacamento* were much more visible by day now, and they had begun patrolling the narrow, rutted side streets as well as the main drag.

A couple days after my return from the States, I learned that the Spanish priest, *padre* Gregorio Donoso, who ran the *Centro de Integración Familiar* (CIF) in Pachalúm, had been pulled out of Rabinal by the leaders of his order.[80] He was there right before I left, and when I came back he was gone. During my brief absence *las autoridades* had also sent one Luís García Caballeros packing as well (or so I was led to believe at the time); he was the CIF administrator, and a teacher by training. I knew Luís as 'Güicho,' and for two years we had coordinated frequently on community development in the *aldeas*.

Everything had changed in Rabinal. My three-week absence was like a punctuation mark. And in the chapter that followed—a chapter that for me lasted another eight months, and for the people of Rabinal many more years—the plot grew more and more twisted, and the conflict more internecine.

CHAPTER 14

Three Fates

O Zeus, what can I say?
That you look on us and care?
Or do we, holding that the gods exist,
Deceive ourselves with insubstantial dreams
And lies, while random careless chance and change
Alone control the world?

— Euripides, *Hecuba*, 487-91

Waking up in the middle of the morning, I hear through an open window the unmistakable sound of a gas-powered lawn mower outside. Soon the richly nostalgic scent of freshly cut grass is wafting into my room. I am easily given to those nostalgic daydreams that transport me to a childhood growing up in central New York, so I find I have to resist that desultory pleasure in order to remind myself where I am. I am in Guatemala. Well, then, since when do people spend their time mowing lawns in Guatemala? Who, for that matter, has ever heard of a lawn mower in Rabinal?

Still half asleep, I do not recognize the room I'm in, and the bed I'm lying on feels firmer than what I'm accustomed to. The crisp, white sheets have an antiseptic smell about them. That's because I'm in the hospital. And leave it to the Peace Corps—guided, no doubt, by SOPs that come direct from the Embassy—to put me in the best hospital that Guatemala City has to offer. Which might explain why someone is mowing a well-manicured lawn outside.

But how the hell did I end up in a hospital bed in Guate? To answer that question, we'd have to retrace our steps. So let's go back a little.

To begin with, just a week or so earlier I had broken up with Mireya. Or, to be more precise, Mireya had left me, out of pure frustration, and it looked for all the world like we would never see each other again. Ever. We had spent an evening sitting on a bed talking in *La Tranquilidad*, but even before that evening had started I was already in the middle of a deep bout of depression that was clouding both my senses and my reason. The recent death of my father undoubtedly had something to do with my state of mind, but there was more to it than that. It was actually a tidal wave of self-doubt and self-deprecation, the likes of which I hadn't experienced in a long time, mixed with a sense of desperation over the state of the world we were living in, and this whole entire malaise was paralyzing my thought, my speech, and my actions. It was pure catatonia, it was acedia on steroids, and it was rendering me a pointless, useless lump of a man. I am not exaggerating; I was a mess.

Mireya tried at first to draw me out of myself, but I just dug in and got stubbornly entrenched in a myopic world view that no longer seemed to include any regard for her. I'm sure I said things I shouldn't have said. After trying for an hour or more to shake me back to my senses, Mireya finally picked up her purse and walked out. I can't remember if we had made love at all that evening, but if we did then we must have done it before we started talking. Because that evening, somehow, talking ended everything.

I got back to Rabinal the next day, and I tried to apply myself and get back to work, but it was no use. I had just lost the love of my life, I had thrown it all away, and now without Mireya I felt I could hardly continue anymore this whole stupid charade of service to my fellow man.

I was also at the time nursing, and getting a little concerned about, a small festering wound on my left shin that for weeks had just refused to heal. I had bumped my leg on something hard some few days *before* I had left for the States on emergency leave, and from my sad, pitiful vantage point now, that was a pretty long time ago. After the initial 'ouch!' of the bump, it hadn't hurt anymore while it was supposedly healing. But then days passed and it wouldn't heal. In fact, it was starting to hurt, and the wound was now exuding a yellowish pus, a sure sign of bacterial infection.

So, I hauled ass back to Guate, I showed my wounded shin to the doctor in the Peace Corps office, and he immediately put me in the hospital. If left unattended, he told me, a festering wound like this could easily lead to a malignancy, with cancer eventually penetrating down to my tibia. And/or possible blood disease. Great.

At the Herrera-Llerandi Hospital in Guate's upscale Zone 10 I was put in a room with another gringo, a marine from the Embassy, and we talked and shared a few stories. I can't remember what he was in for, but we were both equally conscious and capable of conversation, so we talked. The marine had a Guatemalan girlfriend who visited him daily. The girl had an unmistakable upper-class bearing; always tastefully dressed, and fluent in both languages. The two of them talked for a couple hours every day in their corner of the room, while I either read or worked on a letter.

The letter I was working on was a letter to Mireya. I had to try and repair the damage and salvage our relationship. A relationship which, I fully realized, she might have already consigned to the irretrievable past. Nevertheless, I had to try.

I went through several drafts of my letter, groping about, clumsily at first, to try and nail the right approach, just the right words. In retrospect, this was without question the most important letter I ever had to write. Hours later, when I felt I finally had something that she might at least read to the last page before throwing it away, I got an envelope from the nurse and sealed it all up. Then I waited for the visit of my roommate's girlfriend. She came that afternoon, without fail, and the two of them spent an hour talking and caressing each other on his bed by the window. All very civil and reserved. I'm sure they wished they could have done more together, but I was right across the room.

I was sitting upright on my bed with another freshly changed antiseptic bandage on my shin, just waiting for the right moment (and at the same time trying to gather the chutzpah) to ask the soldier's girl if she would please do me one *huge* favor. If it wasn't too much trouble, could she please, please take this envelope I had and drive it over to the INAFOR offices *en la Zona 13* and deliver it to a *señorita* over there by the name of Mireya? Mireya Sánchez. *En la Unidad Administrativa.* The marine's girlfriend was delighted to help out, perhaps in part because I had intimated, without going into details, that this was an attempt at a reconciliation. She understood, and she happily complied.

Now, some people always manage to reap the reward they so richly deserve, while others win the day just on an earnest promise rather than past performance. In case you haven't already guessed, dear reader, I was in the latter category. The next evening Mireya came to see me in the hospital, accompanied by her niece who was also her closest confidante, and to whom (as I found out later) I owed a lot for the reconciliation that happened.

With Mireya at my bedside holding my hand, I promised I would try to be a better man for her.

My mission, then, from that point on, was to work on that. To try and become a better man.

* * *

It was *Semana Santa*, 1981. By now there was so much that had already happened in Rabinal. Nobody, though, had any idea what was still to come. I was hearing almost daily stories and rumors about what was going down in the *aldeas*. Clearly lives were being lost, yet I was somehow shielded from ever seeing a single body. That lack of direct evidence, however, did not mitigate or deny the facts that were obvious to everyone in Rabinal. There was an unspoken curfew in town now, and nobody ventured into the streets after about 7 p.m. I used to enjoy attending a *boda* reception at the invitation of a friend—but now such joy and frivolity lasting into the wee hours of the morning were no longer to be. People were still getting married, but they celebrated in the morning, in the early afternoon.

I sat in the gray cinder block *comedor* on Rabinal's main drag near the church, eating my lunch of *chuleta marañon* with a Coke. The commanding officer from the *destacamento militar* was dining at another table a few feet away from me, with two of his grunts sitting there on either side. One of them had set his Galil—a long assault weapon even when the stock is folded—right on the dining table beside his plate. While we were eating, a solemn religious procession passed by outside on its way to the church. The slow, steady beat of the drum as the *cofradia* passed by called us all to attention. We all got up and walked to the doorway to watch, including Doña Anita and her husband, who had been cooking together in the back kitchen.

It was Maundy Thursday, and this was the kind of solemn religious procession that you see in every Guatemalan *pueblo* on the red-letter days of the Catholic calendar. The procession walked slowly by while we were out on the sidewalk in front of the *comedor*, and it was not quite gone when the officer in his crisp khakis turned around and faced the rest of us, yanked out a silver crucifix hanging from his neck, grasped it tightly and ostentatiously, like a talisman, and then announced in a firm, resolute voice to the rest of us on the sidewalk, "*¡Yo soy católico también!*"

That's it, my friend. That's all there is to say. The procession continued down the street, we all went back in and finished our lunch, and after that each of us went back to his daily business.

* * *

The next day, Good Friday[81], I was walking across the plaza by the church when I ran into Rosendo Xolop, the man whom I'd commiserated with on a bench by the *Calvario* on the Day of the Dead several months earlier. Rosendo was holding with both hands a pretty little bunch of flowers—for his wife, he said. As I found out later from someone else, the two had had some sort of disagreement, maybe a fight, perhaps over a real or perceived infidelity. I'll never know the details, nor does it matter. What mattered was that Rosendo was walking across the plaza, carrying a bunch of flowers home to his wife to try to make things right.

That evening I was sitting in my hammock reading when I heard another one of those sporadic gunshots. This had been happening a little more frequently lately. While it was certainly unnerving, though, I still felt safe because I was the *gringo* in town. Loosely connected to the U.S. Embassy—as I'm sure the commanding officer in town was well aware. I thought I enjoyed some measure of protected status in town—whether real or imagined.

I momentarily raised my head, wondering what might have happened out there in the night, but then I simply returned to my reading. The darkness grew deep, and I listened to VOA for half an hour on my shortwave radio, smoking a cigarette in the dark, before finally going to bed. I think I slept very well that night.

The next day a friend came up to me and told me that the night before, near the *molino* (the local gasoline-driven mill where women came every morning to get their corn milled into flour for tortillas), scarcely three blocks from the three-room house I was renting, an army lieutenant walked into a little *tienda* right behind Rosendo Xolop, who was standing at the counter, and called out his name. Rosendo turned around, and the lieutenant calmly raised his gun and put a bullet in his forehead.

I still remember Rosendo walking across the central plaza of Rabinal the day before, grasping a small bunch of flowers in front of him. And of course I will always remember the Day of the Dead.

I still think about Rosendo every so often. He returns to me in my dreams, and I tell him I am sorry, I wish I had helped him. He doesn't answer. And, unlike Rosendo, I must live with that.

* * *

Juan Pablo Osorio had been my Guatemalan counterpart and friend in Rabinal for two-and-a-half years. Juanito was on the INAFOR payroll, receiving a small salary to oversee the work in the tree nursery and to accompany me in my own work, which included the soil conservation classes that I gave out in the *aldeas*. The man did his job well in the nursery, and seedling production grew considerably year after year. By the time the rains arrived in June of 1981, we had an inventory of over 130,000 hardy tree seedlings ready for outplanting.

In one of our earliest conversations when I first arrived in Rabinal in '79—barely one week after the departure of my predecessor Don Washco—Juan Pablo had set the tone for our relationship when he said to me, "You know, I never asked for another volunteer to come here." Clearly I had my work cut out for me if I was to cultivate some kind of working relationship that would be, well, workable.

Juanito had a better educational grounding than most of the other INAFOR counterparts who worked with my fellow volunteers elsewhere in the country. He was attending *tercero básico* classes in the evenings, which meant he was at a level roughly equivalent to our high school. I helped him a few times with some elementary algebra problems. And when he told me one day that he was learning about Cervantes' masterpiece *Don Quixote* in class, on my next trip to Guate I bought him a copy of the book. It took him a while, but he eventually read the whole thing. I asked him almost every day how the reading was going, and he'd tell me all about the latest chapters he had read. I'll never forget the enjoyment I derived from our long conversations about the Knight of the Sad Countenance, about the jousting with windmills, the righting of perceived wrongs all across the plain of La

Mancha, and about the hero's poignant demise after finally returning to his hometown. And from our conversations I could tell that Juanito had come to love the book as much as I did.

Juan Pablo and I had started out with some considerable distance between us, but we ended up as intimate friends. By all accounts Juanito was a devoted family man, with a wife and two small kids and his parents all living with him in his ramshackle little house with a corrugated metal roof. His wife Rosalía, a slender and pretty young woman with a couple gold teeth in her mouth, was invariably dressed in her traditional *huipíl* and *corte*, her long, lustrous black hair falling to her waist behind her. In addition to taking care of all the cooking and housework that she did for her family, Rosalía earned a few extra quetzales coming by my house every Friday to pick up my dirty clothes, and then I'd stop by their house to retrieve the bundle on Sunday, always finding every item spotless and neatly folded.

Often when I entered their one main room redolent of wood smoke from the constant cooking fire, I'd find them sitting together watching the Mexican variety show *Siempre en Domingo,* or sometimes even a rerun of *Dallas,* on their little twelve-inch, black and white TV that always had trouble pulling in a signal from the stations in Guate.

One might say Juan Pablo and Rosalía were made for each other.

So it came as quite a surprise when I learned one day that Juan Pablo had been unfaithful to his poor wife Rosalía. This was not something I learned through any sort of prying with family members, much less by direct interrogation. Rather, the tryst simply exploded into public view one day, either because of some suspicious behavior that maybe sparked a conversation at home, followed by a scene, or maybe somehow there was an encounter on the street, and words were had between Rosalía and the other woman.

At any rate, one day Rosalía came by my house all by herself, something she *never* did before unless she was stopping by to pick up a bundle of dirty clothes. But it wasn't Friday. She came inside under the carport weeping bitterly and there she told me about her husband's infidelity, and then she buried her sobs in my embrace. My tentative embrace became a consoling hug. It was a necessary gesture of empathy on my part, in fact under the circumstances I'd say it was absolutely necessary. Yet at the same time it felt passing strange to hold my coworker's wife in my arms as we stood there on the veranda. Especially since local customs and basic respect had always dictated that I never touch so much as the elbow of a Mayan woman of any age. Much less a married one.

Poor Rosalía wept buckets as I held her there in my arms, and between sobs I promised her I would try and talk with Juan Pablo.

Meanwhile, back at their place Juan Pablo's father was busy organizing an evangelical prayer vigil that was to be held right there in the house in order to bring his son around to repentance. This, I knew, was the last thing that Juan Pablo needed. And, in fact, he would have nothing of it. While the family and their parishioner friends and relatives and even the minister from their Nazarene church were all crowded into the little house praying out loud and singing their hymns of redemption, Juan Pablo came over to my place where we talked in the dark on my veranda, and we each drank a warm beer, and then we walked over to the *comedor* down the street. Juan Pablo hadn't eaten anything all day and was famished, so I bought us two dinners of *pollo frito* and we drank a couple more beers and we talked long into the night about life, about women, about love, and even a little about fidelity. He spent that night at my house, sleeping on top of the CARE food bags with an extra sheet and blanket that I gave him.

A few days later Juan Pablo did reconcile with Rosalía, and things slowly returned to normal. I suppose with the kids and all there was just too much at stake to let this become a permanent rift. Instead, a stiff and tense sort of normal prevailed.

Our own relationship as friends and as co-workers, however, would never again be the same. For in my efforts to reach out to Juan Pablo during his marital crisis, I had unconsciously crossed a line. I had wanted to help Juan Pablo get back on the right path, I had desperately wanted him to come back to his wife whom I felt deeply sorry for. But in the end, I guess I had been trying too hard. And I had gotten *too close.* My own earnest efforts surely threw into chaos Juan Pablo's understanding of the proper relationship between master and servant. And the man was, after all, the ineluctable product of decades, if not centuries of cultural conditioning about the proper relationship between master and servant. Like it or not, I was the "master" here. And now I had violated a sacred cultural norm, for which in the end I would surely pay a price.

We resumed working together for a couple weeks in the tree nursery, but then one day Juan Pablo delivered to me an unexpected, handwritten letter in which he very solicitously and very formally requested that I put in a request on his behalf to INAFOR so that he might be granted a month and a half of unpaid leave. In his letter he made a point of citing "health reasons," but of course I knew there was more to it than that.

I have saved Juan Pablo's letter to this very day, mainly, perhaps, because of its sentimental value. He signed it, "*Tu íntimo amigo.*" I can't possibly throw that letter away, not even now, so many decades later.

Juan Pablo did indeed return to work six weeks later. He was back together again with his wife and family; he was going to church more often. (*Culto*, they called it. Nazarene evangelicals.)

Our work together had pretty much returned to normal. As I already related previously, Juan Pablo was still on the job on that awful day in October when the firebombing occurred, and even weeks later when we had to deal with the matter of getting Tomás Lajuj's INAFOR identification card re-issued. And he continued supervising our tree nursery operations for a few more months going into 1981. During this time period Juan Pablo bought himself a second-hand motorbike, and one day I even saw him riding his whole family down the street on it, Rosalía riding behind, side-saddle, with their little girl squeezed between them and four-year-old Darwin sitting on the gas tank between his father's arms.

But then one day Juan Pablo arrived at my gate with another one of his handwritten letters. This time he was announcing that he was quitting his INAFOR job. He and his family were already packing up and getting ready to move to Guate, where, he said, he hoped to take a course to become an electrician.

We sat and talked for a few minutes, and of course I asked him if he felt really sure about what he was doing. He did, he said. Thus the conversation ended, and Juan Pablo walked out of my house for the last time. I went out back and sat down on the ground in my yard, and I just stared blankly into space. And I will frankly admit that this time it was me who was sobbing. Sobbing because I couldn't possibly have imagined a more perfect, royal fuck-up. True, the act of infidelity had been Juan Pablo's doing, yet still I felt there might have been something I could have done, some more measured approach in dealing with him every day, something, just *something* I could have done to make him stay. Whether it was rational or not, I felt somehow responsible for losing Juan Pablo. Donaldo, my predecessor in Rabinal, had chosen a good, capable, intelligent man to be his counterpart, his protégé. He had trained him for two years, he had navigated every type of obstacle to keep him in the job, he had even helped nurture Juan Pablo's labor relationship with his superiors at the INAFOR subregional office. And now it was on my watch that we lost the man. A good man.

It took me many, many years to finally discover the true reason behind Juan Pablo's abrupt departure from Rabinal. What he was unable to reveal to me at the time was that he had been detained by the army and tortured for several days in a dark room located in the settlement know as Pacux, the place where the *campesinos* coming from Rio Negro were supposed to take up residence after being flooded out of their ancestral lands by the great river. (The army maintained tight control over the Pacux settlement, and even utilized its spaces as an unofficial annex to their military garrison nearby.) Juan Pablo was tied up and beaten there, held staked to the ground without food or water for almost four days, while the soldiers shouted abuses at him day and night, calling him a goddamn *guerrillero* who works with the gringo in town. Juan Pablo was finally released in the end, with a tortilla and a stern warning not to breathe a word to anybody about what the soldiers had done to him, lest they come back for him later and "bust his ass." So when Juan Pablo finally got back to his wife and family, they packed up to leave, and Juan Pablo sat down to write the words of farewell that I was now reading.

In the first few days after Juan Pablo's departure I had to assume full control of the tree nursery, and in the first few days I was spending much of every day supervising the men there. (Fortunately they did not need a whole lot of supervising, since they all knew their jobs.) I needed a new counterpart pretty quickly, though. And, as it happened, right there in the *vivero* was a man for the job. Chico had worked in the nursery for some time, earning only his weekly bags of Food for Work. He was young—barely nineteen or twenty—but he had his shit together, and he certainly seemed enthusiastic. So Chico it was, and I sent a letter to the INAFOR subregional office with his name and his *Cédula de Vecindad* number to get him on payroll. I didn't wait for an answer from INAFOR; I started training Chico immediately.

I began his training with basic pesticide precautions.

CHAPTER 15

A Needful Errand

Surely the wise man will forever shrink from war,
yet if war come, the hero's death will lay a wreath
not lustreless on the city. The coward alone brings shame.

—Euripides, *The Trojan Women*, 400f

One afternoon before the rains came, I was sitting on the patio when somebody—a young man or a woman, I can't remember—arrived at my gate and called out for me. I got up and walked out to the gate, and the message I received there was short: *Doña* Candelaria over at the *tienda agropecuaria* on the other side of town wanted to talk to me, and she wanted to do so really as soon as possible—if possible. The plea sounded genuinely important, and the person calling on me was polite but quite serious. I told my visitor I would try to get over to see *doña* Candelaria that evening. I hadn't seen *doña* Candelaria's son Güicho in several weeks, and for a minute I wondered if this might be about him. But I checked myself because I didn't want to jump to any conclusions. I had even persuaded myself that everything must be all right; Güicho's simply out of town, that's all, maybe taking a course somewhere, and his mom simply had some other thing on her mind right now, God knows what. I'd have to go find out. My visitor departed, and I went back to whatever I had been doing.

Dinnertime rolled around soon enough, and I was really famished, so my plan was to walk over to *Las Diamelas* on the plaza for a nice beefsteak dinner with *frijoles volteados* and maybe a beer, and then I'd stroll down the three extra blocks to *doña* Candelaria's *tienda* to see what she wanted. Satisfied with my simple plan, I got up to sweep the patio because it really needed it, I dumped the full ashtray into a box to take out later, and I headed out, locking the gate behind me and lighting another cigarette for the short walk to the restaurant.

The dinner was quite satisfying, and I almost wanted to order another beer, but then I remembered the *diligencia* I had to take care of. I paid up at the register and put down my tip at the table and I headed out. An orange sun was starting to settle over Cubulco as I strode westward, and I hoped I wouldn't be arriving too late for this rendezvous. But as I approached the *tienda* I was relieved to see that it was still open, so I walked right in. I asked for *doña* Candelaria and she came out in a jiffy, greeting me warmly and then inviting me to come out back with her, past the store counter, and beyond that point I found she had a lovely little patio with plants all around and a couple comfortable chairs.

Doña Candelaria invited me to sit down, and with some urgency asked a young family member (daughter? niece?) to bring me a soda.

"I am so glad you could stop by and visit us," she said. "Can I offer you something to eat?" But of course I was already quite full, so I politely refused. I wanted to pay for the soda, but she insisted it was on the house. *Doña* Candelaria then got to the point of the rendezvous.

"We have a situation here, *don Cristián*, that I will tell you about in confidence, but my question for you is, do you have dollars that I can buy? I can buy almost any amount you might be willing to sell me, but I need these dollars rather urgently." Without yet answering her main question, I responded with my own. "What has happened, *doña* Candelaria? Why has this sudden need come up?" With her son Güicho out of sight for weeks now, I began to suspect what the answer might be, though I could scarcely imagine what shape the answer might take.

"*Es Güicho, mi hijo*. He's had to flee from Rabinal because of the situation here, and he is now in Mexico." Ahh, I thought, *la situación*. It all made sense. *La Situación*. I recalled my conversation with Güicho in the pickup truck on that rainy day coming back from Chichupac. Seemed like ages ago. Yes, of course, *La Situación*. It was the same Situation that had led a platoon of soldiers to murder nearly two dozen Mayan civilians in *aldea* Pichec a few months earlier.[82] The same Situation playing out right here in town when an army lieutenant from the *destacamento* put a bullet in the head of Rosendo Xolop on Good Friday. The same Situation that ended the life of the well-known psychologist and dedicated journalist Irma Flaquer who had been kidnapped two blocks away from her apartment while driving home from a birthday party in Guatemala City and then "disappeared," never to be seen again.[83] *La Situación*. I understood now. The Situation had arrived at my doorstep.

"Can you help us, *don Cristián*? You see, with Güicho in Mexico now, he's going to need some money to live on while he finds his way there. I have a way to send him money, I can't tell you how, but I have a way. But quetzales will do him no good in Mexico; they're worthless there. He needs dollars. I can help my son if I can find the dollars to pass along to him. You're a *norteamericano*, *don Cristián*; don't you have access to dollars?"

I sat there on *doña* Candelaria's pleasant patio with the lush, green plants all around, and I considered. I took a sip of my soda and I asked my host to let me think for a minute. I sat there and I recalled my experience of the Day of the Dead some six months earlier. I had sat down on a rustic bench near the Calvario chapel with Rosendo Xolop, and he was completely drunk there and weeping bitterly—*remember?*—and he was begging me—*begging* me—to help him get out of the country because he feared for his life. And I had said to Rosendo, between slugs of my *octavo de Venado Especial*, I said to him, Come on, Rosendo, it can't be as bad as all that. Surely there's a way to manage these affairs so you'll come out okay …

That time I had failed miserably to do what was necessary. I couldn't fail again.

But at first I really had no idea how to go about this. I said to *doña* Candelaria, "Look, I understand the situation, *doña*. Believe me, I really do. And I would like to help out, but, but to be honest, I just don't know how." During the pause that followed *doña* Candelaria kept on looking at me with eternally hopeful eyes, despite my words that offered no encouragement. "You see, although yes, I am a gringo, I really don't have such easy access to dollars as you might imagine. At least not here. I don't carry any dollars, I don't have any at the house or in the bank in Guate, and I'm not even sure how I could get my hands on any unless I were to travel back to the States." At this point I wasn't showing all my cards. I was turning it all over in my mind.

"Surely you can think of a way," *doña* Candelaria replied. "I know you're an intelligent man, *don Cristián*, and I'm sure you can find a way to get some dollars that I can send to Güicho."

"Give me this evening and let me think about it. I will stop by tomorrow on my way to the *vivero* and give you an answer." *Doña* Candelaria readily assented, and we left it at that. I thanked her for the hospitality and I complimented her on her lovely home, and then I stepped out onto the street and walked back home. While I walked alone through the now darkened streets, I thought to myself: well, Chris, that was a nice, quiet exit that certainly didn't draw any attention.

Then again, who the hell was I kidding? I was the only *gringo* in town, and at six-foot-three I stood out like a pineapple in a crate of mangoes. I'd have to try to be more careful in the days to come.

Once I was back at the house I sat down in my hammock and lit a smoke and just sat there thinking. There *was* a way, of course. There was certainly a way for me to get dollars. All I had to do was tell them at the Peace Corps office that I wanted to head back home to New York for some vacation time, and I needed an advance of five hundred dollars out of my readjustment allowance, so I'd have cash for the trip. There was a clause in the Peace Corps policy specifically allowing this.

But if you get the cash to make the trip, then you have to make the trip. And spend the cash. Unless. *Unless*. Unless I told them I'd scheduled this vacation—yeah, my family and friends are all expecting me, so I'll pick up the dollars at the Peace Corps office, and *then*—oh *look*, everything just fell through! How unfortunate! Like, *what happened?* Never mind, you can make up a story. Keep the dollars for *doña* Candi. Skip the trip.

But you just *went* to the States a few short months ago, on emergency leave. Well yeah, I know, but I really need to go again. Family issues. And what about plane tickets? Would I need to show them first at the office that I had plane tickets? Hmm, potential obstacle there. Well, but *heck*, you know I don't even have the money for plane tickets, ha-ha, heck no, so my mom is *sending* me the tickets—her treat, she said, and she told me she'll wire them down here in a few days.

So, then: you pick up the dollars at the Peace Corps office on the promise that you'll show them the plane tickets soon, you take the dollars back to *Doña* Candelaria in Rabinal, and then you tell the office it simply didn't work out; mom couldn't send me the tickets after all, so I guess I'm not going anywhere. Yes, I know, I'm *so* bummed out about this, but don't worry, I can either hang on to the dollars, or I guess I can easily change them back to quetzales if I need to. (!!) … Man, I bet I could just send the office a nice little telegram to let them know about the change in plans. Save myself a trip. Hell, I certainly wasn't stealing anything; I was simply circumventing the rules a bit in order to do what was necessary.

This was pure genius.

I could hardly wait to go back and tell Güicho's mom. So the next morning I started out earlier than usual for the *vivero*, but when I got to the *tienda agropecuaria* at the halfway point I found the steel double doors were shut tight, and there was no way to even peer through a window. I had arrived so early that the place hadn't even opened for business yet. I thought of knocking, but then I thought better of it. Instead I gave up and continued on down to the *vivero*, where I spent half the morning doing a seedling inventory, checking the bodega to see what supplies we needed, and filling out a requisition to send in to the CARE office. I was really anxious to go back and give it another try with *doña* Candelaria, so I tried to make short work of it all in the *vivero*, and then I told Juan Pablo that I was headed back to the house to work on my mapping and air photo interp. Which was true—eventually.

On my second try with *doña* Candelaria I found the *tienda* open for business, and in fact *doña* Candi had just finished bagging some items for a customer at the cash register. Upon seeing me she immediately invited me through the gate that was built into the long countertop, and we sat down again on her patio.

"*Señora,* I came by to tell you I have a plan." *Doña* Candelaria smiled broadly and her eyes lit up, and she clasped her hands in eager anticipation of the details. But I didn't give her all the details that I had carefully scoped out the night before. In fact, I gave her almost none. She didn't need to know; and anyway it would've sounded boring, maybe even confusing. I just told her not to worry, I had a plan that would work, and I'd be able to get her five hundred dollars in a few days.

She offered me another soda, but it was kind of early in the day and I wasn't thirsty. We said our goodbyes and I left, and I walked on down to the market in the plaza. It wasn't market day, but nevertheless there was at least one little ramshackle *tienda* in the row that was open, and I found there exactly what I needed: a little, hand-loomed *típica* purse, smaller than a 3x5 index card, that most people would customarily use to keep their spare change in. I had a different, but related purpose in mind. I bought the purse for about a quetzal. I still have this little purse today, and I cherish it. It is stashed away in a box here in my office, and I never want to lose it. Because there was that one time, a long time ago, when it served an important purpose.

A day or two later I took the bus into Guate and I made a beeline for the Peace Corps office. I delivered my carefully planned *spiel* to the clerk there who handled these things, she bought the story lock, stock and barrel, and before I knew it I was filling out a form for the advance on my readjustment allowance. And only then was I informed I would have to wait a day or two, because they certainly didn't have that amount of cash in the office—not in dollars, anyway.

That was a snag I hadn't anticipated, but not the end of the world. I had to pick up my paycheck anyway (in quetzales!), so I did that and hustled over to the *Banco de Occidente* to cash it, and then I went to a hardware store to get some things for the new water pump that we now had in the *vivero*. After that I walked over to the coffee emporium on 7th Avenue, where I bought a couple pounds of their BBB brand—that delicious export quality that I was so addicted to. With little else to do after that, I spent the rest of the day pretty much just bopping around Zone 1, sitting in the shade in the *Parque Concordia* for a while, walking some more, checking out the *disco* store for new cassette titles. I eventually got to a public phone where I could call Mireya at the INAFOR office to tell her I was in town and I hoped to see her if she'd be free in the evening. We made plans to meet at the Café Lido by the cinema of the same name—our usual rendezvous point.

After the telephone call I decided to head down 14th Street to the *pensión* where I'd be spending the night—*La Tranquilidad*, my usual haunt. The *pensión* where I'd also soon be spending a few precious hours of paradise *con mi Mireyita*.

Walking down 14th Street I relaxed and let my mind wander, just relishing the thought of the evening that lay ahead, when I was suddenly stopped by two stocky *ladino* men with formidable biceps. One of the men shouted at me to stop in my tracks, keep my mouth shut, and drop my canvas Boy Scout knapsack on the ground. Both men wore plain clothes—white shirts and black dress slacks—and each had an Uzi, one of which was drawn on me. Then they ordered me to open up the knapsack and empty the contents on the sidewalk.

"Like *now*, quickly!"

I'm kneeling on the ground now, nervously struggling to unbuckle the flap of my knapsack, and I slowly pulled out two brown, brick-shaped packages (*CUIDADO—could be a bomb!*) wrapped tightly in cellophane, with the big letters BBB and the caricature of a happy little brown-faced girl on the front of each one. "*Es solo café*," I offered meekly. "WHAT ELSE DO YOU HAVE IN THERE?" shouted one of the men, waving his Uzi. So I pulled out—very slowly—my change of clothes, my toiletries, my notebook, and two pens, because I always wanted to have a spare on hand.

The men, who appeared to be bodyguards of some sort, finally seemed satisfied with the results of the search. But then, as I nervously stuffed all the things back into my knapsack, one of them asked me, "And where are you headed?" That was actually a tough one to answer, as I was merely killing time that afternoon and really headed nowhere. But my hesitation in answering made them all the more reluctant to release me. Then I suddenly snapped to and found the inspiration to come up with a good truth-lie: "I'm headed to the Peace Corps office in Zone 2! I'm a Peace Corps volunteer, and I'm a United States citizen!" (Might have helped to *start out* with that line in the very beginning, but oh well.) They may or may not have known what the Peace Corps was, but anyway my answer was good enough to get me dismissed with a gruff, "*¡Siga en su camino!*" And so I walked on without looking back.

That evening I met up with Mireya at the Lido. We had both had dinner already, so I just ordered an espresso and a slice of cheesecake. Mireya watched me eat, and we chatted for a while in the tiny, crowded cafe. I asked her if she might happen to have any dollars left over from her trip to Mexico back in November, but she didn't, she said, she had spent them all, so that was that. Just trying every avenue. I finished up and paid the bill and we went over to the cinema next door, where "The French Lieutenant's Woman" was showing, based on John Fowles' wonderfully inventive and very sensual novel.

After the movie we walked over to *La Tranquilidad*, we went upstairs to the room I'd taken earlier in the day, and we sat on the bed together and talked. There in the privacy of the hotel room I explained to Mireya what I'd been doing the past couple days. I told her about my promise to *doña* Candelaria that I would do what I could to help her son, and I acknowledged that yes, in light of his prolonged absence it did appear likely that Güicho had joined the Movement. (Though *doña* Candelaria was actually keeping mum about that; ostensibly Güicho had "fled to Mexico.") I shared every detail with Mireya, and I told her how I just wanted to help my friend *con mi granito de arena*.

It was getting late, and we both just couldn't wait any longer, so we finally turned back the covers and made passionate love on that bed. In a spirit of pure celebration we played in bed together for a long time that evening, until Mireya finally said she had to get back to her place if she was going to get to work on time the next day. We got dressed, we went downstairs, and I walked Mireya out to the bus stop.

The next morning I thought at first I might skip breakfast because I wanted to get over to the Peace Corps office as quickly as possible to see if they had my dollars ready. I felt a bit dissipated from the night before, though, so instead I walked up to 6th Avenue where I found my favorite place for breakfast, Danny's Pancakes. Danny's offered at least a dozen varieties of pancakes and waffles, and some very good coffee to go with it. I got a table behind their quaint stone courtyard and placed my order.

Satisfied with the nice, big breakfast, I was relaxing with a good remainder of coffee that was left, because they always placed a pot on every table, even for a party of one. At the next table over, I noticed four women were seated, and they were talking in English about their recent experiences—maybe as recent as the day before—in towns of the country's western highlands. I overheard their conversation and recognized some of the place names—Sololá, Santa Cruz del Quiché, Santa Catarina Ixtahuacán. Each of the women wore conservative attire with a light tan skirt draping below the knee; sensible, black pumps, and a bright crucifix around the neck.[84] Their conversation, which I could follow almost word for word, shifted to the topic of the airport, and it became clear that at least one of them was soon to depart to return to the States.

This was my chance, maybe, to score some more dollars, so with due alacrity I got up and walked over to their table. I introduced myself and explained what I was doing in Guatemala; I explained a little about Rabinal, and I told them about Güicho. I told them what my mission was on this brief foray into the city, and then I asked them if they had any dollars to spare. Fortunately, I had just collected my pay the day before, so I was not short on quetzales. The Sisters of Charity (for that was their order[85]) were immediately sympathetic. They each did some quick mental calculations to estimate how many dollars they'd need to keep on hand, and in the end I scored about seventy-five bucks. A good start, which hopefully would be added to before the day was over. I thanked the sisters profusely, and we all got up and went our separate ways.

Walking the rest of the way down 6th Avenue towards the Peace Corps office after breakfast, I wondered if they might have my five hundred dollars ready, or if I'd have to spend another night in Guate. The prospect of spending another evening with Mireya did not displease me. Still, when I got to the office I was delighted to find that my dollars were waiting for me there. I signed a paper for the secretary and then I was home free—five hundred dollars in cold, hard cash right there in my hands.

My next stop was the restroom, where I pulled out of my knapsack the little *típica* purse I had bought in the Rabinal market. I folded the thick wad of bills once tightly in half, placed the wad of bills in the purse, zipped it tight, and then I stuck the purse in the sole of my left tennis shoe. Standing over the toilet in the stall, I took a few steps in place to check for fit, and it wasn't too bad. It would flatten out. But I'd have to try to walk as little as possible so as not to damage the bills. I felt pretty satisfied this would work, so I left the bathroom, departed from the office, and took a *bus urbano* instead of walking the three clicks up to the *Salameteca* station where I'd get my bus back to Rabinal.

The first three hours of the ride back to Rabinal were uneventful. I was a little nervous about anybody getting too close to my feet, so I hunkered down and tried to keep as still as possible. The bus made its customary stop in El Rancho, where the women with their wide baskets balanced on top of their heads came on board and squeezed their bodies down the narrow aisle calling out the names of their delectable treats. "*¡Semilla de marañon!*" "*¡Chocobananos a quince len!*" But I wasn't interested in a snack; I was just staring at my shoelaces and waiting for the driver to blow his horn so we could get on our way again.

We did get on our way again, and the next leg of the trip was the one that I always enjoyed: the steep, winding, picturesque climb from the desert of El Rancho up to the cloud forest of the *cumbre de Santa Elena*. We were approaching the turnoff at the *cumbre* when our bus slowed down unexpectedly. I peered ahead through the windshield, though I was seated several rows back, and I saw two army jeeps, one with a 50-caliber mounted in the back, and a group of maybe eight soldiers with their Galils at the ready. One of the soldiers was flagging us down, so we stopped.

"*¡Bajense todos aquí, por favor!*" The order was to get out and stand in a line on the grassy shoulder, and so we did. It was then that I noticed that out of the whole group of soldiers, one of them wore a black balaclava over his head. That was a little disconcerting. We all lined up on the shoulder, facing the asphalt, while two soldiers boarded the bus with guns drawn and slowly walked to the rear and then back to the front, scanning from side to side.

Standing there in the damp fog of the *cumbre*, I was truly afraid we might all be frisked. My wad of bills was right under my foot in my left shoe, but I was still nervous. Fortunately, though, the soldiers just looked us up and down without any physical contact, and then they told us we could get back on board and continue on our way.

The rest of the trip went fine. An hour and a half later I finally walked up to my front gate in Rabinal, and I don't recall a time when I felt happier to be back home. It was only late afternoon, though, so I figured I might as well take care of delivering the goods sooner rather than later. I dropped my *mochila* in a corner without unpacking it and went to the *pila* out back to wash off all the dust from the long trip. Next, I took off my sneakers and pulled the flattened *tipica* purse full of dollars from the left one. I took the bills out of the purse and was pleased to see they had survived the trip pretty well. Didn't even smell too much.

I made it over to *doña* Candelaria's *tienda agropecuaria* well before the dinner hour. I didn't even have to ask for her, as she happened to be right there by the cash register.

"*Hola, doña* Candelaria, I've just returned from Guate."

"*¡Pase adelante, señor don Cristián!*" And she pulled open the gate that was built into the countertop and urged me to come on through and join her in the courtyard out back.

We didn't spend long together on this visit. *Doña* Candelaria offered me a soda again. Then I reached in my pocket and showed her the wad of bills, apologizing for their condition even though they didn't look too bad. About five hundred seventy-five dollars, if memory serves me.

Doña Candelaria excused herself so she could run and get her quetzales for the exchange. She went to a back room in the house, and then she came rushing back to our little sitting area in the midst of her beautiful green plants. She asked me how much she owed me, and I simply told her, "Well, for five hundred seventy-five dollars you only have to give me five hundred seventy-five quetzales. The rate is still one to one." And it was true, that was still the official rate. But times were difficult in Guatemala, and the black market was already on the rise. I could have asked *doña* Candi for more, and she would have gladly given it to me.

So now I had a thick wad of quetzales on hand that I had no immediate use for. Well, maybe the excess cash would come in handy later. I never found out how the dollars I provided might actually have been used. For food? For rent? For bullets, maybe? The only knowledge I was privileged to possess was that they would somehow help to support *doña* Candelaria's son Güicho who had fled to Mexico. While I doubted the veracity of *doña* Candi's account of her son's whereabouts, I never doubted for a minute that I was helping my friend Güicho to do what was necessary. Helping, at least, with my small *granito de arena.*

A few days after my meeting with *doña* Candelaria (a judiciously chosen interval, I thought, to help cover my tracks), I sent a telegram to the Peace Corps office to let them know I had unfortunately had to cancel my planned trip to the U.S. I wasn't going anywhere, after all. "Things just didn't work out."

Doña Candelaria

* * *

Around the beginning of the rainy season I made one of my customary forays into the capital city to pick up my paycheck and run the usual errands. And to see Mireya, of course. As I waited for my *Salamateca* in the plaza I heard the cicadas still buzzing away in the distance, for there had only been some light *lloviznas* so far, and the hard rains had not yet started to fall.

The trip to Guate was mostly uneventful, and after a short visit to the Peace Corps office to pick up my check and get my gamma globulin shot, I was barely able to hit the *Banco de Occidente* in time to cash my check before it closed for the day. That much accomplished, I was off to McDonald's nearby to grab a late lunch. When I got to McD's it was not too busy, as it was already past peak for the day. I ordered my burger and fries and sat down at a table all by myself. Not too many people around, and that was nice because I hated getting caught in the lunch hour rush in Zone 1.

There was this one guy only a little older than me who sat a couple tables away sipping a Coke. A normal-looking Guatemalan guy, sort of middle class, who, with his crisp and pressed shirt and pants and smart pair of black loafers, looked for all the world like one of the bank tellers from across the way on a late lunch break. As soon as he got up from his seat, however, I noticed he carried a holstered sidearm on his hip. He got up and walked towards me, carrying the tall soda cup in his hand, and I watched with only mild concern as he approached me.

"Seat not occupied here? May I sit down with you?" I felt I couldn't easily say no, and so he sat down and set his soda on the table.

"Traveling through Guatemala, *amigo*? Tourist?" I might have easily extricated myself from this whole delicate situation by lying, but my inherent fear of firearms inspired me to respond with the truth. I told him who I worked with and what I was doing. It sort of appeared to me (without any certainty, mind you) that he actually knew what the Peace Corps was. We introduced ourselves by name, though I do not remember his. I just wanted to finish my lunch.

"And where do you work, *amigo*?" he asked. And I told him.

"Ahh, Rabinal! Home of the famous Rabinal orange! That's a town where we have a lot of work to do." By now I knew this guy's number, and

I was starting to get a little worried. I hadn't told him a lot, but I thought maybe I had already told him too much. Still, he pressed on.

"You know, we could use some good information from Rabinal. We really could use someone there who knows his way around. You say you've been living there for more than two years? You must know a lot of people there! Tell me, *amigo*, would you be interested in helping us out? It's not much we need—just some names, you know, and the things people are doing. Little things like that could help us a lot. You'd be helping us protect our national security. National security is a good thing, no? It is important."

I immediately thought of Güicho, who was now somewhere in Mexico—supposedly. I gave the guy with the gun the smart answer, "Yes, of course!", as far as national security goes, and then I gave him the dry, official answer, as far as helping out goes. I was well versed in the answer: "No, I'm sorry I can't help you out. I can't because as a Peace Corps volunteer in this country, as a United States citizen, I cannot get involved in local politics under any circumstances. It's been nice talking with you; I have to go now."

I didn't tell this guy with the gun (who was almost certainly G-2, the often ununiformed intelligence branch of the military) that I was already sort of involved.

I walked out the door with my canvas Boy Scout knapsack, and the guy remained seated inside. As before with the two Uzi-toting bodyguards I had encountered on 14th Street, I didn't look back. I hadn't been planning on returning to the Peace Corps office that afternoon, but under the circumstances I had to. The office was only about a mile from McD's, so it was an easy walk.

When I got to the Peace Corps office I went inside and was relieved to find that the P.C. country director Ron Arms was in his office and apparently not too busy. I asked if I could come in and sit down for a minute, and Ron offered me a chair. I told him what had just transpired during my lunch at McD's, and I tried hard to remember and relate as many of the details of our verbal exchange as possible. Ron asked me if I had felt threatened in any way, and I told him I really hadn't. A little unnerved, perhaps; that was all. Our conversation was short, and at the end, as I was headed for the door, Ron assured me that he would be sharing this incident with the appropriate attaché at the Embassy.

"Yeah, you be sure and tell the *military* attaché at the Embassy what happened, and tell him he should talk to his goddamned Guatemalan counterparts over at the army base and he should tell them their goons ought to fuckin' *knock it off* and stop fucking around with us Peace Corps volunteers!"

I thought that to myself, but I did not say that to Ron.

CHAPTER 16

A Walk to Raxjút

Susanna, the Peace Corps nurse, had been working in Rabinal for some few months, but I rarely got to see her—even though she lived right down the street, in the very house that just happened to be my own first lodging when I had arrived in town two years earlier. Susanna taught health and nursing and worked with the other nurses at the government health clinic in town, while I was mostly down at the tree nursery, or else out somewhere on an *aldea* visit. During this period, however (roughly between March and July of 1981), my travels to the countryside outside of town were becoming less and less frequent, as the security situation seemed to grow more unstable with every passing day. And the rumors of violence became impossible to ignore. By the time the rains came in June, I could be found either in the *vivero* or in my house, where I worked on one of two projects: the forest inventory of the whole *municipio*, and the technical guide I was writing for the local INAFOR personnel. My forays into the field were lately confined to only the nearest *aldeas*, like Chiticoy or Guachipilín.

Susanna once shared with me some scenes from a typical day at the clinic where she worked, and the images they conjured in my mind were alarming: *campesinos* wandering in from the *aldeas*, sometimes from the town itself, stumbling through the door of the clinic in a daze, some with head lacerations, others with their arms or torsos slashed by a machete, not to mention the occasional bullet wound. There was shit going down in the *campo* that we never saw. But Susanna, lovely Susanna—a strong woman she was—saw a lot of the ugly outcomes.

One afternoon I was back from the *vivero* when Susanna stopped in front of my gate and told me we needed to talk. I invited her in, we sat on my veranda and we each lit up a cigarette, and she told me what was up: she had been approached by the colonel from the *destacamento militar* located on the other side of town, and he had told her that he wanted to meet with both of us to discuss the situation in Rabinal. *La Situación*. He wanted to talk with us about that shit going down in the *campo*, how and whether it might impact our work, and what if anything we needed to do. The meeting was already scheduled: it was to be the very next morning, at Susanna's house.

Now, before we go any further, the reader of this story needs to know that Susanna was (and I'm sure still is) a very attractive woman with a long mane of bright red hair, a charmingly freckled complexion, and a frank and candid manner that could be arresting at times, despite her deficiencies in Spanish.

It seemed to me a little suspect that the army colonel would approach Susanna about this meeting that we needed to have, and that the meeting was to be at her house, even though I had lived in Rabinal more than three times as long as she. I thought maybe I should be girding myself to assume some sort of protective role towards Susanna when we met, but in the end that seemed a bit problematic. If not downright ridiculous. The colonel, after all, would have the gun. Not to mention the unquestioned authority.

So we met the next day. The colonel drove up to Susanna's front door in his open jeep, with two of his soldiers in back toting their Galils. The colonel carried just his sidearm. Susanna and I were inside waiting for them, not particularly apprehensive, just waiting. My only slight reservation was that I hadn't had a haircut in a while, so I suppose I had a little bit of that subversive look about me. Wished I had shaved, too.

At any rate, under these circumstances our little meeting began.

"My name is Colonel Solares, and I want to tell you that I asked for this meeting today mainly to see how the two of you are doing. As you know, we have had a rather special situation here in Rabinal the past few weeks, and I wanted to make sure the two of you are okay."

We told the colonel that we both felt reasonably secure at the moment; we simply avoided taking any unnecessary risks. I told the colonel that I had curtailed most of my visits to the farthest *aldeas* in the mountains, and that I was now focusing most of my work right here in town. I was hardly going outside of town at all, I said.

"Yes, we have had these troubles, as you know, with certain criminal elements in the mountains around here," the colonel acknowledged. He called them criminal elements. "But I want to personally assure you, *señor* Cristián, that we are your defenders here in Rabinal, we are here to defend all the peaceful people who live here, and I want to tell you that we now have this situation *completely under our control.* Trust me, *señor* Cristián, you can now go out to any community you wish, and you will be perfectly safe. You should not curtail any of your activities thinking it is unsafe to venture outside of town. We are here to make it safe for you to do your work."

… Or words to that effect. Of course, we had no choice but to accept the colonel's assessment of the situation at face value. And so, we left it at that. Susanna didn't mention to the colonel the awful cases of violence she had seen in her clinic lately, and I of course did not say one word about cooperating again with the army on any future reforestation efforts. Keep'em at arm's length. Or further, if possible.

Near the end of our short meeting the colonel looked around the room where we were sitting, and he told Susanna she had a very nice little place. I got the feeling he was casing the house for future reference. I had noticed him casting more than a couple stealthy glances at Susanna's attractive figure, and he seemed degrees more casual in his manner of addressing her; more formal with me. This whole meeting clearly had another purpose, I thought; it wasn't just a security briefing.

The meeting ended, and the colonel reunited with his two soldiers who had been standing guard outside the door. They drove back to the *destacamento* on the other side of town, and we never met with him again.

* * *

Within days after the meeting we had with the army colonel, two new incidents occurred involving our men in the *vivero*, and both were equally disconcerting. First, my new counterpart Chico failed to show up for work one day. It didn't take long to find out he had been scooped off the street and loaded onto a truck in an army "recruitment drive." I suppose he had had a target on his back for a while, since he was only nineteen or so when I signed him on weeks earlier.

So, I made some connections with people I didn't usually relate to a lot, and eventually I got to sit down and meet with the new *comisionado militar* in town—Rosendo Xolop's replacement after he was gunned down by our local colonel. I tried to explain to the new *comisionado* that the army had taken from us my own right-hand man who was actually on the government payroll with INAFOR and so, in my view at least, should therefore have received some kind of dispensation when it came to military service. The *comisionado*, who was a younger version of Rosendo, dressed in simple civilian clothes just like his predecessor, looked at me stone-faced throughout my courteous and very deferential appeal, and then at the end of it he somewhat evasively said that he would look into the matter. Judging from his cool response I wasn't expecting much. Frankly I thought I had probably failed in my attempt to free Chico from military service.

But miraculously, a couple days later, Chico showed up at the *vivero*, ready for work. Yes, he'd actually been released by the army, with no further obligation for the time being. Then Chico told me a little about what he had been through over the past few days. It was classic brainwashing. Very little food, he said, and constantly interrupted sleep which amounted to almost no sleep at all. And then indoctrination all day long. The army's brainwashing methods were very effective. Indeed, that is how they got young Mayan men all over the country to hold a gun and kill other Mayans—men, women, and children—in a town, any town, far from the soldier's home.

It was a very troubling ordeal, not least of all for poor Chico, but at least this once it ended well.

Which could not be said about the second incident in the *vivero* during that rainy season.

Antonio Ramirez was a rail-thin man of about thirty who had worked in our *vivero* for at least a year. He was a hard worker, though he did have his occasional drinking binges. He didn't earn an INAFOR salary, but rather Food for Work. And, like the other two or three FFW workers we had in the *vivero*, every Friday when I distributed those fifty-pound bags of white enriched flour from the stores I had in the back of the house, he'd say to me *muchas gracias* and then make a bee-line over to the bakery near the plaza, where they'd give him cash for the flour. Because cash was what he and his poor wife and mother needed to survive.

One day, maybe late August or early September of 1981, Antonio did not show up for work. Only it wasn't another drinking binge this time. The night before, an army truck had shown up in the *colonia* where he lived, and the three of them—Antonio, his wife, and his mother, in addition to many others—were simply picked up and hauled away. And that was that. I never saw Antonio again during the rest of my time in Rabinal.

But I *did* see him again: It was one year later, and I was sitting in my fifth-floor corner office in Guatemala City, working in my new capacity as a CARE rep. I was signing papers at my desk when Antonio Ramirez suddenly appeared in the doorway, and my jaw dropped. I have no recollection today how the devil he found me, but find me he did. He sat down and we talked a little while, haltingly, and he told me what had happened that night almost a whole year earlier. Men and women, somewhere between one and two dozen, were rounded up in the *colonia* right across the street from our *vivero* and they were all carted off in an army troop carrier. God knows why. Antonio and his wife and mother were hauled in that truck over the mountains, headed towards Salamá. In Antonio's account, the truck stopped high up in the mountains, and Antonio (and perhaps others) were allowed to step outside to relieve themselves. Such a courtesy offered by the soldiers left me a little incredulous. But while Antonio was off to the side of the road taking his piss, one of the soldiers seized the opportunity to grab and rape his wife at gunpoint. Hearing the screams, and knowing he was absolutely powerless to do anything to save his wife, Antonio zipped his fly and then bolted down the steep, rocky slope. He managed to escape, but while escaping he heard a single shot fired. It was his mother they had shot. Or perhaps his wife, because she was never to be seen again, presumed dead. Antonio ran for his life down the steep, rocky mountainside full of thornbushes and maguey, while the soldiers called to him angrily to turn around and come back. But Antonio kept running and tumbling down the mountainside till he was out of sight. And over the course of several weeks he managed to walk all the way to Guate. Where he found me. In a sprawling city of over one million souls.

Since I really had a lot of work to do that day, I gave Antonio my home address and told him he should stop by and visit. And the next day, a Saturday, he did. Stone drunk; totally wasted. We talked outside through my carport gate, but I can't remember very much of that conversation. I'm sure he would have been more than grateful had I invited him inside for a real dinner. He clearly could have used a good meal. But I didn't do that. I was married now, and my perfectly bankrupt sense of judgment in the moment told me that maybe it wouldn't be a great idea to invite a stone drunk *campesino* into the house to share dinner at the table with us. Instead I gave Antonio some bills out of my wallet and I wished him good luck.

This too I have to live with.

* * *

Walking with Evaristo

You will remember the young man called Evaristo Cuxúm from an earlier account I gave when we saw him in a jail in Salamá. He'd been charged with insurrection stemming from an ugly incident involving the trucks that were hauling tons of barite rock on the road that passed through Patixlán, which was the village where he lived.

Now it is August, 1981, a year and a half later. Well into my third year in Rabinal, there were by now, as I've said, troubling signs of violence in the whole area. Truth is, I had been hunkering down in the town for months without venturing out to any but the nearest *aldeas*. It just seemed a little risky. Therefore, since March I had found myself mainly focusing on the tree nursery and whatever else I could do in town.

Barely a month had passed since that colonel from the local *destacamento militar* had called the meeting to sit down with Susanna and myself. He needed to talk with us, he said. I think he mainly wanted to scope us out and get a better understanding of what we were doing in town. But he also clearly had enjoyed the opportunity to scope out Susanna, who was buxom and pretty. For my part, I wanted to try and get a clearer idea of what we could and could not do in the field going forward. My work required me to visit the *aldeas*, many of which were quite a distance away. I could find things to do here in town, but hardly enough to justify my continued presence in Rabinal for very long. In response, the officer had acted as if absolutely nothing was wrong: "*Si, claro, hombre,* go on out to the *aldeas* and do your work as before. You should have no problem whatsoever," he had told us.

While I was still trying to decide how much faith I should put in the colonel's assessment of local conditions, Susanna made her own decision, and within a few weeks after our little meeting in her front hall she packed up and left Rabinal. She managed to get reassigned to an area that was less subject to the winds of war. I believe it was El Progreso, or maybe San Agustín Acasaguastlán just outside the capital.

So I was once again the only gringo in Rabinal.

Another couple weeks passed, and I felt relieved that I wasn't hearing about any fresh cases of violence in the *campo*. In early August Evaristo and I therefore went ahead and made plans to do a conservation course in the *aldea* known as Raxjút, which was way, way up in the mountains near Concul. A long walk, no question, but Evaristo told me he had learned there were some small farmers in Raxjút who were very interested in doing soil conservation work. Who knows how he found this out. *Teléfono de bejuco.*

I thought about it. Yes, Chris, it's really time to get back out into the field after all these months. There's so much still to do. Everything will probably be fine. So, I got back in touch with Evaristo and we went ahead and did it.

We started out very early one morning around August 6th. We hiked together, just the two of us, up the rock-strewn slope of Piedras Azules south of town, and then we followed a long trail through the mountains, Evaristo leading the way. A couple hours into the mostly uphill walk we came across a wide, grassy clearing with a single avocado tree, maybe thirty feet high, standing in the middle of it, heavily laden with ripe fruit. This was right by the *aldea* known as Plan de Sánchez. We stopped to take a break there, and Evaristo, full of energy as ever, climbed up into the tree.

"*A ver, señor Cristián!* Stand right there and I'll throw some down to you." And then Evaristo began tossing avocados down to me, one after another, each one unblemished and just shy of full ripeness. In all likelihood the tree with its abundance of perfect fruit belonged to someone living there in Plan de Sánchez, or at least it might have stood there as a valued asset for the whole community. But the bounty of nature simply invites sharing, even if we didn't have express permission to partake. So we partook.

Acutely aware that I was a rather undeserving recipient, I nevertheless stored each of the forest green colored fruits in my knapsack. I eventually had to ask Evaristo to stop tossing them down to me, for I feared we might end up with a heavier load than we could possibly carry for the next few miles. Evaristo reluctantly obliged and climbed back down. Everything around us was quiet, and we rested a little while beneath the generous shade of the tree.

I will relish and remember that moment for as long as I live: *Evaristo climbed into the tree and tossed avocados down to me.* We both were filled with a spirit of play that animated this whole unforgettable trip through the mountains.

After the rest break we resumed our walk, for it was still a long way to Raxjút. We talked and joked as we hiked along the narrow footpath passing by Plan de Sánchez. By the time we got to Raxjút we were both pretty tired from the uphill climb of nearly ten kilometers, but we were ready to gear up for a little training session on soil conservation if that's what the people wanted. As it happened, though,

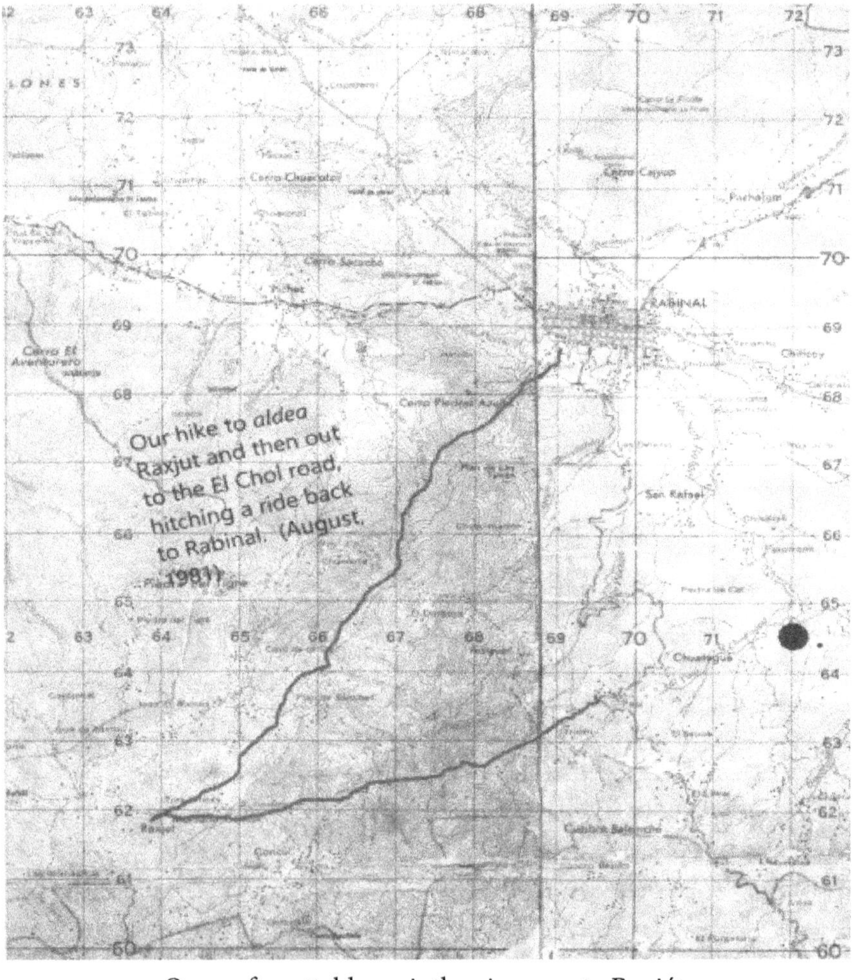

Our unforgettable, pointless journey to Raxjút.

NOBODY in Raxjút was expecting our visit, much less a training session. Apparently the *teléfono de bejuco,* that informal grapevine that everyone depended on to transmit news, orders and gossip across the countryside, had this time broken down. We came to the house of the local leader whom Evaristo knew, but we had unwittingly barged in on a birthday party that was already in progress! I mean, they even had a small, decorated cake on the table, which was positively surreal, since there's no way to bake a cake way out in the *campo*. There was no road to Raxjút, and the nearest bakery was all the way down in the *pueblo.*

I can't remember whose birthday it was, but the family insisted we sit down with them and partake, which we both did. We spent a little while in the midst of these simple festivities, sitting down at the table of a poor family and eating birthday cake with them, but then it got late and we knew we had to make our way back to Rabinal. Clearly there would be no conservation course that day. We both thanked the family for their hospitality, and then we hit the trail again. At Evaristo's suggestion we took the calculated risk of not returning the way we had come, but taking instead the much shorter trail through Concul out to the road to El Chol, where we hoped we could hitch a ride with someone back to Rabinal. The traffic count on the El Chol road on an average day was, at best, about two or three vehicles per hour. And maybe only one of those going in our direction.

Somewhere around Concul it started pouring, and we continued walking though we were getting soaked to the bone. By this time I started to think that this whole trip was maybe not such a good idea, but I kept walking. We had no choice but to keep going, so we both kept walking through the rain, talking and joking along the way between claps of thunder.

We finally made it out to the road somewhere near the *aldea* called Chixím, and at length we got a ride back to town. We had to walk a long time on the road before a pickup showed up, and it was still raining. The trip to Raxjút and back had lasted the whole day, and was utterly and unquestionably useless, since we had accomplished nothing. Still, it was one of the most unforgettable days of all the days I spent in Rabinal.

It is also the way I want to remember Evaristo.

* * *

Now, to close this chapter, I must tell you about a certain man in Guatemala who loved to jump out of airplanes. By all accounts he was a manly man, and he thought the thrill of jumping out of a plane was simply the most exciting and invigorating experience imaginable. Every time when he jumped out of a plane and fell headlong through the azure heavens, he felt a sense of almost spiritual rapture watching all of God's Creation—all the gorgeous mountains and the broad, green valleys—drawing closer and closer, knowing that in the very moment when he chose to will it he could escape certain death by simply pulling a cord strapped to the right side of his manly torso.

But because he knew that others might think his jumping out of airplanes a merely self-indulgent amusement, this man, whose name was Manuel Benedicto, decided he would establish a school where he could teach his comrades in arms to jump out of planes just like he did. And so he founded the *Escuela de Paracaidismo* in the Guatemalan armed forces, and now by attending this brand-new school, scores of enthusiastic, fresh-faced cadets could learn how to jump out of planes to defend their fatherland.

As for the man himself, Manuel Benedicto Lucas García had learned how to jump out of planes while he was studying military engineering at the celebrated École Spéciale Militaire de Saint-Cyr, which is located in a lovely rural corner of France's storied region of Brittany. The school itself, known simply as Saint Cyr, shines brightly in the annals of French history as a veritable equivalent of West Point in the United States. So it was, in fact, quite an honor and distinction for Manuel Benedicto to be enrolled there taking classes.

It was the year 1955, and these must have felt to Benedicto like truly halcyon days that he would always remember and cherish, for during this period of three stimulating and character-building years, our Benedicto, or "Benny" as they called him, was living far, far away from the intrigues at the National Palace in Guatemala City, and far from the messy aftermath of that 1954 CIA-sponsored *coup d'etat* (the nominal leader of which Benny had vocally opposed).

At Saint-Cyr, Manuel Benedicto specialized in combat against guerrilla forces, and he studied the tactics used by the French army in its anti-guerrilla actions in Indochina. It was there that he learned the lessons of the brutal defeat of French forces at Dien Bien Phu which had left so many thousands dead. And, while there, he also had many stimulating opportunities to converse with and learn from those brave French officers who were leading the charge against the forces of liberation in a faraway desert colony called Algeria.[86]

Our man Benny learned his lessons well in the august lecture halls of Saint-Cyr, and he brought his newfound knowledge of counterinsurgency and psychological operations and suppression of popular struggles back with him to Guatemala so that he could put into practice all of these valuable lessons on his native soil.

But he always loved learning new things, Benny did, so in 1965, now as an army captain, he went abroad again to take additional studies. This time it would be a five-week course in combat intelligence at the U.S. military's infamous war college formerly known as the "School of the Americas," located at the army base formerly known as Fort Benning, Georgia.[87] Upon returning to Guatemala after his stint in Georgia, our Benny carried out counterintelligence work as an operations officer in the nineteen-sixties. Then in 1970 he went back to the SOA once again, this time for a nine-month course in the school's Command and General Staff College.[88] And in 1971 he was made deputy director of Army Intelligence while General Carlos Arana Osorio was president.

From the idyllic French countryside of Saint Cyr to the city of Algiers, to the banks of the Chattahoochee river in Georgia, and finally back to the hills and mountains of rural Guatemala. There can be no doubt that General Benny was well-trained for his mission in life. The trouble was the nature of his mission.

All things considered, it seems that my old friend Pitamber back home in Ithaca had been wise and prescient when he said to me that evening after we saw *The Battle of Algiers*—months before I even set foot in Central America—he said to me, "you must understand, Chris, you *must* understand that this story about Ali La Pointe and Colonel Mathieu that we saw on the screen tonight—this is the way of *all* popular struggles for liberation everywhere."

At last I finally felt I grasped the truth of Pitamber's assertion, and at the same time I was finding yet a new way to interpret Barry Commoner's first law of ecology: *everything is connected to everything else.*

On August 15, 1981, a week or so after my magical and pointless journey to Raxjút with Evaristo, Guatemala's president, Fernando Romeo Lucas García, appointed his brother Manuel Benedicto to

Manuel Benedicto Lucas García at a military garrison in Santa Cruz del Quiché (Photo credit: Robert Nickelsberg, The Washington Post/Getty Images. Reprinted with permission.)

become army Chief of Staff.[89] That was on a Saturday, and I imagine I was probably sitting in my hammock on the veranda reading a book, or paging through the latest Newsweek. Or maybe I was writing a letter home. I did not know about the appointment until I read about it in the paper, and even then I could not have understood its portent. But it would not take very long to find out.

Benedicto Lucas García (or "*General* Benny" as he was now known to some) immediately initiated a strategy of *tierra arrasada*, or scorched earth, under the very apposite codename *"Operación Ceniza"*—Operation Ashes. In this strategy, developed between General Benny and U.S. Lieutenant Colonel George Maynes (with the additional help of advisors from Israel and Argentina[90]), 15,000 Guatemalan troops were deployed on a broad sweep through Mayan villages all across the western highlands. Tens of thousands of Mayan *campesinos* would be killed, though it is said that the effect was only to further increase support for the insurgency.[91] Still, there were even more massacres, like the one in Rio Negro, as well as those that occurred in many other villages of Rabinal and in other parts of the country.

It is said that

> Benedicto Lucas García actually designed Guatemala's policy of genocide. He had studied in France and fought in Algeria with French forces. He was a man of enormous experience, and when he came back to Guatemala he used this experience from the French in Vietnam of 'strategic hamlets,' massacres to intimidate the population, and eventually a policy of genocide.[92]

And, lest the support General Benny received from the United States be left ambiguous or unclear:

> The late Lieutenant Col. George Maynes—a former U.S. Defense Attache in Guatemala, and a graduate of the University of Texas at El Paso—worked with Guatemalan Army Chief-of-Staff Benedicto Lucas Garcia in the planning and development of the counterinsurgency program which was implemented by the Lucas Garcia regime in the highlands ... Maynes had close relations with Gen. Benedicto Lucas, functioning as an advisor in counterinsurgency matters. In an interview with investigative journalist Allen Nairn, Lt. Col. Maynes stated that Benedicto Lucas consulted with him on a regular basis.[93]

So, then, to put a fine point on it, the U.S. military was actively assisting the Guatemalan army in planning and executing a campaign of genocide that would exterminate many of the very people—small farmers and community leaders—with whom the U.S. Peace Corps volunteers worked on a daily basis.

Much of the killing was done by the notorious "G-2" military intelligence unit of the army. Years later, General Benny would describe this unit which was under his command in this way: "If the G-2 wants to kill you, they kill you. They send one of their trucks with a hit squad and that's it."[94]

And General Benny still lives as of this writing! He has a place in Cobán, where they say it rains thirteen months out of every year. He is no longer a manly man who jumps out of airplanes; he is now just a stubborn old *anciano* with a hobbled gait who continues to insist that everything he did, every mission, every maneuver and tactic that he ordered, was for the love of his country.

General Benny even has a Facebook page! I've seen it myself, and his page reports that he has one hundred eighty-eight friends. (Fewer than I have myself, but maybe he's working on that.) And you can read some of the fawning comments there from his friends and relatives—comments like:

> Mary
> It's a great pleasure to see you; you are loved and admired with everlasting fondness.
>
> Tatto
> May God continue to bless you, my General!
>
> Luis Arturo
> An honor to greet you, my General! Blessings to you.

It's all so very touching. Poor General Benny was in jail at the time, charged with crimes against humanity, so I'm sure he appreciated all the good vibes his friends and relatives were sending him. Now he is a free man again, having been recently released by a Guatemalan appeals court that acted in shameless defiance of a 2018 sentencing by the Inter-American Court of Human Rights.[95]

A free man.

And on his Facebook page General Benny still asserts in big, prominent letters:

> If I killed, I killed in combat, meeting the enemy face to face like a man, like a soldier. Not like a coward or a psychopath.

Remember General Benny's tough, manly words, dear reader, as I continue my story.

CHAPTER 17

Tierra Arrasada

Strife is both father and king of all;
some he has shown forth as gods and others as men;
some he has made slaves, and others free.

— Heraclitus, Fragment 25

Nearly all of us who were in Guatemala during those years saw some rough times there. And, yes, there were some good times, too. Some damned good times. Yet faced with all the troubling descriptions of those darker moments of terror and horror, one cannot escape the question, "Why would anyone in their right mind volunteer to be a witness to all that?"

The easy answer to that question, which for some people might even put the matter to rest, is that none of us had the *slightest clue* what we were getting into when we signed up. But I think there is more to it than that. After all, once you've seen the hard rains a-fallin', *why stay*?

I think maybe it's because the experience of tragedy shapes our common humanity—it shapes *us* as humans. The ancient Greeks knew this. Nobody willfully goes out into the world looking for the experience of tragedy. But tragedy happens. And when it does, and we see it with our own eyes, it teaches us something about the world we live in, and it teaches us a thing or two about ourselves as individuals. Among other things, it teaches us something about our own capacity for empathy and compassion.

A cynic will say that it's very egocentric to take one's personal life lessons from the horrible tragedies of others. But that view presupposes that the tragedies we saw somehow 'belonged' to others, to the Guatemalan people. They did not, for they were *human* tragedies.

We as volunteers from a far-off land might have been less vulnerable, to be sure, but we were not less human. We saw and we felt, as humans.

I am still reminded of that enigmatic quote that I had pinned to the wall above my desk in Rabinal. That quote from Miguel de Unamuno's *The Tragic Sense of Life*:

> The greatest height of heroism to which an individual, like a people, can attain is to know how to face ridicule. Better still, to know how to make oneself ridiculous and not to shrink from the ridicule.

To make oneself ridiculous and not to shrink from the ridicule—like Don Quixote himself. The radical point I want to make here is that we were all, all of us gringos, in some sense *ridiculous* in the Guatemalan towns where we lived and worked for two or three years. This notion may seem rather disarming at first, so I want to be clear about what I mean.

That time, my friend, when you visited the local *cofradía* to get "the full experience," when you entered the darkened room off the central plaza where six or seven men in their ceremonial dress were chanting in response to the drumbeat and the archaic flute; while you silently watched them passing around the bottle of *aguardiente,* along with a shared, rough-hewn cigar, you stood there and felt close to it all, immersed in an experience punctuated only by the solemn drumbeat. But the truth of the matter is you were merely skipping like a stone on the surface. The profoundly mystical experience that the *cofrades* were sharing was entirely lost on you. You could not enter that realm. You were right there in that dark room with them, yet you were miles away from the state of being they were in. That is what I mean by ridiculous.

Or, to take a darker example: I'm on a packed Salamateca bus sitting at a standstill in the main plaza of San Miguel Chicáj on a wet September morning in 1981 (yes, *real time now*), and the bus has remained at a standstill for several minutes while dozens of *campesinos* are all anxiously clamoring to get on board. Me, I just want to get to the INAFOR subregional office in San Jerónimo, and this delay is frustrating, exasperating. But something bad has happened somewhere. Close by; not far. And there simply is not room enough for everyone, but still they are all struggling to get at least a foot on the doorstep up front. With a foot on the doorstep, they can at least hang on to the bus for dear life until Salamá. I wonder what the hell is going on, until I glance out my window and then, *then* I see it: a red pickup parked on the other side of the street over by the *alcaldia*, the bed of the pickup piled high with dead *campesino* bodies. Ten, fifteen bodies, all piled up there, one on top of the other, stacked like firewood. Our bus is still standing there in the plaza, and the red pickup *just won't move* because it is parked there, and there is no driver present. I glance at the pickup, afraid to look too closely; I look away. I look out the window again, and I look away. In one of my furtive glances I see blood slowly dripping, still uncoagulated, dripping from a body on top, down to the bodies below. For the rest of my life I shall never forget those drops of blood slowly dripping. The bus is still stopped, the noisy commotion still mounting at the entrance up front. And I think to myself, "When the *fucking hell* are we going to get *moving*. For the love of Christ, I can't take this anymore. Please, God, take this away from me."

The view out my window while sitting on that chicken bus that stood idling for an eternity in San Miguel Chicáj was without question the most horrible scene I had personally witnessed in Guatemala. And my presence at that scene in that moment was nothing less than ridiculous. There I was, a fair-skinned, bumbling *gringo* who at six-foot-three towered above everyone around me; a college graduate from a loving family in upstate New York; a self-absorbed East Coast malcontent who loved to inwardly critique and criticize everything; a Peace Corps faker who loved to read but actually knew little about forestry, much less agriculture; an interloper who now wished he had a camera with him and yet knew damn well he wouldn't have had the guts to snap the picture if he had had one there; or, had I one with me and if I *had* snapped the picture, never would have been able to look at that picture even once for the rest of my life without totally breaking down.

These men piled high in the *palangana* were *dead*. And I, I was ridiculous. No hero, to be sure; just ridiculous. Yet I was also a witness. David French, who was posted right there in San Miguel, was a witness, too. And that, in a way, made us brothers that day.

All this happened in San Miguel Chicaj, September 1981. I have no record of the exact date. As it turned out, the horror in the plaza by the *alcaldia* was followed by a downright surrealistic denouement.

The object of my trip, as I said, was to get to the INAFOR office in San Chomo, and I did eventually get there, maybe half an hour after those desperate moments staring and not staring and staring again out the bus window in that plaza.

The moment when I walked through the door of the INAFOR office and was about to greet the secretary sitting at her desk (still feeling shaken by what I had seen), a young INAFOR staffer came running into the room through another door behind the desk. His hands and arms were spattered with bright red blood up to his elbows. He held his arms up high, the way a surgeon holds his hands and arms up in the air after going through a sterile wash right before surgery. The blood that was all over him was not his own.

"Quick, we need a big pan of water out there!" the young staffer shouted urgently. "And bring me something from the sink over there in the corner, Rosita, before I faint from all this stinking shit!"

"My God, what happened, Juanito? That's blood, not shit all over you!"

"*¡Que jodidos!* Screw it; never mind and just help me out here, *por Dios santo*!" I stood there gaping wide-eyed at Juanito (who worked in accounting), still with visions in my head of the horrible scene in San Miguel Chicaj, when a few words from his lips suddenly dispelled the sense of a new tragedy unfolding.

"*Ese chingado cabro* sure had an awful lot of blood to shed!" Juanito looked around the room at us, and then finally cracked a smile. "But don't worry, he's almost ready to be skewered and put on the fire. The boys are finishing up with him right now. We'll be having a feast this afternoon!"

For me the whole scene was almost too much to bear. My rattled brain now was mixing up the grotesque and bloody images from San Miguel Chicaj with the comic yet equally bloody scene I had just witnessed in the INAFOR office, and those crazy synapses in my head were acting now like an invisible hand shuffling cards, so that any card, absolutely *any* card might be the next one to turn face up.

—Oh, *oh*, here is the Hierophant, who in his own good time shall explain everything to you. Why, Calchas!—*¡mi amigo!* What the devil are you doing here? What can you tell me? Look, says Calchas, there lies the Fool—he fell from the hand and is face up on the floor. You are the Fool, *Cristián*. And the Fool knows. Nothing. And he does. Nothing. Beware, though, for Death lingers nearby, and will not be tricked. I've seen Death,

I whisper to Calchas. And where is Justice? Isn't there a Justice in the deck? Only Swords are left, says Calchas the seer. Many different Swords. One Sword for you, one perhaps for me, and then everyone else here shall be wiped out by the King of Swords. Just wait.

It was time to go. I finished my business with the INAFOR secretary, and then I talked with Santizo, who gave me a couple bags of seeds—*Pinus oocarpa* and *P. tenuifolia*. "Yes, thank you Santizo, that'll be a big help for next year."

Will I still be here next year? Things are getting pretty crazy in Rabinal, but maybe things will calm down again. I don't want to leave yet. *Quiero convivir con la gente. Para ser testigo. To be a witness.* That's my mission, now, I thought. I finally realized what my mission was.

I left the INAFOR office and I eventually caught a bus back to Rabinal, though it took time for one to pass by. When we passed through San Miguel Chicaj again, I felt a sudden impulse to get off, because I wanted to look for David, who was posted in San Miguel to teach beekeeping. So I stepped off the bus at the corner of the plaza, almost at the very spot where I had seen the red pickup truck full of dead bodies earlier in the morning. But the pickup was gone, and now there was no trace left to suggest that there ever had been anything amiss.

So I walked over to David's place, a little adobe cottage on a corner a block or two from the plaza, and luckily I found him at home. We sat and talked for a while, and he offered me some strong black coffee in a blue metal cup, and I remember how the edge of the metal cup scalded my lips.

Had he seen it this morning? Yes, he had seen it. I had seen it, too. That was all that either of us needed to know. We both had seen it. By now it was around noontime, and there was nothing left to see. Except for the lovely green mountains outside David's window on this exceptional day.

"Y'know," I said, while I looked up at the mountains outside his window, "Sometimes I wonder why I don't just say 'Screw it all,' and just walk up into those mountains and join the guerrillas up there."

And then David said, "I know what you mean. Y'know, they *are* right up there, almost where you're pointing. They're up there right now." Then we both sat silent, pondering the idea, half-seriously. I only stayed a little while longer, and I guess we talked about other things, but I can't remember what else we talked about. Then I left and caught another bus back to Rabinal. There was work to do—though I can't remember what, exactly.

Forty years on, I can't hardly remember anything else anymore. Only that.

* * *

Evaristo Triumphant

If you've followed my first two stories concerning Evaristo Cuxúm of Patixlán, then you've caught a glimpse of the smart, young, energetic community leader who made such an unforgettable impression on me. I visited Evaristo many times in Patixlán, where we did more than a couple conservation courses together. I visited him in jail in Salamá once, and scarcely a month before this day I am about to relate we had walked together on our unforgettable, pointless journey to Raxjút.

Since March there were no longer any parties or even small get-togethers in the evening. Everything was pretty much shut down and quiet after 7 p.m., and I had more or less gotten used to it. Thus it came as a bit of a surprise that Independence Day festivities were actually planned for the central plaza on the eve of the big day. Me, I just had to go. After all, there would be a safe, large crowd there in the evening, so what could possibly happen on the eve of such a patriotic holiday?

But the evening would be different. And anyway, there would be a safe, large crowd there this evening, so what could possibly happen on the eve of such a patriotic holiday?

When I got to the plaza, I learned that marathon runners representing Rabinal would be arriving in the early evening hours to light a torch up in the gazebo, which was always the focal point of celebrations in the plaza. And indeed, more or less punctually around seven-thirty or eight, the whole *pelotón* came running into the plaza. Several dozen of them. Someone told me they had run all the way from Salamá, some twenty-seven clicks to the east.

Three of the *maratonistas* ascended the steps of the gazebo to the upper level, and incredibly one of them was our Evaristo Cuxúm. (So many *campesinos*. Why Evaristo? But there he was.) I can't remember which of the three tipped his torch flame to light the torch that was mounted on the railing. Maybe it was Evaristo; maybe not. But Evaristo was definitely there, and the whole event must have been a moment of great pride for all of them.

The festivities continued for a little while, but not for too long. The townspeople were already pushing the limits of the unspoken curfew, so things petered out and the crowd thinned quickly after that glorious torch-lighting. It was a moment, though. It was really a moment. I walked back home, stopping in a *tienda* along the way to buy a liter of Cabro, and called it a night. Walking back out, again I heard the firecrackers going off ... or were they gunshots?

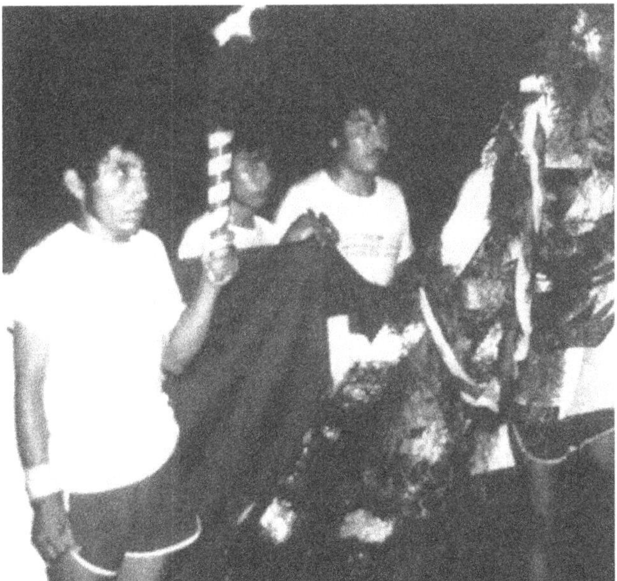

Marathon runners finishing triumphantly in Rabinal's main plaza on the evening of September 14, 1981. (Photo credit: Augusto Jerónimo, RIP.)

* * *

Now it is September 15th, 1981—*Independence Day*. Things were pretty bad in and around Rabinal. The soldiers were everywhere, all toting their Israeli assault rifles. Even more ominous was the presence of the un-uniformed but well-armed *kaibíles* or *judiciales* who were in town. While walking through the main plaza I caught alarming glimpses of things that appeared out of the ordinary and that seemed to augur ill—only I failed to grasp what was imminent. A couple *ladinos* were standing in the park, unfamiliar figures who looked very much out of place, both dressed like cowboys back from the cattle run, and each of them carried on his shoulder not a backpack, not a traditional hand woven *morral*, but a dirty white sack, and the contents of the sack protruded upwards such that it could be plainly seen: sticking out of each man's sack was the muzzle of an automatic rifle. No uniforms. Something was amiss here.

Now, *now*, dear reader, precisely at this point is where I struggle mightily with my memory. For my memory simply wants to fail me here, and I do not understand why. Because I remember so many other parts of this history so well. But what happened in the plaza late that morning on September fifteenth was unspeakably awful, and maybe for that reason my brain now refuses to retain any clear memory of the details.

Except for *one* detail: maybe around nine in the morning, when still nothing yet had happened, but the *judiciales* in the plaza (the two I saw and others with them) were already preparing to make it happen, I stepped out of my house and started walking towards the plaza. I'd been told there were to be some holiday festivities in the plaza, and I just wanted to go check it out. There was to be a musical band or a parade or something. With plenty of firecrackers at the end, no doubt. Hey, it was Independence Day.

I had scarcely walked four blocks down the street—the same dusty street where Eugenio and I had encountered those cute, coquettish *colegialas* Judith and Sandra more than two years earlier—when I was stopped. I was stopped not by a soldier, nor by a police officer (of whom there were still only two in the whole town), nor even by a civil defense patroller carrying a wooden silhouette of a rifle. I was stopped by Armando Garzona, the owner of the local hardware and dry goods store where I had bought my new radio/tape deck on credit a year earlier. The same guy who some two years prior had given me a ride back to Rabinal in the bright red cab of his diesel stake-bed truck.

Armando stood in the middle of the street in front of his store, and he urgently told me to turn around and go back home. The plaza where I was headed wasn't safe right now—no, *señor,* not safe at all.

"You mustn't go into the plaza right now, Cristián. There are soldiers there with guns. Trouble is brewing. *Está caliente la situación.* Go back home, now, and stay there!"

What was about to happen? What did Armando know? Because

nothing at all had happened yet. But he obviously wasn't as clueless as I was. Did he know that the army had blockaded all of the points of entry into Rabinal? (I wasn't aware of that myself until years later when I read the reports.) Did he know that a couple of trucks were sitting idling in the plaza, just waiting for a signal afterwards to begin their cleanup job? (This, too, from later reports; I didn't know it at the time.)

All I know is that Armando knew *something*, and maybe he knew a lot, because before I turned around to head back he said to me the words I shall never, ever forget for as long as I live:

"Estos indios, Cristián, ¡hay que matarlos todos!"

Once I got back home I sat in my hammock and pondered what might be going on. Thinking about it now, I must have heard distant noises from the plaza, *I must have heard the noises of gunfire.* Though I am at pains to report that this is precisely where my memory fails me, for I don't *specifically* remember hearing noises. But I *must* have heard something. I was sitting quietly on my veranda, and the plaza was less than six hundred yards away. Why can't I remember it? Or did I hear the noise, and because I had no expectation of violence, I simply dismissed it as the distant sound of firecrackers?

It was Independence Day, after all.

What actually happened, though, is now a matter of recorded history:

> The testimonies of those who survived narrate what happened in the market square that day [in Rabinal] while the municipal authorities and the state security forces were celebrating the 160th anniversary of Guatemalan independence.[96]
> Because it was September 15, there was a parade in Rabinal and the Army knew that the people were going to gather in the town. After the parade they closed the four entrances to the town and started a shootout in front of the Church. 200 people (over 12 years old) on the roads that were covered, later they drew a list and began to torture and kill. Those responsible had two trucks ready to transfer the dead and the detainees, who were taken away alive, tortured and murdered on the Santa María hill and thrown into a ravine.
> —Report from the Recovery of Historical Memory (REMHI), massacre number 116.

Another of the testimonies collected in the REMHI

report affirms:

> On September 15, 1981, in the market square of the municipality of Rabinal, Baja Verapaz, soldiers from the Rabinal detachment, accompanied by patrolmen, commissioners, and judicial officers executed some 200 people with bullets. It was the day of independence and the soldiers had summoned all the people to attend the parade. Patrolmen and the army pointed at people. They walked with lists in hand. Those who were nearby also died. The square was filled with the dead, the blood, the dogs licking. After this massacre, members of the army went to the villages to continue the killings.
> Of all the victims, according to the CEH, Case No. 9160, only the following were identified: Margarita Cortez Tecu, Emilio Guanche Tecu, Mateo Mejía Moreno, Malecio Tecu Cortez, Florentin Xitumul Osorio, Pedro Cuxúm, unidentified victims: 200.

I realize, only now after so many years, that when Armando Garzona practically ordered me to turn around and go back home that morning—saying to me in the next breath, "these *indios*, Cristián, *all* of them must be killed!"—it is quite possible that he was saving my life. It is a sobering thought that will haunt me forever: just before the slaughter of innocents in the plaza, my own life was spared by a fucking racist.

So what if I had evaded Armando Garzona standing there in the street? What if I had just ignored him? What if I had made a nimble end run around him? Here's where my overly vivid imagination starts to run away with me. What if I had made it to the plaza and actually saw the *judiciales* standing there ready to shoot? What if I could have shouted, "*¡Alto! ¡Pare fuego! ¡Soy gringo, y soy TESTIGO!*" Me, the fucking six-foot-three gringo who would have towered above everybody else. But none of that happened. No, nothing like that happened. The reality is that Señor Nada was just sitting in a hammock back at the house, smoking a cigarette, while two hundred citizens of Rabinal were being slaughtered in the plaza.

There was nothing I could have done. But that doesn't make the memory of that day any easier to bear.

Oh, and those two trucks that were parked in the plaza that morning? The trucks that were loaded up with all the dead bodies after the massacre? One of them, I discovered only years later, was that very same stake-bed truck with the bright red cab belonging to Armando Garzona.[97] The same truck which I had seen him driving one day back in 1979, driving up a dusty avenue in Salamá—that day when he saw me on the street on crutches and offered me a ride to get back to Rabinal.

The mist of time rises, the picture becomes clearer, and the pieces finally all line up. One: Armando facing me on the street and ordering me home. Two: "*¡Estos indios, hay que matarlos todos!*" And Three: a red stake-bed truck parked in the plaza at that very moment, *Armando Garzona's truck*, just waiting to clean up after the bloody outcome. Me, I felt I was totally in the dark that day, but my readers can put together the pieces of this story.

This massacre was part of a series of similar actions by the army that quickly escalated. According to the report of Guatemala's post-war Commission for Historical Clarification, from 1960 to 1996, 626 massacres were committed throughout the country. The Recovery of Historical Memory (REMHI) project managed to document that 16 massacres were committed in Baja Verapaz in the twenty-four months from 1980 to 1982. Ninety-five percent of all the massacres were committed by the army in a period of seven years, from 1978 to 1985.[98] *Tierra arrasada*. Scorched earth. Mayan villages all over the Western Highlands wiped out, in some cases all but erasing their names from the map.

Some ten months after the massacre in Rabinal's plaza, members of the Civil Defense Patrol commanded by military commissioners of the army perpetrated another massacre in the *aldea* of Plan de Sánchez, deep in the mountains south of the *pueblo*. There, some 256 Achí *campesinos* were murdered, all accused of belonging to the guerrilla.[99] Women and children among them.

Plan de Sánchez. Right where Evaristo and I had passed by that one day on our journey out to Raxjút. That place where we found the most beautiful, majestic specimen of *Persea americana* standing all by itself in the middle of a mountain meadow, its branches sagging under the weight of a thousand delicious, ripe avocados.

Four civil patrollers and a military commissioner were sentenced for this massacre in 2012.

* * *

The next day I walked through the plaza again early in the morning, headed towards our *vivero forestal*. In the middle of the plaza I was suddenly approached by the wife of Evaristo Cuxúm. She was walking alone. It was exceedingly rare to be addressed by a married *indígena* woman walking alone, no matter the time of day. But Evaristo's wife walked up to me and, with a look of anguish bordering on abject terror in her face, asked me if I had seen Evaristo anywhere. Stupidly, and with absolutely no inkling as to what might have happened, I tried to calm her down and I assured her that maybe Evaristo had headed back to Patixlán on his own. Surely, if she would just go back there, she would find him back in the *aldea* waiting for her. I actually said this to her. Evaristo's wife walked on hurriedly, clearly unsatisfied by my stupid answer.

As it turned out, there had been a further massacre in and around Rabinal on the night of Independence Day, beginning right after the festivities in the plaza concluded. Though I saw no bodies, no evidence, I learned that scores of *campesinos* had been killed more or less indiscriminately that night. Evaristo was among the dead. A confidante in town whose word I knew I could trust told me that Evaristo was actually not shot, but strangled. How he knew this, I have no idea—but my source sounded credible. And that piece of information suggested to me some sort of targeting. (I should add that another community leader, Mariano Lopez Alvarado of Xococ, who I told you about earlier when I spent the night at his house, was also among the dead.)

I took no pictures during this whole event, but my good friend and town photographer Augusto Jerónimo did. Sometime later he visited me in Guate and gave me an Ektachrome slide showing Evaristo and the other *maratonistas* standing atop the gazebo with their ceremonial torch.

This, then, is the story of the life of Evaristo Cuxúm Alvarado of Patixlán. Or at least that part of his life when I had the privilege of knowing him. *Evaristo was just a man.* I have to keep telling myself that. But he was also a hero of Rabinal.

And over the course of forty years I've thought to myself many a time (and I hope this will be understood in the right spirit) that knowing and walking with Evaristo was in some sense like walking with Christ through the Stations of the Cross.

CHAPTER 18

Leaving Rabinal

I wonder how many of my readers have ever faced the obvious, the inevitable, yet through a supreme effort of will simply refused to acknowledge it was coming. Let's say, for instance, you are facing an imminent layoff at work, and the handwriting is on the wall for everybody to see. The economy in a shambles; unemployment rising. Competitors have already laid off their own, and now those companies are lurching forward into an uncertain future with whatever they have left. *And you're up next*, but you don't want to face reality, because you love your job—or at least you feel quite comfortable in it, thank you very much—and you can't possibly imagine doing anything else. And then reality hits.

This scenario, as unsettling as it may sound, is not unlike the reality I was refusing to face up to during my last few weeks in Rabinal.

Were we still on the cusp of something? Or were we already *way* past the cusp now and careening headlong towards the apocalypse? Or was the worst possibly over now? Could things actually get better if we just waited for a little while? How long a while? *How long?*

Like the Stateside worker in his comfortable job that he can't imagine doing without, I had grown comfortable in Rabinal, and that sense of comfort had clouded my vision. I felt comfortable with the community; comfortable with my friends and neighbors; comfortable with my Spanish; and comfortable with my job, despite the occasional setbacks, the frustrations, and the ambiguities of success. Most of all, I felt comfortable with Mireya; I felt, in fact, that I could no longer live without her. Even extending for yet another year with the Peace Corps—in Guatemala—*in Rabinal*—was to my mind not out of the question.

I felt so damned comfortable that, despite the daily signs of growing instability, I couldn't see the handwriting on the wall. But things were definitely falling apart.

* * *

One night shortly after the Independence Day massacre I was reading late into the night in my hammock strung up on the veranda. My two cats Leo and Felix were both long gone, and my only company on the veranda that night was a huge, black June bug that kept buzzing slowly to and fro around the dim ceiling light. The constant movement and the low-pitched, droning buzz of the June bug were unwelcome distractions from my reading, but fortunately these clumsy, lumbering albatrosses of the insect world are an easy kill. I got up and grabbed a shoe, and with just a light whack, hardly aiming, I knocked the critter to the floor where I then stepped over it with the barest amount of pressure until I heard the satisfying crunch of its shiny carapace. The ants would arrive afterwards to take it from there, and I knew that by next morning only the barest remnant of the inch-long carcass would be left on the floor.

I decided to pack it in and call it a day, so I went over to the pila and washed up, turned out the outdoor light and went into my room. I lay in bed smoking a cigarette and listening to VOA on the shortwave when the deep stillness of the night was suddenly interrupted by heavy army boots tromping hurriedly down the street right in front of my house. There were many footsteps—less than a platoon, but I guessed there were more than four or five soldiers. I didn't dare look outside my window. I quickly zeroed out the radio volume, and I waited in the dark. I sat on the edge of my bed in a room illuminated only by the tiny power LED on my shortwave and the dull, intermittent glow of my cigarette. The soldiers had already passed, and yet I imagined they could smell the cigarette smoke drifting outside and maybe they could have guessed that the gringo was here. But I doubt they would have cared, as they were clearly on their way to something else. I thought about the 'CUC' graffiti in six-inch letters that was plainly visible on the white plastered wall right outside my house, and I hoped it wouldn't attract any undue attention as the soldiers passed. I wished it wasn't there, so plain for all to see. But it was dark out, so I felt I was safe.

It only took a few seconds for the soldiers to pass, but the anxiety caused by those heavy footsteps in the dark remained for a while longer. A few minutes later I heard automatic weapons fire in the distance—maybe three blocks away, just a short burst or two. And then the stillness of the night enveloped everything once again. I killed the radio and my cigarette, and I went to sleep.

I never found out what might have happened that night in my neighborhood, and I was afraid to ask anyone. One might conclude that it was just another night in Rabinal's "new normal," but the terror of that night stuck with me, and it made me begin to question what I could possibly accomplish going forward, even in the daytime.

* * *

About a week or so after Guatemala's Independence Day, a group of men appeared at my front gate. They were all regular *campesinos* just like those I had worked with all the time in the *vivero* or (in better times) out in the *aldeas*. But these men were now on a mission: they were newly inducted members of the local Civil Defense Patrol formed in September by the army in town, and their mission was to recruit others to join them.

The army in Rabinal had assembled and armed more than a thousand Mayan men and organized them into one of the first "civil patrols" of the decade. In a matter of months, the army implemented this system on a widespread basis all across Guatemala's countryside. In creating these militias, Gen. Benedicto Lucas effectively created a structure which superseded local government and was directly subservient to white *ladino* military authority.[100]

The *campesinos* who arrived at my gate—there were five or six of them—had come to tell me I needed to join their squad without further ado and go on patrol with them. The men looked like any of the small farmers I might have worked with on a terracing project out in the *campo*. They were unarmed, but if memory serves me a couple of them carried long sticks or poles. I knew that when they were on patrol the army would provide at least a few of these *patrulleros* with some of their old, single-action rifles.

The assertiveness of their verbal summons took me by surprise, and I had to think fast in order to decide how best to respond. I explained to the men that I was not a Guatemalan citizen and was therefore exempt from service. But the leader of the group simply replied, with a broad sweep of his arm, that *to-o-o-o-dos los hombres* who live in town must serve on the PAC. *No, señor, all* the men in town must serve.

I wasn't sure if it would help to explain that I was with a North American agency called the Peace Corps, but I told them anyway. "Peace Corps," even when translated as "*Cuerpo de Paz,*" sounds completely innocuous to an American ear, but the poor in the countryside, when they heard the word *cuerpo* in this context, might immediately think of the notorious *Cuerpo de Detectives*, or the *cuerpos* in the army itself, such as the *Cuerpo de los Kaibiles*, the Guatemalan special forces that were trained by the U.S. Marines. *Cuerpo de* anything might not help me right now.

The men appeared suspicious, or perhaps a little confused by my answer. Not the usual answer they got in their door-to-door recruitment drive. It didn't help matters that that darned CUC graffiti was still in plain sight on the white plaster wall of my carless carport. (*El Comité de Unidad Campesina*—this was the group that had left the flyers on my doorstep in months past; the same group that had supposedly thrown the Molotov cocktail into our tree nursery.) My visitors seemed nonplussed, so I finally suggested to them, in a tone of nervous exasperation, that they should just go and check with the commanding officer over at the *destacamento militar* on the other side of town, and he would certainly verify my claim that I was off-limits for PAC recruitment.

The men walked off to the next place, not entirely satisfied with my answer.

But saying 'no' to the recruitment efforts of the local PAC invariably met with dire consequences if you were a poor *campesino*. About half a year after my own refusal, twenty-five *campesinos* from the *aldea* of Xesiguan had fled to the mountaintop *caserío* of Rancho Bejuco in the nearby town of El Chol because the adult men in their group had recently refused "voluntary" recruitment into the local Rabinal PAC. So, under the able guidance of one Lieutenant Colonel Ovalle Sálazar, the civilian members of the PAC hunted down the refuseniks and their families and murdered them all, including seventeen of their children, in Rancho Bejuco on January 29, 1982.[101]

After my own refusal facing the PAC members at my gate, they never returned to bother me again. I could relax in my hammock and read a book while a posse of PAC recruits went down the street outside, performing their daily reconnaissance walk. I have to live with the comfortable privilege of my exemption which, though it troubles me from time to time, I realize is a pretty light burden to bear compared to death.

* * *

October 7, 1981

It will hardly come as a surprise, then, that Independence Day, Sept. 15th, 1981, was the beginning of the end of my time in Rabinal. Rosendo Xolop, Evaristo Cuxúm and Mariano López were all dead, along with scores of others—hundreds, actually. Padre Gregorio, under threat of imminent danger, had been pulled out by the leaders of his order. Güicho, it was clear to me now, had left to join the Movement. Thank God they got out alive, for both men are heroes to me. But the greatest hero of all was poor Evaristo.

During the fall of 1981, nobody was out in the street at night. This had been the case throughout most of the year, but the absence of activity in the evening was now more pronounced than ever. I still walked down to the *vivero forestal* several times every week, but there was little I could do there. People weren't exactly climbing over the fence begging for trees to plant, and the seedlings were growing tall in their little black poly bags. Venturing out to the *aldeas* was risky. I started feeling guilty for not accepting the risk in order to DO SOME DAMNED WORK in the field. But instead, I remained in the house a lot of the time. Much of that time I spent working on mapping and air photo interpretation for the natural resource inventory I had initiated a couple years earlier. This, at least, was something to keep me occupied. Quiet, patient work with a Rapidograph pen and stereoscope in the stillness of the evening or on a rainy afternoon. I still kept thinking, naively, that maybe, somehow, this could all 'blow over' after a while.

I didn't imagine, I couldn't have imagined, that following September 15th, I had less than two months left in Rabinal.

Like most of us volunteers around the beginning of every month, in October I got on a bus to Guate to visit the Peace Corps office and pick up my paycheck. Upon entering the building in Guate's Zona 2, I stopped to talk with our APCD, Basilio Estrada. I told him about some of the recent events, but I recall being a little cautious with Basilio so as not to overstate the seriousness of the situation, and I tried to emphasize that I still felt pretty secure about continuing my work there. (... Work? What work? Hell, I was really just staring at maps and air photos every day.)

Basilio told me that Country Director Ron Arms wanted to talk to me. So I walked over to his office next, picking up my paycheck from Sheny along the way. Ron Arms invited me to sit down, and then he gave me a guarded and very partial description of the measures that the Embassy is always taking to gauge the situation everywhere in the country. He said he had news from the Embassy about Baja Verapaz, and he was very concerned about letting me go back to Rabinal.

Oh, God.

The news that Rabinal was actually under the microscope over at the Embassy was unsettling to say the least, but it also filled me with the energy I needed in order to seize on every conceivable argument I could think of that might put his concerns to rest.

"Don't worry, Ron, I'm being very careful"... "My Spanish is good now, and I am capable of having detailed, confidential conversations with the people I know in Rabinal." ... "I have friends there, and rest assured they will be the *first* to tell me when it is really too risky to remain there." ... "And anyway, the *destacamento militar* is way, way over at the other end of town from where I live (pretty weak argument, that), and the soldiers don't even come through my neighborhood very often." (A lie.) On and on I rambled in this manner, with my adrenalin-fueled silver tongue. I simply didn't want to leave the town I loved.

After listening to all these arguments, Ron Arms was prepared to make a deal with me. He'd let me return to Rabinal, but he wanted to pay me a visit there. Then some sort of decision would be made.

I returned to Rabinal the next morning, and the days that followed felt pretty much the same. By now even my next-door neighbor Juan Avelino had fled town. He was an ag extensionist, a *perito agrónomo,* with DIGESA who had been very active in the *campo*. He was, in fact, the one who had introduced me to Evaristo Cuxúm.

A few days later Ron sent me a telegram saying he was coming over to Rabinal to see me. He wanted to assess the situation for himself. He drove up to my house, alone, on October 7th.

As soon as he arrived in the early afternoon, I had late-breaking news for him: the army authorities had just announced a general meeting of the townspeople to be held in the central plaza the very next day. I had heard this from one of those pickups that drive slowly up and down the streets with a PA megaphone on the roof. Just like when they had announced the strychnine baits all over town.

We talked about this fresh development, and ultimately decided that we'd both have to attend, if only just to hear what the authorities had to say. Maybe Ron and I had the luxury of deciding whether to attend, but for everyone else in town the meeting was obligatory.

After dinner in my favorite *comedor*, *Las Diamelas,* we walked back to the house and talked long into the night. We actually talked about a lot of things, not only the situation in Rabinal. We ended up talking about liberation theology, and Ron recommended a book to me: *Cry of the People*, by Penny Lernoux. It was about the faith-based *comunidades de base* throughout Latin America. I kept that title in my head and read the book many years later. To return the favor, I recommended to Ron a book I had recently finished, the one that my hometown pastor had sent me—the biography of Dietrich Bonhoeffer, by Eberhard Bethge. The story of a man of God, a German Protestant theologian in the 1930s who ended up participating in the failed bomb plot to assassinate Hitler, and then, with only days remaining before Hitler's fall, was hanged for it.

Later (and by now it was getting *very* late), while sitting on the veranda I launched into my well-prepared, exhaustive arguments to explain why I should be allowed to remain in Rabinal. I have to admit, I really poured it on, but in a patient, deliberate manner. I knew this was my last, best shot.

I was just wrapping up my forceful and compelling arguments, feeling rather grateful that Ron Arms had been attentive throughout. But as I was finishing, knowing I had done the very best I could to persuade Ron to let me stay in Rabinal, in that moment something happened. As if on cue, a burst of automatic weapons fire rang out a few blocks from the house where we were sitting. Just one short burst, rat-a-tat-tat *y punto*, but it was not the sort of punctuation mark I was anticipating.

Ron *could* have simply said, "Well, that settles the matter, doesn't it?" But he didn't, and once again I felt grateful. After all, we still had a meeting to attend in the central plaza the next morning.

We had talked until very late that night, and when it was lights-out I showed Ron a row of CARE bags of enriched flour that I had laid out for him as a cushion on the cement floor of my house. My customary gesture of hospitality for my overnight visitors.

* * *

October 8, 1981

We rose early the next morning. I can't remember what we did for breakfast—maybe coffee and *pirujos* or *pan dulce* right there in the house, or maybe we went out to a *comedor*. At any rate, it was around nine-thirty when we thought we'd better head over to the central plaza for this meeting that the *ejército* had announced the day before. Neither of us knew quite what to expect.

We arrived at the plaza. I'm not great at estimating crowd size (especially at this distant remove), but there must have been eight to nine thousand people crowded into the central plaza, if not more. But certainly not the "thirty thousand" that was later reported in the newspapers. Everybody had been summoned to appear, including from most of Rabinal's *aldeas*. In the northwest corner of the plaza the people from *aldea* Xococ were holding up a very long, white *manta* (imagine four or five bedsheets sewn together end to end) with the words painted on it, "*Patrulla de Auto-Defensa Civil de Xococ.*"

The events of September 15th, less than a month earlier, were still on everybody's mind and had left all the people of Rabinal deeply traumatized. So it's fair to say there was a lot of tense anticipation pervading the whole crowd in the plaza as we waited for something to happen. Everybody was facing the church, where soldiers occupied the top of the steps. There was also a marimba at the top of the steps, and the *marimbistas* were playing cheerful traditional melodies for the crowd. There was a wooden speaker's podium set up there with a mic, but no speaker yet. The most unforgettable sight of all: there were soldiers manning two tripod-mounted machine guns high up in the twin belfries, their barrels trained on the crowd below. Ron and I were standing about a hundred feet from the steps near the front of the crowd.

After a little bit of marimba entertainment, the speeches began. First the local *comandante* of Rabinal's *destacamento militar* spoke, and then he introduced the higher-up *comandante* who had come in from Cobán. After so many years I can't remember what exactly they said, but they were words to the effect of, "You needn't worry; we are here to protect you … We know you have all seen much trouble lately, much violence. But we are here to protect you from those communists who want to seize your land and make slaves of you!" The one part of the Cobán general's speech that I'll NEVER forget was when he said, "And who do you think has perpetrated all this violence? *¡Son MALOS guatemaltecos!*" Yes indeed, it was all the work of the BAD Guatemalans.

Well, that much was undeniably true, wasn't it?

The *comandante* from Cobán then turned it over to the next speaker: a low-ranking army regular who was introduced, somewhat perversely, as a voice of the people, a brother to us all. This private (for he couldn't have held much higher rank) then launched into a well-rehearsed diatribe against the guerrillas, mixed with an equally forceful plea for everybody to stay calm and continue going about their daily business.

We were now well over thirty minutes into the assembly, and the army private was still in the middle of his animated harangue when … *it happened.* While the soldier kept speaking over the P.A. system, there was a disturbance somewhere in the middle of the crowd, and many people started pushing excitedly to get away. Within a few seconds, many more people started pushing through and running. Pretty soon, everybody was running, all fleeing to the side streets to get away from the central plaza. The chain reaction of fear and commotion quickly got out of control, and I tapped Ron Arms who was standing at my side, and I said to him, "*¡Vámonos, Ron!*" And we ran, too.

Less than a minute after that mysterious mêlée that began in the middle of the plaza, almost *everybody* was in the side streets, walking away briskly or running. Nobody seemed to know why the hell we had all fled the plaza. What exactly had sparked the commotion in the center of the plaza, a commotion that had quickly escalated to a general stampede, was a mystery to everybody. For me, personally, it was the last great enigma of my time in Rabinal.

But army commanders don't like to acknowledge enigmas, much less acquiesce under their mysterious force. It didn't take long before we heard the marimba break into another bright, familiar tune on the church steps, and the colonel from Cobán grabbed the mic at the podium and started to call everyone back. Most of us were scarcely half a block away, so we could still hear him distinctly.

People paused timorously in their tracks and listened to the *comandante's* amplified voice and the marimba, and then slowly we all turned around and walked back to the plaza. Once we were mostly all back, the *comandante* said a few more words that I can't remember, and then the assembly was summarily adjourned. I'm sure they wanted to say more to us that morning, perhaps much more, but it seemed as though the unexpected mêlée had spooked them into a premature silence. *They* sure didn't know what the hell had just happened, and neither did those of us in the crowd.

The moment in the plaza was so singular and unforgettable that that evening I walked over to the house across the street from where I lived, *la familia Jerónimo*, and I sat down to talk with them for a while. They too were in the plaza that morning (hell, *everybody* was); so what did they think had happened? Augusto Jerónimo's wife Carmen gave me a calm answer, which she stated succinctly but with conviction, indeed with certainty: "*Fue la mano de dios.*" The hand of God had somehow caused the mysterious movement of people that we all had witnessed. After all, the army had occupied the steps of the church in order to don the mantle of God's authority to peddle their lies. With gunners in the belfries.

Now me personally, I'm not attached to any organized religion these days, nor was I then, though for almost all of my life I've believed in God. So I have to say that Carmen's simple explanation on that night of October 8th, 1981, just seemed eminently plausible. Army on the church steps; gunners in the belfries. *Fue la mano de Dios.*

Ron Arms went back to Guate the next morning. After a couple weeks of laying low, I wrote a letter to Ron and mailed it to him. I simply reiterated everything I had told him in person, but now with the luxury of time to choose every word carefully. I told Ron,

> I personally feel calm and secure here in Rabinal. As you know, I am limiting my work activities to around town, which still leaves me with quite enough to do, at least for some few weeks or months. As I emphasized during your visit here, I have excellent relations with persons of influence here, as well as wide contacts among those from the *aldeas*, and with a small circle of confidantes who would advise me if they felt there was real trouble in the air.
>
> Your visit to Rabinal came during an extraordinary period in the life of this town, which naturally had to color your impression of the state of affairs here. I respectfully

> offer the opinion that that state of affairs was very special and has changed significantly since your visit; that, indeed, those couple of days represented sort of a turning point.

'Turning point,' I said. *Qué esperanza.* But I mailed the letter anyway, and then I waited. There was nothing more to be done.

The coded telegram from the Peace Corps office came a few days later. (My Peace Corps buddies from that time will recall the clever little telegram code that we all had a key for typed out on a slip of paper.) I was pretty much expecting it and was surprised it actually had taken so long. I started packing my bags, and I gave my bedframe, my foam mattress and a few other things to my Guatemalan counterpart. A Peace Corps pickup driven by Carlos, the office errand boy, arrived on November 6th. This was some "errand" for Carlos—a bit more fraught with peril than his usual daily trips over to the post office in Guate to send telegrams or to pick up mail. After loading my scarce cargo into the pickup bed, I sat on the tailgate for a long while in front of my house, talking with Augusto Jerónimo's brother Gilberto, and promising him I would get back there someday, somehow, *someday.* And then I wept, sitting there on the tailgate with Gilberto beside me.

We said our goodbyes, and then I climbed into the cab, and I left Rabinal.

The main road heading for the capital (that is to say, the decent dirt road) climbs out of the broad Urram valley through a number of tight curves and switchbacks, and as it ascends into the *sierra* there is one point on the road which is the very last point where one may catch a final glimpse of the town that one has left behind. When we reached that point on the road, I asked Carlos if he would do me a favor and pull over onto the shoulder and just idle there for a minute while I took one last look at the *pueblo* that I had come to love.

"You mean *here*?" asked Carlos, as we approached a curve with a panoramic view of the valley off to the right.

"Yes, right here, if you could, please."

"We can't stay here too long. This is not safe."

"Just for a minute, Carlos—please. Just one minute." Carlos obliged, against his better judgment, and I got out of the pickup. I stood on the edge of the road in the warm breeze and gazed out over the valley and the oblong patchwork grid of streets and houses that had been my home for almost three years. The town looked so small—

and so positively *peaceful*—from this distance. I watched a blue curl of smoke rise above the rooftops where somebody was probably burning off a patch of brush to plant some maize in the spring. No sound, except for the softly idling motor right behind me. I turned around and walked back to the truck.

"Okay, let's go," I said.

I don't think I had been a full minute standing there on the edge of that precipice. There was no point in lingering any longer, and anyway Carlos was getting nervous. We got going again, and I settled back into my seat for the long ride to Guate.

Epilogue

How does one sum it all up? How might I begin to make sense of thirty-four months of celebration and tragedy in a place called Rabinal? There has never been a place in the entire world closer to my heart than *el pueblo de los Achí*. Yet there's never been any place where I've confronted a greater sense of terror or sadness. Or heroism.

So how to put a period at the end of the sentence? How to extract anything even remotely resembling meaning or purpose from the tragedy? Is there a lesson? Is there a way forward?

Maybe. I suppose I can at least take a stab at finding out.

I
After Rabinal: What's Left?

It took me a while to get over the shock of my evacuation from the town where I had spent nearly three years of my life. During my first week in the capital I was commuting on foot every day between the Peace Corps office in Zone 2 and the *pensión* where I was staying, a modest hulk of a building situated a couple blocks downhill from the National Police headquarters. The very name of the *pensión* seemed like an absurd irony: *La Tranquilidad.* Yet tranquility was what I found there many nights—at least those nights that I was able to spend with Mireya. Mireya helped make the city bearable.

I went into the Peace Corps office every day and tried to take care of the things that needed to be taken care of. I saw the Peace Corps nurse, then the doctor, and before he even got the test results back the doctor concluded that I certainly had amoebas, because every volunteer had them by the end of their tour. He put me on the Flagyl again for a couple weeks and that worked to clean my system out, though it also meant I couldn't drink alcohol for a while.

Nights alone in the *pension*, I started trying to read Dietrich Bonhoeffer's *The Cost of Discipleship*, but I couldn't get very far in it. It wasn't a difficult read, but it started to seem to me like an impossible standard to live by. Living and preaching in Nazi Germany, Bonhoeffer saw what it was necessary for him to do, and after meditating on the Word and confiding only in his closest friends, he went ahead and did it. And then he was arrested, imprisoned, and hanged for it. I too had caught a glimpse of what needed to be done, but it was not my destiny to go down that road, even after the whole sordid truth of the matter was laid out plain enough that September morning in San Miguel Chicaj. It's different when it's happening in your own country. And, after all, as much as I loved Guatemala, it was not my own country.

Well, then, screw the reading for now. Even Bonhoeffer, who is a hero to me. *Especially* Bonhoeffer. I am human, I am fallible, I am weak and not very brave, and now I've found that the convictions I thought I possessed are actually still in a period of gestation. They are still forming. Just keep watching, Chris, keep listening, and let them form.

In the meantime, I just have to find a way forward.

* * *

My official Completion of Service date was February 13, 1982—some three months away. Well, then, what to do with the time that remained? Though I couldn't return to Rabinal, I did not want to leave Guatemala. Returning to the United States at this time would have meant leaving Mireya, and that I could not possibly do.

So we decided to get married. We discussed the whole matter one night while sitting on the bed in my little room in *La Tranquilidad*, and right at the beginning I dismissed the alternative of maybe returning to the States alone and somehow trying to maintain a long-distance relationship for a while, before returning again for Mireya. Hell, that would *never* work. I also couldn't see staying on in Guatemala after the Peace Corps, with no obvious job prospect on the horizon. So if we weren't going to say goodbye to each other forever, then getting married as soon as possible was the only logical alternative. As soon as we had that marriage act in hand, we could begin to apply for Mireya's green card at the embassy. And hopefully she would be holding the card in the palm of her little hand before my Completion of Service date.

The decision to get married was a rational calculus, mutually agreed upon. I know Mireya must have felt keenly the absence of romance in the decision. For, unlike all the dreams and fantasies that a young, eligible woman may have in her head, there really was no magical moment when I would kneel before Mireya, place my hands on her lap, and utter the words, "My love, will you marry me?" Instead, it was all so logical. Almost methodical. *Damn.*

While we prepared for our marriage date, I went every day into the Peace Corps office and tried to occupy myself with trivial tasks. Some of them not so trivial. I had to write a Completion of Service report on my time in Rabinal in order to win my plane ticket home, so I got to work on that job. Whenever I reread that report today I am reminded of the painful difficulty I had trying to find the right words to wrap up the whole experience into one neat, tidy package not to exceed roughly ten to fifteen pages. I didn't know how much I could say, and I was afraid I couldn't say what I really wanted, what really had happened. Though the COS report was ostensibly little more than a rough guide for future volunteers who might serve in the same site, the whole experience in Rabinal had by now imbued me with a weird sense of paranoia, and I became afraid of who else outside of the Peace Corps might see my written words. So when it came to identifying key community leaders for the benefit of future volunteers, I kept it all very concise and sanitized.

I also wanted to try and finish my field guide on reforestation and soil conservation practices, since I had worked on it so diligently all those afternoons and nights in Rabinal, and I still needed to finish the darn thing. But I needed a proper space somewhere for such concentrated work. The wide open common area upstairs at the Peace Corps office, with its deep lounge chairs and constant foot traffic going by, was definitely not the proper space.

One thing that was no longer on my to-do list: the comprehensive forest inventory that I had begun for the *municipio* called Rabinal. That whole effort was now impossible to complete after my evacuation. Over the course of more than two years I had collected data and created several thematic maps on mylar and on paper; I had even written a good bit of the text for the study. But the next major stage of development would have required field reconnaissance, and now that was not going to happen. So my forest resource inventory, which for two and a half years I had hoped might become some kind of notable achievement capping off my term of service in the Peace Corps, simply died on the vine.

* * *

Fortunately, I had to haul ass for only a few more daily hikes between the *pensión* and the office, and then I lucked into a spot in an apartment that some Peace Corps volunteers were sharing over in Zone 4. Everybody there was okay with me taking up residence in the maid's quarters, a cubicle measuring maybe eighty square feet that opened to a terrace complete with clothesline, washing board, and the ubiquitous *pila*. And since we were getting married soon anyway, I persuaded Mireya to abandon the spot she shared with others out in Zone 12 and move in with me in this well-appointed little hovel, which in a few short weeks would become our matrimonial suite.

We now had a date firm for the marriage—right before Christmas, which I suppose in itself makes us a slightly unusual couple—and thanks to a friend of Mireya's who had a relative who was an attorney, we now had someone to officiate. Yes, we were to be married by an attorney—in his office.

I still had a pocketful of quetzales left over from the dollar advance on my readjustment allowance which I had given to Güicho's mom and received quetzales from her in return, and so now a good chunk of that came in handy to pay for a wedding suit as well as for the attorney who would officiate. I needed a witness for the ceremony too, so I cornered a Peace Corps pal who volunteered to perform the role. Even though he was simultaneously advising me not to go through with this marriage.

Mireya and I married a week before Christmas, exactly three years to the day from the date my plane first landed at La Aurora airport. So now we were—I couldn't believe my good fortune—husband and wife. I had found a priceless treasure in Mireya, and Mireya had found a gringo who didn't have two nickels to rub together.

* * *

I started to cultivate a pretty consistent rhythm of going into the Peace Corps office every day to continue working on my field guide to reforestation and soil conservation activities. I found some space with a table and chair in a storeroom near the front of the office, and I managed to talk the secretaries into giving me a good manual typewriter that I saw sitting unused in a corner. So I now had an "office" of sorts. An office where I could even close the door and work quietly, all by myself.

Still, progress on the field guide was slow and laborious. I had less than three months left before my COS and the trip back home, and yet some of the topics I was writing about required patient, meticulous attention. And also some good graphic depictions of the subject matter. While I had some moderate ability at drawing, given the press of time, the lack of proper drawing instruments and the lack of money to buy any, my artwork ended up looking pedestrian at best. I did end up completing a field guide after a manner of speaking, but it fell far short of what I was hoping to accomplish. The fat, three-ring binder still sits in a drawer somewhere here in the house, never to be shared with any field worker anywhere.

Less than a month after my evacuation, the army called on the people of Rabinal to assemble once again in the central plaza. Because I was now absent from the scene, my only source of information on this event is a fragile, yellowing news clipping from *La Nación* that I've kept all these years.

> **Rabinal: A Peasant Crowd in Support of the Army**
> More than 30,000 residents of Baja Verapaz held a large and spontaneous rally on Thursday the 3rd in the central square of Rabinal, to express their repudiation of international communism and request weapons to combat it.

The press was more beholden than ever to the army's direction

GUATEMALA SABADO 5 DE DICIEMBRE DE 1981 — LA NACION *Guatemala* — PAGINA 3

Rabinal: concentración campesina de apoyo al Ejército

Más de 30,000 habitantes de Baja Verapaz, efectuaron nutrida y espontánea concentración, el jueves 3 de los corrientes en la Plaza Central de municipio del Rabinal, para expresar su repudio al comunismo internacional y solicitar armas para combatirlo. (Foto de RR.PP. del Ejército).

and purpose. A "spontaneous" gathering of the townspeople? The army had *called for* the gathering that day, for Chrissake, and the army had organized the whole show which was delivered (once again) from the steps of the church. The gathering was about as "spontaneous" as the one I had attended in October when I was accompanied by the Peace Corps country director.

Later I received a firsthand report from a Rabinal friend who visited me in the capital. The army's elaborately staged dog-and-pony show in Rabinal's central plaza had certainly been a big deal, no question about it; never mind the incredible exaggerations in the press. And then, my friend told me, a few days later the army positioned howitzers by the soccer field on the west side of town, and from there they lobbed shells over the mountains to the south, and the shells rained down and exploded over the *aldea* of Xesiguán, the same village where a couple years earlier I had helped farmers set up and manage a tree nursery.

* * *

Towards the end of the year, not long after tying the knot with Mireya, I paid a visit to see CARE rep John Mosher who worked in a fifth-floor office out by the tree-lined streets of Zone 9. I had already heard through the grapevine that John was being transferred to CARE in Colombia, so it looked like a position might be opening up in the CARE/Guatemala mission. John confirmed the news when I met with him, and yes, CARE did have a position announcement already out, and yes, I would be most welcome to apply for the job. Thus began a whirlwind finale to my Peace Corps tour, as I tried to juggle the completion of my field guide with the fulfillment of documentation requirements for Mireya's green card and visa, and now on top of that the tedious task of completing an application and résumé for the CARE job. If I could land that job, I might not have to worry about resettling back in the States with Mireya for another few years.

Meanwhile Guatemala's presidential election was right around the corner, and I was encouraging Mireya to be sure and cast her vote. I was still just full of our American concept of citizenship, according to which one has a duty to participate in fair and free elections and make an informed choice among the supposedly competitive candidates. So I spent some time in lengthy conversations with Mireya, and I found I had to deploy my best effort at persuasion, because recent history had not exactly predisposed Mireya to perform this "civic duty." I use the scare quotes advisedly here because ever since the coup in Guatemala in 1954, the army generals who rose to the presidency typically picked another general to succeed them, and then sham elections every four years became little more than a pro forma exercise to confirm the incumbent's choice. Given the bleak prospects for real democracy in those years, Mireya was preparing to make a perfectly rational decision not to participate in the whole circus.

We sat down to dinner one night in the apartment, and I was already mentally preparing myself for a renewed campaign aimed at the conversion of souls. Or at least this one soul who was my love, my partner. Mireya was pretty determined not to waste time going to vote—but I was going to change her mind!

Just as we sat down at the table, however, a curious thing happened. The delicate, diaphanous lace curtains that hung over the wide window by our dining room table suddenly moved of their own accord, silently wafting away from the window as if a gentle incoming breeze had disturbed their stationary pose. Except the window was shut tight, and there was no breeze. The gently billowing curtains in a windless room almost seemed like some kind of mystical manifestation of the Holy Spirit, for in that very instant no other explanation came readily to mind. Do you believe in the Holy Spirit, Chris? Well, gosh, maybe you should start believing.

But the instant passed, and it was followed scarcely two seconds later by a jolting, thunderous explosion that shook the foundation of the house and rattled all the windows. I jumped from my chair, and our housemate Andy came running out of his room at the same time. Okay, so it was clearly a bomb—but where? We were all okay, so Andy and I decided to go outside and check it out. Mireya told us we were both crazy to go outside; we should just stay in the house and wait for the ten o'clock news, *por dios santo*.

Out on Seventh Avenue there were sirens everywhere, and a couple army jeeps streaked past, each with a soldier standing up in back holding the grips of a mounted machine gun. We saw commotion down the street, so we walked in that direction. We didn't have to walk far. Four short blocks from our apartment we stopped in our tracks and saw it: there stood the modern, twenty-story Financial Center building, once gleaming and wrapped in glass, with all of its expansive windows now completely blown out on nearly all of its floors. The enormous building appeared to remain structurally sound, but curiously faceless, with countless offices on each floor now fully enveloped by the cool December breeze. When we arrived at the scene there was no smoke, no fire. Just hundreds of office papers—letters, purchase orders, status reports, memoranda both pointed and pointless—all of them now just so many errant missives fluttering through the air and falling almost weightlessly down to the ground below. The Financial Center was home to the *Banco Industrial* as well as Guatemala's Ministry of Finance, so the whole building represented a preeminent bastion of the Guatemalan economy. But it was clear that the hundreds of bankers and bureaucrats who worked there wouldn't be getting back to their jobs for a while.

That day I learned for the first time that shock waves from an explosion travel faster than the speed of sound.

Who knew?

* * *

During the last days right before my COS date and the plane trip home everything was hectic. I'd been granted an interview with CARE at their headquarters, which back then was located in downtown Manhattan, so I was preparing for that ordeal as best I could. Organizing my pitch; sending out to get my college grades released; reading about CARE, organizing my pitch. I spent a lot of time organizing my pitch. Meanwhile we were both getting a little frantic over Mireya's green card, because she didn't have it yet. The last step in the process was an in-person interview at the Embassy, but we had not yet even been notified of an appointment date. A letter from the consulate finally came less than two weeks before my COS, giving Mireya an appointment that same week. At least she didn't have to prepare for this interview; she simply had to be her natural, beautiful self.

When we got to the Embassy on the day of the interview, there were well over a hundred Guatemalans waiting in line for admission to get inside. This was not unusual; this was the way it was every single day, Monday through Friday, in front of the embassy. We walked right up to the gate at the front of the long line, showed our consulate letter with the appointment date to a guard there, and I showed him my U.S.

passport. He waved us in with a low sweep of the hand. I sheepishly followed Mireya through the gate, acutely conscious of our privilege that all the Guatemalans waiting in line could only dream of.

Mireya's interview with the consular official was short and sweet, her visa application was approved, and a couple days later we visited the Embassy again to pick up her green card. Which, of course, was not actually green.

The date finally arrived for the flight back home. In the cab ride to the airport I warned Mireya she wasn't properly dressed for the cold winds of February in upstate New York. She'd find out. We overnighted in New York City for my CARE interview the next morning, and after the interview we hopped on a Greyhound for the remainder of the trip, and then we waited at my mom's house in central New York until a selection decision would become known. That was an excruciating wait for both of us. I didn't know if I'd be returning soon to Guatemala to start a fascinating new job, or possibly entering the unemployment rolls in my hometown. And Mireya, for her part, didn't know if she would ever be returning to her INAFOR job in Guate, nor whether it might be just a couple weeks or possibly years before she would see her family again.

The wait dragged on for more than a week, and then I finally got the call. I was in, and we were headed back to Guatemala. The sense of relief was palpable. It was as if, three months into our marriage, we were finally about to start a life together.

* * *

Back once again in Guatemala City, I sat in the early hours of the morning at John Mosher's old desk on the fifth floor of the Plaza Tívoli, dressed in the same suit I'd gotten married in, and I gazed out the window to admire the sunny, tree-lined street below and the hazy blue prominence of Pacaya Volcano on the horizon. What a view I had from this office! It was a gorgeous morning, and I could tell the view outside my window would definitely be a distraction every day. But I had a lot of things to take care of that morning, as it was my very first day on the job with CARE.

It was Tuesday, the twenty-third of March. *Prime number*, I thought to myself. Hmm...I like that. Primes can be lucky, they say. Nice, I think we got this. Eleven primes less than thirty-two, and this is—oh, but wait a minute (I find out only much later), only *some* of 'em are lucky, and twenty-three ain't one of them! Look it up. *Eikositriophobia*. Some people believe. *Shit*. It turns out even William S. Burroughs was fearful of 23!

(What can I say? In three short months, life with Mireya was already teaching me to respect the irrational, the mystical. And foreshadowings sensed in dreams.)

Okay, forget about these idle ruminations. Stuff to do here, c'mon. Eight-thirty, sit down with country director Ginny Ubik for a warm welcome and some initial orientation. Then make the rounds through the whole office. Introduce self to the bookkeeper, to the purchasing agent, the P.L. 480 traffic manager and his assistant, the vehicle fleet manager, and Patty, the pretty receptionist out front who always has her head buried in the NIV Bible between visitors and phone calls. Be nice to her; she'll be typing up all my scrawls and scribbles every day.

It's almost ten now. I'm back at my desk, talking with my very first visitor of the day, an INAFOR subregional *jefe* from Region V (which coincidentally includes Baja Verapaz). We're sitting there talking about trees and plans and what the subregional *jefe* will need in order to make reforestation happen and make it a success. The wide, pane glass window behind me draws in an abundance of morning sunshine, and I imagine my visitor must be seeing the shape of my head in semi-silhouette, though I can see him very clearly against the background of my *mapa de la República de Guatemala* hanging on the wall behind him.

There's a bothersome droning noise growing a little louder outside the window behind me. I keep on talking about CARE and trees and plans (as before noted), when suddenly my visitor interrupts me. "Pardon the interruption," he says, pointing out the window, "but that looks rather odd over there, *no crees?*" So I turn around in my chair and gaze out the window. Well, I'll be damned, there is an olive green Huey hovering scarcely a block away, hovering in place at an altitude not much higher than the fifth floor where my visitor and I are sitting. *Eso sí parece algo raro.*

As we stared slack-jawed at the unusual sight of this helicopter hovering nearby, Rosario, the secretary from accounting, came rushing over from the opposite side of the office: "*¡Todo el radio está en cadena!*" she exclaimed. The radio stations *are all in a chain*! And sure enough, there was no more Camilo Sesto to be heard on Radio Sonora, no more tuneful renditions by Rocio Durcal or Juan Gabriel. Nor advertisements for *productos* Bayer or *jabones* Ambar or *pilas* Ray-O-Vac. Every single station *en toda la República* was now playing, in perfect unison, the field marches of John Philip Sousa, one right after another, interspersed with a few popular marimba tunes. But mostly Sousa. "The Thunderer," "El Capitan," "King Cotton," "The Washington Post March." And, pulling up the rear, as if an afterthought, Guatemala's own national marimba orchestra playing "*Mi Lupita.*"

¡Hay golpe! It's a fucking *coup d'etat*. Damn. So much for my meeting in the afternoon with the people over at DIGESEPE.

We all stood around listening to two, no, maybe three transistor radios spread throughout the office. The vibrant tones of the Sousa marches in a major key sounded weirdly cheerful yet at the same time ominous. Then all of a sudden there was silence on the airwaves—a pregnant pause, as the writers of pulp fiction like to say. We all stood around and looked at each other. A minute or so later the radios crackled in unison, and a spokesperson for the Guatemalan armed forces came on the air with a short message.

"*... Los jovenes oficiales del Ejército de Guatemala han tomado la determinacion de levantarse en armas como respuesta al clamor popular* ... " The young officers of the Guatemalan army have determined to take up arms in response to the popular clamor ...

We wouldn't know it until it came out in the papers the next morning, but there were howitzers positioned in the central park, each one aimed at the National Palace, which back then was the seat of government. A tank was parked in front of the national library across the way. (It was the more cost effective, asphalt-friendly variety of tank, with tires instead of treads.) And I wouldn't learn this until many years later, but even as we all listened to the radio on the fifth floor of the Plaza Tívoli in Zone 9, President Fernando Romeo Lucas Garcia over in the palace in Zone 1 was still refusing to relinquish power. So a group of well-armed rebellious officers seized the president and escorted him down through a long basement corridor, at the end of which he faced his own mother and his sister who were both tied up and held at gunpoint by a group of soldiers.

Checkmate.

But of course we do not hear about any of this in the moment.

All we hear is John Philip Sousa, an occasional marimba melody, and the same army officer repeating the exact same message every half hour or so. After an hour waiting for news that never arrives, Ginny Ubik gets up and tells us all to just leave our work on our desks and go home. It's not yet noon, yet it's impossible to do anything else but call it a day.

So I take off and walk a few blocks in the placid sunshine over to Mireya's office at INAFOR which is located in the *Edificio Cortéz.* Hoofing it because, with less than four hours on the job, I don't even have an assigned vehicle yet. We meet up at her place of work, and pretty soon all the INAFOR workers get leave to go home as well. So we walk across the street to a supermarket. First rule during a *coup d'etat*: stock up, because you never know. Of course, everybody else knows this rule as well, and so the supermarket is impossibly mobbed, and the long line to cash out snakes through the same narrow aisles where others are still pulling items off the shelves. Some people were dumb enough to try and maneuver a shopping cart through the chaos in the impossibly narrow aisles, and that only made matters worse.

But at length, through assertive pushing, tight squeezes, and some impossible reaches, we manage to gather a couple armfuls of various items and we cash out after close to an hour's wait in the long line. Escaping finally from the mayhem, we still have to walk all the way back home, which is a couple miles down Seventh Avenue—Mireya, as always back then, in her heels. Even with our load of groceries, though, the walk back home turned into a surprisingly pleasant stroll, as we now had no particular schedule for the remainder of the day.

Back in the apartment I immediately switched on Mireya's little red Hitachi TV, adjusted the flimsy rabbit ears, and as soon as I caught a signal I found the *cadena* was the same thing we were hearing on the radio, only now with a twelve-inch screen showing black and white stills of Guatemala. And, of course, the flag. Proud and brilliant quetzal perched over crossed flintlocks. The Sousa and marimba tunes droned on merrily, and every half hour or so the same disembodied voice told us to stay tuned while the "young officials" of the army responded decisively to "the clamor of the people." But as the dinner hour approached the disembodied voice added something new to his message: at nine o'clock this evening there would be a special address to the people of Guatemala. So stay tuned.

But *who* will be addressing the people? Is Lucas still around, or is he already history? Okay, so there was a coup, it's plain to see, but what's happening right now? Who's in charge here? For hours an entire country of eight million people remained in the dark. Mireya and I sat down to eat dinner, and we waited.

We were all in a state of nervous suspense to learn the outcome of everything that had transpired during the day. But we didn't have to wait much longer. Promptly at nine o'clock in the evening everybody in the country tuned into their favorite channel or station—at this point it didn't matter which one—and at the appointed hour we all met our new head of state: General Efraín Ríos Montt. In an address that lasted maybe fifteen minutes, the mustachioed general, dressed in camouflage fatigues and sitting with his back straight as a rod and with both palms of his hands resting on a table (*my, my—all spit and polish!*), explained how the "young officials" of Guatemala's army had just decisively responded to the public's outrage over the results of the most recent sham election which would have handed power over to president Lucas's hand-picked successor (who happened to be his defense minister). The general on the TV then praised the comportment and professionalism of his officers and assured his listeners that the "operation" was now complete, that it was a success, and that he himself, our good general, had been chosen by acclamation among all the other commanding officers to lead the new government. (Never mind that in Quetzaltenango, Guatemala's second largest city, there was still at that hour a pitched battle raging at the army base there between Lucas loyalists and the *golpistas*.)

Having announced the change in government, and after thanking all his brave and patriotic supporters in the army, the general wasted no time laying down the law for his adversaries representing *El Movimiento*, the armed resistance.

"Listen to me closely. *Only the army in this country may bear arms*," he told the rebel forces slowly and loudly. "*Only*. The army. May bear arms!" he repeated, in case they did not hear. "So lay down your arms, members of the *guerrilla*, lay down your arms TODAY, *or the army will take your arms away from you!*" And that, of course, would be messy.

During this particular passage in the general's address, his voice rose to a menacingly vitriolic pitch that sounded like a crude impersonation of the wrath of God. Not surprising, perhaps, coming from an evangelical Christian who regularly listened to the fire and brimstone preachers of his beloved Church of the Word. We now had a preacher in camouflage acting as the country's head of state.

At the conclusion of the general's address, people didn't know quite what to think. There was a sense of relief that the day's events had come to some kind of conclusion. No need to panic; all the food we had stocked up in the fridge would eventually get eaten. The words "young officials," which had been repeated on the airwaves over and over again throughout the long day, conjured up aspirational images of some obscure group of rebellious (maybe progressive?) officers who obviously opposed the failed policies of all those old, stodgy, stick-in-the-mud generals who commanded their units. Rebels in the ranks who were ready and poised now to set a brand new course for the nation. Hearing about the daring initiative of these anonymous *jovenes oficiales*, and then finally hearing about the successful conclusion of their *golpe de estado*, many people in Guatemala tentatively embraced the spirit of change and hoped for the best.

But hope would not last long. In his first televised appearance, Rios Montt appeared to be first among equals in a military triumvirate that would chart a path going forward, a path that ostensibly was to lead to free and fair elections. Within days, however, it became clear that Rios Montt himself was the only one in charge, and the stage props who went by the names of Gordillo and Maldonado Schaad quickly became invisible entities. And it didn't take long after that for the new *jefe de estado* to apply his evangelical fervor to a new campaign of counterinsurgency that aimed to eradicate all of the "godless communists" who opposed the ruling elites in the country. The new campaign was called *Fusíles y Frijoles*—"Bullets and Beans," to preserve the catchy alliteration. Arm the peasants and feed them while they're holding their rifles. And if you don't wish to be armed (within the Civil Defense Patrols organized by the army), then you must be a godless communist. You will be dealt with.

The scorched earth campaign planned and executed by Gen. Benedicto Lucas (the brother of the now ousted president) would evolve into an even bloodier campaign of terror. And the campaign continued for many more years. The seventeen months of Ríos Montt's rule turned out to be the most brutal of the country's thirty-six year civil war. Human rights organizations estimate that some ten thousand people were killed during the first three months of his government. On average, Guatemala registered nineteen massacres per month between March and December 1982. More than four hundred indigenous communities were completely destroyed during this time.[102] Including several in Rabinal.

And within a year of my departure from Rabinal, Armando Garzona, the man who had stopped me on the street on Independence Day, 1981, and said to me, "*Estos indios, ¡hay que matarlos todos!*" became the mayor of Rabinal. (Ten years later, his brother Roberto would become mayor.) *La familia* Garzona was one of the key *ladino* families of influence in Rabinal, so it stood to reason (at least in the eyes of some) that a Garzona should have a chance to be mayor. But it would never stand up to moral scrutiny. Never.

> O generations of men,
> Fleeting race of suffering mankind,
> Look, look on your hopes!
> Look at your lives,
> All those happy hopes
> Cut down with failure and crossed with death.
> See, in endless long parade,
> the passing generations go,
> Changing places, changing lives.
> The suffering remains.
> Change and grief consume our little light.[103]

And so we reach the point where I choose to end this narrative of the time I spent in Guatemala. I remained in the country for another five and a half years working on various projects with CARE, and during that time I was able to make three or four very brief trips back to Rabinal. There was a first communion for Gilberto Jerónimo's little daughter. Then there was the inauguration of a potable water system in the *aldea* of Guachipilín. And later, the funeral of a good friend, Victor Morales, who managed the tree nursery in town after I was evacuated, and who tragically succumbed to cancer.

On one of those visits—I think maybe it was the funeral visit—I found myself walking through the plaza on market day when a man suddenly called out to me, "*¡Hola don Cristo!*" It was Juan Cortez, the man from Xesiguan with whom I had once worked to get a small tree nursery started in his little village. Way back during the first few months of my life in Rabinal.

The nursery had failed a year later due to lack of interest in its upkeep (as reported earlier). And a couple years after that—just a month or so after my evacuation—the howitzers positioned by the soccer field on the west side of town lobbed their shells over the mountains to the south, and most of them detonated all over Juan's village.

A friend in Rabinal had told me about that assault, and afterwards I had little reason to believe I would ever see Juan Cortez again in my life. So, when Juan waved his hand and called out to me in the middle of the plaza that day in 1985 or thereabouts, I froze at first because it was like seeing Lazarus risen from the dead. But I snapped out of it and was able to return a warm greeting, and we stood there and talked for a while. We talked about the heat of the afternoon, and we talked briefly and guardedly about *La Situación*. And then we parted ways and got on with the rest of our lives.

* * *

By the spring of 1998 I had been back living in the States for some ten years when Mireya and I decided to pay a visit to Guatemala again. It was time. The government of Guatemala had just signed peace accords with representatives of the guerilla movement less than two years earlier. So far as we could learn from the press and from Mireya's family in Antigua, there seemed to be every indication that the country was headed towards a new beginning, a new era of peace and justice and respect for basic human rights.

We made the trip in April, staying with Mireya's family in Antigua for the solemn festivities of Holy Week. And then, the week following, I rented a car and we drove to Rabinal for a visit.

Physically, little had changed in the town. The same dusty streets everywhere, the same gazebo in the park where Evaristo and the other marathon runners had once lit the ceremonial torch. And, since it was late in the dry season, the familiar cicadas droning on in the distance, singing their cacophonous, monotone hymn. I walked around town and I visited my old friends Augusto and Gilberto Jerónimo. We talked for a long while. We talked a little about the past troubles in town, but mostly we tried to focus on the present and the future.

And it was during this visit to Rabinal when I learned that Güicho himself, whom I had completely lost contact with, was alive and well and teaching in a school in the *aldea* of Chiac. Güicho had survived, thank God. Unfortunately, my visit to Rabinal was all too brief, and I never got to reunite once again with the man who had given me a ride through the mountains one rainy morning back in 1980; the man who had set up the movie projector with a generator in Nimacabaj while I watched heat lightning silently flashing on the horizon. The man who had talked to me about creating a brighter tomorrow for Rabinal, for the country, if we all could just add our little *granito de arena*.

But, thankfully, Güicho and I have recently had an opportunity to renew our very special friendship. We found each other quite by accident a few years ago on social media, and now we keep in touch with each other more or less frequently. Ever the activist, Güicho told me how just last year he was busy organizing the townspeople and talking to a crowd gathered at the Santa Elena highway junction high up near the cloud forest above Salamá, exhorting his enthusiastic audience to keep the faith and sustain the nationwide traffic blockade, *and never give up* until the Pact of the Corrupt Ones is finally vanquished and Guatemala's new, freely elected president (the living son of Juan José Arévalo, the country's first progressive president) is finally sworn into office. I even saw a video of his speech to the crowd, and it was moving.

Indeed, Guatemala today is on the cusp of a bold new era bending toward freedom, justice, and prosperity. And under the capable leadership of Bernardo Arévalo it certainly promises to be a salutary break from the past, provided all the old oligarchs and corrupt officials of the past seventy years can be held at bay. The threats to undermine positive change in Guatemala still remain, and President Arévalo's path forward is far from clear of obstacles. But that must be the topic for another book.

II
A Confession to Richard and James

I wish, oh how I wish I still had in my possession two very special letters that I received from Stateside correspondents while I lived in Rabinal. One was from my hometown pastor, the Rev. Richard Manzelmann, who actually wrote me a short note along with the two books he sent me. The other letter was a longer one in which my old literature professor Jim McConkey replied to a rather turgid and awkward epistle I had written him because I simply wanted to reach out and let him know what I was doing with my life.

I can't remember a single detail of what either of them wrote to me, yet I feel quite sure what both men would have had on their minds as they wrote: I think both my pastor (who always loved reading *The New Yorker*) and my beloved teacher (who occasionally wrote for the magazine) must have been hoping I'd be keeping some kind of record about my experiences, some kind of testimony as a witness to the unfolding of history in that tiny corner of the world called Rabinal.

As a matter of fact, I did keep a haphazard, partial record of my time in Guatemala: I still possess most of those scrawls and scribbles—fragments of mostly purple prose that are so incomplete they would not even fill one half of a standard, high school composition book. The rest of what I have is just pure memory. Memory that plays out again and again like a never-ending movie in my head.

Even as I sat in my hammock in Rabinal I kept repeating to myself over and over again a simple phrase that had become almost like a mantra for me: "looking forward to the looking back." I longed for such a time, someday in the near or distant future, when I might be able to look back on the whole experience and just take stock and tell the story. Because one thing I knew for certain: during every single moment in Rabinal I knew that I was living a story worth telling.

After I had an epiphany walking on the road past Patixlán one day early in my tour, *I looked forward to the looking back.* And after that singular, incandescent moment of fellowship with the other passengers on a bus headed out of town a couple years later, *I looked forward to the looking back.* Even on that day after I glimpsed the horror through a bus window in San Miguel Chicaj—though it had to be with an inescapable sense of revulsion—I found myself *looking forward to the looking back.*

And yet after I returned to the United States months passed, then years and even decades passed without my ever committing myself to that necessary, concerted, systematic effort at looking back. Until now, more than forty years later.

Richard had a right to expect more of me, and so did James. From Richard I had learned that to be a Christian was to be a witness; it was not an optional act but a duty. He also had taught me, through the example of the German pastor Dietrich Bonhoeffer, what it really meant to do what was necessary in a time of crisis. From James I had learned, through the example of St. Augustine's *Confessions* which we read in his class, about the supreme importance of memory as a source of narrative; indeed, as a source of knowledge, including self-knowledge. Richard and James both gave of themselves to equip me both morally and intellectually for the role of witness that I was destined to perform—and then I squandered my time on earth for more than four decades before taking up that mantle and doing what was necessary with the blank sheet of paper in front of me.

They both had a right to expect much more from this young *norteamericano* who once stood in the middle of Rabinal's plaza and witnessed a small piece of history unfold. Who stood there and witnessed (if *doña* Carmen de Jerónimo's confident assessment is to be credited) *the hand of God* as it passed invisibly through the whole crowd in front of the church, where gunners were positioned in the twin belfries.

I confess now to my mentors, to Richard and to James, I confess that I wasted precious time, I followed wayward paths, and I forgot my duty to do what was necessary. I wish I had told this story twenty-five or thirty years ago. It might have served a more important purpose back then. Now, though, my words are all but useless to anybody except a very few who perhaps, along with me, simply yearn to remember. Even when it hurts to remember. I confess now to Richard and James that *por mi culpa, por mi propia culpa*, I am far too late now in offering my testimony.

I wish I could have shared this whole story with my mentors, and I feel devastated now because I took so damned long to finish it. But why? Why do I feel such spiritual and emotional distress? I suppose in part it is due to a selfish sense of pride in my creation, no matter how flawed it may be. My teachers should have had a chance to see it. Maybe they would have felt proud of me—or, what is more likely, simply gratified to see that I finally made at least some kind of effort. The way a schoolteacher feels, after weeks of patient coaching, when a struggling student turns out, way, *way* after the due date, a little essay that is—why *yes*, praise the Lord, it's actually intelligible! It can be read and understood by others, despite all the awkward structure and the sloppy handwriting!

So here I am, now, turning in my homework at last.

Afterword

SOCRATES: There are some, then, who desire evil?

MENO: Yes.

SOCRATES: Do you mean they think the evils which they desire, to be good; or do they know that they are evil and yet desire them?

MENO: Both, I think.

SOCRATES: And do you really imagine, Meno, that a man knows evils to be evils and desires them nonetheless?

MENO: Certainly I do.

—Plato, *Meno*

In the final analysis, I only witnessed barely three years of Rabinal's thousand-year history, and after more than forty years of silence my testimony (if you can call it that) comes rather late. Far too late to make any kind of life-saving difference. And decades too late to contribute anything meaningful to the quest for justice, or even "historical clarification."

That begs the question, of course, as to why I even took the time to produce this record. For me, the answer to that question is not hard. I simply wanted to praise and remember: to praise a handful of heroes whom I had the privilege of knowing in this life, and to remember the steps we walked along the path together. Heroes like *padre* Gregorio Donoso. Like Luís David García Caballeros (Güicho) and doña Carmen de Jerónimo. Heroes like Evaristo Cuxúm from Patixlán, and Mariano Alvarado of Xococ. Teachers, community leaders, innovators. People who were ready to lay down their lives for justice and equality. So many heroes, heroes living and dead, from the town where my soul still dwells.

Most people will never in their lives learn about the history of a place called Rabinal. In fact, most people will never even hear the name of the town. And hardly anybody outside of the department of Baja Verapaz will ever know the names of the heroes I have named here. I guess I just wanted to do something about that.

Thousands died in Rabinal during the time I spent there, and in the months right after my departure. In the country as a whole, the 36-year civil war left some 200,000 dead, and 40,000 disappeared, and over a million people were displaced both within and outside of the country's borders.[104]

Yet the town called Rabinal survives. Rabinal is still very much on the map.

How can we begin to make sense of an act of genocide? On one level, the level of (let's call it) common understanding, the question seems nothing less than absurd, for there is no sense in senseless acts. Yet the mind still gropes for meaning. That's why I wanted to ponder the whole experience in Rabinal to see what I could learn.

I
A Quest for Meaning

> I am a slave, I know,
> and slaves are weak. But the gods are strong, and over them
> there stands some absolute, some moral order
> or principle of law more final still.
> Upon this moral law the world depends;
> through it the gods exist; by it we live,
> defining good and evil.
>
> —Euripides, *Hecuba*, 798ff

Hecuba wasn't always a slave. She was once the queen of Troy. But after ten long years of war that took the lives of her husband and her sons and reduced all of Troy to a pile of rocks, she herself was reduced to slavery, surviving only at the mercy of the victorious Athenians. Contemplating her own fate and the fate of her people, Hecuba waxes philosophical in this passage, and she finally asserts, with a voice of authority born of her unspeakable suffering, that the mighty gods themselves, who wreaked so much havoc with Troy's fortunes and fate, are actually subservient to *a higher law* in this universe. A law that is higher than the gods. A law that, indeed, makes the gods' existence possible.

It is a cosmic assertion that I ponder myself even today. For the epic tragedy that unfolded on the sands of Ilium thousands of years ago has replayed itself over and over again, hundreds of times through the ages. And it happened again—not for the last time—in Rabinal in the year 1981. One could say it is Nietzsche's Eternal Return writ large. So, if shit is going to happen over and over again, and violence and injustice are simply endemic to our human race, then maybe we had best simply learn to take it as it comes, ponder the outcome for a bit, and then just try to move on. Thinking too much about suffering will never make suffering go away.

> Why should man fear since chance is all in all
> for him, and he can clearly foreknow nothing?
> Best to live lightly, as one can, unthinkingly.[105]

So said Jocasta to her suddenly inquisitive husband (and son), King Oedipus. Forget the past. Best to live lightly, unthinkingly, like a stone skipping over the surface of the water.

Except that when the victims are the people you knew, the people you worked with every day, when the town that has suffered so terribly is the one place in the world that you had come to love more than any other because the people had welcomed you in the first place, and over time came to regard you as a member of their community, if not as a brother, then the search for meaning becomes imperative.

So, over the years I kept searching for some scrap of meaning in the tragedy that I had seen unfold in Rabinal. Any scrap might do. What can we learn from the horror?

Here are the stages of learning. Or at least, this was my path.

* * *

By 1988 I was back in Ithaca again, enrolled as a grad student in Cornell's natural resources department. Mireya and I, along with our three-year-old daughter and all our possessions that had once filled a house in Guatemala City, were now all crammed into a modestly appointed unit in the married student housing complex on North Campus.

Though my classes were interesting and challenging, my mind during this time period was often seized by memories of everything

I had seen in Rabinal. One afternoon I found myself alone in our apartment, having just returned from a particularly fast-paced class in quantitative methods. Sitting on the sofa, my mind gradually decompressed from the very heady linear programming lesson we had covered in class, and I settled into a decidedly more qualitative state in which I began to mourn the tragic losses in Rabinal seven years earlier. (This is the way my mind wanders; I can't help it.) Only this time it was not just an idle recollection from the past—this time I totally broke down in uncontrollable sobs thinking about and mourning for the people who had suffered so much in Rabinal. It all came back to me in a sort of tidal wave, all at once.

This came out of nowhere. I was a total mess sitting there on the edge of the sofa, but at the same time I had the presence of mind to think of something: Chris, I thought to myself, *this is it*. It is happening. This is what you've been holding in, dreading for years, and now it has finally hit you. What did the great ones whom you admire so much do when faced with an existential crisis? What did Augustine of Hippo do?

Augustine, a man who had long been held hostage by the memory of his sins, experienced such a crisis one day on the eve of his conversion. Then, as he found himself sobbing alone in his room, he heard a voice, a child's voice, which instructed him to take up the Book and read. And so he did:

> I stemmed my flood of tears and stood up, telling myself that this could only be a divine command to open my book of Scripture and read the first passage on which my eyes should fall.

I suddenly felt inspired to try and emulate Augustine, after my own sciolistic fashion, so I seized my copy of the Bible from a shelf nearby, I placed it on the coffee table in front of the sofa, and I let the book fall open quite randomly to whatever page it might fall open to. And on that page I read the following:

> O LORD, how long must I call for help before you listen, before you save us from violence? Why do you make me see such trouble? How can you stand to look on such wrongdoing? Destruction and violence are all around me,

> and there is fighting and quarreling everywhere. The law is weak and useless, and justice is never done. Evil men get the better of the righteous, and so justice is perverted.

The sense of some kind of miracle happening right then and there was palpable. Out of the more than sixteen hundred pages in the entire volume, how was it that in my reenactment of Augustine's epiphany the Holy Scripture sitting on the table had fallen open to this very page which spoke so directly to my inner turmoil?

It was the Book of Habakkuk, a book I had never seen before. Habakkuk was one of the more obscure prophets in the entire Old Testament, and so far as I know the *only* one who had ever dared to question God's plan. I saw this moment sitting on the sofa with the Bible open in front of me as a pivotal experience in my life, so I decided I would stay with Habakkuk for a while and just ponder the enigma.

But the pondering drove me mad. I pondered the message of Habakkuk for days, weeks, months. Years.

In the opening scene, Habakkuk exclaims to God, "Even when I cry out to You 'Violence!', You will not save." Habakkuk is perplexed by God's seeming inactivity, even while he sees all around him that the violence continues and justice has become a complete hoax. I like a man who asks questions.

In the beginning I wanted to place my trust in the enigma of God's power just like Habakkuk did. I wanted to trust in God. Even if it meant facing an enigma that I could not understand. God may appear to be slow to act, but bear with Him. His timing is PERFECT because He is always in control. We need only to keep a watchful eye and wait for Him to fix it all.

This is the point where Habakkuk climbs out of the valley where he started out; he climbs up to a high mountaintop (in my mind's eye I imagined him climbing up to the ancient altar atop *Cerro* Kaj'yup), and there he goes from wailing and railing against God to singing, singing praise now for God's power and wisdom.

This is the point where I, Christian, a flawed Christian at best, started looking for other sources of wisdom.

So I started reading the Greek tragedies. I eventually read every single one of them, and they brought me some solace. After much meditation on the lessons from Greek tragedy, I began to ask, along with Agamemnon's friend and messenger Talthybius:

> O Zeus, what can I say?
> That you look on us and care?
> Or do we, holding that the gods exist,
> Deceive ourselves with insubstantial dreams
> And lies, while random careless chance and change
> Alone control the world?[106]

Though I still maintained a belief in God, I had begun to adopt a more humanistic view of things. God the Creator? Yes, perhaps. I could definitely see Genesis as a plausible metaphor not inconsistent with the Big Bang and evolution. But God the Fixer? Not bloody likely, as far as I could see. So much, *so much* remains broken.

Verses like these stuck with me for a while, but I was still wandering alone through the fields of the ancient tragedies, and I was a bit lost. Reading one after another of those great stories, still looking for answers. It was not until later, in Aeschylus, where I finally found something like the answer that I was seeking:

> *We must suffer, suffer into truth.*
> And even in our sleep, pain
> which cannot forget
> falls drop by drop upon the heart,
> until, in our own despair,
> against our will, comes wisdom
> through the awful grace of God.[107]

The awful grace of God. What can *that* possibly mean? In order to understand this enigmatic quote from the *Agamemnon*, I want to quote at some length a Union University news release I read recently about a sermon by one Robert Smith Jr., a Professor of Christian Preaching:

> "We talk about grace, but always benevolently. [But] what about grace in a malevolent way? We're so selective in our lifting up passages about grace." Smith spoke at a chapel service to Union students about God's awful grace, and said that type of grace is necessary if Christians are to appreciate God's amazing grace.
>
> He quoted a passage from the Greek playwright Aeschylus, who wrote [the lines quoted above].
>
> "Is this the inception of insanity, to talk about grace

> as awful?" Smith asked … Is this bare blasphemy? Is this pure perversity? … Or has [Aeschylus] put his finger on the pulsating heartbeat of an attribute of God that we want to avoid?"[108]

Never mind that Aeschylus himself was not talking about any Jewish or Christian God, but rather about Zeus, who was first and foremost in a pantheon of Greek gods. Never mind, because I think this Baptist preacher from Alabama might be onto something here:

> [Smith] suggested that amazing grace and awful grace are not antithetical to each other, but coexist. They are, he said, *opposite sides of the coin of grace "within the currency of the divine economy of God."* [Emphasis added.]
>
> He used Psalm 23 as an example to make his point and suggested that Christians too often are in a hurry to get to the banquet table described at the end of the psalm.
>
> "You can't get to the table where he prepares a banquet … until you have walked through the valley of the shadow of death," Smith said. "And the one who prepares the banquet table before you is the one who says, 'You don't have to fear evil, because I'm with you in the valley as well as at the banquet table.'
>
> "It is the awful grace of God that takes you through the valley in order that when you come to the banquet table of the amazing grace of God, you can appreciate the trip that he has brought you through."[109]

Whether we read it straight off of Aeschylus' script, or recast it in the light of Christian teaching, I think I can now understand how the awful grace of God might somehow prepare us for future enlightenment. It's not an easy lesson to internalize, but it's an important one. Maybe that's why Robert F. Kennedy quoted these very same verses from Aeschylus during an impromptu speech he gave in Indianapolis on that day in April 1968 when Martin Luther King Jr. was cut down by an assassin's bullet. In that speech Bobby Kennedy was trying to offer some measure of consolation to a crowd of people who were stunned, shocked and weary from the latest tragedy that had just played out here in America the Violent. (He could not have imagined that two months later another crowd would need similar consolation in the wake of his own assassination.)

The lesson from Aeschylus, that we must "suffer into truth," was the first important piece of wisdom that crystallized my understanding of everything that had happened in Rabinal. It was still an enigma, no doubt about it, but somehow it was now an approachable enigma. If that makes any sense.

* * *

We ultimately have to face the reality of persistent evil in the world. And in Guatemala during the time that I lived there, there was no shortage of evil to contend with, from the scorched earth terror campaign of Gen. Benedicto Lucas to the man who stopped me on the street on Independence Day and said to me, "*Estos indios, ¡hay que matarlos todos!*"

So I kept on searching for guidance, from whatever source.

My search brought me eventually to the *Upanishads*. In order to conquer Evil, the spiritual teacher Eknath Easwaran tells us, in his meditations on the *Upanishads,* that we must

> [act] without attachment to the results. The victory of good over evil is guaranteed—but not by the doer. We cannot win that victory, but we can make ourselves instruments of it, precisely by not thinking of ourselves as the doers but by 'making ourselves zero,' in Gandhi's phrase.[110]

Victory is guaranteed, but not by the doer. Okay, so we're faced with yet another enigma here. But what's that thing he said at the end of the quote? *Making ourselves zero.* I see. I see, now. So it all comes back, then, to Gandhi, to the *Upanishads*. Mohandas K. Gandhi, the man who was my adolescent hero so long ago in a world that, like today, was swirling with violence and injustice. Our purpose, then, is *to do what is necessary* to fight Evil, and to simply respond to Evil with Good, not with apathy or paralysis. One might even say, perversely paraphrasing General Benny, "to face *Evil* like a soldier, not like a coward or like some passive, indifferent idiot." Guatemala's Gen. Benedicto Lucas, brave and sadistic in equal measures, was on the wrong side of history, yet here is a rephrased lemma I could actually live with.

Suffer into truth. Make oneself zero. Respond to Evil with Good. Or as the poet Lao Tzu put it,

Use up all you are
And then you can be made new.

Learn to have nothing
And then you will have everything.[111]
If you can put yourself aside—
then you can do things for the whole world.
And if you love the world, like this
then you are ready to serve it.[112]

Words, words, words. Enough, I say, *damn them all*. In the end, I really just want to sit on the ground one night atop *Cerro Kaj'yúp*, right there beside the sacrificial altar, and peer deeply into the bright, starry heavens and proclaim, along with Miguel de Unamuno and to no one in particular, that

> [u]ncertainty, doubt, perpetual wrestling with the mystery of our final destiny, mental despair, and the lack of any solid and stable dogmatic foundation, *may be the basis of an ethic*.

For that, I think, is in the final analysis probably the best we can hope for. Wrestle with the mystery. Suffer into truth.

* * *

II
Coda: What's Left

Some people collect autographs. That was never my thing, really. But while I've never "collected" autographs per se, I do happen to possess a couple that are very special to me. They come from two different bookends of my life: One I obtained when I was still that fresh-faced, idealistic youth sailing my golden barque towards a gleaming palace in the sky. The second autograph I have—this one priceless—comes from a period in my life when I was praying for guidance on a rudderless vessel careening towards chaos.

Each of the two autographs I possess has a story behind it. Let me tell you the first story: I was fourteen when my sister Diane, twelve years my senior, was working as a flight attendant for TWA. It was 1969, the year of the first moon landing, and Diane must have known how closely I was following the space program from one exciting mission to the next. So, when Neil Armstrong himself happened to be a first class passenger on one of her flights, back in the galley she offhandedly remarked to one of her coworkers, "Wouldn't it be crazy if I could get Mr. Armstrong's autograph to give to my little brother?" She wasn't about to pursue the thought any further, it was merely a passing fancy, but a little later a sympathetic and somewhat mischievous coworker took her by the hand to where the famous astronaut was seated, and she simply said to him, "Excuse me Mr. Armstrong, sir, but I have a small request to make. You see, Diane, here—this is Diane—she has a little brother who is just so excited about the space program and everything, and, and—could you possibly sign an autograph for Diane here, so she could give it to her little brother? Please?"

While nursing a drink that he had nestled in his armrest, the first man to set foot on the moon obliged the young woman's request: he took out his briefcase and opened it, and he pulled out one of maybe a dozen or so eight-by-ten color portraits of himself dressed in full astronaut regalia. He asked for the name of Diane's "little" brother (who actually would be starting to grow whiskers in a couple more years), and then he took out his felt-tipped pen and wrote, "Best Wishes to Chris. Neil Armstrong."

Felt-tipped pen. Damn, it must have been a cheap one. Or maybe it's just that I kept this prized picture of Neil Armstrong mounted proudly on my bedroom wall for several years, where maybe it got exposed to a little too much sunlight. Because today that once valuable autographed picture is fit only to be relegated to a file drawer under my desk—the markings once scribbled in haste by the first man on the moon now so faded as to be nearly invisible. It's almost as if the god Apollo himself, in a capricious mood that was his wont, had cast a spell ordaining that this valuable artifact of mine shall waste itself away over the years, to eventually become nothing more than worthless paper. Just as Neil Armstrong himself eventually faded from American consciousness over the years, so must all the physical evidence that you ever regarded him as a hero.

So it goes.

I'm lucky, though, that I possess another valuable autograph that I've had for some time, and that one still remains sharp and clear to this very day. It, too, has a story behind it.

I was sitting in my hammock in Rabinal catching up on the news one Sunday morning, when Evaristo appeared at my front gate. Though I had only met him a couple weeks earlier during a short course on soil conservation that I delivered out in Patixlán, I recognized him because his was the patch of farmland where we had done the demonstration terracing work.

"*Pase adelante*," I said, "The gate's open." Evaristo smiled and sat down in a chair on the patio and we exchanged pleasantries for several minutes, which is the way my conversations with all my visitors always began, no matter what the purpose of the visit. At length Evaristo came around to why he was paying me a visit. It was about another project we had started in Patixlán, namely a community fruit tree nursery, and he handed me a yellow half-sheet of paper. The nursery was all set up, and the seedlings now under daily care, he reported, and the paper he handed me listed the names of all his neighbors and relatives who had helped him do the work. Ten of them in all, with Evaristo's name appearing in his best penmanship at the top. The deal was that they'd all receive Food for Work as an incentive, so I took out a scratch pad to total up the days and multiply it out. I had all the bags of flour and bulgur and CSM from CARE in the back room, but since Evaristo had arrived at my house alone, I promised I'd coordinate with Juan Avelino next door to get all the food (several hundred pounds) delivered to them in the DIGESA pickup. We settled the whole matter in short order, and I told Evaristo I'd try to get out to Patixlán within the next few days to take a look at their nursery.

That's how I obtained the autograph of Evaristo Cuxúm Alvarado. This happened some time before Evaristo was briefly jailed for "insurrection," and it was long before we struck out on our magical, pointless journey to Raxjút together. Before he climbed up a tree in a mountaintop meadow and threw ripe avocados down to me on the ground below.

And it was long before Evaristo ran the marathon that ended triumphantly at the gazebo in Rabinal's central plaza in the early evening on Independence Day, 1981. An evening which became his last among the living.

After Evaristo left my house that day at the beginning of our acquaintance, all I really knew I had was a scrap of paper with a handwritten list of names, his own name appearing at the very top. But now, having walked with Evaristo through the Stations of the Cross, now I know I will have to cherish and save that yellow scrap of paper forever. For on that paper, there at the very top, is the autograph of a true Guatemalan hero.

This autograph on a fragile slip of paper, and the discolored

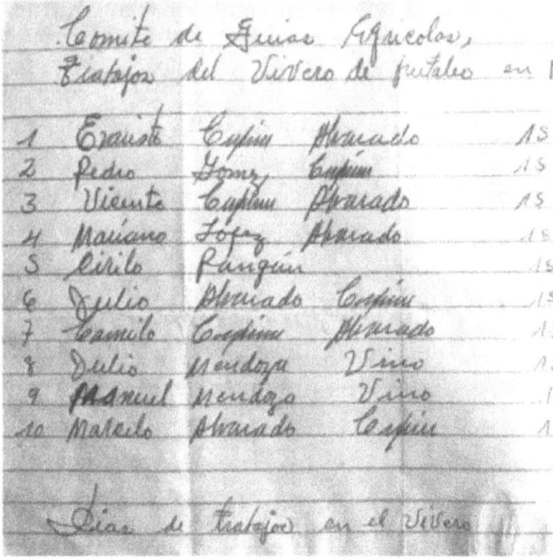

Comité de Guías Agrícolas,
Trabajos del Vivero de frutales en Pat[illegible]

1	Evaristo	Capím	Alvarado	15	días de trabajo
2	Pedro	Gómez	Capím	15	"
3	Vicente	Capím	Alvarado	15	"
4	Mariano	López	Alvarado	15	"
5	Cirilo	Ranquín		15	"
6	Julio	Alvarado	Capím	15	"
7	Camilo	Capím	Alvarado	15	"
8	Julio	Mendoza	Vino	15	"
9	Manuel	Mendoza	Vino	10	"
10	Marcelo	Alvarado	Capím	10	"

Días de trabajo en el Vivero

Evaristo with his family, *aldea* Patixlán (1980)

photograph I have of the man himself standing beside his family in Patixlán—these are the only physical things I have left from Evaristo.

But is that really all that's left? All over Latin America there is a well-known saying that everyone in the world dies three deaths. The first death occurs when your body ceases to function. The second death occurs when the body is interred in the ground. But the third death is the most poignant of all, for it occurs when there is nobody left in the entire world to say your name.

I am still left, and so are you, dear reader. *And you, Evaristo*—I walked with you once. Now I say to you, my friend: We still have miles to go together. *¡Caminemos otra vez juntos, mi hermano!*

END

1997 - 2024

Acknowledgements

It is indeed hard to write, and to keep writing, while holding down a job that pays the bills but has nothing to do with writing. I started this memoir, *qua* memoir, more than ten years ago while working as a water resources "circuit rider" with a nonprofit organization in upstate New York. Some years before that, the whole story was going to be a novel based on my experiences. I wrote Chapter One of my so-called novel a little before the start of the new millennium—and it appears now, substantially unaltered, as Chapter 5 of this present volume. For the most part, I simply changed 'he' to 'I,' *et voilà*.

Writing off and on over the past twenty-five years, I can say that for the most part I have found writing to be a very lonely, solitary experience. But all of that changed during the last half-year or so of the writing process. Suddenly, I had a handful of readers, an editor, and a publisher who were all looking at my work and providing useful input. And in these last few months I even began to share some chapters with my wife Mireya.

I am deeply grateful to my editor, Robyn Harrison, for all the patient and detailed assistance she provided, not to mention her constant encouragement. I cannot count the ways in which Robyn helped me to make this a better book. She read the entire manuscript numerous times, and it is fair to say that every single reading brought forth new suggestions and corrections that were essential to address. Any errors that remain in this volume are my own, of course, and mine alone.

I also wish to thank Marian Haley Beil of Peace Corps Writers for her invaluable guidance and assistance in preparing this manuscript for publication.

I owe a huge debt of gratitude as well to several friends who took the time to read my manuscript and comment on it. My heartfelt thanks go out to John Schelhas, Doug Clark, Scott Wallace, Raul Tuazon and Glenn Blumhorst for all the time and thoughtful consideration they devoted to this effort. All five of these gentlemen, like me, have been abroad and have "seen the elephant"—a picturesque phrase from a century and a half ago that referred to those individuals who had endured the dangers and privations of the American frontier, or again, those who had seen the blood and smoke of pitched battle in the heartland. Together and separately, the six of us all saw the elephant in Central America. John Schelhas, who worked near me and occasionally alongside me in Baja Verapaz department for almost a year, was among the first to read what I had written, and he saved me some embarrassment by catching more than a couple errors and faux pas. Doug Clark helped me reassess the story that I wanted to tell when he challenged me to think harder about whether my aim was to write autobiography, or a story about Rabinal. (In the end, Doug, I think the answer is both—but mainly Rabinal.)

I am grateful to journalist Scott Wallace for his sage advice on the importance of early foreshadowing, as well as his concerns about the overall length of the book. I ultimately cut out a lot thanks to Scott's suggestion, though probably not as much as he would have liked to see cut.

Raul Tuazon provided insights that made me think harder about the purpose of each vignette that I had written. I discovered that at least a couple of my digressions, while great fun to write, actually served little purpose in terms of advancing the main story line. (Who knows, maybe I'll get to use them somewhere else another day.) Raul also helped me to better appreciate the whole arc of my story as a journey towards self-awareness.

I also wish to thank Luís David García Caballeros ("Güicho") for reading and commenting upon several of my chapters in translation. I had reached out to Güicho in Rabinal in particular because I sought his approval of the manner in which I portrayed him in Chapter 8, as well as the manner in which I portrayed his sweet mother (God rest her soul) in Chapter 15. I am happy to report that I was successful on both counts.

Thanks go out to Daniel Arturo Chen Siana, Helios Villatoro, and Lewis Johnson for the photographs they allowed me to use to illustrate this book. I am also grateful to the late Augusto Jerónimo, who lived across the street from me in Rabinal and who supplied a couple photographs of great historical significance—the scene showing the *iglesia de San Pablo* right after the 1976 earthquake, and the shot of the triumphant *maratonistas* who were murdered that very same night.

And a very special thanks also to Marino Cattelan for his beautiful photograph of Rabinal's San Pablo cathedral which adorns the cover. Marino's skill, his eye for beauty, and his storytelling ability are all on display in every single one of his photographs of life in Guatemala.

There are also a few people now deceased who deserve very special recognition. My profound gratitude to my mentors, the late Professor James McConkey and the late Reverend Richard Manzelmann, must be pretty evident already in the pages I have written, so I needn't belabor that debt any further here. It pains me greatly that they shall never see this book, which is a product of their patient tutelage. And I would hasten to say the same about yet another important mentor I had, my high school ecology teacher the late Douglas Pens. "Mr. Pens," as we knew him back in New Hartford, left his singular imprint on my formation as an environmentalist and as a man. Thank you, Mr. Pens, for your lessons about understanding, protecting, and honoring Nature.

My wife Mireya supported me during this entire writing project with unflagging cheerfulness and encouragement, and with more patience and forgiveness than I deserve. She also read the entire manuscript, noting places where her memory of events did not necessarily square with mine. In several instances, it turns out, her recollection is better than mine and I made adjustments accordingly. Now that the work is finished I can say to Mireya, as I said once before when I finished another writing project in graduate school, so very long ago,

Ahora sí, ya se terminó. Pero mi amor por ti perdura para siempre.

And finally, to the people of Rabinal, I offer my humblest thanks for receiving me as a guest in their community, and for sharing their wisdom and confidences with me over the course of three years. May Rabinal forever prevail and prosper under the protection of the *rajawales* who guard her destiny!

ENDNOTES

Chapter One

1. The nine-minute video is available at: https://youtu.be/d3NM3xaN-uLk?si=nOiYs9zXBBCjoDvQ

2. Miguel de Unamuno, *The Tragic Sense of Life* (New York: Dover, 1954), 315.

Chapter Two

3. *The Battle of Algiers,* acclaimed as one of the greatest cinematic accomplishments of the twentieth century, offered such a vivid and accurate portrayal of so-called "asymmetric" warfare that it was used as a didactic tool in military training programs, and was even shown to U.S. defense officials in the aftermath following 9/11.

4. An alternative to widespread use of hazardous agrochemicals is the phytosanitary approach known as Integrated Pest Management. In the United States, IPM was formulated into national policy in 1972 when federal agencies began to take steps to advance the application of IPM in all relevant sectors. But IPM was still a novel approach in the 1970s, and in the developing world was still virtually unknown.

5. See https://www.aphis.usda.gov/publications/plant_health/alert-old-world-bollworm-sp.pdf Volaton is Bayer's brand name for the compound known as phoxim.

6. Cf. W. Blum, *Killing Hope: U.S. Military and CIA Intervention Since World War II* (Monroe, ME: Common Courage Press, 1995), 233.

7. U.S. Defense Intelligence Agency, "Military Intelligence Summary (MIS), Volume VIII, Latin America (U), 1980."

8. The name "Kaibil" is derived from Kayb'il B'alam (*Kaibil Balam*), a Mam indigenous leader who evaded capture by the Spanish conquistadors under Pedro de Alvarado. The official motto of Guatemala's Kaibiles: "If I advance, follow me. If I stop, urge me on. If I retreat, kill me." Source: Wikipedia, https://en.wikipedia.org/wiki/Kaibiles

9. Thomas and Marjorie Melville, *Guatemala: The Politics of Land Ownership* (New York: The Free Press, 1971), 21f.

10. Richard F. Nyrop (ed.), *Guatemala: A Country Study* (1983), 21.

11. Blum, *op. cit.*, 74.

12. Norman Lowe, *Mastering Modern World History*, Fifth ed., (Basingstoke: Palgrave Macmillan, 2013), 618.

13. Allan Nairn, "C.I.A. Death Squad" (Editorial) *The Nation*, April 17, 1995, 511. See also A. Nairn, "Despite Ban, U.S. Captain Trains Guatemalan Military." *The Washington Post*, October 21, 1982. And: Greg Grandin and Elizabeth Oglesby, "Washington Trained Guatemala's Killers for Decades." *The Nation*, January 25, 2019.

14. W. Dalrymple, *The Anarchy: The East India Company, Corporate Violence, and the Pillage of an Empire*, (New York: Bloomsbury Publishing, 2019). See also: P. Chapman, *Bananas: How the United Fruit Company Shaped the World*, (New York: Grove Press, 2014).

15. Maudslay, Alfred P. 1899. *A Glimpse at Guatemala*. New York: Cambridge Univ. Press.

16. Verses translated from: https://growingupbilingual.com/es/canto-para-las-posadas/

17. The name "Guatemala" comes from the Nahuatl word "Cuauhtēmallān", which means "place of many trees". The name may also derive from the K'iche' Mayan word for "many trees" or the Cuate/Cuatli tree *Eysenhardtia*. The name was given by the Tlaxcalteca people who came with Pedro de Alvarado to conquer the land.

Chapter Three

18. "P.L. 480" refers to Public Law 480, the Agricultural Trade Devel-

opment and Assistance Act of 1954, commonly known as PL–480 or Food for Peace.

19· Wikipedia contributors, "Achi people," *Wikipedia, The Free Encyclopedia,* https://en.wikipedia.org/w/index.php?title=Achi_people&oldid=1157717354 (accessed August 2023 ,8).

20. David Freidel, et. al. 1993. Maya Cosmos: Three Thousand Years on the Shaman's Path. New York: William Morrow. P. 430, n27.

21. O. Samayoa Urrea. 1995. "Economic and Institutional Analysis of Agroforestry Projects in Guatemala,." IN: Costs, Benefits, and Farmer Adoption of Agroforestry: Project Experience in Central America and the Caribbean. World Bank Environment Paper 14. p. 101.

Chapter Four

22. Or was it a Central American boa? Big difference, I know, but I'm no herpetologist.

23. St. Augustine, *Confessions*, Book III:1, (London: Penguin Books, 1973), 55.

24. Alfred P. Maudslay, *A Glimpse at Guatemala*, (New York: Cambridge Univ. Press, 1899). A. Ledyard Smith, *Archaeological reconnaissance in central Guatemala*, (Washington, D.C.: Carnegie Institution, 1955). John W. Fox, *Maya Postclassic State Formation*, (Cambridge: Cambridge Univ. Press, 1987).

25. Arnauld, Marie-Charlotte. "Relaciones interregionales en el área Maya durante el Postclásico en base a datos arquitectónicos." In: X Simposio de Investigaciones Arqueológicas en Guatemala, 1997 (J.P. Laporte and H. Escobedo, eds.), 119-133. Museo Nacional de Arqueología y Etnología, Guatemala.

26. *Ibid.* (Emphasis added.)

27. Augustine, *Confessions,* IX:25.

Chapter Five

28. V.L. Scarborough and D.R. Wilcox (eds.), *The Mesoamerican Ballgame*, (Tucson: Univ. of Arizona Press, 1991), 227.

29. In ancient Athens, "Pharmakos" referred to a sacrifice ritual, a kind of societal catharsis, used to expiate and shut out the evil, out of the body and out of the city. "Pharmakos" was the name given to a human scapegoat (a slave, an invalid, or a criminal) who was chosen to become an "outsider," being expelled from the community at times of disaster (famine, invasion or plague) or at times of calendrical crisis, when purification was needed. The evil that had infected the city from 'outside' was thus removed and returned to the 'outside', forever. See, generally, the trenchant and highly illuminating discussion of this topic found in René Girard's *Violence and the Sacred* (1972).

Chapter Six

30. I have reconstructed this brief conversation as best I can some forty years after the fact. But the last line contains the exact words spoken by Armando Garzona. Words I shall never forget for as long as I live. (Regarding the event, see Nelton Rivera, "La masacre del 15 de septiembre en la plaza del mercado de Rabinal," *La Prensa Comunitaria,* 2020.)

31. Many years later I took the trouble to find out the names: San Antonio, San Francisco de Asis, San Sebastian, San Miguel Arcangel, Santo Domingo de Guzmán, Santo Tomas Aquino, San Jeronimo, San Ambrosio, San Gregorio, San Agustin, San Pedro Apostol, San Pablo Apostol, San Pedro Martir.

32. Here is a small handful of Guatemala folk remedies – courtesy of my wife Mireya, who is knowledgeable about these things. 1. **Sávila**: aloe vera: use the *liga adentro* to alleviate whooping cough. 2. **Pericón**: Mexican tarragon, for diarrhea and stomach issues. Pericón (*Tagetes lucida*), also known as Mexican tarragon or mint marigold, is a traditional plant native to Mexico and Central America. 3. ***Hoja de trueno*** from the *palo de trueno* (*Ligustrum lucidum*): leaves boiled in a tea, for

urinary tract infections. 4. **Hoja de higo**: boiled with menta, ginger and lemon, used for coughs. 5. **Semilla de ciprés**: boiled as a bitter tea, it's taken for tonsillitis and throat problems. 6. **Pomegranate skin**: boiled as a tea, also for tonsillitis.

33. "Like Oedipus, the victim is considered a polluted object, whose living presence contaminates everything that comes in contact with it and whose death purges the community of its ills." René Girard, *Violence and the Sacred*, (Baltimore: Johns Hopkins Univ. Press, 1972), 95.

34. D.I. Bleiwas and M.M. Miller, "Barite—A Case Study of Import Reliance on an Essential Material for Oil and Gas Exploration and Development Drilling ." USGS Scientific Investigations Report 2014–5230, 2014. See also: N. Peckenham, "Peasants Lose Out in Scramble for Oil Wealth." *The Multinational Monitor* 2(5), 1981. See also: Anon., "Double Crown Resources Announces Success on Multiple Projects; Deal for Guatemalan Barite, Positive Ruling on Legal Claim and Development of Improved Aggregate Material Transport System." *Businesswire* 5/15/2014.

35. T.W. Kading, "The Guatemalan Military and the Economics of *La Violencia*". Canadian Journal of Latin American and Caribbean Studies, 24(47), 2014.

36. The Chixoy Dam and its reservoir forcibly displaced more than 3,500 Maya community members and resulted in the loss of land and livelihoods to 6,000 other families in the area. In 1982, 444 farmers were brutally murdered by the Guatemalan military government for opposing the construction of the Chixoy Dam. (International Rivers Network, 2007)

37. Bayer products. Cupravit was copper-based, and Agallol was mercury-based.

Chapter Eight

38. These news headlines actually appeared in Guatemala's *Diario La Tarde*, Aug. 13, 1981.

39. In order to reconstruct this commentary from memory, I had to struggle to put myself in the shoes of a 28-year-old Güicho, himself speaking over forty years ago, and I naturally had to write it out first in Spanish. Thus, as I wrote it originally:

"Este gobierno de militares asesinos, y los ricachones chupacabras que los apoyan tienen que acabar algún día. *Pues, ya no podemos seguir así.* Mirá vos, lo que está pasando en el campo – están secuestrando a nuestros maestros ahora, y a los líderes comunitarios. Y aquí mismo en nuestro Baja Verapaz está pasando la misma mierda – o peor. ¡Están matando a toda la gente que más necesitamos para progresar! Te digo, Cristian, que las fuerzas rebeldes que están en las montañas – que están luchando todos los días casi sin comer – ellos, ELLOS van a vencer algún día, y entonces vamos a ver unos cambios. Pero mientras tanto, seguimos en la lucha – y tú y yo, seguimos luchando para poner nuestro granito de arena, en estas benditas aldeas – aquí en Chichupac, en Nimacabaj y Pichec y Chitucan."

"Me alegro, Cristian, que estás aquí con nosotros. Para ser testigo. Créeme, no me opongo a lo que haces aquí, pues necesitamos preservar la naturaleza y conservar el recurso forestal para nuestro propio bien – y de nuestros hijos. Pero vas a ver, Cristian, vas a ver que al final de cuentas hay una misión aún más grande que nos espera, y cada quien va a tener que decidir si va a poner su granito de arena ahí también."

40. In the words of one U.S. State Department official at the time: "Somoza may be a bastard, but he's *our* bastard."

41. "Sandinista National Liberation Front." *Wikipedia*, Wikimedia Foundation, 24 Nov., 2023.

42. "Modeling strategy on the successful Cuban revolution, [the EGP and other guerrilla organizations] attempted the *foco* technique, choosing Ixil country as a sufficiently isolated location. In 1975, they killed a leading landowner. The army combed the area for months, began selective killing of suspected leaders, and established bases. Bombing hideouts proved ineffective, and eventually the army created a scorched earth policy, destroying villages. The intense army response meant guerrillas could not protect their supporters. Displaced people

gathered in town centers, repopulated destroyed villages, coerced to participate in unpaid work." Elaine Elliott, in *Maya America*, Vol. 3, No. 3, pp. 111-166, 2021.

43. This and later philosophical fragments from Heraclitus are quoted from Philip Wheelwright, *Heraclitus*, (New York: Oxford Univ. Press, 1959).

44. Quique's original words (from contemporaneous notes): "*Va a llegar el día, Cristián, cuando tendrás que desconocerme. ¿Tenés miedo? Pués tal vez no, pero cuando sientas la necesidad de irte de este país por conocerme a mí, entonces por favor, véte, VETE.*"

45. "Panzós" article at W3WE: Free Online Tutorials and Courses: https://es.w3we.com/wiki/Panz%C3%B3s

46. "Guatemalan Civil War," *Wikipedia*, Wikimedia Foundation, 20 January, 2024. See also: CIA secret cable dated March, 1966.

47. J. Grosso, "Killing Guatemala," *Jacobin* magazine, 2015.

48. Recinos, Adrián, *Pedro de Alvarado: Conquistador de México y Guatemala* (in Spanish), 2nd ed. (Guatemala: CENALTEX, 1986), 205.

49. Available at: https://www.wikiwand.com/en/Committee_for_Peasant_Unity

Chapter Nine

50. Literally: Thirteen seeds. From Saq' Be', the Organization for Mayan and Indigenous Spiritual Studies: "Q'anil symbolizes the seed, that which gives life, which makes it possible for everything to emerge if it is cultivated; it is the power of creation." Available at: http://sacredroad.org/oxlajuj-qanil-todays-chumil-2/

51. Ronald Wright, *Time Among the Maya*, (New York: Henry Holt & Co.,1991), 207.

52. UNESCO (n.d.), "Rabinal Achí dance drama tradition". Available at: https://ich.unesco.org/en/RL/rabinal-achi-dance-drama-tradition-00144 A full transcription of the dialogue of the play, along with

detailed analysis, is provided by Dennis Tedlock, *Rabinal Achi: A Mayan Drama of War and Sacrifice,* (New York: Oxford Univ. Press, 2003).

53. "In accordance with a treaty between Mexico and Spain, an extradition order must pass through the Secretaria de Relaciones Exteriores (SRE) to a federal judge and then on to the Procuraduria General de la Republica (PGR). A SRE spokesperson told reporters the order had been passed on. Mexican officials suspected Alvarez had been warned to flee. After the horse had fled, on Dec. 16, Mexico closed the barn doors with a migratory alert for Alvarez at 172 border crossings. Interior Secretary Santiago Creel and Attorney General Rafael Macedo vowed to apprehend him but told the media they had no idea where he was." By the staff of Latin American Digital Beat (LADB), "Guatemalan Activists Track Down Donaldo Alvarez Ruiz But Mexico Lets Him Slip Away," 2005. Available at: https://digitalrepository.unm.edu/cgi/viewcontent.cgi?article=10264&context=noticen

54. Loosely translated: "Why yes, THANK YOU sir for your good offices—and now you can eat shit and go fuck yourself, you son of a bitch. You murderous turd of shit—go fuck your mother."

55. Carolina Gamazo, "*Las Osamentas Localizadas en Cobán Son de un Cementerio.*" *El Periódico,* Aug. 6, 2012.

56. Wikipedia contributors. (2023, December 24). Burning of the Spanish Embassy in Guatemala. In *Wikipedia, The Free Encyclopedia.* Retrieved 02:29, January 16, 2024.

Chapter Ten

57. As they did, for example, in the case of the kidnapping of the Minister of Health, Roquelino Recinos, in November of 1981. See *El País,* Nov. 24, 1981.

58. "While initially autonomous from the government, the White Hand was absorbed into the Guatemalan State's counter-terror apparatus and evolved into a paramilitary unit of the Guatemalan armed forces, and was responsible for the murder and torture of thousands

of people in rural Guatemala. The group received support from the Guatemalan army and government, as well as from the United States." From Wikipedia: https://www.wikiwand.com/en/Mano_Blanca

59. Dominga herself (a.k.a. Denese Becker) tells the story of her escape from the Río Negro massacre in the PBS documentary "Discovering Dominga," which was broadcast as part of the weekly program "Point of View" on July 8, 2003. The program has since been re-broadcast by HBO, and can be seen in its entirety on YouTube at: https://www.youtube.com/watch?v=WcGGaxvVzFU&list=PL0FA208064A21915C&index=12

60. M. Williams, *Deforesting the Earth: From Prehistory to Global Crisis*, (Chicago: Univ. of Chicago Press, 2003), 395.

61. *Ibid.*, 399.

62. P. Rosado, *et. al.*, "Soil Erosion Control Efforts in Guatemala." IN: E. Lutz, *et. al.*, *Economic and Institutional Analyses of Soil Conservation Projects in Central America and the Caribbean.*" World Bank Environment Paper No. 8, 1994.

Chapter Eleven

63. "Committee for Peasant Unity," Wikipedia article. Wikimedia Foundation.

64. *"Rio Negro Massacres," Wikipedia article. Wikimedia Foundation.*

65. *Ibid.*

66. "Ejército Guerrillero de los Pobres," available at: https://es.w3we.com/wiki/Ej%C3%A9rcito_Guerrillero_de_los_Pobres

67. Figueroa Sarti, blog entry dated Sept. 13, 2012. Available at: http://raulfigueroasarti.blogspot.com/2012/09/el-14-de-septiembre-en-nuestra-memoria.html

68. "Irma Flaquer," Wikipedia article. https://en.wikipedia.org/wiki/Irma_Flaquer. See also June C. Erlick, *Disappeared: A Journalist Silenced*, (Emeryville, CA: Seal Press, 2004).

69. *The Inferno*, Canto III, in: C.H. Sisson (trans), *Dante Alighieri, The Divine Comedy,* (New York: Oxford University Press, 1980). When I read *The Divine Comedy* in Rabinal it was actually Laurence Binyon's *terza rima* translation as found in Penguin's *The Portable Dante.*

70. See "Quote Investigator" website at: https://quoteinvestigator.com/2015/01/14/hottest/

Chapter Twelve

71. Sappho, Fragment 1. https://www.uh.edu/~cldue/texts/sappho.html

72. *Iliad*, 14:241. (Robert Fagles, trans.)

73. Sappho, Fragment 147. https://www.uh.edu/~cldue/texts/sappho.html See also: https://pressbooks.claremont.edu/clas114valentine/chapter/someone-will-remember-us/

74. Homer, *The Iliad*, I:79-84.

75. This airborne leaflet tactic is reminiscent of a country-wide leaflet drop that occurred on June 18, 1954—an opening salvo in the *coup d'état* engineered by the CIA to topple the progressive president Jacobo Arbenz. (William Blum, 1995. *Killing Hope.* p. 78.)

Chapter Thirteen

76. *Lorena = lodo + arena.* These high-mass stoves were fashioned from a wet mixture of mud and sand, just like adobe blocks, with two or three cooking pan sized holes on top that kept heat loss to a minimum.

77. One day in the Guatemalan war: the rebel occupation of Nebaj, 21 January 1979. I had barely finished my second week in Rabinal.

78. Augustine, *Confessions,* VII:24.

79. This was a killing that would have coincided with the revolutionary FMLN's failed "Final Offensive of 1981." That effort to seize the reins

of power in El Salvador failed largely due to lack of popular support among the people. The FMLN leaders had threatened to kill president Jose Napoleon Duarte upon seizing power, since they saw him as a mere puppet of the oligarchs. But the oligarchs in El Salvador actually hated Duarte, while he was a figure much admired by many of the poor and disenfranchised.

80. From Rabinal, Padre Gregorio was next sent to El Salvador to continue his mission aiding the poor. By his own account, *los padres* had told him, "If you could handle Rabinal, then we believe you will certainly be able to handle El Salvador."

Chapter Fourteen

81. April 17, 1981.

Chapter Fifteen

82. Figueroa Sarti, blog entry, 9/13/2012, http://raulfigueroasarti.blogspot.com/2012/09/el-14-de-septiembre-en-nuestra-memoria.html

83. "Irma Flaquer," Wikipedia article. Wikimedia Foundation. Available at: https://en.wikipedia.org/wiki/Irma_Flaquer

84. Very likely the Sisters of Charity of New York: https://scny.org/the-guatemalan-mission-1971-2021/

85. More precisely, the Sisters of Charity of the Blessed Virgin Mary. See: https://en.wikipedia.org/wiki/Sisters_of_Charity_of_the_Blessed_Virgin_Mary?oldformat=true.

Chapter Sixteen

86. Nelton Rivera, "La masacre del 15 de septiembre en la plaza del mercado de Rabinal." Prensa Comunitaria online, 2020.

87. The "School of the Americas" (SOA) is now known as the Western Hemisphere Institute for Security Cooperation, WHINSEC. "Fort Benning" was renamed Fort Moore in 2023.

88. On his second foray to Fort Benning to attend classes at the SOA, Benedicto Lucas was accompanied by his comrade in arms Major Manuel Antonio Callejas y Callejas, who took the same course with him. Later, under the brutal regime of Benedicto's brother, Fernando Romeo Lucas Garcia, Callejas would become a senior intelligence officer in charge of choosing targets for assassination.

89. Colaboradores de Wikipedia, "Manuel Benedicto Lucas García," *Wikipedia, La enciclopedia libre,* https://es.wikipedia.org/w/index.php?title=Manuel_Benedicto_Lucas_Garc%C%3ADa&oldid=156618965 (descargado 4 de enero de 2024).

90. *Wikipedia,* "Guatemalan Genocide: Genocide Under General Benedicto Lucas." Wikimedia Foundation.

91. Richard Brusca (n.d.). "Guatemala."

92. Frank La Rue, "Interviews: Witness to Massacre." (Edited from an interview by Patricia Flynn and Mary Jo McConahay in March 2001.) N.B.: I could not corroborate elsewhere the assertion that Benedicto Lucas "fought in Algeria with French forces."

93. Wikipedia contributors, "Guatemalan Civil War," *Wikipedia, The Free Encyclopedia,* https://en.wikipedia.org/w/index.php?title=Guatemalan_Civil_War&oldid=1208770124 (accessed February 2024 ,19).

94. Allan Nairn, *The Nation*, 4/17/95.

95. *Al Jazeera*, "Guatemala releases military officials convicted of grave crimes," June 10, 2023.

Chapter Seventeen

96. Nelton Rivera González, "La masacre del 15 de septiembre en la plaza del mercado de Rabinal." *Prensa Comunitaria,* 2020. Significant

portions of this reporting are reproduced from: The Recovery of Historical Memory (REMHI), 1995. Available at: https://www.odhag.org gt/publicaciones/remhi-guatemala-nunca-mas/

97. Personal communication from a confidential source, March, 2024.

98. *Ibid.*

99. *Ibid.*

Chapter Eighteen

100. ODHAG, *Guatemala: Nunca Más*, vol. 1: pp. 100–101, 101 n. 1, 107–11, 114, 118–21, 126–7, 131–3, 257, 278–80; vol. 2: pp. 113–29, 135–6, 141.

101. Internet article available at: https://www.wola.org/2023/08/sentence-guatemalas-rancho-bejuco-massacre-indigenous-people-august/. See also: https://breakingthesilenceblog.com/rancho-bejuco/.

Epilogue

102. J. Burt and P. Estrada. 2018. "Commentary: Legacy of Guatemalan Dictator Rios Montt Shows Justice is Possible." Available at: https://www.wola.org/analysis/legacy-guatemala-dictator-rios-montt-shows-justice-possible/

103. Euripides, *Orestes*, 977-982.

Afterword

104. Jeff Abbott, "20 Years of 'Peace' in Guatemala." *NACLA: Reporting on the Americas Since 1967,* January 4, 2017.

105. Sophocles, *Oedipus the King*, 977-979.

106. Euripides, *Hecuba*, 489-492.

107. Aeschylus, *Agamemnon*, 179-184.

108. Anon., "God's Awful Grace Necessary in the Lives of Believers, Smith Says." (News Release, Union University, Jackson, TN, March 17, 2005).

109. *Ibid.*

110. Eknath Easwaran, *The Upanishads*, (Tomales, CA: Nilgiri Press, 2007), 211.

111. M.H. Kwok, M. Palmer and J. Ramsay. (trans.), *The Tao Te Ching of Lao Tzu,* (Rockport, MA: Element, Inc., 1997), 65.

112. *Ibid.*, p. 55.

Guatemala, 1971-2015: A Chronology

(The dates of personal events appear in boldface; other events appear in plain font.)

1971	ORPA (Revolutionary Organization of the People in Arms) formed under the leadership of Rodrigo Asturias, eldest son of Nobel Prize-winning author Miguel Angel Asturias.
1972	EGP (the Guerilla Army of the Poor) established, with headquarters in the oil-rich region of the north of the department of Quiché, in the so-called Franja Transversal del Norte.
3/7/1978	Gen. Fernando Romeo Lucas García elected president of Guatemala.
4/15/1978	The Comite de Unidad Campesina, CUC, is formed; described by its founder Pablo Ceto as a convergence of the leftist insurgency and the indigenous peoples' movements. Though it was a distinct organization, it had close ties to the EGP. The CUC had a quite visible presence in Rabinal during the author's whole time there.
5/29/1978	In the central plaza of Panzós, Alta Verapaz (100km NE of Rabinal), government soldiers attacked a peaceful peasant demonstration, killing many people. The deceased peasants, indigenous people who had been summoned to the place, were fighting for the legalization of the public lands that they had occupied for years. Their struggle brought them directly into conflict with investors who wanted to exploit the mineral wealth of the area, particularly the oil reserves.
June, 1978	President Lucas Garcia declares a state of emergency for the entire Chixoy region where a hydroelectric dam is under construction. Most of the affected communities accepted the terms of the declaration, except for Rio Negro, which was evacuated by force at a cost of many lives.
9/15/1978	**The author's arrival in Costa Rica to start Peace Corps training.**
12/18/1978	**The author's arrival in Guatemala to finish training and begin the assignment.**
1/20/1979	**The author moves out to his Peace Corps posting in Rabinal, B.V.**
1/21/1979	Rebel occupation of Nebaj.

2/13/1979	**The author met with OAS reps in Salamá re reforestation goals for the Río Negro (Río Chixoy) watershed.**
3/22/1979	Manuel Colom Argueta, mayor of Guatemala City and founder of the United Front of the Revolution (FUR) political party, was assassinated, having had a premonition about his death three days before.
7/19/1979	The Sandanista (FSLN) army entered Managua, culminating the first goal of the Nicaraguan revolution. The war left 30,000–50,000 dead and 150,000 Nicaraguans in exile.
12/1/1979	In late 1979, the EGP expanded its influence, controlling a large amount of territory in the Ixil Triangle in El Quiché and holding numerous demonstrations in Nebaj, Chajul, and Cotzal. At the same time that the EGP expanded its presence in the western highlands, a new insurgent movement called ORPA (the Revolutionary Organization of the Armed People) came to prominence.
1980	Early in the year: A strike led by the CUC forced the Guatemalan government to raise minimum wages by 200 percent, from an equivalent of U.S. $1.12 to $3.20 per day . The strike involved 70,000 workers from sugarcane plantations, as well as 40,000 cotton pickers.
1/31/1980	The Spanish Embassy in Guatemala City caught fire during a police siege, killing 37 people, including embassy staff and senior Guatemalan government officials. A group of indigenous people from El Quiché occupied the embassy in a desperate attempt to draw attention to the problems they had had with the Army in that region of the country. Afterwards, Spain severed diplomatic relations with Guatemala.
3/5/1980	Two residents of Río Negro who were in Pueblo Viejo were accused of stealing beans from the dining rooms of the dam workers. They were pursued by two soldiers and an officer of the Policia Militar Ambulante (PMA). Upon arrival at Río Negro, the two residents began shouting that they were pursuing the military. The soldiers were rounded up and taken to the church. A community member, who was drunk, struck the officer of the PMA, who, in his eagerness to defend himself, shot and killed seven people. Immediately, the farmers reacted with stones and machetes and killed the agent.

3/6/1980	The Army commented on the Mar. 5 incident saying that the community had influence from the guerrillas and that was the factor that explained their refusal to leave their lands. The military claimed in their Press bulletin: "For some time the people of the Río Negro village have become troubled by the influence of subversive elements, which have benefited from the problems of land, raised on the grounds that their land will be affected by the flooding of the Chixoy dam. This, unlike other villages which have voluntarily accepted the transfer to safer places and where they have better life expectancies".
9/1/1980	Vice President Francisco Villagrán Kramer, resigns from his position. In his resignation, Kramer cited his disapproval of the government's human rights record as one of the main reasons for his resignation.
9/5/1980	A terrorist attack by the EGP (Guerrilla Army of the Poor) took place in front of the National Palace of Guatemala, then the seat of the Guatemalan government. The objective was to prevent the Guatemalan people from supporting a massive demonstration that the government of General Lucas García had prepared for Sunday, September 7, 1980. In the attack, six adults and a child died when two bombs exploded inside a vehicle.
9/14/1980	Pichec village, Rabinal municipality: Soldiers dressed in civilian clothes with red handkerchiefs, accompanied by members of the PAC, massacred 16 people including newborn children, men and women. Some people were buried alive, others executed with bullets. A civil patrolman from the same community was guiding the soldiers. Identified victims: 8. Unidentified victims: 92.
October 1980	An alliance was formalized between the rebel groups EGP, FAR and ORPA as a condition for Cuban support of the insurgency. Thus was formed the Guatemalan National Revolutionary Unity (URNG).

10/16/1980	Irma Flaquer (psychologist and journalist with La Nación newspaper) disappeared after attending her grandson's fourth birthday party. While she and son Fernando drove back to her apartment, they were stopped by two cars surrounding their car. Fernando was shot in the head and Irma cried out for a doctor for her son. She was grabbed and taken away. Her body has not been recovered and it is believed she was executed.
10/18/1980	**During the night, soldiers from the local army detachment in Rabinal torched and burned down our new bodega/ office we had built in the tree nursery. Then they littered the ground with fake guerrilla leaflets in order to frame the Committe for Peasant Unity (CUC) as authors of the deed.**
1981	In early 1981, the insurgency mounted the largest offensive in the country's history. This was followed by a further offensive towards the end of the year, in which the insurgents forced many civilians to participate. Villagers worked with the insurgency to sabotage roads and military establishments and destroy anything of strategic value to the armed forces. In 1981, between 250,000 and 500,000 members of Guatemala's indigenous community were actively supporting the insurgency.
2/15/1981	Father Juan Alonso Fernández was 48 years old when he was murdered on this date. Ordained a priest in 1960, that same year he arrived at the mission of El Quiché. He spent a few years in Guatemala, then in Indonesia, and then returned to Guatemala, explicitly choosing one of the hardest places. Some armed individuals attacked him when he was riding a motorcycle on the highway between Cunén and Uspantán. They threw him to the ground, beat him, breaking his leg, and then shot him three times.
Jul.-Dec., 1981	The army killed 25 people in aldea Chuategua. Cases of forced cannibalism of notable cruelty occurred in Baja Verapaz, between July and December 1981, in a joint operation between the Army and the PAC of Rabinal, the soldiers cut off the ears of six people and forced them to eat them, CEH Case No. 883, 1981. Chuateguá Village, Rabinal, Baja Verapaz.
8/16/1981	Gen. Benedicto Lucas is named Chief of Staff of the Guatemalan armed forces.

9/15/1981	**The army, with the help of judiciales and comisionados, murdered 205 people in Rabinal's main plaza. CEH Case No. 9160.**
9/20/1981	The army killed 21 people in aldea Panacal, Rabinal municipality. CEH Case No. 2269.
10/8/1981	**The day of the great assembly called by the army in the central plaza of Rabinal. (Obligatory attendance.)**
11/1/1981	32 men massacred in aldea Pichec
11/7/1981	**The author was evacuated from Rabinal as a security precaution.**
11/22/1981	30 more men massacred in aldea Pichec.
11/26/1981	In 1981 the appointment of military commissioners reached massive levels. The new Chief of the Army Staff, General Benedicto Lucas, in a speech in Joyabaj, Quiché, said: "This force is voluntary; in Rabinal there are already 1,000 men and in Joyabaj 800." (*Memory of Silence*, p. 162.)
1/2/1982	35 more men massacred in aldea Pichec
1/8/1982	Massacre in aldea Chichupac: dozens of campesinos murdered, and women raped.
Feb., 1982	A group of armed men, possibly guerrillas, burned the market of Xococ, killing five persons. As a result of the fact that the Army identified the peasants of Río Negro with the guerrillas, residents of Xococ broke trade relations with Río Negro and declared them their enemies. Says an inhabitant of Xococ: "When the war began, friendship was lost" .
2/7/1982	The first action taken by the patrol Xococ was on February 7, 1982, on behalf of the military detachment of Rabinal. They asked some people from the community of Río Negro to come to Xococ. The head of the Patrol Xococ that received them accused them of participating in the guerrilla and of burning their market. The inhabitants of Rio Negro replied that the market was a benefit for them and that they had no reason to burn it. However, to avoid worsening the situation, the persons from Rio Negro promised to build a new market in Xococ. Finally, the patrollers retained their identity cards and ordered them to report back to Xococ the following week to recover them.

2/13/1982	74 people from Río Negro (55 men and 19 women) went to Xococ to recover the identity cards. Once there, they were executed by the patrollers.
3/13/1982	Members of the Army and members of the PAC from a neighboring community carried out a massacre of Achi women and children in Río Negro, Rabinal, Baja Verapaz. 177 women and children were murdered.
3/23/1982	The *coup d'etat* of Gen. Efrain Rios Montt, deposing Pres. Fernando Romeo Lucas Garcia. Also, the author's first day on the job with CARE/Guatemala.
7/18/1982	In the Plan de Sánchez massacre, Rabinal, Baja Verapaz. "Several bombs were dropped by a small plane, but they did not fall on the town. At eight in the morning, the military detachment launched two 105 mm caliber mortar grenades that fell to the east and west of the community. In the afternoon, soldiers from Rabinal and Cobán arrived at the community. The men were not there, but the soldiers raped nineteen women and mocked them, accusing them of being guerrillas. At five in the afternoon they threw two grenades and fired their weapons. The shooting continued until eleven at night. Children were beaten to death. According to witnesses, the children screamed and screamed and then fell silent. The next day the houses were smoking, you couldn't recognize the corpses that were inside the houses, they were pure coal. The bodies that were outside the houses had shots in the head, chest and back. That day the Army executed 227 people. The PAC and military commissioners also participated in the massacre." *(Memory of Silence*, p. 287.)
8/8/1983	The *coup d'etat* of Gen. Oscar Humberto Mejia Victores, deposing Rios Montt.
Mar., 2005	The Chixoy Dam Legacy Issues Study is completed, concluding that the construction of the dam caused loss of lives, lands, and people's livelihoods, and that it violated national and international laws. The study recommended the creation of a negotiations process between the government, communities and financial institutions resulting in a binding agreement.

4/10/2010	After a decades-long struggle, the Reparations Plan for Damages Suffered by the Communities Affected by the Construction of the Chixoy Dam was finally signed and agreed to by all parties, which involved the participation and approval of communities and the government.
1/16/2014	The US Congress passed the 2014 US Consolidated Appropriations Bill, which instructs the US directors of the World Bank and Inter-American Development Bank - which both financed construction of the Chixoy Dam - to "report ... on the steps being taken by such institutions to support implementation of the April 2010 Reparation Plan for Damages Suffered by the Communities Affected by the Construction of the Chixoy Hydroelectric Dam in Guatemala" (see p. 1240 for this provision).
11/8/2014	Guatemala's President Otto Perez Molina asked forgiveness from the communities for the government's role in the social, cultural and environmental destruction caused by the Chixoy Dam. He also presented the Reparations Executive Agreement, which operationalizes reparations for the 33 communities who were drastically impacted by the construction of dam. The Agreement includes more than US$154.5 million to fund individual compensations, infrastructure, development assistance and environmental restoration.
10/15/2015	The first part of the reparation plan that was agreed upon between the State of Guatemala and the survivors and descendants of the victims of the Río Negro massacres that occurred in 1982 during the construction of the hydroelectric plant became effective. The agreement was signed in 2014 and began with the delivery of twenty-two million quetzales to the affected families of the thirty-three communities where the Chixoy hydroelectric plant was built.

In the opinion of the CEH, the number of human rights violations perpetrated by the State against the Mayan-Achi population during the years 1980-1983 allows us to conclude that acts of genocide were committed, inspired by a strategic determination that also had a genocidal character. The objective of the military campaign carried out in the Rabinal area was the partial destruction of the Mayan-Achi people, as a necessary requirement to maintain absolute control over a militarily strategic area

and to separate the guerrilla from its supposed social base. (Memory of Silence, 375.)

This military campaign resulted in the death of at least 3,637 people, including women, the elderly and children, of which 98.8% were Achi, with 16% of the population having been victimized and suffering other serious violations of human rights, such as torture, rape and forced disappearance. Along with the killings, other acts of serious injury to physical and mental integrity, and measures that prevented births within the group.

Abbreviations

APCD	Associate Peace Corps Director
CARE	At the time of its founding in 1945, CARE stood for the Cooperative for American Remittances to Europe. As CARE's activities broadened, this was changed to the 'Cooperative for Assistance and Relief Everywhere.
CIF	Centro de Integración Familiar (also known locally in Rabinal as the Hogar Rural, "Rural Home."
COGAAT	Cooperativa Guatemalteca-Alemana de Alimentos por Trabajo (the Guatemalan-German Food for Work Cooperative)
CSM	Corn-Soy-Milk, one of the several food commodities supplied by USAID's "Alliance for Progress" food program (P.L. 480).
CUC	Comité de Unidad Campesina, the Guatemala's Peasant Unity Committee.
DIGESA	Dirección General de Servicios Agrícolas, Guatemala's agricultural extensión agency.
DIGESEPE	Dirección General de Servicios Pecuarios, Guatemala's animal husbandry extensión agency.
EGP	Ejército Guatemalteco de los Pobres, the Guatemalan Army of the Poor.
FFW	Food for Work

G-2	The military intelligence unit of the Guatemalan armed forces (known as S-2 in the rural sector)
INAFOR	Instituto Nacional Forestal, Guatemala's National Forestry Institute
INDE	Guatemala's National Electrification Institute (Instituto Nacional de Electrificación)
NGO	Non-Governmental Organization
OAS	Organization of American States (OEA, in Spanish)
ORPA	Organización Revolucionaria del Pueblo en Armas, the Revolutionary Organization of the People in Arms
P.L. 480	U.S. Public Law 480, referring to the federal legislation known as the Agricultural Trade Development and Assistance Act of 1954, which created feeding programs such as the Food for Work program administered by CARE.
Q.	Quetzal, the currency of Guatemala.

Bibliography

Listed here are the main writings that have guided me on the path to try to understand and come to terms with the time I spent in Guatemala. Most but not all of these writings are referred to in the text of this volume. Those which are not nevertheless had a great influence on the development of my thinking, and may serve as profitable reading for anyone who is interested in the saga that continues to unfold in Guatemala.

Al Jazeera, June 10, 2023. "Guatemala releases military officials convicted of grave crimes." Available at: https://www.aljazeera.com/news/2023/6/10/guatemala-releases-military-officials-convicted-of-grave-crimes

Anon. 2018. *"Alerta de Plagas: Gusano cogollero (Helicoverpa armigera)."* USDA Pamphlet APHIS 81-35-025S. Available at: https://www.aphis.usda.gov/publications/plant_health/alert-old-world-bollworm-sp.pdf

Anon., 2014. "Double Crown Resources Announces Success on Multiple Projects; Deal for Guatemalan Barite, Positive Ruling on Legal Claim and Development of Improved Aggregate Material Transport System." Businesswire 5/15/2014. Available at: https://www.businesswire.com/news/home/20140515005800/en/Double-Crown-Resources%C2%A0Announces-Success-on-Multiple-Projects%C2%A0Deal-for-Guatemalan-Barite-Positive%C2%A0Ruling-on-Legal%C2%A0Claim%C2%A0and-Development-of%C2%A0Improved-Aggregate-Material-Transport-System.

Anon. 2005. "God's Awful Grace Necessary in the Lives of Believers, Smith Says." (News Release, Union University, Jackson, TN) March 17, 2005. Available at: https://www.uu.edu/news/

release.cfm?ID=848#:~:text=He%20quoted%20a%20passage%20from,the%20awful%20grace%20of%20God.%E2%80%9D

Arnauld, Marie-Charlotte. 1997. *"Relaciones interregionales en el área Maya durante el Postclásico en base a datos arquitectónicos."* In: *X Simposio de Investigaciones Arqueológicas en Guatemala,* 1996 (J.P. Laporte and H. Escobedo, eds.), pp.119-133. *Museo Nacional de Arqueología y Etnología, Guatemala.*

Augustine of Hippo. *Confessions.* Translated by Maria Boulding. New City Press, 1997.

Augustine of Hippo. *Confessions.* Translated by R.S. Pine-Coffin. Penguin Books, 1961.

Baillie, Gil. 1996. *Violence Unveiled: Humanity at the Crossroads.* New York: The Crossroad Publishing Company.

Ball, Patrick, et. al. 1999. *State Violence in Guatemala, 1960-1996: A Quantitative Reflection.* Washington, D.C.: American Association for the Advancement of Science.

Bethge, Eberhard. 1977. *Dietrich Bonhoeffer: Man of Vision, Man of Courage.* New York: Harper and Row.

Bleiwas, D.I., and M.M. Miller, 2014. "Barite—A Case Study of Import Reliance on an Essential Material for Oil and Gas Exploration and Development Drilling ." USGS Scientific Investigations Report 2014–5230. Available at: https://pubs.usgs.gov/sir/2014/5230/pdf/sir2014-5230.pdf.

Blum, Walter. 1995. *Killing Hope: U.S. Military and CIA Intervention Since World War II.* Monroe (ME): Common Courage Press.

Bonhoeffer, Dietrich. 1963. *The Cost of Discipleship.* New York: MacMillan Publishing Co., Inc.

Brusca, Richard. (n.d.). "Guatemala." Available at: https://www.featheredserpent.online/guatemala

Burt, J., and P. Estrada. 2018. "Commentary: Legacy of Guatemalan Dictator Rios Montt Shows Justice is Possible." WOLA Commentary, 13 April, 2018. Available at: https://www.wola.org/analysis/legacy-guatemala-dictator-rios-montt-shows-justice-possible/ .

Central Intelligence Agency. 1966. Secret cable dated March, 1966 (approved for release, Feb. 1998). Available at: https://nsarchive2.gwu.edu/NSAEBB/NSAEBB32/docs/doc02.pdf.

Cervantes, Miguel de. 2003. *Don Quixote.* (John Rutherford, transl.) New York: Penguin Books.

Chapman, Peter. 2014. *Bananas: How the United Fruit Company Shaped the World.* New York: Grove Press.

"Committee for Peasant Unity," *Wikipedia*, Wikimedia Foundation. 15 September, 2021, https://en.wikipedia.org/wiki/Committee_for_Peasant_Unity#:~:text=In%20early%201980%2C%20a%20strike,of%20U.S.%20%241.12%20to%20%243.20.

Dalrymple, William. 2019. *The Anarchy: The East India Company, Corporate Violence, and the Pillage of an Empire.* New York: Bloomsbury Publishing.

Easwaran, Eknath. 2007. *The Upanishads.* Tomales (CA): Nilgiri Press.

Elliott, Elaine. 2021. "A History of Land Tenure in the Ixil Region." *Maya America* 3(3): 111-166. Available at: https://digitalcommons.kennesaw.edu/mayaamerica/vol3/iss3/10/.

Erlick, June C. 2004. *Disappeared: A Journalist Silenced.* Emeryville (CA): Seal Press.

Fagles, Robert (trans.) 1990. *The Iliad.* New York: Penguin Books.

________________. 1977. *The Oresteia: Agamemnon, The Libation Bearers, The Eumenides.* New York: Penguin Books.

Figueroa Sartí, Raúl. 2012. *"El 14 de Septiembre en Nuestra Memoria."* Internet blog entry dated Sept. 13, 2012. Available at: http://raulfigueroasarti.blogspot.com/2012/09/el-14-de-septiembre-en-nuestra-memoria.html.

Fox, John W. 1987. *Maya Postclassic State Formation.* Cambridge: Cambridge Univ. Press.

Freidel, David, et. al. 1993. *Maya Cosmos: Three Thousand Years on the Shaman's Path.* New York: William Morrow.

Gamazo, Carolina. 2012. *"Las Osamentas Localizadas en Cobán Son de un Cementerio." El Periódico,* Aug. 6, 2012. Available at: http://lacunadelsol-indigo.blogspot.com/2012/08/las-osamentas.html

Girard, René. 1972. *Violence and the Sacred.* Baltimore: Johns Hopkins Univ. Press.

Grandin, Greg, and Elizabeth Oglesby. 2019. "Washington Trained Guatemala's Killers for Decades." *The Nation,* January 25, 2019.

Grene, David, and Richmond Lattimore (eds.). 1955. *The Complete Greek Tragedies: Euripides I.* Chicago, Univ. of Chicago Press.

__________________. 1969. *The Complete Greek Tragedies: Euripides II.* Chicago, Univ. of Chicago Press.

__________________. 1958. *The Complete Greek Tragedies: Euripides III.* Chicago, Univ. of Chicago Press.

__________________. 1958. *The Complete Greek Tragedies: Euripides IV.* Chicago, Univ. of Chicago Press.

__________________. 1959. *The Complete Greek Tragedies: Euripides V*. Chicago, Univ. of Chicago Press.

__________________. 1954. *The Complete Greek Tragedies: Sophocles I.* Chicago, Univ. of Chicago Press.

Grosso, J. 2015. "Killing Guatemala." Jacobin magazine. Available at: https://jacobin.com/2015/11/guatemala-molino-corruption-maras-gangs-cia-united-fruit/

"Guatemalan Civil War." *Wikipedia*, Wikimedia Foundation, 31 October, 2023, https://en.wikipedia.org/wiki/Guatemalan_Civil_War?oldformat=true

"Guatemalan Genocide: Genocide Under General Benedicto Lucas." *Wikipedia*, Wikimedia Foundation, 25 November, 2023, https://en.wikipedia.org/wiki/Guatemalan_genocide#Genocide_under_General_Benedicto_Lucas

Hunt, Michael. 2004. *The World Transformed.* New York: Oxford University Press

"Irma Flaquer." *Wikipedia,* Wikimedia Foundation, 30 September, 2023, https://en.wikipedia.org/wiki/Irma_Flaquer.

Jonas, Susanne, et. al. 1984. *Guatemala: Tyranny on Trial, Testimony of the Permanent People's Tribunal.* San Francisco: Synthesis Publications.

Kading, T.W. 2014. "The Guatemalan Military and the Economics of *La Violencia*". Canadian Journal of Latin American and Caribbean Studies, 24(47).

Küng, Hans. 1978. *On Being a Christian.* New York: Doubleday and Co., Inc.

La Rue, Frank. 2001. "Interviews: Witness to Massacre." (Edited from an interview by Patricia Flynn and Mary Jo McConahay in March

2001.) Available at: http://archive.pov.org/discoveringdominga/interview-witness-to-massacre/2/

Lowe, Norman. 2013. *Mastering Modern World History* (Fifth ed.). Basingstoke: Palgrave Macmillan.

"Mano Blanca." Wikipedia, Wikimedia Foundation, 27 July, 2023, https://en.wikipedia.org/wiki/Mano_Blanca?oldformat=true

"Manuel Benedicto Lucas Garcia." (In Spanish) *Wikipedia*, Wikimedia Foundation, 22 November, 2023, https://es.wikipedia.org/wiki/Manuel_Benedicto_Lucas_Garc%C3%ADa

Manz, Beatriz. 1988. *Refugees of a Hidden War: The Aftermath of Counterinsurgency in Guatemala.* Albany: State Univ. of New York Press.

Maudslay, Alfred P. 1899. *A Glimpse at Guatemala.* New York: Cambridge Univ. Press.

Melville, T. and M. Melville.1971. *Guatemala: The Politics of Land Ownership.* New York: The Free Press.

Nairn, Allan. 1982. "Despite Ban, U.S. Captain Trains Guatemalan Military." *The Washington Post*, October 21, 1982. p. 1.

__________. 1995. "C.I.A. Death Squad (Editorial)." *The Nation,* 17 April, 1995. p. 511.

Navarrete Pellicer, Sergio. 2005. *Maya Achí Marimba Music in Guatemala*. Philadelphia: Temple Univ. Press.

Nyrop, Richard. (ed.). 1983. *Guatemala: A Country Study*. Washington, D.C.: U.S. Govt. Printing Office.

Ortiz Borbolla, Sergio. 2023. "Sentence in Guatemala's 'Rancho Bejuco' Massacre of 25 Indigenous People Expected on August 17th." WOLA Media Advisory, 15 Aug., 2023.

Peckenham, N. 1981. "Peasants Lose Out in Scramble for Oil Wealth." *The Multinational Monitor* 2(5). Available at: https://www.multinationalmonitor.org/hyper/issues/1981/05/peckenham.html.

Recinos, Adrián. 1986. *Pedro de Alvarado: Conquistador de México y Guatemala* (2nd ed.). Guatemala: CENALTEX.

"Rio Negro Massacres." *Wikipedia*, Wikimedia Foundation, 22 April, 2023, https://en.wikipedia.org/wiki/R%C3%ADo_Negro_massacres

Rivera, Nelton. 2020. *"La masacre del 15 de septiembre en la plaza del mercado de Rabinal." Prensa Comunitaria* Available at: https://prensacomunitaria.org/2020/09/la-masacre-del-15-de-septiembre-en-la-plaza-del-mercado-de-rabinal/

Rosado, P., *et. al.* 1994. "Soil Erosion Control Efforts in Guatemala." IN: E. Lutz, *et. al.*, 1994. *Economic and Institutional Analyses of Soil Conservation Projects in Central America and the Caribbean.* World Bank Environment Paper No. 8.

Rothenberg, Daniel. 2012. *Memory of Silence: The Guatemalan Truth Commission Report.* New York: Palgrave MacMillan.

Samayoa Urrea, Otto. 1995. "Economic and Institutional Analysis of Agroforestry Projects in Guatemala,." IN: *Costs, Benefits, and Farmer Adoption of Agroforestry: Project Experience in Central America and the Caribbean.* World Bank Environment Paper 14.

"Sandinista National Liberation Front." *Wikipedia*, Wikimedia Foundation, 24 Nov., 2023, https://en.wikipedia.org/wiki/Sandinista_National_Liberation_Front?oldformat=true.

Sanford, Victoria. 2003. *Buried Secrets: Truth and Human Rights in Guatemala.* New York: Palgrave MacMillan.

Scarborough, Vernon L. and David R. Wilcox (eds.). 1991. *The Mesoamerican Ballgame.* Tucson: Univ. of Arizona Press.

Schlesinger, Stephen, and Stephen Kinzer. 1982. *Bitter Fruit: The Untold Story of the American Coup in Guatemala.* New York: Doubleday.

Sisson, C.H. 1981. *Dante Alighieri, The Divine Comedy.* New York: Oxford Univ. Press.

Smith, A. Ledyard. 1955. *Archaeological Reconnaissance in Central Guatemala.* Washington, D.C.: Carnegie Institution.

Stewart, Julie, *et al.* 1995. *A People Dammed: The Impact of the World Bank Chixoy Hydroelectric Project In Guatemala.* Washington, D.C.: Witness for Peace Publications.

Tedlock, Barbara. 1992. *Time and the Highland Maya.* Albuquerque: Univ. of New Mexico Press.

Tedlock, Dennis. 2003. *Rabinal Achi: A Mayan Drama of War and Sacrifice.* New York: Oxford Univ. Press.

Unamuno, Miguel de. 1954. *The Tragic Sense of Life.* New York: Dover.

United States Defense Intelligence Agency. 1980. "Military Intelligence Summary (MIS), Vol. VIII, Latin America (U).

Wheelwright, Philip. 1959. *Heraclitus.* New York: Oxford Univ. Press.

Wikipedia contributors, "Achi people," *Wikipedia, The Free Encyclopedia,* https://en.wikipedia.org/w/index.php?title=Achi_people&oldid=1157717354 (accessed August 8, 2023).

Wilkinson, Daniel. 2002. *Silence on the Mountain: Stories of Terror, Betrayal, and Forgetting in Guatemala.* Boston: Houghton Mifflin Company.

Williams, M. 2003. *Deforesting the Earth: From Prehistory to Global Crisis.* Chicago: Univ. of Chicago Press.

Wright, Ronald. 1991. *Time Among the Maya.* New York: Henry Holt & Co.

Praise *for* WALKING WITH EVARISTO

"Christian Nill has written a highly engaging, disarmingly honest and evocative account of nearly three years as a Peace Corps volunteer in a Guatemalan indigenous community at a time of mounting upheaval and violence. Starting out brimming with idealistic optimism, the young Nill comes to find himself in the unwitting role of witness to terror that casts a pall over the countryside and claims the lives of those dearest to him. An unforgettable and page-turning memoir that left me wanting more."

—SCOTT WALLACE, AUTHOR OF THE *NYT* BESTSELLER, *THE UNCONQUERED: IN SEARCH OF THE AMAZON'S LAST UNCONTACTED TRIBES*

"This eloquent and moving account contributes in its own way to the body of testimonio literature from the period. …[T]his book makes a worthwhile contribution to our understanding of this dark period in history, and we should be grateful to [author] Nill for having had the courage to write it."

—GAVIN O'TOOLE, *LATIN AMERICAN REVIEW OF BOOKS*

"Passionate and personal confessions from author Christian Nill, *Walking with Evaristo* is a captivating account of a nearly forgotten calamity."

—*SELF-PUBLISHING REVIEW*

www.ingramcontent.com/pod-product-compliance
Lightning Source LLC
Chambersburg PA
CBHW031943090426
42739CB00006B/69
9781950444687